THE
CHRISTIAN
COUNSELOR'S
MANUAL

THE
CHRISTIAN
COUNSELOR'S
MANUAL

The Sequel and Companion Volume
to
COMPETENT TO COUNSEL

By JAY E. ADAMS
Westminster Theological Seminary

BAKER BOOK HOUSE
Grand Rapids, Michigan

ISBN: 0-8010-0071-8

First printing, November 1973
Second printing, May 1974
Third printing, November 1974
Fourth printing, July 1975
Fifth printing, April 1976
Sixth printing, October 1976
Seventh printing, March 1977
Eighth printing, March 1978
Ninth printing, December 1978
Tenth printing, November 1979
Eleventh printing, February 1981

LIBRARY OF CONGRESS CATALOGUE CARD NO. 73-87752
PRINTED IN THE UNITED STATES OF AMERICA

FOREWORD

This volume is designed to take its place next to *Competent to Counsel* as its complement, not as a replacement. The two may be used together as textbooks for college or seminary courses. Counselors will find that the reference section at the back of the book provides ready helps to pinpoint possible causes of and biblical solutions for the problems that they confront in the day-by-day work of counseling. Check lists for procedures, failure, etc., have been included to make the ready reference section more profitable. In addition, throughout the reader will find samples of various counseling materials. These may be obtained separately or in complete packets from the publisher of this volume.

I wish to express my deep gratitude to the Rev. William Varner of Willow Grove, Pennsylvania, for preparing the indexes.

TABLE OF CONTENTS

INTRODUCTION

I was gratified when the first printing of *Competent to Counsel* sold out four months after its publication.[1] This interest seems to prove my contention that there is a recognized scarcity of material making a serious attempt to deal with the biblical data concerning counseling and the human difficulties that counseling is concerned to alleviate. Indeed, it was precisely to meet such a need that I wrote. That I was not alone in assuming that conservative ministers would be interested in such a book has been demonstrated to my satisfaction. I was surprised, however, at the number of Christian laymen who also responded with deep interest and concern. This larger response I interpret as a mandate for other volumes that cover additional ground, specialized matters, and advance beyond the first. This present work is one of several in which I seek to fulfil that mandate. The type of readers who have responded with interest has been kept in mind throughout.

Competent to Counsel, while containing a good bit of practical information about the counseling goals, methods, and processes, was, nevertheless, largely polemic. It was important to grapple with the problem and place of Christian counseling in today's world. Of course, very little of that which needs to be done to combat the forces that are impinging upon the Christian counselor was attempted in that volume. It was but an initial attempt. Yet before coming to grips with other antagonists,[2] I feel constrained to do something to meet the need

---

1. At the present writing approximately 75,000 copies have been sold. A translation and printing in German, *Befreinde Seelsorge* (Giessen Und Basel: Brunnen-Verlag GMBH, 1972) is doing well overseas. A Chinese translation is now under way.

2. For example, the whole Skinnerian behavioristic movement that is becoming so popular in colleges and universities under names like "Behavior Modification" or "Behavior Therapy" needs to be handled in depth. I hope in a future volume to give full consideration to this significant movement, laying bare its pagan presuppositions that man is simply another animal, deterministically oriented by genes and chromosomes, who can be taught and tamed by S-R methods involving reward and punishment. Behaviorism, in this country, begun by Watson and newly revived in response to the failures of Freud and Rogers, will be the more

(frequently expressed) for a "how to" manual of the type that Professor C. Gregg Singer suggested in his gracious review of *Competent to Counsel*.[3]

In *The Christian Counselor's Manual* I have tried to fill that need to some extent. I know that it is not exhaustive and, D.V., plan to publish additional books covering various areas in more detail in time. I have published *The Big Umbrella: Essays and Addresses on Christian Counseling* and *Christian Living in the Home*, books that amplify and supplement what I have tried to cover here. Also, pamphlets, *Christ and Your Problems, What to Do About Worry*, and *Godliness Through Discipline* are available as the first of a series of materials designed to assist Christian counselors in the work of nouthetic confrontation. *Christ and Your Problems* may be given to counselees early in the counseling process, since it is intended to help set conditions for successful counseling by stressing Christian hope and personal responsibility to God. The other two pamphlets are intended to help counselors meet the needs indicated by their titles.

In *The Christian Counselor's Manual* I have built particularly upon the first work, *Competent to Counsel*, and everywhere assume it. In the scope of this book I have kept in mind my intention to continue to publish materials covering specialized areas of the field of biblical counseling.[4] I have tried, then, neither to duplicate what I have said before nor hope to cover (except perhaps by anticipation) in depth in the future, D.V. Therefore, at points I have presupposed a basic

---

dangerous, since, because of its laboratory-based stance, it will involve successes of a sort that psychoanalysis and client-centered therapy were unable to produce. Skinnerian manipulation is so significant a development that it must be considered separately.

3. Professor Singer wrote: "This book answers a tremendous need in contemporary evangelical literature. . . . I can only hope that Professor Adams will produce other volumes in which he applies these principles in detail to specific areas and issues which Christian parents, teachers and pastors confront daily as they seek to do the will of the Lord" (*The Presbyterian Journal*, November 4, 1970, p. 20).

4. For example, another book, *Christian Living in the Home*, has been released. That is one reason why marriage and family counseling is handled illustratively and incidentally rather than centrally in this manual. However, I am painfully aware of the need to do *much* more in this area and hope yet to publish other material to help meet crying needs. *The Use of the Scriptures in Counseling, The Function of the Church in Counseling, Cases in Counseling,* and *Theology and Counseling* are volumes that are now in various stages of preparation.

knowledge of nouthetic confrontation as it has been set forth already. While some matters have been sharpened or amplified, I have not always taken the trouble to make the careful qualifications that I labored to express exactly in the former work. I see no need to paint over the picture again and thereby risk muddying the canvas. If, as a result, I should at places seem brash or appear to take too much for granted, it is probably because I have tried to use bold strokes and vivid colors. After all, I am writing this book for my friends; for those who so enthusiastically responded to my previous efforts. I am not trying to sell anyone here; this is an instruction manual intended principally for those who have already bought the product and wish to make the most effective use of it. The apologetic and polemic notes, therefore, largely will be absent.

May I hasten to say, lest anyone should misunderstand, that in Part Two I have made no attempt to be exhaustive either in depth or in breadth. I do think that the principles considered are vital ones and that what I have said has been discussed fully enough to be helpful, but I must make this clear—the principles are offered more suggestively than comprehensively. They are, in a sense, representative and illustrative as well as (I hope) informative. With those disclaimers and this minimum of orientation, now I should like to introduce you to . . .

PART ONE

THE PERSONS

Chapter One

THE PERSONS INVOLVED IN COUNSELING

Always More Than Two

It is by no means self-evident that the persons involved in pastoral counseling are, as Seward Hiltner has written, "the parishioner and pastor" or, as nearly every book on counseling assumes, the counselor and the counselee.[1] In raising this issue there is no attempt to drag in a dozen or more significant others who might "sit in" on the session as a part of the superego of the counselee.[2] Indeed, anyone who has read *Competent to Counsel* will recognize immediately my complete antipathy to any such idea. And, while the matter is on the floor for discussion, let us at once dismiss concepts of transference that might consciously be brought into the picture by projecting upon the counselor the image or figure of some person from the counselee's past or present life context.[3] Certainly, too, we must avoid any notions of genetic determinism that may make parents (whether immediate or Jungian past) responsible for the behavior or feeling of the counselee. No, all of these attempts

---

1. Seward Hiltner, *The Counselor in Counseling* (Nashville: Abingdon Press, 1952), p. 7. I must also dissent from the notion of Clyde Narramore that "the most important element in counseling is the counselor himself." Clyde Narramore, *The Psychology of Counseling* (Grand Rapids: Zondervan Publishing House, 1960), p. 18. Hiltner speaks of three elements: "parishioner, pastor," and "the relationship" between them. God is not mentioned in the foreword, which purports to spell out the "fundamental" points of Hiltner's approach and the basic elements in the counseling context. The approach described is essentially humanistic.

2. I also reject the deterministic concept of the child, parent, and the adult which is advocated in Tom Harris' *I'm O.K.—You're O.K.* (New York: Harper and Row, 1967), a volume on transactional psychiatry (*à la* Eric Berne). This clever presentation is simply a thin disguise for the old Freudian Id (child), *Super-ego* (parent), and *Ego* (adult). Berne, originator of T.A. (Transactional Analysis), was a close associate of Erik Erikson, the prominent neofreudian who emphasizes the ego.

3. For further comments concerning transference and its evils as a counseling tool, cf. *Competent to Counsel*, pp. 100 ff., 207.

3

to enlarge the counseling context fail since, as the Scriptures plainly teach, God holds each one of us personally responsible for his thoughts, words, and actions regardless of external pressures and influences:

> For we must all appear before the judgment seat of Christ, that *each one* [italics mine] may be recompensed for his deeds in the body, according to what he has done, whether good or bad.[4]

All blame-shifting and excuses will evaporate in that day before the searching gaze of the One whose eyes are "as a flame of fire."[5] The sophisticated Freudian or behavioristic theories that now seem so conveniently plausible and that are used to justify and excuse men of their responsibility to God will be shown to be futile and false. In His presence, men in anguish will wonder at the naivete that they once called sophistication.

At Least Three

Well then, of whom is the counseling context composed? How many persons are involved and who are they? The Christian answer is that the biblical counseling context, like the disciplinary context (and counseling and discipline must be seen as integrally related),[6] always involves a minimum of three: "Where two or three are gathered together in my name, there I am in their midst."[7] In truly biblical counseling, therefore, where a counselor and counselee meet in the name of Jesus Christ, they may expect the very presence of Christ as Counselor-in-charge.

---

4. II Corinthians 5:10 (NASB). Cf. also Matthew 16:27; Hebrews 4:12, 13; 9:27; Colossians 1:28.

5. Revelation 1:14.

6. E.g., see Matthew 18:16, where counseling by "one or two others" is considered to be a part of the informal stage of disciplinary action.

7. Matthew 18:20. This verse closely follows the reconciliation passage (Matthew 18:15-17) and is, indeed, a part of it.

Chapter Two

THE HOLY SPIRIT IS THE PRINCIPAL PERSON

Jesus Christ now dwells invisibly in His church in the person of the Holy Spirit. Before leaving His disciples, Jesus assured them that the Father would send them "another Counselor . . . the Spirit of truth."[1] The Greek word that is translated "another" is a specific term meaning literally "another of the same kind." For three and one-half years, in fulfillment of Isaiah's prediction that He would be called a "Counselor," Jesus guided, instructed, rebuked, encouraged, and taught His disciples.[2] He was truly their Counselor. During His ministry, of course, Jesus counseled many other individuals as well.[3]

Now, as Jesus was about to leave His disciples, He graciously calmed their fears by informing them that He would send "another" Counselor like Himself to be with them to teach and guide as He had previously.[4]

---

1. John 14:16, 17.
2. Isaiah 9:6. Cf. also Isaiah 11:2; Zechariah 6:13 (NASB).
3. For a biblical picture of the work of counseling, it is important to study the work of Jesus Christ. I should suggest that He is particularly set forth in the Gospel of John as "counselor," and that encounters such as those recorded in John 2, 3, 4, 9, etc., are specifically examples of Christ's work of counseling. It is instructive to note, although I cannot discuss the matter fully here, that John seems to have built his Gospel around the titles attributed to Christ in Isaiah 9:6. It is John who pictures Him as "the Unique One" ("Wonderful" *pele* Isaiah 9:6, and "only begotten" *monogenes*, which means "the only-one-of-its-kind" rather than "only begotten," John 1:14,18; 3:16, etc., both seem to speak of His uniqueness), as "Counselor," John 14, 16, I John 2:1, as "the Mighty God," John 1:1, 18, etc., "the Everlasting (John 1:1; 8:58) Father," John 10:30-33; 14:8, and the "Prince of Peace," John 14:27; 16:33. Only by understanding the matter in this way can we explain the (otherwise) astounding fact that the New Testament writers entirely by-passed this plainly messianic prediction. It is my hope that of the more than one hundred men who so far have been trained in nouthetic counseling, some one or more of them would undertake the important biblical study of Jesus Christ as Counselor. He was Counselor to men in general and Counselor to His disciples in an even more intimate way.
4. The guiding and teaching function of the biblical counselor is seen clearly in John 14:26; 16:13. His methods as Counselor are described in John 16:7-15. The Spirit as Counselor is so concerned with counseling by teaching and leading into *truth* that He is specifically designated "the Spirit of truth" (John 14:17).

The rendering "comforter" goes back to Wycliffe. But there is good reason, however, to translate *parakletos* in its occurrences in John by "advocate" or a synonym, such as "counselor," or "helper," or "intercessor."[5] He identified this Counselor as the Holy Spirit, the Spirit of truth (i.e., who is the Source of truth and who leads into truth).

His Work Is Holiness

The Holy Spirit is called holy not only because He is to be distinguished from all other spirits, and in particular from *unclean* spirits, but also because He is the Source of all holiness.[6] This point is specifically emphasized in Romans 1:4 where, in an unusual construction, He is called "the Spirit of holiness." The holiness of God's people that results from their sanctification by the Holy Spirit must be attributed entirely to Him as He works through His Word.[7] The "fruit" of the Spirit is just that: it is the *result* of His work. If the counseling is in essence one aspect of the work of sanctification (as I have argued elsewhere[8]), then the Holy Spirit, whose principal work in the regenerated man is to sanctify him (cf. also Ezekiel 36:25-27), must be considered the most important Person in the counseling context. Indeed, He must be viewed as *the* Counselor. Ignoring the Holy Spirit or avoiding the use of the Scriptures in counseling is tantamount to an act of autonomous rebellion. Christians may not counsel apart from the Holy Spirit

---

5. Walter W. Wessel in Baker's *Dictionary of Practical Theology* (Grand Rapids: Baker Book House, 1960), p. 30. The words *noutheteo* and *nouthesia* occur only in Paul. John seems to prefer *parakletos*, putting the emphasis upon the Person who counsels.

6. "Holy" means "set apart *from* and *to*; i.e., "special" or "unique."

7. Cf. John 15:3, where Christ notes that it is by the Word that He prunes (cleans) the branches. Moreover, in His prayer for the church He prays "make them holy by the truth; your Word is truth" (John 17:17). See footnote no. 6, above. For a discussion of the Spirit's use of the Word, see also *Competent to Counsel*, pp. 23-25. Here let me add simply this: the Spirit ordinarily works through means. The Christian does not *order* the Spirit, or mechanically "turn on" the Spirit by the use of biblical truth. While He gave the truth, brought the Bible into being, and has chosen to work through it, the Spirit is neither a force nor a machine. He has put the Bible, not Himself, at our disposal. He is a Person who works when and where and how He pleases. To us has been given the Bible. We ask God to be pleased to make our use of it effective by His Spirit and then move out in obedience to its truth. The results and whole outcome belong to God.

8. *Competent to Counsel*, pp. 20, 21, 73-77. As the Spirit of sanctification, He is the Spirit of change. Wherever the Spirit is at work, change is inevitable.

and His Word without grievously sinning against Him and the coun-selee. Any counseling context that disassociates itself from these ele-ments is decidedly a non-Christian context, even though it may be called Christian or may be structured by a counselor who is himself a Christian but who has (wrongly) attempted to divorce his Christian faith from his counseling principles and techniques.

At the time that he announced the coming of the Spirit, Jesus also told His disciples that they would be sent to do a "greater work" than He had done.[9] This work could be accomplished, He said, only if He left them and sent the Holy Spirit to take His place. The Spirit would be a counselor to them in performing these tasks in a way in which He could not be. His continued visible bodily presence with them would have meant that the work, if it were to be guided by His counsel, would be confined to a few in but one area. But in going to the Father and in sending the invisible Spirit to be with them wherever they went throughout the world, they and all other Christians could benefit from the same counsel at once wherever they were. By the Spirit, He promised to continue to be with them until the end of the age (Matthew 28:20). In this work they were going to be in great need of counsel (cf. Luke 12:11, 12; 21:14, 15). Thus, Christ's leaving and the Spirit's coming were for their benefit (John 16:7).[10]

All Christians Benefit from His Counsel

It is true that the Holy Spirit counseled the apostles uniquely, en-abling them infallibly to remember the words and works of Jesus and helping them to reproduce the same in the form of an inerrant revela-tion. This unique sort of counsel ceased with the close of the New Testament canon, once its purpose had been achieved. Yet the more general counseling work of the Holy Spirit continued after the death of the apostles. Indeed, through His use of this written revelation preached, read, explained, and applied among the members of the

---

9. John 14:12. Obviously not in *kind;* their work would be greater in *extent.*

10. If they should attempt to evangelize the world without the ever-present coun-sel and power of the Holy Spirit, they would fail, for it was He who would "teach" them and help them to "remember" (John 14:26), and "guide them into all truth" (John 16:13). These, and other similar functions attributed to the Holy Spirit, indi-cate that the biblical role of the counselor is essentially *directive.* The counseling work of Jesus by the Spirit is normative for all Christian counseling. As counselor, the Spirit is directive in approach.

Church of Christ, the Holy Spirit today carries on His work of counseling. It is He who regenerates and gives faith to the elect (I Corinthians 12:3), and it is He who enables the believer to understand (I Corinthians 2:9-16) and live according to God's will revealed in the Scriptures. These two purposes (salvation and sanctification) are declared to be the ends or "uses" of the Scriptures (II Timothy 3:15, 16), just as the two conjoint purposes of the worldwide mission comprise the works of evangelism and edification (Matthew 28:19, 20). All true believers receive the baptism (or "anointing") of the Holy Spirit at regeneration and, therefore, receive the benefit of His counsel (I John 2:20, 27). But that counsel has been deposited in the writings of the apostles, and it is by enabling His church to "hear" them in these writings (I John 4:6) that the Spirit has chosen to counsel His church today.

Chapter Three

THE HUMAN COUNSELOR

Who Should Counsel?

While every Christian must become a counselor to his fellow Christians, the work of counseling as a special calling is assigned particularly to the pastor.[1]

Biblically, there is no warrant for acknowledging the existence of a separate and distinct discipline called psychiatry. There are, in the Scriptures, only three specified sources of personal problems in living: demonic activity (principally possession), personal sin, and organic illness. These three are interrelated. All options are covered under these heads, leaving no room for a fourth: non-organic mental illness.[2] There is, therefore, no place in a biblical scheme for the psychiatrist as a separate practitioner. This self-appointed caste came into existence with the broadening of the medical umbrella to include inorganic illness (whatever that means). A new practitioner, part physician (a very small part) and part secular priest[3] (a very large part), came into being to serve the host of persons who previously were counseled by ministers[4]

---

1. Cf. *The Big Umbrella*, chaps. I ("The Big Umbrella") and VI ("You Are Your Brother's Counselor").

2. *Ibid.*, pp. 39-62. Clyde Narramore's threefold classification of the body (physician), spirit (pastor), and soul (psychologist) is not biblical. Trichotomy is not supported by a superficial appeal to I Thessalonians 5:23, where Paul is not distinguishing the parts of man, but simply heaping word upon word to emphasize entirety. Jesus Christ did the same thing when He spoke of loving God with all of one's "heart, soul, mind, and strength" (Mark 12:30). The Scriptures use the terms soul (*pseuche*) and spirit (*pneuma*) interchangeably. Cf. Luke 1: 46, 47, where the two are used in parallelism. Cf. Berkhof, *Systematic Theology* (Grand Rapids: Wm. B. Eerdmans Company, 1941), pp. 193, 195. Especially see Wm. Hendriksen, *New Testament Commentary* (I Thessalonians), Note on I Thessalonians 5:23 (Grand Rapids: Baker Book House, 1955), pp. 146-150.

3. Cf. Perry London, *The Modes and Morals of Psychotherapy* (New York: Holt, Rinehart and Winston, 1964), pp. 156 ff.

4. Prior to Freud and Charcot it was ministers who wrote books on such subjects as depression (melancholia). "From as far back as Hippocrates, the

9

but now had been snatched away from them and placed beneath the broad umbrella of "mental illness."[5]

I do not wish to argue the point that modern ideas of mental illness are invalid. Many others have made this point with impact.[6] Moreover, I have cited some of this material at length elsewhere.[7] I am concerned here to make but two observations only: (1) the psychiatrist should return to the practice of medicine, which is his only legitimate sphere of activity; (2) the minister should return to the God-given work from which he was ousted (and which, in many instances, too willingly abandoned).

That there is much for the psychiatrist to do *medically* to help persons suffering from problems in living whose etiology is organic cannot be questioned. The field is growing. Certainly an understanding of the influence of bodily chemistry upon behavior and emotions is only beginning. For instance, recent study indicates that those pathological problems that result from toxic chemical impact upon perception and, consequently, upon personality are probably greater in number than presently is known. The Christian pastor would rejoice to see psychiatry leave the area of the non-organic to become what (in America though not in Europe) it falsely has claimed to be, a medical specialty.[8]

---

medical profession had to fight its way into the domain of mental illness, an area that had been appropriated by philosophy and theology." *The Encyclopedia of Human Behavior*, Robert M. Goldenson (ed.), vol. I (Garden City: Doubleday and Company, 1970), p. 670.

5. The two general goals and methods of psychiatrists and Christian ministers are identical, clearly revealing the overlap: (1) Both want to change behavior, emotion, and character; (2) Both attempt this through value, attitude, and behavioral change. God has assigned this task as a life calling to those who minister His Word, and to no others.

6. Cf. Perry London, *op. cit.*, "Psychotherapists are not really doctors because the people they treat are not really sick," p. 153.

7. Viz., *Competent to Counsel, The Big Umbrella*.

8. Cf. Perry London, *op. cit.*, pp. 153-156. Note especially the following: "Medical training and license is largely irrelevant to its proper practice . . . ," p. 153; London observes that the medical requirement "was adopted only after Sigmund Freud's demise; he regarded analysis as a non-medical business, and favored training 'lay' analysts," p. 155. Of course, in returning to the medical aspects of behavioral problems, psychiatrists will have to do much more than they have done already for "real progress has been near zero in establishing a biochemical basis for mental illness," Andrew Kopkind & James Ridgeway, "The Mental Health Industry," *Readings in Sociology*, '72-'73 (Dushkin Pub. Group, Inc., 1973), p. 114. Since this is true, medical psychiatry at first will be restricted to grosser problems like brain damage, tumor, etc.

In other words, psychiatry's legitimate function is to serve those who suffer from organic difficulties. The psychiatrist has reason for existence only when he specializes as a physician to treat medically those persons whose problems have an organic etiology. Even then, most likely there will be need for twofold help. While the physician treats the physical problem, the Christian counselor should pedal in tandem. As he works with a physician who treats an ulcer by dealing with life patterns that led to the ulcer, so he may need to work together with a physician using megavitamin therapy. The pastor's task will be to help him to alter sinful life patterns that may have developed in response to the chemical disorder. These may include bad human relationships resulting from suspicion, withdrawal from others, etc.

Counseling Is Ministerial

The Christian minister must be willing (and able) to assume the full task to which God has called him: that of ministering to men and women who suffer from the pains and miseries that stem from personal sins.[9] The subject matter of the Scriptures is the redemptive love of God in Christ for His Church and the Church's response must be love toward God and one's neighbor (the summary of the law). The minister is called to the special task of proclaiming the good news and ministering God's Word to those whom the Spirit regenerates. He is vitally concerned with the love response of the Christian to the love of God. As a calling he must be a pastor/teacher who faithfully leads God's flock in the paths of righteousness and feeds them upon "every word that proceeds from the mouth of God." *Par excellence*, it is his task to minister the Word in preaching and counseling in such a way that weary, torn, hungry, wandering sheep are safely sequestered within the sheepfold. The two functions, counseling and preaching, correspond to the

---

9. The question of referral is a live one. Cf. *Competent to Counsel*, pp. 11, 12, 18, 19, 21, 62, 253, 268 for further discussion of this matter. A minister's wife suggested: "Why send someone to a person who doesn't know as much as you? If a dentist can't fill a tooth, why patronize him?" Cf. "12 Admissions of Mental Error," *Medical World News*, February 9, 1973, pp. 17 ff., which showed that in 12 out of 12 cases diagnosis in leading mental institutions was in error. Other patients in the institution proved to be more able diagnosticians than psychiatrists! Cf. also Hans Strupp, *Psychotherapy: Clinical, Research and Theoretical Issues* (New York: Jason Aronson, Inc., 1973), p. 69, for evidence of experimental research of a different sort that confirms the charge that psychiatric diagnosis is, as he puts it, in a "sorry state."

designations pastor and teacher.[10] To say that the Christian minister is counselor and preacher, *par excellence*, means that he is called to these works as his function or office in the church. It does not exclude much teaching, exhortation, and counseling on the part of every Christian, incidental to his particular gifts and calling."[11]

All of which raises the important matter of whether Christians may legitimately assume the position of counselors as a life task and calling *apart from ordination to the Christian ministry*. Just as all Christians may give witness to their faith, which involves an informal proclamation of the Word (cf. Acts 8:1-4; the *whole* church "announced the message of good news"), so all Christians may (indeed, *must*) do counseling. Yet, not all Christians have been solemnly set aside to the work of "nouthetically confronting every man and teaching every man,"[12] as the Christian minister is. He, in a special way, has been appointed and set aside by God and the church to these two works of ministry by the call of God and the church and the laying on of hands. There is no indication in the Scriptures that anyone but those who have been so recognized should undertake the work of counseling or proclamation of the Word *officially* (i.e., as an office, work, or life calling). This means that persons with a life-calling to do counseling ought to prepare for the work of the ministry and seek ordination, since God describes a life-calling to counseling as the life-calling of a minister.

Many young Christian men have written or visited me in the last two years who want to go into counseling as a life-calling but who have no thought of doing this work as ministers under the aegis of the Church of Jesus Christ. I have tried to show them from the Scriptures what God says about this matter. I have pointed out that the more Christian a counselor becomes in his counseling activities, the more he looks like a minister; i.e., his activities are precisely those to which a minister is called as a counseling pastor.

The best training for Christian counseling is a good seminary education to provide a solid biblical and theological background. The resources upon which a truly Christian counselor relies are the Word, the Spirit, and the Church. There are major differences between the minister and the free lance counselor. The minister has the opportunity to do

---

10. Cf. Ephesians 4:11; Ezekiel 34; Jeremiah 23.
11. Cf. "You Are Your Brother's Counselor," *The Big Umbrella*, chap. VI.
12. Colossians 1:28.

the preventive work that preaching and regular pastoral care provides. The counselor outside of the church has no opportunity to mold a congregation of people into a harmonious, loving body into which counselees may be assimilated and from which they may receive significant help. And, perhaps most important of all, the processes of discipline, which are of utmost significance in scriptural counseling, are not available to the Christian counselor who operates from outside of the church. He opts, therefore, for only *a part* of the full resources that God has put at the disposal of the Christian minister; consequently he can do but *part* of the full task of counseling.

There is no reason to think that a minister who is especially gifted in counseling cannot spend the principal part of his time doing the work of counseling, perhaps as an associate pastor in a congregation or as a presbyterial member who assists the pastors of several local congregations.

The authority of Christ given to "those who have the rule" (Hebrews 13:7, 17; I Thessalonians 5:13)[13] must not be despised. The unordained Christian counselor, working outside of the organized church of Christ, has not received and cannot exercise such authority. Yet this authority in many ways is of great importance in the work of counseling. And, in addition, he must reckon with the fact that in going it alone, he has failed to bring himself under the authority of Christ vested in His church. All would-be Christian counselors should consider and take seriously their own gifts and calling.

Qualifications for Counseling

The qualifications of a minister are the same as those of a counselor. Can a Christian who has not been set apart (by ordination) by the church to this ministry legitimately take up as a life calling the work that God allocates to the minister as *his* life's calling? That is the question that he should ponder.

Qualifications for Christian counselors have been discussed at length elsewhere.[14] These may be summed up as extensive knowledge of the Scriptures, divine wisdom, and good will toward others.[15] These three

13. In I Thessalonians 5:12, 13, it is the ordained elder who "has charge over" (i.e., has been given authority by Jesus Christ over His flock), who as his "work" has been given the task of "nouthetically confronting" (vs. 12).

14. *Competent to Counsel*, pp. 59 ff.

15. Cf. Romans 15:14; Colossians 3:16.

elements correspond to the three sides of the task that the Scriptures call nouthetic confrontation.[16]

Nouthetic Confrontation	Qualifications in a Counselor
1. Discernment of wrong doing in another that God wants changed.	1. Scriptural knowledge of the will of God (Romans 15:14; Colossians 3:16).
2. Verbal confrontation of another with the Word of God in order to change his attitudes or behavior.	2. Divine wisdom in one's relationships to others (Colossians 3:16).
3. Confrontation of another for his benefit.	3. Good will and concern for other members of the body of Christ (Romans 15:14).

Unfortunately some men are ordained to the gospel ministry almost entirely upon the basis of the successful completion of examinations in systematic theology and church polity. In his trials for licensure and ordination, the candidate's personal qualifications frequently either are assumed or ignored. Yet, the qualifications for the ministry found in the check lists in Titus and I Timothy center even more fully upon personal qualifications than upon doctrinal prowess.[17] There is little question, therefore, that the process of calling and ordaining ministers needs fresh examination. The process must be augmented in such a way that, while a presbytery continues to stress doctrinal soundness, it equally examines the personal fitness of the man in general and, in particular, his qualifications to do the work of confronting men nouthetically.[18]

In addition to what I have written about the three basic qualifications of a counselor in *Competent to Counsel*, I must add another implied by by these: he must be a man of faith and hope. As a man of faith, he will believe the promises of God. In the Scriptures God promises to change those who repent of their sins and who walk according to His

---

16. Cf. *Competent to Counsel* for a full discussion of the word *nouthesia* and its three elements, pp. 41-50. Those three elements may be summarized as (1) *change* by (2) *confrontation* coupled with (3) *concern*. Interestingly, Strupp observes that there is an "amazing dearth of empirical data on the personal & technical qualifications of a good psychotherapist." Hans Strupp, *op. cit.*, p. 57.

17. Titus 1:6-9; I Timothy 3:1-7. With Paul, I am sure, I should not wish to disparage the great importance of doctrinal soundness. Yet, it cannot be denied that the *emphasis* today has changed from that of the New Testament.

18. I am not speaking here of the other side of the ministry, which pertains to the ability of the candidate to preach and teach the word. The two cannot be separated; the qualities that enable a man to preach and those that qualify him to confront others with the Word of God are plainly interrelated.

commandments. As a man of faith he becomes also a man of hope. Without hope, he cannot communicate the hope and encouragement that many counselees need.[19] He must be convinced that the Bible is true and be ready and able to direct others to its promises with assurance and conviction. This means that his orientation will be toward God's solutions, not merely toward man's problems.

Authority in Counseling

There is need for divine authority in counseling. Only biblical counseling possesses such authority. The counselor, as an ordained man of God, exercises the full authority for counseling that Christ gave to the organized church (I Thessalonians 5:12, 13). To the extent that all Christians must counsel (Colossians 3:16; Romans 15:14), they exercise the authority that Christ has conferred upon them as saints.

Because the misuse of authority is a source of numerous problems not only in counseling, but in living every aspect of life (and, of course, the counselor is concerned about every aspect of life), it is important to understand something about the functions and limitations of biblical authority.

We shall begin by noting that the Scriptures contrast two kinds of authority: God's authority and man's authority (Acts 5:29—"We must obey God rather than men"). In the instance cited, the state was overstepping the authority that God had granted to it. It must never be thought that because God gave authority to the church, to the home, and to the state that in such instances these several authorities of God were in conflict. God is not a God of confusion. The passage makes certain that the conflict in authority came not from the exercise of God's authority vested in the church with God's authority vested in the state, but rather from the fact that state officials had overstepped their authority. Thus, they had gone beyond (transgressed) the legitimate authority that God granted them and were, therefore, acting upon their *own* authority (which need not be recognized as a valid authority at all). God's authority is one. It is the same whether it is granted to parents, to rulers, or to the elders of the church. The limits of that authority are set forth in the Scriptures (e.g., Romans 13:1-7). The principle set forth in Acts 5:29 is reaffirmed in another realm in Ephesians 6:1—"Children, obey your parents [but then notice the qualification] in the Lord" (i.e.,

---

19. Cf. *The Big Umbrella*, "Grief As a Counseling Opportunity," pp. 63 ff.

insofar as those parents act within the limits of the authority that was granted to them by God). Clearly then, God's authority is limited by the biblical data which are found in God's commandments.

Counselors, who exercise the authority of God, are not authorities *in their own right*. Although they must use the authority vested in them by God, they must not exceed the biblical limits of that authority. Nor by their authority may they conflict with the valid God-given authority of the state or the home. Counselors who advise illegal acts or who teach children to dishonor parents violate God's authority rather than act according to it.

Nouthetic counseling is subject to the directives of the Bible and is not a law to itself. It is counseling that uses (and does not exceed) the authority of God. Therefore, it is neither arbitrary nor oppressive. Nouthetic counselors must learn to distinguish clearly between good advice that they think grows out of biblical principles and those principles themselves. The latter ("You have no grounds for divorce; it would be sin!") they may enforce with the utmost authority; the former ("Why not set up a conference table in order to begin to learn how to speak the truth in love?") they must present with more caution. It is possible that one's deductions from scriptural principles may be false. The counselor must always allow such deductions to remain open for question by the counselee in a way that he cannot allow a plain commandment of God to be questioned. A conference table may be useful, may grow out of biblical principles, but cannot be commanded; speaking the truth in love *must* be.

Since the Scriptures are the Standard by which a counselor's authority is known and regulated, it need not be feared.

As an exercise, consider the following statements to determine which are proper and which are improper uses of counseling authority. (Rewrite those that are wrong in an acceptable manner.)

1. "Confess this sin to God and forsake it."
2. "Sell your car and pay off the loan."
3. "You must study the Scriptures and pray regularly."
4. "Every morning you must read the Bible one-half hour and pray for twenty minutes."
5. "One way to begin to implement the commandment to 'love your neighbor' is to make a list of items you know will please her and do one each day this week."

6. "You must break off that homosexual relationship today!"

7. "Tranquillizers will do you no good; don't take any more."

8. "Your worry must go; you are going to have to learn how to focus your concern on today rather than on tomorrow."

9. "Catch up on your ironing by the next session."

10. "Obey God's command, whether you feel like it or not."[20]

Counselors Must Be Directive

Because it is authoritative, biblical counseling is directive. The New Testament word for counseling (*nouthesia*) implies scriptural direction. Counseling *as* directing was universal in biblical times. This was the meaning of counseling in the Old Testament, and through subsequent history it remained the same; it meant: "to give advice or direction."[21] It has been only in quite modern times that the concept of counseling did an about-face so that for some the word came to mean *listening* rather than speaking. Now we hear of *non-directive counseling*. Biblically speaking, those words represent a contradiction of terms. Of all of the terms that Carl Rogers might have chosen, this combination is at once the most strategic and the most tragic. The Rogerian title is like that ingenious combination of *Christian Science*, in which respected words are misused to designate their opposites.[22] The Rogerian title, however, unlike that used by Mrs. Eddy, has found such wide acceptance that (against all history) vast numbers of intelligent people today equate counseling with something other than giving direction and advice. Rogerian concepts of counseling are squarely at odds with the unanimous testimony of the biblical data concerning counseling. This means that, in order to do biblical counseling, the human counselor must know the good counsel of the Scriptures, and develop those skills by which he may confront others directively in deep concern.

---

20. Before turning to Appendix F for discussion of these ten statements, see if you can distinguish between them for yourself.

21. Cf., for instance, Isaiah 40:13, where in the parallelism of Hebrew poetry *directing* is equated with *counseling*. See also *Competent to Counsel*, chap. VI. The kings' counselors and the counselor-at-law are wise men who supply answers. See preeminently Isaiah 9:6.

22. The combination probably does not stem from Mary Baker Glover Patterson Eddy herself; similar terms are found in the writings of Phineus Quimby and Francis Lieber.

The Personality of the Counselor

But does not directive counseling require a certain personality type? Indeed, the question has been asked, "Can every counselor be directive, or does the sort of confrontation described in *Competent to Counsel* and in this book fit only a certain sort of personality?" In other words, do counseling methods grow out of a counselor's personality and develop because they are appropriate to it rather than grow out of his basic presuppositions? Or, perhaps even more pointedly, does a counselor tend to adopt those presuppositions that are in accordance with his fundamental personality type? Does the man mold the method or does the method mold the man?

The question is important for several reasons. If personality is the determining factor behind the various types of counseling, then of course the counseling presuppositions and methods set forth here are relative and do not rest upon a divine imperative. They cannot be said to be based upon or guided by clear biblical principles, and their authoritative distinctiveness is lost. In short, if the personality of the counselor is the determining factor in the type of counseling one elects to do, then this volume was written in vain.

If there is anything that must be maintained at all costs, it is the integrity of the Scriptures as the authoritative standard for Christian counseling.[23] All ideas of relativism must be abandoned. It is only upon biblical presuppositions that counseling may be based, and these are necessarily the same for every Christian counselor. The fundamentals of method, insofar as they inevitably grow out of these presuppositions, again will be the same.

This unity of person, principle, and practice does not exclude personal

---

23. In a generally sympathetic review of *Competent to Counsel*, John S. Bostrom claimed that using the Bible as a textbook for "modern physics or geography or shipbuilding" is analogous to my use of the Bible to meet human needs. John S. Bostrom, M.D., *The Christian Medical Society Journal*, Fall, 1971, p. 15. He is quite wrong. The Bible was not written for the former purposes, but it decidedly was written for the latter. Dr. Bostrom, by his inept analogy, shows that he has missed the most fundamental point of all. The Bible was not written to deal with the intricacies of shipbuilding, but surely it tells us *all* that we need to know about interpersonal relations. In the Bible are all things necessary to know how to love God and one's neighbor. Counseling directly pertains to the intricacies of those matters.

variety growing out of the individual gifts of each counselor.[24] As in preaching, where within the biblical framework of proclamation there are individual styles, so in counseling each counselor will develop his own style. Personality differences to this extent are clearly valid.[25]

However, since God's message carries its own authority, like the preacher the counselor must accommodate his personality to the message rather than seek to do the reverse. The authority is God's. Although mediated through various styles, the fundamental authority of God in counseling must be evident in all biblical counseling. Any personality traits that interfere with, rather than mediate the message must be altered. That is why the Lord changed the apostle Peter from a weak, vacillating, fearful disciple to the bold fearless disciple who told the authorities, "We must obey God rather than men" (Acts 5:29).[26] The more faithfully a counselor ministers God's Word, the more he changes by conforming to it.

In order to counsel according to methods that are appropriate to biblical presuppositions, a would-be counselor may find that a rather radical change of personality is necessary.[27] This change is precisely what we have seen occur in the lives of a number of the seminary and pastoral trainees who participate in our program. Men frequently express appreciation not only for the changes that the course has brought about in them as pastors, but also consistently comment on the changes that have been made in their personal lives and in their marriages. Wherever the Spirit of the Lord is at work, one of the discernible evidences of His presence is changed personalities. Men can and do change. Peter and Paul did; so can you. Sanctification (personality change toward holiness) is the work of the Spirit through His Word.

24. Flexibility of style *within* the biblical framework is itself a biblical principle based upon *biblical* presuppositions. The Bible plainly speaks of individual gifts to be exercised in the common work of ministry.

25. Cf. Matthew 11:16-19 (Luke 7:31-34). Christ compares John's approach and His own. Neither the dance nor the dirge moved the wicked generation. John was a voice shouting in the desert; Christ did not lift up his voice in the streets.

26. Cf. also Acts 3:14, 15: "But you disowned the Holy and Righteous One, . . . and put to death the Prince of life." Boldness (Acts 4:31) and confidence Acts 4:13) now characterized his personality since he had "been with Jesus" and since he had received the Holy Spirit.

27. As a matter of fact, all methods always mold the man. How important then it is for the Christian counselor to adopt Christian methods!

One trainee, after his first day in a counseling session, said, "I could *never* talk to people that way; I'm simply not capable of it. I have neither the courage nor the inclination." He was encouraged to wait and see. During successive weeks he was caught up in the counseling program, into which he entered enthusiastically and from which he emerged a transformed person. The program itself had brought about changes that have affected his entire subsequent ministry.

Based upon the fundamental Christian conviction that men can change as the Spirit works within them, we must insist upon the idea that every man who has been called by God into the ministry has been given the basic gifts for the pastoral ministry and, therefore, can do nouthetic counseling. The gifts required for biblical counseling are precisely those that God requires for the pastorate. A number of changes may be necessary in order for him to achieve proficiency in counseling, but these changes can be made. After all, the Christian counselor is engaged in the very work of effecting God's change in the lives of His children; if he does not believe that it is possible for change to occur in his own life, how can he expect to see change in others? How can he call upon counselees to change and assure them that such change is possible? Conversely, the man who himself has undergone the changes necessary to become a truly Christian counselor will be full of hope for change in others and will helpfully communicate this confidence to them. Every man who has been called by God to the task of biblical counseling experiences change.[28] The demands of the work are greater than any man may assume in his own strength. The requirements of the work greatly stretch him. He *cannot* remain the same.

---

28. Not all change happens immediately. A counselor cannot wait for perfection before he begins to counsel; he will *never* begin at that rate. Indeed, the greatest changes will come *through* counseling. When he fails, he must learn how to admit it and move ahead. That sort of experience leads to growth as he mends his net. A human counselor is believable partly *because* he is a redeemed sinner. Because he too has to face the same problems and has found Christ in His Word sufficient both to keep him from sin and to extricate him from it, he can offer hope. If he has been willing to subject himself to the judgment of the Word, others will allow him to bring that judgment to their lives too.

Modeling (apprenticeship or discipling) is the fastest way to teach the art of counseling. At the Christian Counseling Center in Hatboro, Pennsylvania, we have been using this method to train ministers for more than six years with good success.

Chapter Four

THE COUNSELEE

You Already Know a Lot

Twenty minutes into the first counseling session a counselee said in astonishment and disbelief: "You know me! *How* do you know me; I just met you?" When nouthetic counselors ask depressed housewives, "How is your ironing?" or "Have you stopped making the children's lunches?" or "Has the green hairy stuff started growing in the refrigerator yet?" they often respond like one woman who asked: "Are you a mind reader?" Yet, there is nothing so remarkable about these simple insights into human behavior. As a matter of fact, they are, as Sherlock Holmes used to say, "Elementary my dear Watson, elementary."

A sign in the Detroit Airport terminal reads: "When you see a man reading the *Wall Street Journal*, you already know a lot about him." And *before* the counselee walks into the counseling room, a Christian counselor already knows a lot *more* about *him*.

Sources of Knowledge

There are three sources of information available to the Christian counselor (the first primary and foundational, the other two secondary and derivative) from which he may draw hard-core data and on the basis of which he may make judgments, set goals, and project courses of action. These are (1) the Scriptures, (2) his (and others') counseling experience, and (3) the dynamics of his own sinful heart.[1]

The Scriptures are the primary and normative source from which the Christian counselor's presuppositions and principles must be drawn; the other two sources will help him to flesh out these principles in the concrete terms of everyday life.[2] Such fleshing out is vital to the

---

1. That one can know a lot about others by looking into his own heart seems to be the meaning of Proverbs 27:19. Cf. Keil and Delitzsch on this passage.
2. Apart from the Scriptures, a counselor is virtually helpless. The Scriptures teach that "the heart is deceitful and desperately wicked" and ask, "Who can know it?" (Jeremiah 17:9). In verse 10 God replies: "I the Lord search the

21

vibrant communication with counselees that is so essential to effective counseling.[3]

No Surprises Necessary

The Scriptures themselves suggest the principle that encourages one to make use of the two secondary sources mentioned above:

No test has overtaken you but such as is common to man.[4]

If no Christian faces unique tests in life, and if Paul can say to the church at Corinth (living in an entirely different age and culture) that what happened to the Israelites is pertinent also to them (cf. vss. 6, 11), the counselor may be assured that he will face no truly unique problems in counseling. There are just so many basic common themes of sin and no more. There may be times, for one reason or another, when, because he is unable to discover the nature of it, a problem might *seem* unique. But the counselor may be assured that it is not. He has faced the problem in others and possibly struggled with it within himself in one form or another. His difficulty lies only in his inability to recognize and identify the problem for what it truly is. This inability may stem from his own failure, the failure of the counselee to disclose clear or adequate data, or from both, but never from the fact that he is facing a unique problem.[5] The Christian counselor may take heart from this important truth.

The problem patterns that counselees exhibit today may be seen (at

heart, I test the mind." Apart from what God knows of man's deceitful heart, a counselor is in grave difficulty. God's knowledge of man's heart is revealed only in the Scriptures. The heart is deceitful even when it speaks of itself. Therefore, the dynamics of one's heart, like those of his counseling experience, must always be determined and judged by the Scriptures. What He tells us is not inviting (cf. Mark 7:19-23).

3. Counselees vibrate responsively whenever the counselor states principles not merely as generalizations, but in the Monday morning language of everyday life. Counselors must make every effort to become as specific and concrete as possible. Good preaching and good counseling merge here as they do at many other points. Cf. Jay Adams, *Pulpit Speech* (Nutley, N. J.: Presbyterian and Reformed Publishing Company, 1971), p. 17.

4. I Corinthians 10:13a. Cf. *Competent to Counsel*, pp. 58, 90, 131 ff., 254, and *Christ and Your Problems* for fuller expositions of this verse. Cf. also II Corinthians 1:3, 4. Paul says, "God . . . comforts us in all our affliction so that we may be able to comfort those who are afflicted with the [same] comfort."

5. The counselor often may elicit the unknown information from a counselee by suggesting a string of possibilities concretely: "I can do little to help when the problem is so vague. Now if I knew that we were dealing with a specific problem like masturbation, homosexuality, or adultery (here the specific sugges-

least in germ form) in the account of Adam and Eve in the garden of
Eden. The only unique aspects (that may throw a counselor off the
track) of the counselee's problem are to be found in the secondary
features of the problem, but not in the basic problem itself. The
secondary superficial or surface features are always unique to the time,
place, and persons involved. But when these are stripped off and the
inner core of the problem is exposed, it will be found to be (at base)
nothing new under the sun.

Solutions for Every Problem

Just as the Christian counselor knows that there is no unique problem
that has not been mentioned plainly in the Scriptures, so also he knows
that there is a biblical solution to every problem.[6] He knows, too, that
Jesus was tested "in all points as we are" and that He successfully met
every test "without sin."[7] Since Jesus has faced and solved all of life's
basic problems, the counselor knows that in His work and words as
recorded in the Scriptures he may discover the needed solutions.[8] Indeed, the Scriptures say that God has revealed to His church "all things
pertaining to life and godliness," and that God has given His Word in
written form in order to enable His people to engage in "all good
works" by "thoroughly equipping" them for every exigency of life[9] The

---

tions used should include tentative conclusions that the counselor wishes to explore), we could go right to work on the problem. For instance, if masturbation
were the problem, then. . . ." Often such specific suggestions with the hope of a
solution in view will be seized upon immediately by the counselee. Sometimes,
when a word like "adultery" is first spoken by the counselor, it is easier for the
counselee to speak about the problem.
    6. Cf. I Corinthians 10:13b: "God is faithful who will not allow you to be
tested beyond that which you are able to bear and with the test also will make a
way of escape in order that you may be able to bear it." The counselor may extend hope confidently to the Christian counselee upon the basis of God's promise.
He may say, "There is no problem that you have to which God does not offer a
solution in His Word. It is my task to understand your problem, help you to
discover God's solution to it, and to encourage you to do (by His help) what
God requires you to do about it."
    7. Hebrews 4:15.
    8. Christ's works and words must not be limited to the gospel accounts; the
whole New Testament is the record of His continuing work carried out by the
Spirit for and through His church (cf. Acts 1:1. Stress in the original upon the
word "began" emphasizes Christ's continuing work). God did not give us a
Red Letter Bible. See The Big Umbrella, p. 99.
    9. II Timothy 3:17. The man of God thus is made "perfect" (i.e., "complete"
or "completely prepared").

biblical picture, then, is that of God's complete provision for the needs of His people. It is this that is everywhere stressed in the figure of the shepherd: e.g., "The Lord is my shepherd; I shall not lack."[10] As the rest of the psalm plainly shows, the oriental shepherd cared for all the needs of his sheep: feeding, healing, leading, resting, and protecting them. In order to do so, he was fully equipped with "rod and staff." The pastor-teacher, whose task it is to emulate the "Great Shepherd of the sheep," similarly has been equipped to carry on the same work. And, as a matter of fact, *every* believer may share in the full supply of divine equipment to the degree that is necessary to accomplish God's will.[11] Thus, those who function as counselors in the shepherding ministry of Christ possess all that they need to carry on the ministry of shepherding.

What the Counselor Needs to Know

What does a Christian counselor know about counselees before they enter the counseling room? A great deal. As a matter of fact, because he has God's written Word, he knows everything that it is necessary for him to know.[12] The only basic questions that remain to be answered during the counseling interview are:

1. What is the specific problem (or problems) in this case? This question implies that the counselor wants to understand the problem thoroughly *on all levels.*[13]

2. Specifically, what biblical principles apply in this case?

3. What must be done to bring these principles to bear upon the case in order to understand and solve the problems? These three questions imply and necessarily raise a number of additional ones that will arise in Part III and cannot be discussed here.

In summary, it may be said that the counselor seeks to learn not what unknown or unique problem the counselee may have, but rather which

---

10. Psalm 23:1.

11. Hebrews 13:20.

12. The data that a Christian minister possesses concerning man and sin is impressive. From the third chapter of Genesis alone he may be aware of man's tendencies toward blame-shifting, self-seeking, pride, desire/feeling orientation, rebellion against authority, guilt, fear, depression, shame, covering up, hiding, and the breakdown in communication.

13. Cf. *Competent to Counsel* for a discussion of three sorts or aspects, or levels of problems, pp. 148 ff., 200 ff. I shall not duplicate here what I have said there in detail.

one(s) of many *already known* problems he may be handling unsuccessfully.

It is possible for the Christian counselor, therefore, to meet the counselee in humble confidence. He knows that as God enables him to understand the Scriptures and the counselee, he will be able to provide the assistance that is requested. His major obstacle as a counselor—and it can be a large one—is the possibility of his own failure to study prayerfully what the Scriptures say about men and their needs. Every young pastor should spend much time carefully exegeting the Bible and *at the same time* looking at his own wicked and deceitful heart as it is laid bare by the Word. He also should observe the lives of the members of his congregation in the light of what he discovers in each passage. He must never study the Scriptures abstractly, but always must read them personally.[14] While differing widely from his solutions to the problem, I must certainly agree with Oates when he writes, "It is just at these points that a minimum of training is given the pastor as to the distinctively *pastoral use of the Bible*."[15]

How Prior Knowledge Helps

Sylvia was the 20-year-old daughter of missionary parents who during all her life had labored in Africa. Now they were forced to return to the States to care for Sylvia, who, during two years of treatment on the field and in America, had been institutionalized several times and who was unanimously labeled by several psychiatrists (Christian and otherwise) as a schizophrenic. Beyond occasional one-word replies (usually of a yes/no variety), Sylvia would not talk.[16] Since she had been vir-

---

14. A Christian cannot accept the view of transactional therapist Thomas Harris, who wrote, "The truth is not . . . bound in a black book. *The truth is a growing body of data that we observe to be true*." Tom Harris, *I'm O.K.— You're O.K.*, *op. cit.*, p. 230. God's truth *is* in the Bible, all of it that is necessary for His children to live lives of godliness. Yet the whole world is God's too. The world is a great picture book from which we may learn, but not apart from the interpretation of that world by the written Word.

15. Wayne E. Oates, *The Bible in Pastoral Care* (Grand Rapids: Baker Book House, 1971), p. 9. Oates makes false disjunctions between pastoral and non-pastoral uses, but he is correct in noting that the use of the Bible has been taught in many theological seminaries in ways that could hardly help (and probably has hindered) the minister in the everyday ministry of the Word. At Westminster Theological Seminary in Philadelphia we have been keenly aware of this problem and have been developing ways and means of overcoming it.

16. Psychiatrists wrongly said, "*could* not talk."

tually silent for the whole of two years, nearly everyone assumed that she was "out of touch with reality."[17] In sheer desperation, when they heard of the Christian Counseling and Educational Center, her parents brought her for counseling. At the end of the third week, the breakthrough occurred. Following that session Sylvia began to talk. And what she said told the whole story.

When Sylvia was old enough to go to school, her parents sent her to the mission school over 350 miles away. Only for brief periods during each year did they see each other and, except for furlough, this pattern continued until she graduated from high school. It was then that the trouble first became apparent. Over those years Sylvia seemed to be a happy docile child; outwardly there was no reason to suspect otherwise. Yet within seethed a bitterness toward her parents that had been growing for more than ten years. She came to resent not only her parents, but also the mission and the God that they both represented. She deeply resented not having a father and mother like other children; she came to realize that she hardly knew them at all and chafed at the thought. But she had never told a soul. For these ten years the bitterness hardened until she was ready to graduate; it was then that her resentment could no longer be hidden and appeared in the strangely rebellious action that the psychiatrists had labeled "schizophrenic." While resenting her parents, she also feared driving them away for good, so she refused to speak at all lest she reveal her true feelings.

The breakthrough came about as follows: when the counselors discovered that Sylvia had spent many years of deprivation apart from her parents, they inquired fully into this area. Her parents were honest and helpful. They believed that they had been "doing the Lord's work" and that this justified their behavior toward their child. During the first two sessions, they came to see that their conduct toward her in many ways had been sinful. They became deeply repentant.

The counselors, assuming that Sylvia was *in touch* with reality, directed pointed comments toward her, explaining that there was hope for solving the problem—whatever it was—and developing the theme that they recognized that her life without her parents had been difficult to take, but that she was a grown woman now and that if she did not

---

17. A much overworked phrase that (apart from its use to describe organic difficulties) in most instances more accurately describes the counselor's viewpoint than the state of the counselee.

learn to face problems rather than running from them, she would never come to know her parents. Running away from problems, they suggested, might eventually cause her to run from her parents (and everyone else) into a mental institution. A balanced combination of hope, warning, exhortation, and encouragement characterized the almost entirely feedbackless conversation.[18] It was following that session that Sylvia broke through the barrier and told her parents (as she had been urged to do) about her resentments.

From then on, counseling consisted of reconciliation and the structuring of a new relationship designed to reacquaint parents and child and as much as possible to make up for lost time.[19] Eventually, after a year or so at home, during which Sylvia got a job and earned a large portion of her tuition, Sylvia went to a Christian college, where she became an excellent student, getting good grades and entering fully into the social life and activities of the student body.

How was the counselor able to achieve these results so early and under conditions in which it was virtually impossible to obtain information directly from Sylvia? Two things may be noted. First, after he had gathered the minimal data that he could from Sylvia, the counselor (in Sylvia's presence, assuming she was in touch and thus capable of understanding the situation fully) questioned the parents in detail about the circumstances. The data he gathered led him to sketch a rather clear picture that pointed toward possible resentment on the part of the child. Secondly, he was able to reach this tentative conclusion (and to speak directly to Sylvia about it as a live possibility), since he knew from the Scriptures that the sinful nature of men often responds in resentment when so neglected. From talking to many missionaries and their children, he knew that the two greatest problems encountered by them were (1) separation from children and (2) interpersonal problems resulting from living with other missionaries in very close proximity or severely restricted settings (particularly in compounds or similar contexts). In this case, the evidence pointed clearly toward difficulties in the first area rather than in the second.

---

18. One wonders what Rogerian "listening" would have accomplished when there was nothing to listen to.

19. The parents and Sylvia, for instance, were directed to compose together a list of activities in which they had never engaged as a family but would have liked to. They listed such items as going to the zoo, picnics, birthday parties, etc.

In this way, the Christian counselor, using the Scriptures practically (they say much about resentment and bitterness), relied upon the information that was in his possession. He then discussed his conclusions with Sylvia and her parents and urged her to repent of her resentment if his conclusions were true.

Sylvia might have retreated behind the screen of silence as a protection from being found out. Fear of discovery may lead to such behavior when one feels guilty over matters that have never been cleared up. Self-pity, also, might have led Sylvia to embark upon a life of silent introspection in which she attempted to construct a fantasy world that she hoped would be more pleasant than the real world around her. As the case developed, however, the constellation of clues (verbal data from parents and non-verbal data from Sylvia[20]) seemed to point in this case toward anger and resentment rather than toward depression from either self-pity or the feelings occasioned by guilt over particular transgressions.

Counselees Can Change

I do not want to repeat what I have said in *Competent to Counsel* about change, but rather, in the following discussion of this important subject I shall assume that the reader is familiar already with that material.[21]

Against all positions that deny either the possibility of significant change (stemming from deterministic views of genetic, social, or environmental influence) or that hold out change as a possibility only after long periods of time, the Christian cheerfully asserts the possibility of thorough, rapid change. This is a very crucial plank in the Christian counselor's platform. As a basic assumption, he presupposes the possibility of radical change in the personality and life style of the counselee. He believes in conversion and in the sanctifying power of the Spirit. He

---

20. As, for example, the muscular tension she evidenced whenever her parents spoke of their separation and the frowns and other facial contortions that accompanied this. Incidentally, such data also indicated that Sylvia *was* in touch with reality and fully understood the content of the conversation. For more information on gathering non-verbal data in counseling, see "Halo Data," pp. 257 ff.

21. Cf. *Competent to Counsel*, esp. pp. 74-77, 171 ff. More will be said throughout about the changes that God effects through counseling that honors His Word and Spirit. When dealing with habit, God's method for change will be handled in detail.

believes that it is possible for one, who, because of his sinful nature, developed sinful living patterns and was taught wrongly by both precept and example from early days, to become a vital Christian possessing the fruit of the Spirit. He is certain that if a headhunting Auca Indian can change so radically that he abandons his primitive pagan life style and is able to tour the United States giving testimony to his new-found faith, then an American housewife, who may have experienced less love and security in her childhood than she might have wished, also may become a responsible Christian woman. She is not doomed inevitably to live the life of a (verbal) headhunter because of what her parents did to her! The possibility of change is not limited to primitive tribesmen. Indeed, even Americans who grew up "on the wrong side of the tracks" have been known to become outstanding Christian leaders. In many cases, their backgrounds were used by God as an impetus to service for Him.

Change is possible; that conviction must be maintained as a foundational fact of Christian counseling. *Radical* change, the most radical change known to man, is described in the Scriptures as a *new birth*.[22] The use of this figure of speech indicates the radical nature of the change. Nothing less than an entirely new start toward living life is in view.

Everywhere the Scriptures either demand change or assume its possibility. Since not all change is good, the Scriptures were written to give direction to that change; the Holy Spirit, their ultimate Author, was given to provide the disposition and power to follow those directions. Hope in counseling belongs primarily, therefore, to the Christian counselor. He *knows* that God is in the business of changing lives. Every change that God promises is possible. Every quality that God requires in His redeemed children can be attained. Every resource that is needed God has supplied.

Age is no hindrance to change. I shall not discuss this matter thoroughly here. More will be said later on. The question has been considered in a pamphlet entitled, *Godliness Through Discipline*.[23] Just let me make one or two observations, therefore. In God's providence *older*

---

22. John 3.
23. Jay Adams, *Godliness Through Discipline* (Nutley, N. J.: Presbyterian and Reformed Publishing Company, 1972), pp. 8-9.

persons are called upon to face some of life's most radical changes.[24] It is they who must commonly face loss of friends and loved ones, loss of health, retirement, and even death itself. It is they who must break more patterns and ties. Yet mature Christian living ought not to fossilize, but rather should teach one how to live as an alien and stranger in this shifting world of change.[25] With a taproot sunk deeply in the unchangeable Christ, one can learn to live a relatively rootless life here with joy. Change is what the Christian ought to expect, ought to demand of himself, and ought to learn to live with. He knows that there is "no continuing city"[26] here; his "citizenship is in heaven."[27] Counselors with this hope can undertake the task of counseling with joy and expectation. By the grace of God, there is every hope of change!

---

24. Cf. comments in "Hope," p. 65.
25. Hebrews 11:13.
26. Hebrews 13:14.
27. Philippians 3:20. The highs and lows and radical swings of life are not too much for the true servant of Christ who can "learn to be content" in whatever state he finds himself (cf. Philippians 4:11-13).

PART TWO

THE PRESUPPOSITIONS
AND PRINCIPLES

Chapter V

PRESUPPOSITIONS AND PRINCIPLES
BASIC TO COUNSELING

A Limited Number of Presuppositions and Principles

There are many fundamental presuppositions and principles of Scripture that bear upon counseling. Indeed, it could be demonstrated that every biblical assumption or principle relates either directly or indirectly to some aspect of the counseling situation. That is true since the subject matter of counseling is precisely the same as that of the Scriptures. It is, therefore, necessary for the counselor to be well grounded in the Word of God. Theological and biblical training, then, is the essential background for a counselor; not training in psychology or psychiatry.[1]

In order to meet human needs, which are as varied as those life principles contained in the Scriptures, one must have a thorough systematic knowledge of the whole counsel of God. The study of psychology in depth coupled with a smattering of scriptural data can lead only to the grossest misstatements regarding man and the solutions to his problems.[2] Yet this is the training of most of the self-styled "pro-

---

1. Cf. *The Big Umbrella*, pp. 15-19, where this is discussed in more detail.
2. Cf. Gary Collins, *Search for Reality* (Wheaton, Ill.: Key Publishers, 1969), p. 21: "First, neither psychology nor theology has a clear statement about the nature of man." He continues by saying that there is no "Biblical view of man." Such statements reveal a profound ignorance of the history and results of theology and exegesis. For centuries the Christian view of man has been defined in detail. The title of Collins' book indicates the futility of his attempt to find reality in the eclectic fusion of Christian theology and psychological speculation. In the process, one inevitably finds himself taking up the *search* for reality; yet every Christian should know that the *search* was ended by God's revelation of His Son, Jesus Christ. Why must Collins *search* when he owns a Bible? Quentin Hyder's book, *The Christian's Handbook of Psychiatry* (Old Tappan: Fleming H. Revell Company, 1958), offers another example. Hyder, doubtless a conservative Christian, nevertheless treats Old Testament ideas of sickness and madness in a condescending manner (p. 27) and allows the reader to choose between the creation of man and evolutionary views: "If you believe in special creation. . ." (p. 40). No wonder then that he believes "that many mental disturbances can be properly

33

fessional" Christian counselors. Even in seminaries the mistake is made of hiring teachers of pastoral counseling whose sole or primary training is not theological. Ministers who know the Scriptures must move in to develop these biblical principles; they cannot expect the "professionals," who have neither the training nor (in many cases) the inclination, to do so.

I wish to point out now that in the study of the presuppositions and principles that underlie practice, the design of this book demands that I *limit* the number of principles considered in this chapter.[3] On the basis of what criteria may such a limitation be made? Arbitrarily, I have chosen two:

1. I have *assumed* (without discussing) the common knowledge of many of the most basic principles of the Christian faith (e.g., man is born dead in sin, salvation is by grace through faith, etc.). My own theological position is Reformed (Reformation theology). It is those views commonly held by Reformed theologians, therefore, that I have assumed throughout. You are entitled to know this important fact.

2. I have elaborated only upon those biblical presuppositions and principles that counseling experience has shown to be *vitally* related to counseling in a more direct manner, yet may not be recognized as such.

Limitation was inevitable; I could not in this chapter reproduce a book on systematic theology. In accordance with this purpose, then, let us turn to the first presupposition, together with its corollary and applicatory principles.

Life Must Have Meaning

Frankl, in contrast to B. F. Skinner, is correct in observing that meaning (or perhaps a better word would be "purpose") is fundamental not only to a full and productive life, but also to the well being and, in some instances, the continued existence of a human being.[4] The day-by-day

treated by psychiatrists who make no profession of religion," contrary to Galatians 6:1 (cf. *The Big Umbrella*, pp. 146-151).

3. I am hurrying on to Part Three, which contains the materials that form the heart of this book. As a manual, rather than a theoretical work, the greater emphasis must be preeminently practical.

4. Even William Sargent writes, "We have to believe in something, to have some purpose in life, however bizarre the life of faith may turn out to be, now or later," *Battle for the Mind* (New York: Harper & Row, 1959), p. 27. See the present writer's evaluation of Frankl in *The Encyclopedia of Christianity*, vol. IV

activities in which men are caught up have short-term meaning. Effort profitably expended during the day may produce a sense of satisfaction and well being at its close (cf. Ecclesiastes 5:12). It may also bring the short-term benefits of wealth, possessions, power, or fame. Frankl rightly has observed that man cannot live without at least such day-by-day goals and purposes. Yet, these results (precisely because they are of a short-term nature) do not satisfy the human craving for a *fuller* explanation of the meaning of human life. Here Frankl and the other existential psychiatrists can offer nothing, for they do not believe in the God of the Bible; for them the future is but a long dark tunnel.

Apart from meaning related to God, the apparent meaning that one finds in the pleasures of this life soon evaporates. This is the disconcerting message of the book of Ecclesiastes: all temporal activity is meaningless ("vanity," or "emptiness") apart from the God of meaning. For a time (as the writer says) one or another activity seemed to bring purpose into his life, but, upon subsequent hard reflection, he concluded that each was no more than vanity. That is also the sad conclusion to which the existentialists lead us. But Solomon goes beyond: the "conclusion of the whole matter" lies rather in the fear of God, which is the beginning of wisdom. Ecclesiastes succinctly records, from the wide-ranging experience of its divinely inspired human author, what every man discovers (sometimes too late) in his own limited experience.

The contrast between the long-term and the short-term views of life is made frequently in the Scriptures.[5] Yet present activity and responsibility are never neglected because of preoccupation with the future. Indeed, the summary accounts recorded in Hebrews 11 make it clear that the notable saints mentioned all gained their power to act meaningfully in the present precisely from their orientation toward the future. The biblical principle is that it is only the long term that can fuse short-term purposes and goals into a meaningful overall pattern. God is the Alpha and Omega, and His Son, Jesus Christ, is the One who is the same yesterday, today, and forever. Thus all purposes take on

---

(Marshallton, Del.: The National Foundation for Christian Education, 1972), pp. 244-246.

5. Cf. Hebrews 11:10, 14-16, 24-26; 12:2, 10, 11; I Timothy 4:7-8. The biblical concept of faith is particularly associated with living meaningfully *now* because one lives *toward* that eternal land and city which are *yet to come*.

ultimate meaning only in relationship to Him. Apart from Him, they are simply isolated short-term objectives which randomly come and go without any necessary connection and, thus, no ultimate purpose. Indeed, if there is no ultimacy of purpose in one's daily activities, there is no purpose at all. It is only to such ultimacy that Paul could appeal in encouraging slaves to do their work well: "from the Lord you will receive the reward. . . . It is the Lord Christ whom you serve" (Colossians 3:23-24). Counselors today must point disillusioned, disheartened businessmen and housewives to the same fact.

This fact is of great significance in counseling. First, it may be noted that men who live for short-term goals alone live wrongly and at length must reckon with the folly of such a life orientation. Many of them will end up in counseling precisely because they have come to see that the ultimately meaningless "meaning" upon which they have staked their lives no longer holds meaning for them at all. They eventually reach the point where they must admit with Ecclesiastes, "All that I have done is 'vanity.' " Persons in this condition need to be confronted with the gospel of Jesus Christ. It may be that the Spirit of Christ has brought them into their present despair in order to bring them at length to Jesus Christ, the Prince of life. In Him alone may be found the possibility of living "abundantly."

Breakdowns

Such persons frequently exhibit behavior that leads some to conclude that they are suffering from a "nervous breakdown."[6] However, what has collapsed is not their nerves, but their foundation for, and whole outlook on, life. Having built their lives upon day-by-day living for short-term successes, literally they have found themselves to be on the short end of life. They have reached a significant life impasse and they have not been able to overcome the problem, since their lives are *oriented* solely toward the attainment of short-term objectives. They need an entirely new orientation. Thinking and acting in short-term categories alone, they may have stumbled from one unsatisfying experience to the next, but in none have they discovered fulfillment or

---

6. We cannot consider here the unfortunate euphemism *"nervous* breakdown." It is enough to point out that nerves do not break down. For data on the history of this terminology, cf. Jules Masserman, *A Psychiatric Odyssey* (New York: Science House, 1971), pp. 271 ff.

peace. When they come for counseling, they may be dispirited, disillusioned, and bitter. The short-term solutions upon which they have depended (running, lying, blaming, etc.) are of no use in solving the problems of ultimate meaning. The chickens have come home to roost (cf. Proverbs 5:22; 28:10, 18; 29:5, 6). Now, having exhausted all known resources, they find that they have painted themselves into a corner. Such counselees are not "out of touch"; they are *out of resources*. They have come to the end of them*selves*. They can see no place to turn: "all is vanity." Action comes to a standstill; they cease functioning because they do not know how to function meaningfully. This is what a *breakdown* is all about; one has run out of resources.[7]

Such people need to discover the meaning that is found in Jesus Christ alone. Frequently in God's providence they are ripe for the gospel.[8] Counseling, apart from the evangelistic presentation of the gospel will be of no avail.[9] Counselees themselves often are quick to see that all such counseling fails to speak to their needs. Indeed, they frequently conclude that such godless counseling is nothing but more vanity (as in fact it is). Those who grasp at something less than the gospel to solve life's problems soon find that they have hold of a straw; frequently their disappointment is bitter.

---

7. Persons may run out of resources for other reasons, and thus "breakdowns" may occur in other contexts (e.g., grief). Cf. *Competent to Counsel*, pp. 171, and *The Big Umbrella*, pp. 86-90.

8. Cf. *Competent to Counsel*, pp. 170 ff., and *The Big Umbrella*, "Grief As a Counseling Opportunity," pp. 63-94. For other comments on "Evangelism in Counseling," cf. *The Big Umbrella*, pp. 95-112.

9. Shock treatment (ECT, or electro convulsive therapy), administered frequently in these cases, constitutes nothing more than another fruitless short-term remedy. The good effects of shock are not lasting. Sometimes they make persons "more anxious," Wm. Sargent and Eliot Slater, *An Introduction to Physical Methods of Treatment in Psychiatry* (New York: Science House, 1972), p. 63. There are risks of fracture, *ibid.*, p. 72. When they work, shock treatments simply relieve the counselee of the pressures of stress by temporarily erasing recent memory. Loss of memory makes counseling difficult. When the memory returns, the problems (which in the meantime may have grown larger) must be faced again. ECT causes convulsions with an effect "very similar to that of a mild concussion" and "One should also be cautious with the man who uses a highly trained memory in the exercise of his profession," *ibid.*, p. 73. It is difficult, if not impossible, to justify the use of ECT. Shock treatments are, perhaps, the best symbol of the fruitless attempt of frustrated psychiatrists to solve non-temporal problems by short-term temporal means.

When counselees like this come for help, it is often with a hope-against-hope attitude. Wanting to hope, they dread the possibility that their hopes may be raised (again), only to be dashed (again) to the ground. Counselors will find it necessary to rebuild hope before proceeding further.[10]

Christian counselees too can lose sight of the long-term goals of the Scriptures and can suffer the despair and disillusionment that comes from a failure to focus one's faith on the "God of all hope." Such despairing believers must be reminded of the promises of God. Their sin of shortsightedness must be pointed out by bringing the future into proper focus and perspective in its relationship to the present.

---

10. More must be said *infra* about hope. At this point it is necessary to observe that those suffering from the bitter feelings of depressions must be distinguished from counselees with "breakdowns." Both lead to nonfunctioning and may be confused. In *depression* the counselee's attitude is "What's the use?" He no longer cares. He is filled with guilt and usually wallows in self-pity. In a *breakdown* (when past patterns have been broken *up*), the counselee's attitude is "What can I do?" He is cornered; the bottom has fallen out. He is confused and frightened. He will be frozen, perhaps speechless and immobilized. His resources have failed. He must be pointed to the true resources that are found only in Christ and His Word. In depression, confession of sin and reversal of action from recent irresponsibility to known (and perhaps formerly assumed) responsibilities is the answer. The basic message to the depressed person is found in Revelation 2:4, 5. The categories are not mutually exclusive. Breakdowns may lead to depression. Perhaps in most (if not all) breakdowns there is an element of depression. Yet not all who are depressed are suffering from a **breakdown**. These distinctions sometimes hold true as emphases only.

Chapter Six

HOPE

Hope of Change

Closely akin to meaning is hope. In the Scriptures God speaks of the importance of hope. He places hope in unique conjunction with love and faith in I Corinthians 13. There hope ranks second only to love: "Faith, hope and love, these three; but the greatest of these is love."[1] Love is the greatest, for when faith turns to sight and hope blends with realization, love will continue. Yet, for *now*, hope is not only necessary, but in some instances must be ranked even above love. In I Thessalonians 1:3, for example, Paul again speaks of the same trio of qualities; yet in this situation (where the great need of the Thessalonian church was for hope), love comes second: "the work of faith, the labor of love and the perseverance (or endurance) of hope." While faith is the source of works and labor issues from love, endurance (especially under trial) comes only from hope. It is such perseverance through the difficulty of early failures and the awkwardness of newly changed patterns that counselees so desperately need. In order to continue along the path of change, they must have hope.

Hope in the Scriptures always is a confident expectation; the word hope never carries even the connotation of uncertainty that adheres to our English term (as when we say cautiously, "I hope so"). There is no "hope so" about the biblical concept. When Paul wrote to Titus about the "blessed hope," for instance, he was urging him to look forward to the "happy expectation" of the "appearing of the glory of our great God and Savior Jesus Christ." He had no thought of uncertainty about the fact of this event.

The counselor must love people. That is one reason why he counsels. Because he does, he will be deeply distressed whenever he discovers that a counselee has lost hope. But even that distress must be balanced by enthusiastic hope. It is his task always to sound the note of biblical optimism

1. I Corinthians 13:13.

39

that is warranted by the promises of God. A counselor must be, above much else, a man of hope. He himself must believe what he says about hope, or he will communicate the opposite. He must be fully persuaded of the faithfulness of God in fulfilling His promises. Nothing less than this will give him the confident enthusiasm that is needed in speaking of hope (expectation) of change with conviction and assurance. Enthusiasm truly is contagious when the reasons for the counselor's enthusiasm are biblical. In Romans 15:14, Paul speaks of the encouragement and endurance that spring from hope. Nothing short of such biblical encouragement can enable one to endure the often discouraging task of helping sinful men change in a world warped by sin and cursed by God.

Who needs hope? This is an important question for every counselor. Not only must he be able to answer it, but he must know the biblical reasons for hope in each situation. A large share of the initial work of counseling may involve urging biblical hope upon those who come in desperation and despair. Knowing what sorts of counselees often need hope should alert the counselor to look for clues and make inquiries in cases where hope might seem to be a matter of significance. It is important, then, to consider the question in some detail.

Everyone Needs Hope

In one sense, *every* counselee needs hope. Sin has worked its defeating and disheartening effects in all of our lives. There are times when every Christian is dispirited. Often this attitude deteriorates into the sin of despair. Counselors, therefore, may be sure that they will see more than their share of sin's blighting effects. Doubt and discouragement, and sometimes despair, so frequently assert themselves in conjunction with other difficulties, that the counselor soon must learn how to confront and overcome these complicating problems. Until these have been cleared away and have given place to hope, usually it is fruitless to try to handle other matters. No wonder, then, that *immediately* after the fall, *in the very midst* of punishment and judgment, God also gave hope (Genesis 3:15). While discussing the misery of the curse, God also promised the coming of the One who would deal definitively with sin and sweep away its misery. While speaking of the thorns of the ground, God also gave the first prophecy of His son, who in His own body would bear the curse of the thorn for His people. What God did, we who try to counsel in His shadow must do too.

There is in the gospel a double hope: (1) the hope for the *eschaton* (the last time, the future), which is bound up with the coming of Christ, the resurrection of the body, and the erasure of sin, pain, and tears. This, with its crowning hope—the presence of Christ—is the great hope of the Christian. It includes the hope (expectation) of final perfection. But that is not all. Christianity is not merely pie in the sky bye and bye when you die; indeed, Christians can start slicing today! (2) There is hope for a new abundant life right now. The misery that comes from living sinfully can be alleviated. The believer can enjoy the peace, comfort, and assurance of the fullness of the living Christ here in this life. In times of trouble, then, when our sin has brought misery into our lives, *all* of us need to be reminded of the hope of the gospel (Colossians 1:5).[2] But let us turn specifically to those classes of counselees who most frequently need a heavy stress upon hope.

Specific Problems Requiring Hope

First, *people with long-standing problems* need hope. Jesus did something unusual in healing the man born blind (John 9); he used means. He spit on the ground, mixed clay, smeared it on the eyes of the blind man, and told him to go to the pool of Siloam and wash. He assured him that if he did so he would return seeing. Did Jesus need to use means? Was His power somehow limited? Certainly not. Whenever Jesus used such means it was in order to demonstrate something either to the person to be healed, or to others around him, or to both. In this case, Jesus was dealing with a man who had never seen. He had never seen the sun set, a sunrise, the face of another person; he had never seen anything or anyone at all. If ever he had once dared to hope that he might one day see, long ago he had probably lost all such hope. After all, who ever heard of a man who was born blind healed so that he could see? Jesus, therefore, in order to raise hope smeared clay upon his eyes. As the clay grew heavy and dried in clots on his eyelids, the man's hope began to well within. He thought, "If only I could wash away my blindness as I can wash away this clay!" He rushed to the pool, followed Christ's directions, and came back seeing. People like this man, whose problems have been of long duration, need hope.

---

2. The hope of the gospel is the one unfailing certainty. Healing cults, witch doctors, placebo effects, etc., all demonstrate the temporary power of hope even when falsely grounded.

It is apparent that Christ did the unusual in order to give hope to a man with a long-standing problem.

Secondly, *people with peculiarly difficult problems* need hope. Although nearly every counselee thinks that his problem is the most difficult one ever faced, some problems are greater than others. Some counselees who recognize the extreme complexity of the presenting problem have little hope of anyone ever untangling it. They themselves may have tried (perhaps often) but have failed to extricate themselves. Such persons need to be assured that there is hope in *Christ*.[3] That hope lies in the power of His Word ministered by His Spirit (cf. Romans 15:4, 13).

The woman with the issue of blood who had suffered at the hands of many physicians is a good example of one who needed hope for this reason. People who for years have consulted in vain with psychiatrists or other counselors often need to be reassured of the scriptural promises.

Juli had frequented various psychiatrists on and off for the past ten years, but nothing had been accomplished. When she came she both wanted change and did not. She had worked out a way of handling the problems that was less than satisfying but, she thought, better than the ways that she had tried before. At first, therefore, she resisted any change that would rock the boat. It was not a seaworthy vessel in which she was sailing, but it leaked more slowly than some others and was still afloat. Because she was headed for shipwreck, it had to be torpedoed by her counselor, who showed her from the Scriptures that she could not continue to lie her way out of difficulties or run away from problems. He also held out hope by showing the real solution in the Bible.

Thirdly, *people who have been sold a bill of goods* about their problems need hope. Those who have been told that they are sick when they are not need to understand that there is no strange, incurable illness that is at the root of their problem.[4] They must come to see that they are in difficulty because of their sin. People who have been labeled by psychiatrists or others as schizophrenics, catatonics, etc., often begin

---

3. Take, e.g., the engineer who was mentioned in *What to Do About Worry*. Here his problems looked like a forest too thick to penetrate. By learning Christ's way of handling problems—felling each day's trees that day and leaving the rest for tomorrow—he was able to cut his way through.

4. Cf. *The Big Umbrella*, "Is Society Sick?," ch. II.

to live according to the hopelessness of those labels.[5] These people need a clear explanation of what the real problem is, so that hope once again can be restored to them.

Frequently it is helpful to show such persons from another area of their lives in which they are successfully handling similar problems that they *are capable* of doing what God requires to handle the problem under discussion. If, for instance, at work or school responsible relationships have been maintained, they can be developed at home as well. If one can control his temper elsewhere, he can learn to do so at home.

Fourthly, *people who are harassed by fear* need hope.[6] Fear can immobilize and even paralyze. It is a potent force that can be overcome only by the stronger force of love.[7]

Fifthly, *persons whose hopes have been dashed repeatedly* in the past need hope. They have had high hopes again and again, only to be disappointed and hurt each time. At length they have become not only distrustful of any assurances of hope, but while desiring to hope may actually hold it at arm's length. They stiffarm hope out of fear of additional pain and disappointment. These counselees must be shown the *biblical* basis for hope (such as I Corinthians 10:13).[8] Hope failed before because it was wrongly based; "God is faithful," and His promises *never* fail.

Sixthly, there are *those who have tried and failed*. They may be both hopeful and skeptical at the same time. They may be confused and worried. They may be angry or even deeply resentful toward God. Often, when the true reasons for failure are shown, they must be brought to repentance for their attitudes before going further. Such persons

---

5. Labeling that is not biblical is false and, therefore, harmful. To call a man psychotic, neurotic, psychoneurotic, schizophrenic, etc., is dangerous and should be avoided. Close adherence to biblical categories when describing human beings and their problems is mandatory. De Bono writes, with good reason, "The units of experience, the packets of information require a name. Once they acquire a name they are frozen and immutable, for a label is usable only if it has an unvarying meaning." Edward De Bono, *Think New* (New York: Avon Books, 1968), p. 112. Strupp writes that it is a "well-known fact that diagnostic labels are of very questionable value; . . . they may obscure more than they elucidate," *op. cit.*, p. 69.

6. Cf. *infra*, pp. 413 ff.

7. Cf. *infra*, pp. 414, 415.

8. Cf. *Christ and Your Problems*, pp. 11-13.

may be of two sorts: those who have tried the *wrong* solutions and those who have tried the *correct* ones. It is the latter especially who require extra effort. Perhaps they have tried prayer. Many Personal Data Inventories reveal that Christians turn to prayer as the panacea for their problems. In response to the question, "What have you done about it [your problem]?" many counselees write: "I have prayed," and that is all. There can be no objection to prayer; indeed, if it is the right sort of prayer, it cannot but be encouraged.[9] But when one's solution to a problem *stops* with prayer, then the matter must be reopened. The Bible says pray, but it also gives many other specific directions. When we pray for our daily bread, we do not expect it to come floating out of the sky on a parachute. God *could* send bread this way (remember the manna), but He has not told us to expect to get it in that manner. Instead, He assures us, "If anyone will not work, he must not eat."[10] That means that when we pray for daily bread, we are praying for the Lord to give us the opportunity and strength to earn it. Yet, in the solution to problems, many counselees seem to forget that prayer must be followed by the biblical course of action commanded.[11]

In addition there are those who do the right thing but give up too readily. They will drill until noon, but give up because it took too long and it is getting too hot; at 1:00 P.M. they would have struck oil! They will drill through the sand until they hit rock, but then they quit; it has become too difficult. Three feet deeper and they would have hit a gusher! Hope leads to *perseverence* that gives one the patience to continue in spite of delay or difficulty (I Thessalonians 1:3).

Seventhly, *older persons often need hope.* They sometimes believe that they have passed the point where change is still possible. They must be shown that the Bible places no age limitations upon sanctification. Indeed, God in His all-wise providence has *so* ordered life that some of the greatest changes of all must be borne by the aged. Loss of occupation, health, and loved ones, for instance, require some

---

9. Some people never seem to consider the fact that all prayer is not proper. James makes this point in his eminently practical letter: "You ask and do not receive, because you ask with wrong motives . . ." (James 4:3). Prayer is conditioned (cf. I John 3:22; 5:15; James 5:16; John 14:13, 14).

10. II Thessalonians 3:10.

11. Cf. *The Big Umbrella*, pp. 92-94. Talk alone is inadequate and can be destructive. Problems must be viewed as *projects*, not *topics*. Discussion of problems should result in *programs* for Christian action, not in *opinions* alone.

of the most dramatic changes in life. Only a truly mature person is capable of handling such radical change. Maturity in Christ should prepare and equip one for change, not debilitate him. If one has learned through the years how to live with and rejoice in Christ's change, he should be better able to handle change than a child with little or no such experience. Maturity in Christ, then, itself should lead to hope.[12] The aged often repeat the saying, "You can't teach an old dog new tricks." Perhaps that is true of old dogs; but an old man, created in the image of God, can learn them!

Eighthly, *depressed persons need hope.* By insisting that they resume duties and chores that have been allowed to slide and by working through other sinful acts and patterns to repentance and its fruits, hope is reborn. Hope never comes by sympathizing with self-pity. In these cases action, not talk, soon brings hope.

Ninthly, *suicidal persons also need hope.* They are preeminently persons with no hope. Taking them seriously about their sin is absolutely essential. Hope comes when someone recognizes and acknowledges how hopeless the counselee is in his present situation.[13] From agreeing that such a life is not worth continuing, the counselor can show the possibility of a new and different sort of life in Christ.

Tenthly, *persons who have suffered life-shattering experiences* need hope. Grief over the loss of (1) a *person* by death, moving, adultery, divorce; (2) *possessions* or (3) *position* (status, job, one's good name) may lead to such need.[14] "Nervous breakdowns" constitute another frequent example.[15]

---

12. What tends to make change hard for the aged is not their age itself. It is harder to break the *many interrelated associations and patterns.*

13. Cf. *supra*, pp. 38 ff. Suicidal persons often see themselves caught between the horns of a dilemma. They see the outcome of their problem in strictly either/or terms. Often, as Christ showed the Pharisees (Matthew 22:23-33), there is a third way (God's way). The basic assumptions (because not biblical) may be wrong. Clearing these up biblically may point to the way between.

14. Cf. *The Big Umbrella*, "Grief As a Counseling Opportunity," ch. III. Hope in grief is the antidote to despair. Grief tends to move toward despair, but hope holds it back in proper balance (I Thessalonians 4:13; cf. Hebrews 6:18, 19: hope is the anchor that stops the drift). Note the following diagram:

$$\text{(HOPE)} \xrightarrow{\text{bound to}} \text{(GRIEF)} \xrightarrow[\text{to move toward}]{\text{checks tendency}} \text{(DESPAIR)}$$

15. Viz., pp. 36 ff.

Finally (although the list is not exhaustive), *those who are without Christ* need hope. To them there is no hope apart from the hope of the gospel, i.e., the hope that comes from believing the gospel (cf. Romans 8:24[16]).

How to Give Hope

In all of these instances the Bible is more than adequate to give such hope. That is why Paul wrote: "All those Scriptures of long ago were written for our instruction, so that through the patience and encouragement of the Scriptures (that is the patience and the encouragement that the Scriptures give) we might have *hope*" (Romans 15:4). Apart from the Scriptures there is no basis for hope. But the Scriptures were written to give hope. Christian counselors, therefore, should strongly emphasize God's promises that are found in the Scriptures whenever they discover counselees who seem to have lost hope.[17]

One way to raise hope is by taking people seriously when they talk about their sin. Often in the very first session a woman, for example, will say something like this: "Well, I guess I haven't been much of a mother." Or, "I haven't been a good wife." Nouthetic counselors take all such comments quite seriously. They consider all self-deprecatory comments important and always investigate them fully. They refuse to minimize or allow minimizing of a counselee's negative self-evaluations.[18] So when a counselee says something of this nature, a counselor almost immediately will bring the discussion to a halt and say, "That's serious. A Christian woman should be a good mother (or wife). Tell me how bad a wife (or mother) you are."

One of two responses is likely to be forthcoming immediately: first, if the woman has been saying that she is not much of a mother or wife in order to seem "pious," then she will immediately begin to back off

---

16. The King James reads "saved by hope." Literally, Paul wrote, "saved in (or *with*) hope." Hope comes by faith in Christ.

17. A pamphlet, *Christ and Your Problems*, has been developed for distribution by nouthetic counselors. This biblical study of I Corinthians 10:13 is calculated to give hope while challenging to personal responsibility before God. This pamphlet may be handed to counselees at the conclusion of the first session.

18. Here are some actual examples of minimizing: "Now Mary! Don't say that; you've been a *good* girl." "Things aren't *that* bad." "Don't forget, you have so much to be *thankful* for!" "Don't disparage yourself so much!" "Look at all you *have* accomplished." "Come on now, you're *not* a failure." "Try to look at the *bright* side."

and row in the other direction: "Don't get me wrong now. . . ." In such cases, of course, the counselor knows what he is dealing with—hypocrisy rather than sincerity—and he must do so accordingly. But in most instances the response he will get will be gratifying. Indeed, it is often electrifying: her hopes rise, she begins to talk freely, and the whole story is likely to emerge at once.

June was a Christian girl some twenty years of age, quite stout and very depressed. On her Personal Data Inventory[19] she had written, I am disgusting, stupid, ugly, rotten, and a complete failure." Her mother immediately jumped in upon hearing this inventory read out loud in the session, saying, "Don't believe her. She is a wonderful girl. She won the Sunday School contest, was able to go to camp for a week free," etc., etc. (I have already commented elsewhere on the problems connected with such minimizing.[20]) The counselor stopped her mother abruptly and said, "Now listen, June knows more about her life than you or I or anyone else but God, and if June says that she's disgusting, stupid, ugly, rotten and a complete failure, she must have some good reasons for saying so." Turning to June, the counselor continued, "June, tell us how disgusting you are. Tell us just how stupid you've been. Tell us what it is that makes you so ugly. Tell us about the rotten things you've been doing, and tell us also, June, something about the ways in which you've failed." June's head had been hanging down since she entered, but when the counselor said this, she looked up as if to say, "Is he for real?" She must have concluded that he meant it, because for the first time she began to talk freely and her story poured out.

It is important, therefore, to take people seriously when they talk about their own sins. Often a self-deprecatory comment is a trial balloon that the counselee sets afloat in order to see what the counselor will do with it. It is important to grab the string quickly, pull it down and burst it to see what is inside.

Following a case of adultery there is almost inevitably great hesitancy on the part of the innocent party to trust the offender again. Yet after reconciliation, hope will come quickly if it is *allowed to develop* indirectly. Since the forgiven offender's word has been proven untrustworthy in the past, that word must be backed by action. What cannot be

---

19. Cf. *Competent to Counsel*, pp. 271-274. A revised sample is included in the Appendix A of this book, pp. 433-435.
20. *Competent to Counsel*, pp. 67, 112 ff., 140, 142 ff.

communicated by telling must be shown. When he does so, the bits and pieces of evidence that change has taken place point to true repentance (they are fruit appropriate to repentance). The offended party quickly begins to regain hope. Evidence, in terms of efforts expended to begin afresh God's way, is worth more than words by the bookfull. Counselors, therefore, will wisely give many concrete assignments to the forgiven partner during the early sessions in such cases in order to afford him (or her) maximum opportunity to demonstrate the genuineness of the professed repentance. If these assignments involve single-stranded problems, progress toward reestablishing confidence can be made more rapidly.

In a different sort of context, appreciation for genuine effort also may encourage and fan the spark of hope. The Lord Jesus Christ spoke of expressing appreciation when he noted that He will say "Well done," to "good and faithful servants." (Also see Proverbs 31:28, 29.[21]) Encouragement by appreciation for doing what is required is an effective means of giving hope. To know that others have noticed and care tends to spur one on to further efforts. In remedial reading, for instance, it has been found that many children, regardless of the material that they are using, do not care one way or the other about the lack of interesting material that they may have to read so long as they have *success* in reading. That seems to be motivation enough.

Thus the first important fact is that *counselees need meaning*, and the second is similar to it: *counselees need hope*. Every counselor must keep these two facts in mind, especially at the beginning of a sequence of counseling sessions.

---

21. Doubtless, one reason for this woman's continued effort in the development and use of her gifts was the encouragement she received from her family, who freely expressed their appreciation audibly. Cf. "A Word to the Wives," Jay Adams, *Christian Living in the Home* (Nutley, N. J.: Presbyterian and Reformed Publishing Company, 1972), pp. 69-85.

Chapter Seven

PRAYER: THE BASE FOR CHRISTIAN COUNSELING

Hopefully it will not be necessary to argue for the necessity of undergirding prayer in the work of counseling. Those for whom this book is written will acknowledge readily enough how important such prayer is. Their only problem, like that of the writer, will be to implement adequately this knowledge and conviction. The power and purifying presence of the Holy Spirit must be invoked by the human counselor as he acknowledges his own sins and inabilities. However, the issues of whether, when, where, who, and how prayer may be used *as a part of* the counseling session may occupy our concern for a time.

The counselor should prepare for counseling *largely* by prayer for himself and for his counselees. Prayer for the counselee may grow naturally out of reading the notes in the file in preparation for the next session. Such prayer, mingled with reflection upon the counselee's problems and the possible solutions that one may find in the Scriptures, probably will be found most satisfactory. When prayer grows out of and becomes a part of intelligent thought, both its content and fervency are likely to be greater. Often God may use such prayerful thought to help the counselor to develop fruitful plans for the next session.

A student wrote:

> We note in James 5:16 that it is the prayer of the righteous man which is especially helpful to the sinning member.[1]

It is important to observe that prayer is one of the three determining factors in the counseling situation supposed by James. So, it is clear that prayer may not be considered taboo in the counseling session. As James indicates, prayer itself may be the essential element of the counseling process. As a matter of practice, under ordinary circumstances, prayer always ought to be offered *at least* at the close of the

---

1. Daniel R. Meiners, "Prayer and Pastoral Counseling," November 10, 1971. An unpublished term paper for a course in pastoral counseling at Westminster Theological Seminary.

session. At other times, *during* a session prayer may be appropriate. It may be the natural outcome of a decision or commitment. It may be the fervent cry of the counselee for forgiveness as the Word that was ministered brought conviction of sin and repentance.

Here lies a danger, however. Counselors must become sensitive to when the Spirit has moved a counselee to the point of prayer or when, on the other hand, it is the counselor's own desire that is being forced upon the counselee. No pressure can be exerted here; no hesitancy to allow one to pray can be tolerated if the Spirit has used His Word to convict. Prayerful concern on the part of the counselor about this matter will lead to spiritual discernment.

Prayer at the close of each session tends to be less ritualistic and formalistic than prayer at the outset, since it may focus upon the vital content of the previous hour. Often at the outset of a session the counselee may be so excited, so angry, so upset as almost to preclude meaningful prayer at that point. And yet, it is precisely in some of those cases where prayer is the one and only answer at the moment. If, for instance, a counselee enters with some such comment: " I am so upset (angry, etc.) that I don't know what to say . . . ," the counselor may reply: "All right. Don't say anything to me yet. Let's talk to God about it first. Among other things we'll ask Him to take this bitterness (or whatever) out of your heart so that we can begin to deal with the important issues that you are having difficulty discussing."

Prayer may be suggested as homework. Not only should regular prayer be advised for all counselees, but prayer may be prescribed specifically as a part of the solution to a problem.[2]

There are at least two dangers to be avoided in counseling that are connected with an abuse of prayer: (1) depending on prayer alone when the Scriptures direct additional action; (2) turning prayer into a self-pity session.

Often when the Personal Data Inventory question no. 2, speaking of the problem, asks, "What have you done about it?" it is answered by one word: "prayed." Usually the counselor must make the point that the biblical answer is different. Instead it is *ora et labora*, "pray and

---

2. For example, a discussion of discouragement may lead to a consideration of Luke 18:1, where Jesus advocates prayer as an answer to the problem. Thus the counselee may be told as a part of the solution to pray as Jesus said whenever he begins to become discouraged.

work." Sometimes a counselor may make the point this way:

"You don't pray 'Give me this day my daily bread' and then sit back and wait for it to float out of the sky on a parachute, do you?"

"No."

"What then do you do?"

"I work for it."

"How come?"

"Because the Scriptures say somewhere that if you want to eat you have to work."[3]

"Right! God ordinarily answers your prayer by giving you the health, the strength, and the opportunity to work; not some other way. Now, the problem that you presented probably cannot be solved by prayer alone either. We shall have to look at the Bible to see what God says that you must *do* about the problem."

The other problem is more difficult. We will reserve comments at this point and refer the reader to subsequent sections in which the place of talk in counseling and the problem of self-pity are discussed.

---

3. Cf. II Thessalonians 3:10.

Chapter Eight

THE RECONCILIATION/DISCIPLINE DYNAMIC

We must consider next an important biblical principle that provides a basis for hope by spelling out the biblical dynamic that leads to change. The principle may be stated simply as follows: interpersonal problems between Christians must be solved. Perhaps this principle is best exemplified by the reconciliation/discipline dynamic. This dynamic is described in Matthew 18:15-20. The reconciliation/discipline dynamic puts an end to loose ends in Christian relationships. That is what it is all about; Christ intended for it to do just that. One of the greatest difficulties between husbands and wives, parents and children, and various members of a congregation who have had poor interpersonal relations is the problem of loose ends. Loose ends are those interpersonal problems between Christians that remain unresolved.

Problems between Christians should not continue unresolved. When they do, strength is sapped from the congregation and members work at cross-purposes. Unresolved problems hurt everyone and dishonor Christ's name. There is no place, therefore, for such loose ends in the church. God does not allow for loose ends; rather He insists that every personal difficulty that arises must be settled. Whatever comes between Christians must be removed. Every such difference must be cleared up *by reconciliation*.[1] And, for that purpose, God graciously provided a method by which this can be accomplished.

---

1. People often ask: "Wouldn't it be better just to let a matter die and not raise the question afresh, thereby starting more trouble?" The issue resolves itself to this: *whether or not the offended person really finds it possible to let the problem die.* Proverbs 10:12 says, "Hatred stirs up strife, but love covers a multitude of sins." Plainly every rub and offense cannot be raised and settled. We must learn, in love, to forgive and pass by many slights, annoyances, and offenses. Christ is not speaking of these in Matthew 5 and 18. There (Matt. 5:23) He is considering a case where a brother "has (or 'holds') something against" another (*echei ti kata sou*) and when it is necessary to regain (Matt. 18:15) one's brother (*ekerdesas*). Rather, he speaks of those offenses that brethren find it difficult to "cover." If a matter is likely to rattle around inside or carry over till the next day, it should be handled. To put it another way, if an offense drives a wedge be-

52

In Matthew 5:21-26 Christ says, if you are offering your gift at the altar and you realize that you have done something against your brother (or he thinks you have), drop your gift and *first* go and get the matter straightened out with your brother.[2] Then (*tote*, "at that time"; then and only then), He continues, may you come back and finish your act of worship.

These words clearly indicate that there is an urgency to reconciliation. God says, "go *first*." Indeed, in Christ's example, reconciliation takes precedence over worship. Surely that must be one of the striking features in the example chosen; by using so bold a contrast as that between worship and reconciliation, He intended to underscore the importance and the priority of reconciliation. Unreconciled relationships, therefore, constitute *emergency priorities* that may not be handled casually or at one's leisure.

In Matthew 18, the other side of the question is handled: if your brother has done something against you, again you must go. It is always your obligation to make the first move (as also it is his); you may never say, "He should have come to me!" Jesus doesn't allow for that. Whether *you* have done something to *him* or *he* has done something to *you*, in either case (Matthew 5; Matthew 18), *you* are to go. Christ left no loopholes; He covered all of the bases.

Picture two brethren who have had a quarrel and go off in a huff. When they both cool down, ideally they ought to meet one another on the way to each other's house seeking reconciliation. Christ says that *both* of them are obliged to seek reconciliation; it does not matter who was at fault.

The Three Steps

Reconciliation, then, is the answer to loose ends in interpersonal problems between Christians. But what happens if one of the parties refuses to be reconciled? Christ also anticipated that question in Matthew 18. First, one brother or sister must go to the other *privately* in the attempt to square matters (that may not mean just one visit; he must make

---

tween Christian brothers, the wedge must be removed by reconciliation. To say it a third way: anything that causes an unreconciled condition to exist between brethren must be dealt with.

2. Note the *Kakei* and the *echei*, both of which are in emphatic positions: "if *there* you remember . . . leave *there* your gift," i.e., *there*, right on the spot, "in front of" (*emprosthen*) the altar.

every possible attempt to do this). But if he exhausts that means, if he tries and tries, yet to no avail because the other steadfastly refuses to be reconciled, then he must take a second step. Jesus directs that in such situations he must take one or two others with him and go to seek reconciliation again. These others become arbiters or counselors who try to persuade the brother to be reconciled.[3] They become involved and try to bring the two parties together once again by helping them to straighten out the relationship and possibly assisting them in reaching a solution to any problem or problems that may have been the occasion for the separation. They too must work at this (perhaps making several visits if necessary) until they have achieved reconciliation or are convinced that they have done all that it is possible for them to do to no avail. Reluctantly, if they have failed, at this point they become witnesses, and the whole matter must be brought officially before the church. Then formal discipline takes place. The church (represented by its elders) now officially (i.e., through its officers acting in the presence and with the authority of the risen Christ) seeks to bring about reconciliation. But if the elders also fail (after exhausting every means), the member must be solemnly excommunicated.[4]

At this point the matter has moved over the line from mere reconciliation to formal discipline. But even the discipline, n.b., has reconciliation in view. Excommunication is not an end in itself but, at least temporarily, it settles the matter. Hopefully, this serious act itself

---

3. Notice that the possibility of one or more (a team of) counselors is contemplated.

4. A believer as a member of Christ's church is entitled to all of the privileges and blessings of church discipline. Neither the individual who is offended nor the church has the right to withhold either informal or formal discipline from the offender. It is sin to do so. Remember, Christ has promised to be present in a special way in the process of church discipline: "There am I in the midst." Excommunication never takes place for committing the sin that occasioned the process in the beginning. Excommunication always occurs when one rejects the authority of the church of Christ; he is excommunicated for contumacy. One is excommunicated, then, not for adultery, but for failure to repent and be reconciled. The sin that occasioned discipline may have been relatively "small" in its effects, but to *that* sin is added the *enormously* significant sin of the rejection of Christ Himself as He demands repentance through His representatives. Excommunication occurs when men act like Nabal: "He is such a worthless man that no one can speak to him" (I Samuel 25:17). As Christ puts it: "He will not hear (listen to) the church." The people of God were destroyed and God declared that there is "no remedy," not because of their sin, but because of their refusal to repent of it; their stiff-necked attitude toward God (cf. II Chronicles 36:11-21).

at length may bring the offender to repentance. If the supposed brother or sister will not hear the church, he becomes as a heathen and publican (that is, outside of the church, excommunicated). When he becomes like a heathen and a publican, even then members of the church must seek to counsel him with a view to restoring him in repentance. Paul's comments on the purpose of church discipline in I Timothy 1:20; II Thessalonians 3:14, 15; I Corinthians 5:5, 9, 11; II Corinthians 2: 5-8 are clear about this matter.

The Purposes and Benefits of Discipline

Discipline must be carried out in a loving way; it is done to preserve the honor of God's Name, to assure the purity of the church (cf. I Corinthians 5:7), and to reclaim and reconcile the offender. Unless all three of those elements are present, the discipline exercised is not biblical. It is not possible to seek the glory of God in discipline by failing to give heed to His aims and methods. The welfare of the church is not served by selfishly eliminating people with a "good riddance" attitude. Paul speaks of his great sorrow over the excommunication of a church member. The church always must keep in view the hope and possibility of the reconciliation of an excommunicated member. He may truly be an erring *brother*. They must pray for and urge him to repent and return to the fellowship of Christ's church.

Christ has set forth the reconciliation/discipline dynamic as an either/or. Counseling, then, is always the other side of discipline. In one sense, that is all that it is.[5] It is getting involved in the reconciliation process.

The reconciliation/discipline dynamic provides great hope. Because God has indicated that He does not want any loose ends in the church, and since He has provided an effective dynamic for tying up loose ends in every instance, there is plainly no need for them. Every problem can be solved God's way.

---

5. Since discipline has as one of its objects the reclamation of the offender, discipline also may be looked upon as one tool or means that the Holy Spirit uses to bring about nouthetic change. In that sense it is a form of counseling; i.e., discipline seeks the welfare of the offender by attempting to bring about change through *official* confrontation by the church. It is plain that discipline and counseling are inextricably intertwined. One reason for failure in counseling is found in the almost total neglect of biblical discipline. The third stage may be considered to be *official* counseling.

Discipline has been almost totally neglected, not only by liberals, but also by the modern conservative church.[6] That is one reason why so many harmful loose ends among Christians are draining off the power of the church. Christians, as individuals, also suffer greatly from the neglect. Proper biblical church discipline *must* be revived.

Take, for instance, two significant factors that are missing as a result of the failure of elders to exercise proper discipline over their flocks: (1) the privilege of helpful arbitration and counseling on the part of one's brethren (that we all need at some time or other) is neglected. Christians are allowed to flounder alone in their sin and its baneful consequences. Most matters could be set to rest rapidly at stages one or two in the reconciliation process if it were rigorously applied. Instead, matters are allowed to progress from bad to worse, with no serious attempt to do anything about them. Every member of the church of Christ has been granted the privilege of the reconciliation procedure by Jesus Christ, the Head of the church. Yet, His officers too often have taken that privilege away from them at great cost to the individual and to the cause of Jesus Christ.

(2) Of even greater importance is the fact that the presence of Christ is promised wherever the reconciliation/discipline dynamic is properly set in motion: "Where two or three are gathered together in my name, there am I in the midst" (that verse was *not* intended to give warrant for *small* prayer meetings). Jesus was assuring His disciples that where they faithfully followed His injunctions about reconciliation and discipline, He would personally guide and direct the course of events.[7] He reassured them of this because He knew of the reluctance

---

6. Failure to understand and acknowledge Christ's dynamic has led Wayne Oates to foolish and unscriptural conclusions about discipline. In a quite unbiblical dichotomy, borrowed from K. E. Kirk, he writes: "The pastor who uses the Bible as a lawbook casts himself into the roll [sic] of a legalistic judge of his people. When he does this, he cannot but cast himself into the roll [sic] of one who excommunicates, one who penalizes." *The Bible in Pastoral Care* (Grand Rapids: Baker Book House, 1971), p. 29. Oates has missed the balance between reconciliation and discipline. The pastor is one who excommunicates (not individually, of course) *only* after he has been one who seeks to reconcile. Indeed, as one who excommunicates, he is still one who seeks to reconcile, for reconciliation is one purpose of excommunication.

7. Indeed, Jesus' use of the future perfect passive in vs. 18 was intended to encourage reluctant Christians to use church discipline: "Whatever you bind (loose) . . . *shall have been* bound (loosed)." Christ is saying: your act on earth is but a reflection and outworking of what has already been judged by God

they would have in doing as He said. Yet, in spite of His plain assurances, men still refuse to follow His injunctions.

A counselee said: "My wife, Wilma, is living with another man. She has been living with him for four years. I have done everything I can do to get her to return; there is nothing left to do."

The counselor inquired: "You have gone to her, then, Cliff?"

"Certainly," he replied. "I have done so time and time again; yet she simply will not come back. In spite of all that she has done I love her, and I want her and I am ready to forgive her if she repents and returns."

The counselor continued: "You've gone to her and that didn't work. Then, of course, you took one or two others from your church?"

"No, I haven't," Cliff said.

"You said that you did everything, yet you haven't taken even the second step. The Bible tells you what to do in Matthew 18. Wilma is still a member of your church, so ask a couple of the officers of the church to go with you to talk to her. You have only *begun* to do what God commands. Surely He will bless you for doing so, and who knows whether He will grant your desire."

Obviously discipline in Cliff's congregation had broken down. The counselor urged him to persist until he could convince one or two others to go with him. He finally persuaded a couple of the deacons to accompany him. The three of them had a heart-to-heart talk with Wilma. As a consequence, she left the other man and returned to Cliff. For four years they had been going through agony unnecessarily, simply because he had failed to follow God's Word.

Of course, it does not always work that way. Yet, the reconciliation/discipline dynamic offers hope. God has not left us helpless. There is a biblical method for dealing with problems between professed Christians—*all* problems! The reconciliation/discipline dynamic is the basic biblical motif against which we must live our day-by-day lives as sinners who, though saved by God's good grace, continue to run headlong into one another.

At a pastors' conference the following case was mentioned:

in heaven. The words "binding" and "loosing" were terms familiar to Jewish ears and were used roughly as the equivalent of our terms "prohibit" and "permit." Thus, one was prohibited or permitted communion with the Lord's people.

Pastor:

A husband and wife were spreading gossip about the church board throughout our congregation and to other nearby congregations. Here is what we did: an elder and the pastor visited them during the regular yearly house visitation program. The couple brought up their problem with the board. A long discussion followed. The pastor and elder tried to clear up a misunderstanding of the board's position. This began and ended with the reading of the Scriptures and with prayer. We said that if we had hurt or wronged them in any way, we were sorry. The husband and wife are continuing to gossip about the church board and are very critical about everything. What should we have done? What can we do now?

It seems that there were several things that should have been done differently. For example, the visit was made during regular yearly house visitation; that is to say, a *special* visit was not made. If there was gossip going on, a special visit should have been made to deal specifically with *that problem*. The problem already was on a level that involved the church. It was not on the private level or the one-or-two-others level. The gossipers had put the matter into the public domain. The gossip had spread throughout the congregation and to other congregations and pastors. The problem already had reached the highest level. Therefore, the pastor and elders were correct in considering the matter as a body.

But the manner of the visit that was conducted obscured the visitors' purpose. The people involved in the alleged sin were given no reason to believe that they were being visited to be dealt with about their gossip. And as far as we know, they were not dealt with about their gossip; there is no indication that they were. As a matter of fact, the problem with the board was raised not by the visitors, but by the sinning couple themselves. Yet, even then, the pastor and elder continued to speak not about the gossip, but rather about whether the board was right or wrong. They succumbed to the temptation to take an "easier" way out. An attempt was made to clear up misunderstandings about what the board was really doing. That is all well and good and probably should have been done, of course. But the principal problem that had to be handled *first* was not the misunderstanding; it was the conduct of these church members. Suppose the misunderstandings had been cleared up. Still, the matter of gossip would not have been handled. How long will it be until more gossip is spread and the next problem arises?

Instead of these mild, oblique approaches, we must learn, in such cases, to be irenically direct. The reconciliation/discipline dynamic must be applied. Presumably the pastor and elder thought: "Well, house visitation is coming around soon. Let's wait 'til then to do something about the problem. We'll visit and perhaps the matter will come up naturally and we will be able to discuss it then." Instead, the visitors should have focused their comments directly upon the question of gossip. The issue concerning the board should have been separated from the issue of gossip. The pastor and a couple of elders should have made a special appointment with the offending members to confront them specifically about the latter issue alone. Then the issue concerning gossip could not have been diverted to a discussion about what the board was doing. That could have come later on. Indeed, it could be discussed properly only *after* the prior issue of the sin of gossip had been settled before God and His church. The allegedly gossiping members were not prepared to pluck a splinter from the board's eye until the plank in their own was removed.

The pastor and the elder were on the defensive rather than the offensive. They were failing to exercise the authority that Christ vested in them. Of course, they should have said that they were sorry if they really believed that in some way they had wronged the couple. There is no indication, however, that they thought so. The apology seems insincere. But the main point is that nothing was said about the gossip.

Gossip is a very destructive sin; for the glory of God, the welfare of His church, and the sake of the offenders, it should have been dealt with. No wonder these members are continuing to gossip; nobody ever talked to them about *that*. No wonder they are very critical about everything. Nobody has dealt with *them*. It is not too late to do so. But when the officers do so this time, they *do* have something to apologize for: they should ask forgiveness for not having assumed their obligation sooner. In the providence of God, who makes even the wrath of man to praise Him, perhaps asking forgiveness for this failure to deal forthrightly with the matter of gossip will be used by His Spirit to soften their hearts to hear the firm but kindly meant rebuke.

Where to Begin

Since discipline has been neglected so widely in the church today, where may a pastor begin in correcting this situation? Here is a suggested procedure:

1. Begin by instructing your elders (church board) and convincing them of the need for discipline.

2. Then, preach plainly about the matter, instructing the congregation in God's will.

3. Finally, begin exercising scriptural discipline in the *very next incident* that arises.

Marriage, Divorce, and the Reconciliation/Discipline Dynamic

As a concrete example of the crucial nature of the reconciliation/discipline dynamic, let us consider the growing problem of divorce among Christians. This is a problem with which every Christian pastor increasingly will find himself confronted. John Murray sketches several situations in the back of his landmark book, *Divorce*, as paradigms for handling practical cases.[8] They are helpful, but limited in use. A pastor soon discovers that there are many situations that do not fit into the framework of these paradigms. However, the addition of one further factor to what Murray has said so well about marriage and divorce will bring such problem cases within their framework and will enable counselors to bring every case to a successful conclusion. This factor is the reconciliation/discipline dynamic.

The argument begins in I Corinthinans 7. Murray has exegeted the passage brilliantly. Paul first reiterates Christ's word concerning two believers, namely that there is no reason short of adultery for dissolving their marriage (I Corinthians 7:10, 11). But then he takes up another question about which the Lord did not speak directly while on earth (vs. 12). By the Spirit's inspiration the Lord's Word on that new matter is now about to be written by the apostle himself. That Word deals with the additional question of the marriage of a believer to an unbeliever. The believer is to continue the marriage if the unbeliever so desires. However, because his partner has now become a Christian, the unbeliever may no longer wish to continue living with him. In such cases the believer is to let him (or her) go (vs. 15). Whenever this happens, Paul says, the believer is no longer "in bondage"

---

8. John Murray, *Divorce* (Philadelphia: Presbyterian and Reformed Publishing Company, 1961).

(vs. 15). Murray argues successfully that this means that the Christian is free of his marriage bonds, may obtain a divorce and remarry.[9]

The problem remains, however, as to what must be done when two professing Christians fail to keep their marriage together and reconciliation does not take place. Let us say that a husband who is a professing Christian refuses to be reconciled to his wife. Perhaps he has even left her. Reconciliation has been attempted by the wife. If she continues to insist upon reconciliation (according to Matthew 18), but fails in her attempts at private confrontation, she must take one or two others from the church and confront her husband. Suppose she does and that he also refuses to hear them. In that case she is required to submit the problem officially to the church, which ultimately may be forced, by his adamant refusal to be reconciled, to excommunicate him for contumacy. Excommunication, Christ says, changes his status to that of a heathen and a publican, i.e., someone outside of the church (Matthew 18:17). Now he must be treated "*as* a heathen and a publican."[10] That means, for instance, that after reasonable attempts to reconcile him to the church and to his wife, he may be taken to court (I Corinthians 6:1-8 forbids *brethren* to go to law against one another[11]) to sue for a divorce (only, of course, if the excommunicated one deserts his partner).

By following the reconciliation dynamic, hopefully there will be reconciliation in most cases.[12] Whenever the principles of biblical

---

9. The right of remarriage is inherent in the biblical concept of divorce (cf. Deuteronomy 24:1-2, ". . . and when she is departed, she may go and be another man's wife." In a somewhat redundant, but nevertheless convincing and highly useful book, Guy Duty has shown (1) that the biblical idea of divorce always carries with it the right of remarriage, and (2) that *porneia* ("fornication") in biblical usage (such as in Matthew 19:9) was used more widely than the English term. Guy Duty, *Divorce and Remarriage* (Minneapolis: Bethany Fellowship, 1967).

10. The force of *hosper* is "treat him as." William F. Arndt and F. Wilbur Gingrich (Chicago: The University of Chicago Press, 1951), p. 908.

11. This fact is important. A church trial leading to excommunication must always precede any civil trial, since civil trials between believers are explicitly forbidden. This means that hasty action is slowed down and a process aimed at reconciliation not only is begun, but must run its full course unsuccessfully *before* legal proceedings may be begun. Thus Christians are afforded ample opportunity to consider the consequences of their actions before taking further action that might precipitously bring about new and greater evils.

12. This is to be expected among Christians. Cf. Proverbs 14:9 (T.E.V.).

reconciliation are followed faithfully, discipline rarely reaches the highest level of excommunication. Most marriages not only can be saved, but by proper help may be changed *radically* for good.[13] But in those few cases where reconciliation is refused, the believer who seeks it is not left in a state of limbo. He has a course of action to pursue, and if it leads to excommunication and desertion he is no longer obligated to remain married indefinitely.[14] This is true only if the believer's marriage partner during the whole process of discipline has failed to demonstrate evidence of repentance and faith, if that partner has been excommunicated, and if he (or she) wishes to dissolve the marriage. Continued rejection of the help and authority of Christ and His church finally leads to excommunication.

An excommunicated party who continues to be unrepentant must be looked upon and treated as a heathen and publican. He shows no signs of a work of grace. When he has been put outside of the church and still evidences no signs of salvation, the believing partner may deal with him as with an unbeliever. This means that if he leaves the believer under those circumstances, the latter is no longer under "bondage." The word in I Corinthians 7:21 ff. governing the relationship of a believer to an unbelieving marriage partner then comes into effect. By plugging in the reconciliation/discipline dynamic to the marriage-divorce-remarriage problem, the solution to ninety-nine percent of these cases that heretofore may have seemed unsolvable immediately may be seen. Most parties hopefully will come to reconciliation, but those who will not repent and be reconciled should be disciplined. Either way, matters are not left at loose ends.[15]

---

13. Often the weld is stronger than the metal before the break.

14. Often refusal to be reconciled leading to excommunication ends in separation from bed and board or desertion.

15. It is of vital importance for the church to pronounce judgment officially whenever cases of discipline have been adjudicated, *even when they have been settled by reconciliation.* The fact of settlement should be noted on the minutes of the board of elders. This is important for the sake of the parties involved so that in years to come they always may be able to refer back to the pronouncement of the church that the matter was closed satisfactorily.

Chapter Nine

RECONCILIATION

Reconciliation is a change of relationship between persons (God and man; man and man) that involves at least three elements: (1) *confession* of sin to God and to any others who have been offended; (2) *forgiveness* by God and by the one who has been offended;[1] (3) the establishment of *a new relationship* between the offender and God and between the offender and the offended party (parties). In reconciliation, enmity and alienation are replaced by peace and fellowship.[2]

There is no need to discuss this matter at length, since I have already dealt in detail with confession and forgiveness in *Competent to Counsel* (cf. especially pp. 110-124, 220-241). Here, perhaps, it is most important to take up two matters not fully discussed there: first, what the establishment of a new relationship involves; secondly, whether forgiveness requires forgetting.

A New Relationship

When God forgives a repentant sinner, He never leaves the matter there. Forgiveness not only marks an end, it is a watershed that also constitutes the beginning of something new. God insists that the matters which the repentance concerned must *be cleared up*. That is to say that true repentance at length will bear "fruit" that is appropriate to it.[3]

This fruit always involves change. Change in human relationships not only leads to the abandonment of the old ways (putting off), but also to the establishment of a new relationship (putting on). The new relationship may develop out of a request for (or offer of) help following

---

1. If the offended party refuses to grant forgiveness, then the process in Matthew 18 comes into effect: first, the repentant brother approaches him about the matter. Secondly, if this fails, he takes one or two others, and so on. Cf. Luke 17, where Christ makes forgiveness of the repentant brother *mandatory*.

2. Cf. William Childs Robinson, *Baker's Dictionary of Theology* (Grand Rapids: Baker Book House, 1960), pp. 437, 438.

3. Matthew 3:8.

the granting of forgiveness (cf. Ephesians 4:28, 29 and comments in *Competent to Counsel*, pp. 228 ff.). If a new relationship based upon biblical change and help is not established, then it is likely that one or more of the parties will revert to his old ways again. If so, again an unreconciled condition will develop. This failure frequently results in a kiss-and-make-up pattern. The same old problem is never really settled but becomes the reason for continued and repeated confrontation, confession, and forgiveness.[4] The answer to this problem lies in the concern to take steps immediately to establish a new biblical relationship between the offender and the offended party once forgiveness has been granted.[5]

Forgive and Forget?

When one has forgiven another, there ought to be a complete change in the relationship that follows. That change, however, does not mean that everyone must immediately *forget* the past. There is no such commandment in the Scriptures. Forgiveness is not a shock treatment that

---

4. At times counselees complain over an inability to forgive themselves after having received forgiveness from God or others. If, for instance, he has injured or maimed another seriously in a display of violent temper, a counselee may say, "I simply have never forgiven myself for this crime." Yet, the problem of continued guilt is not a question of inability to forgive oneself. To view it as such is to cloud the real issue and thereby to miss the path that leads to a solution. The real difficulty usually stems from the fact that the counselee feels guilty because he knows that, although the unfortunate *act* has been forgiven, *he is still the kind of person who did it.* The incident is forgiven, but guilt will not fully disappear until he knows that the patterns of life of which it was but one example have been destroyed. When the habit patterns have been changed (i.e., he becomes a non-violent person, for instance), he will no longer suffer the pain of *guilt.* He may feel sorrow upon occasion for his former act, but not guilt. Counselors, therefore, in dealing with any who complain of continued feelings of guilt after receiving forgiveness for sinful behavior will explain the source of these feelings as the acknowledged need for a basic life change and will help the counselee to begin to work on changing the underlying patterns. At a later point I shall discuss how the use of the biblical method for change that sticks can solve the problem by the two-sided process of putting off and putting on.

5. It is important to help counselees guard against any harmful side effects of confession to another. Awkwardness may occur at subsequent meetings, particularly if these occur infrequently, after a significant lapse of time, or only by chance. This awkwardness, although it may be no more than that, may be misinterpreted by either party as coldness. Misunderstandings like this can be avoided by *pursuing reconciliation to the end* by determining to maintain regular continued contact, in which open communication and joint work on the new relationship lead beyond awkwardness to a true friendship, understanding, and brotherly love in Christ.

instantly wipes out memory of the recent past. On occasions there may continue to be some fear that the same transgression may be committed again. This may be true particularly where a sexual offense, such as adultery, homosexuality, or incest, has occurred. It is understandable and proper that the offended party should be somewhat wary for a time. Nevertheless, under proper conditions forgetting (even of such unsettling offenses) will take place more rapidly than at first may be expected.

If forgetting in time does not follow forgiving, the counselor ought to look for the reason.[6] He may find, for instance, that the offended party has been brooding over the offense in self-pity. Such brooding is decidedly unscriptural and does not fit into the biblical concept of forgiveness. Forgiveness means no longer continuing to dwell on the sin that was forgiven. Forgiveness is the promise not to raise the issue again to the offender, to others, *or to himself.* Brooding is a violation of the promise made in granting forgiveness.

Now let us turn our attention to problems connected with the process of building a new relationship with the forgiven person. Often questionable motives may be mixed into the reconciliation situation that may cause one to doubt the reality of the repentance or forgiveness. The question may take at least two forms: (1) has there been genuine repentance?; (2) has real forgiveness actually been granted? The counselor may find it necessary to ask such questions directly and pursue them until he reaches an answer.

---

6. The biblical concept of forgiving and forgetting often has been misrepresented. The Bible speaks of "fruit appropriate to repentance." One forgives, but he does not immediately forget; rather, he remembers and looks for the *fruit* or the *results* that eventually accompany true repentance. It takes time for fruit to to grow. When fruit is discerned, forgetting *then* becomes possible. Perhaps the most evident fruit and one that does as much as any other to facilitate forgetting is the desire and willingness of the forgiven offender to build a new relationship with the one who has forgiven. The process may be diagrammed as follows:

Problem

Fruit

Forgetting

Forgiveness

In counseling the offended one, the counselor may discover that although speaking of forgiveness, the party wishes to make the offender suffer more. He (or she) may seek to achieve this through various subtle means. One frequently used method involves the adoption of a martyr stance. The counselor looks for depression, crying, self-pity, etc. He listens for comments like these: "Even though I try not to, all that I do is to think about John's sin day after day; I can't seem to erase it from my mind."[7] "What did I do to drive Mary into this?" "Why did this happen to me?" "I just keep on thinking about what it must have been like for Fred to go to bed with *her!*" By such attitudes and statements he causes the supposedly forgiven offender over a period of time to suffer for his sin. These attitudes do not savor of the grace of true Christian forgiveness.[8] God did not act like this when He granted forgiveness in Jesus Christ.

Forgiveness does not necessarily mean forgetting immediately, then, but it does involve a commitment not to raise the issue again.[9] Biblical forgiveness also involves the promise to avoid holding the offense over the offender's head, the promise to tell no one else about it, and the

7. The counselee may be challenged about *how* he has "tried." Either he may not be trying the right things (in which event he may be instructed as to how to break habits of brooding and self-pity), or in the event that he has not really tried, he may be challenged to do so. Brooding and self-pity sessions must be shattered at their inception.

8. While God in His providence sometimes may wish to bring about the consequences of sin in this life for His wise purposes (cf. Psalm 99:8, Berkeley), we have no right to take providence into our hands. However, even when God does this, *He does not intend to make the forgiven sinner suffer.* Christ suffered for him; neither man nor God may require further atonement.

9. "But," someone may object, "when God forgives, He forgets (cf. Jeremiah 31:34)." Yet, no one presses the point literally. God *cannot* forget. The *forgetting* in the passage is actually an anthropomorphic Hebrew parallelism for *forgiving*: "For I will *forgive* their iniquity, and their sin I will *remember* no more." The two are closely equated in this anthropomorphic reference to God because they are bound up in *human* forgiveness. True human forgiveness leads to forgetting. When one refuses to bring up the matter again (even to himself), he soon forgets. When we cannot forget, it is because we actively remember. Forgetting with reference to God can mean no more than the willingness to "bury" the issue, to raise it no more. Cf. also Isaiah 43:25. This is what is required in human forgiveness. To forgive *is* to "forget" in the sense that one has buried the hatchet. Forgiveness is a promise not to remember an offense *against* another again. To "remember" is used in the sense of "bring up again" (cf. III John 10). Cf. also E. J. Young, *N.I.C., The Book of Isaiah*, vol. III (Grand Rapids: Wm. B. Eerdmans, 1972), p. 162: "The things that you have done contrary to My law, I will not call to mind."

promise not to dwell on it oneself. As one consciously and prayerfully avoids such practices, he discovers that increasingly it becomes possible to forget. Indeed, there is no other way to forget. Granting forgiveness, then, does not produce instant forgetfulness, but rather entails the promise to adopt attitudes and practices that will lead to forgetting.

On the other hand, forgetting is facilitated, not only by the acts and attitudes of the offended one, but also by the willingness of both parties (and in particular the demonstrated desire of the offender) to establish a new (biblical) relationship that will preclude the same sort of offense in the future. On the part of the forgiven offender this willingness often may take the form of seeking help from the one who was offended. On the part of the other, there must be a willingness to work to establish such a new relationship and to offer to give such help.

When self-pity prevails, a new relationship will not grow. When help in changing is not sought and the old ways and the old relationships are allowed to continue, the parties set themselves up for a reoccurrence of the offense. Mutual effort to discover and solve issues God's way must be encouraged by the counselor. The only way to cement a new relationship that will enable both parties to forgive and forget past offenses and to avoid and/or handle future failures as well is by means of such effort.

Forgiveness First Is Granted, Not Felt

"But suppose I do not feel like forgiving my brother, am I supposed to do so anyhow? Won't doing so without *feeling* forgiving make me a hypocrite?" This objection is frequently raised by sincere Christians who become perplexed over hypocrisy by wrongly equating hypocrisy with acting against one's feelings. This objection also is used *hypocritically*, I may add, by others who wish to excuse themselves from the hard (but Christian) duty of granting forgiveness.

By a thorough understanding and application of Luke 17, it is possible to resolve the question quite satisfactorily. In verse 3 Jesus warns: "Be careful of yourselves." The warning is necessary; there are many ways to err about forgiveness. The warning is pertinent to many Christians who are caught up in the easy rationalizations by which they try to excuse themselves from the obligation to forgive their brothers. Jesus continues:

If your brother sins against you, rebuke him, and if he repents, forgive him.

The obligations of Galatians 6:1 and Matthew 18:15 are repeated here. An offended brother must approach the offender and seek to bring him to repentance and endeavor to bring about a reconciliation. "When another sins against you," the counselor must explain, "God says that puts you under an obligation to rebuke him." No wonder Jesus warned "be careful of yourselves." That is hard, but not quite so hard as what follows.

Jesus then stresses the *results* of ensuing repentance, not its *cause*. He plainly states that if as the result of the rebuke the offending Christian says that he is repentant, the offended brother must forgive him.

Hands usually go up all over the room whenever I make this statement. One asks: "But shouldn't we wait for the fruits of repentance before forgiving?" Another says, "What if I don't *feel* forgiving toward him?" A third: "Do you mean to say that I am to forgive him merely because he *says* that he is sorry?"

Jesus knew all about such objections. He answered them fully in the verses that follow. Let us consider the next verse, then:

And if he should sin against you seven times a day and seven times in a day should return to you saying "I repent," you shall forgive him.

Take the first and third questions above—must we grant forgiveness merely on the basis of one's *statement* that he repents, or must we demand fruits fitting for repentance first? Clearly the words of Christ preclude waiting. There could be no clear evidence of change within the hypothetical time period that Christ suggests: seven times in the same day! Indeed, if a brother does the same thing seven times in the same day, the only evidence that you could have would be entirely negative.[10] After being rebuked, repenting, and being forgiven once, he continued to sin (possibly even in the same way) six more times. It is certain, then, that Jesus does not condition the granting of forgiveness upon the behavior of the offender after forgiveness, but rather hangs the granting of

10. Fruit takes time to grow. It also takes care and nourishment. A Northerner, looking at the shiny green leaves of a citrus tree, may not know what kind of tree it is. But if he waits long enough, he will know *when the fruit appears* whether it is an orange or . . . a lemon! By their fruit shall you know them, has nothing to do with the truth that is taught in Luke 17.

forgiveness upon the brother's verbal testimony *alone*: "and seven times in a day should return to you *saying*, 'I repent.' " It is the *saying*, not subsequent *doing* on his part, that should activate the offended one to grant forgiveness. And . . . said Jesus, he should grant that forgiveness *even if it should be requested seven times in one day.*

"That is too difficult," you may object. Well, your objection is precisely the response that the disciples made to this injunction. They replied: "Lord, give us more faith!" (vs. 5). "This is too hard for us," they complained; "if you want us to forgive that way you will have to give us greater faith." Now we can understand why the Lord prefaced the discussion with a warning (vs. 3).

At first the disciples' request for greater faith sounds quite reasonable —and pious. But it was not met with a sympathetic response by the Lord. He took a dim view of their request, shunting it aside, treating it as an excuse rather than as a sincere plea:

> But the Lord said, "If you had as much faith as a grain of mustard seed, you could say to this myrtle tree, 'Be rooted up and be planted in the sea'—and it would obey you."

His reply amounts to saying:

"The problem is not lack of faith as you allege. It does not take much faith to do great things. Even a small amount (as small as a tiny mustard seed) could do wonders. What you need is not more faith; you simply need to exercise the faith that you have and stop making excuses."

The problem, then, is not a problem of faith; the problem is much more straightforward, uncomplicated, and simple. It is a problem of *obedience.* Christ told them what to do and they were to *obey.* The parable of the servant points this up:

> But which of you who has a servant plowing or tending sheep will say immediately when he has come from the field, go and eat? But will he not say to him "Prepare so that I may eat," and "Get ready and serve me while I eat and drink, and after this you will eat and drink?"

This is a *hard* word, but necessary. It could not have been easy for the tired, hungry servant to prepare a meal for his master when he, himself, was so hungry. His *feelings*, as he savored the aroma of the food that he was preparing, told him to forget the hard task of feeding his master and urged him to eat the food himself. But he had been ordered by his master to prepare and serve the meal, so—*hard as it was, thankless*

as the task might be (vs. 9), and *against his feelings*—he *did* what
was commanded. The Lord Jesus makes the point:

> So also when you have done all things *commanded* you, say, "We
> are unprofitable servants, for we have done that which it was *our
> duty* to do" (vs. 10).

It is now clear that forgiveness is a "duty." It is "commanded." It
is no more hypocritical to obey the Lord in granting forgiveness *against
one's feelings* than for the slave to prepare and serve the meal *against
his feelings.*[11] Nor is it meritorious to do this duty: one is still an unprofitable servant (i.e., he is one who is only doing what is expected
of him and no more) when he does so—even though it may be *hard*
to obey.

Faith and feeling are irrelevant to the matter of granting forgiveness
to a brother. What one must do is to commit himself to the *hard* task of
promising not to raise the matter of the offense again. That is the
essence of granting forgiveness. When one sincerely avoids mentioning
the offense to his brother, when he refuses to discuss it with anyone
else, and when he puts it out of his own mind by declining to think and
dwell upon it in resentment or self-pity, the *feelings* of forgiveness soon
will accompany the promise and commitment.

This, then, is how counselors must address themselves to counselees
who balk at granting forgiveness. They must not be misled by ideas of
lack of faith, supposed feelings of hypocrisy, etc. Instead, like their
Lord, they must knife through all such excuses and incisively lay bare
the root of the problem: disobedience. In no other way can they help
the counselee.

---

11. Christians confuse hypocrisy with feelings. I get out of bed every morning
against contrary feelings. That does not make the act hypocritical. I would
be hypocritical *only* if I pretend that I enjoy getting up.

Chapter Ten

PRESUPPOSITIONS AND METHODOLOGY

In considering the methodology of counseling, it is important first to speak of the place and importance of methodology, then to compare and contrast biblical methods with some of those that are employed by others. The issue at stake is: what methods may Christians use in counseling? Counseling methodology is so integrally related to counseling philosophy that (in the words of Perry London, who makes no pretense of being a Christian) if you want to understand the core ideas of a system, "analysis of technique serves understanding more than any other possible approach to this discipline."[1] Yet Baker, writing in a conservative Christian magazine, naively speaks of the "moral neutrality" of methodology or technique![2] Thereby, he places an aspect of life outside of the concern of God.

The issue, to be sure, takes one form when speaking about the techniques of mechanics who service an automobile and another when discussing the techniques of the repairmen who seek to change the life and values of another human being. The values involved in the methodology of auto mechanics are more indirectly related to methodology. Some excuse for failing to see the impossibility of neutrality with reference to the former might be understandable, but how can one speak of "moral neutrality" with reference to the control and manipulation of men? Surely the crucial importance of methodology, therefore, may not be by-passed.

Counseling methodology, as London rightly has said, is "a moral question that is always answered by the therapist in practice."[3] Indeed, it could not be otherwise. *What* we do to another man and *how* we do

---

1. Perry London, *The Modes and Morals of Psychotherapy* (New York: Holt, Rinehart and Winston, 1964), p. 32.
2. Cf. Dwight B. Baker, "Psychology and Christianity: Getting to Know You," *Eternity*, April 1970, p. 58.
3. *Ibid.*, p. 10.

it is tightly bound up with what we *believe* about that man. If, with Skinner, we assume that man is only another animal, we shall seek to train him as we would train our dogs and do it in precisely the same way. In other words, we shall adopt methods that are appropriate to training animals. If we use Skinner's methods, we treat man as if he were only an animal. On Skinner's presuppositions, methods used in training a man and a rat will differ only insofar as the man and the contingencies necessary to control him may be considered more complex. There will be no *basic* difference. If we acknowledge the existence of the image of God in man, however, this very belief will demand a methodology discrete from that which is used in training a dog. Dogs, for instance, may not be called to repentance and faith in Jesus Christ; neither may they be converted and persuaded by the Spirit of God to live according to His Word.[4] But according to Christian presupposition a man may; indeed must. Christian methodology, therefore, is conditioned radically by Christian beliefs. Christians insist that counseling methodology *necessarily* must grow out of and always be appropriate to the biblical view of God, man, and the creation.

The chart on the following page may be of help in noting the relationship of methodology to presuppositions in some of the more prominent schools of counseling.

Basically the chart distinctly divides other counseling approaches from the biblical one.[5] The first non-Christian method I have labeled *Expert Knowledge* and the second *Common Knowledge*. The third (Christian) approach begins with and grows out of *Divine Knowledge*. Now the distinctions between the first two subdivisions are not absolute, of course, yet they fairly indicate the general thrust of the methodological approaches of the various schools of counseling.

Expert Knowledge

Freudianism

The first approach is adopted by those who believe that counseling

---

4. Nor do dogs do experiments on men and write up their results in learned journals.

5. At bottom, the Christian believes that there are only *two* approaches: the Christian; the non-Christian. The first two approaches in the chart are mere subdivisions of the latter. The basic antithesis of the Christian position to all others is demarked by the division in the chart.

General Approach	Specific Type	Man's Problem	Solution	
1 Expert Knowledge	Freudian	Poor Socialization	Resocialization by expert	
	Skinnerian	Environmental Conditioning	Reconditioning by expert	I non-Christian approaches
2 Common Knowledge	Rogerian	Failure to live up to potential	Resources in self	
	Integrity Groups	Bad behavior toward others	Resources in self and group	
3 Divine Knowledge	Christian	Sin against God	Spirit's Resources in Word	II Christian approach

Figure 1

Methodology and Presuppositions of Some Leading Approaches to Counseling

can be done only from the point of view of expert knowledge. They hold that counseling must be restricted to some small coterie or elite group of technocrats. People of this sort develop castes and priesthoods (secular or otherwise).[6] To the counseling priesthood alone is assigned the task of counseling. Among the leading theorists of this school are Freud and Skinner. According to this kind of approach, the experts must do it for you. Only the experts know how. They alone possess the

---

6. Cf. London's designation: "secular priest," *op. cit.*, pp. 156 ff. As De Bono points out, "Experts are not usually the first to leap out of the hole that accords them their expert status, to start digging elsewhere, . . . so experts are usually found happily at the bottom of the deepest holes, often so deep that it hardly seems worth getting them to look around." Edward De Bono, *Think New* (New York: Avon Publishing Co., 1968), p. 48. Experts have large investments and deep commitments; they often find challenge hard to take.

proper knowledge, methods, and techniques. To them belong both the requisite knowledge and skills. They are held in awe by laymen in a fundamentally gnostic pattern.[7]

Because the origins of the counselee's problems are viewed as essentially external—the result of events that have *happened to* the counselee—he is considered to be at their mercy.[8] He is helpless apart from external expertise. Just as he had little or nothing to do with getting into difficulty in the first place, so there is little or nothing that he can do to get out of it. One sign of the expert approach to counseling is the wide use of esoteric jargon and institutionalized techniques.

Freud has been the most prominent example of the expert knowledge approach. According to Freud, man's main problem is poor socialization. The typical counselee's psychoanalytic history will show that in the past this helpless patient became the victim of other people in society. He was helpless then and he is helpless now. Possibly he has been kicked around since he was a kid. Perhaps a strong grandmother set up rules and rituals by which he had to abide. He may have been raised in a Victorian-like home. Conceivably, the beliefs and practices of his church were very narrow and he was forced to move within the cramped boundaries of its restrictions. So, victimized by one or more of these pressures from without, the counselee was socialized by others who built up in him a conscience (or Superego) that was overly strict. This conscience now is in conflict with his normal desires (Id), and it is this conflict that is the source of his current difficulties. Every time he violates a "do" or "don't," he feels guilty (not because he is, but because he has violated his unreasonably strict Superego or conscience[9]). Since the *Id* (the natural impulse for sex and aggression) is not allowed to come to conscious expression, the impulses must

---

7. See E. Fuller Torrey's comments on the witch doctor and psychiatry, *The Big Umbrella*, p. 108. Freud himself put it this way: "We form a pact with each other. The patient's sick ego promises us the most complete candor, promises, that is, to put at our disposal all of the material which his self-perception provides; we, on the other hand, assure him of the strictest discretion and put at his service *our experience* in interpreting material that has been influenced by the unconscious. *Our knowledge* shall compensate for *his ignorance* and shall give his ego once more mastery over the lost provinces of this mental life. This pact constitutes the analytic situation" (italics mine). Sigmund Freud, *New Introductory Lectures on Psychoanalysis* (New York: W. W. Norton and Company, Inc., 1933), p. 212.
8. The victim theme is prominent. Cf. *Competent to Counsel*, pp. xvii, 9, 33.
9. Cf. the discussion of real and false guilt in *Competent to Counsel*, pp. 14 ff.

emerge in covert ways. The angry policeman who was socialized into him stands at the door of conscious expression with a night stick, ready to keep every Id-impulse from leaving home. By threatening or clubbing them, he has succeeded in chasing them back inside. So poor socialization by *others*—Grandma, the church, other people—is the problem; *they* did it to him.

Now the expert is necessary to undo what others have done. Through the process of psychoanalysis, the expert takes a long expedition back into the counselee's past. He overturns every flat stone to discover what vermin lurk beneath. Over a long long period of time through such analysis the expert discovers those crucial things that happened to his counselee. He becomes aware of the many forces that have been unleashed against him as the process of socialization took place. This is accomplished by the process of free association, dream analysis, and other esoteric methods that are appropriate to the basic assumption.

Next, the psycho*analytic* expert, now turned psycho*therapist*, himself *becomes* (assumes the role of) those persons from the past. He becomes the church authority, the strict father, grandmother, *et al.* But this time as *he* plays their role, all of these persons turn out to be very gracious, understanding, and permissive; quite unlike their real-life counterparts. Thus the therapist resocializes the counselee; if the latter is helped the counselee says (again): "He did it for me."

Of course, only experts are eligible to do such esoteric work. No common, ordinary, garden-variety pastor, for example, could get involved in this work. The methods of psychoanalysis are far too complex and specialized; they take years of unique training in theory and skills. No mere pastor could analyze the dream symbols, interpret the free association, and put them all together successfully. He never could learn to develop and handle a transference relationship adequately enough to bring about the needed resocialization. Thus the pastor is told that the counselee needs "professional help." This phrase is the hallmark of the Expert Knowledge approach.

The Freudian expert moves into the picture to restructure the counselee's value system. He attempts to chop his consience down to size. He wishes to remove the policeman's night stick and to teach him how to become polite to escaping Id-impulses. At length the policeman learns to tip his hat as they leave home by the front door. It takes an expert to do all of this.

The Freudian therapist uses two expert techniques that grow out of his expert diagnosis of the problem: psychoanalysis and psychotherapy. He also has expert jargon. Freudianism involves professionalism to the highest degree. In fact, only those who themselves have undergone long hours of analysis are allowed to become members of the psychoanalytic caste.

Since the counselee's problem arose from the outside, and since it must be solved from the outside, the counselee himself is virtually passive. The assumption that a man is not responsible for his condition leads to the notion that he is not responsible for getting himself out of that condition. Thus, if convinced of the psychotherapist's dogma, at times such persons will not cooperate. This may lead to the *tyranny* of the expert, who *against the will of the counselee* exerts his expert testimony to effect the counselee's committal to a mental institution.[10]

The Expert Knowledge approach is based squarely upon the presupposition that man is not responsible for what he does. This is a fundamentally non-Christian assumption. Consequently, the methods used by the expert also turn out to be anti-Christian.

Now usually there is an element of truth reflected by every false position.[11] Yet the truth is distorted as it is reflected in a dented bronze mirror. Only dimly does it approximate the truth itself. Yet we must not miss those elements as we progress, because it is these that make non-Christian views seem plausible and, therefore, dangerous. The element of truth reflected in Freudianism is that people *do* exert significant influence upon one another. Obviously parents influence children, church authorities influence members, etc.

---

10. Cf. Thomas Szasz, *The Manufacture of Madness* (New York: Harper and Row, 1970) and Ronald Leifer, *In the Name of Mental Health* (New York: Science House, 1969).

11. False teachings, whether they be the teachings of cults like Mormonism or whether they be pagan systems of counseling, usually make gains by capitalizing upon those areas that have been neglected by the church. Rather than to rush to adopt the views and methods of such groups, one should thank God for the chastening He has given and return to the Scriptures, the one and only proper source for *all* that is necessary to life and godliness. Group therapies, for instance, have shown the need for stressing community and fellowship among Christians. The answer to the problem, however, is not to bring Integrity Therapy or Transactional Analysis or Encounter Groups into the church; rather, it is to search the Scriptures faithfully to discover what God says about groups, beginning with such passages as Hebrews 10:24-25.

The Bible says much about the good and bad influence that Christians may exert upon others and the influences others may have upon them.[12] But the day-and-night difference between Freudianism and God's truth is this: God holds us responsible to do something about influence. We may not consider ourselves matchboxes to be tossed about by the rolling waves and high winds of influence. When one is under the influence of another, it is *because* he has allowed himself to come or to remain under it. According to the Scriptures, God holds men responsible for the kind of life style that they adopt and according to which they live. One must rethink biblically what he has learned. He must "test all things and hold fast" only to "that which is good" (I Thessalonians 5:21). God expects Christians to reject or shake off all wrong influences.

Let us take an example. Regardless of how he has been influenced, God holds a Christian responsible to work when he can. The Scriptures command: "If any would not work, neither should he eat."[13] This biblical principle reaches down into concrete situations; it may largely *determine* a given counseling process. The following remarkable case demonstrates much of what has been said.

Roger, a young man twenty-three years old, was bribed by parents into coming to a counseling session[14] (that is a poor way to bring a person to counseling). For more than two years he had been regularly visiting a psychoanalyst who had not helped him in the slightest. Roger reported that the psychiatrist had told him that he did not know what his problem was, but that one thing was certain: he was very, very sick. (Roger carefully stressed the two "verys" to impress the counselor.) He further reported that he was told that treatment would take a long, long while (he stressed the two "longs" as well). He also reported that he was told that there could be no assurance that anything done for him would be successful. Presumably the psychiatrist had convinced this strapping young man with a robust body and good mind that he was sick. Consequently he was lying around doing nothing except watching television. He claimed that he couldn't go to work or do anything more, although so far as he knew *the only reason why* he couldn't was because the expert had said so. Medical tests had given Roger a clean bill of health physiologically, but in spite of that fact, he was certain that he

---

12. E.g., Proverbs 13:20; 28:7; 29:3; I Corinthians 15:33.
13. II Thessalonians 3:10.
14. "If you come then we will allow you to. . . ."

had a serious mental illness. Roger was sure that there wasn't anything that he could do about it. He had received expert advice to the effect that he was sick; and only an expert, of course, could help him. But as of the moment the expert had not yet come through with more than a diagnosis.

The counselor asked him what his problem was. Roger said that during the two years that the psychiatrist had been treating him he could not discover what the problem was. The psychiatrist still did not know. He was asked what the symptoms of his mental illness were. He did not know. His parents knew of none but laziness. Several physicians could find nothing else. Yet Roger was certain that it was going to take a long, long time to discover what the problem was. After all, a problem this deep really required an expert! Clearly no pastoral counselor could help; this was a task for a *professional*. But the mere pastoral counselor dared to ask again (pressing the point): "What expert advice have you *received*?" He stammered, "Well, uh, uh, uh." He couldn't come up with any specific advice that he had been given during the entire two-year period. The two years had yielded nothing except the advice that since he was so ill he should assume no responsibilities. The counselor pursued the matter:

"What has happened during this time? Have you improved significantly as a result of these two years of consultation and rest?"

"No," he replied, "I am no better. Things are exactly the same, or perhaps a little bit worse."

The counselor reasoned with him (to no avail): "Well, now look, you've been going for two years to this expert who admits that he doesn't know what is wrong with you. You haven't received any expert advice so far, and you say that there hasn't been any change at all. Aren't you beginning to grow a little suspicious of his expertise? Would you like us to take a crack at it?"

"Oh no, thank you," Roger responded. "I know you mean well but, you see, I need *expert* help!"

Roger was ensnared by the concept of the expert. The simple fact is that there is every reason to believe that this young man was not sick. He had physical strength and ability. The counselor had suggested (vainly):

"Even if you are a little mixed up and you're having some problems about sorting things out, why not get up off the sofa and *try* to do a few things?"

The pastoral counselor hazarded this: "I suppose at times you feel a little guilty sponging off your parents the way you do, don't you? Couldn't you at the very least do a few simple tasks around the home? Perhaps in a short time you even could take on a part-time job—deliver newspapers, dig ditches; after all, the doctors say that you are in great physical shape."

"No," he replied, "my psychiatrist tells me that I am too sick to work. I have mental illness."

Throughout he kept using the expert's favorite jargon term, mental illness. At last the counselor stopped him: "Now wait a minute, do you mean that you have an organic problem?"

"No, there is no organic problem," he answered.

"There's no brain damage, then?"

"Correct, there is no brain damage."

The counselor explained: "I know what mental illness is if you're talking about brain damage. For example, if I were to part your hair with a crowbar you would have mental illness; there is no question about that. But the issue is, what do you mean when you speak of mental illness; what do you really mean by that?"

He said, "I am talking about the mind."

The counselor probed: "Do you mean by the mind something physiological?"

"No, nothing physiological."

"Well, did some kind of bug crawl into some part of you and make you sick?"

"No."

"Well, what is sick?"

"My mind."

"But not *organically* sick?"

"No."

"And what is it that made it sick?"

"A disease."

"Was it an organic disease; a disease caused by a virus, bodily malfunction, or an injury?"

"No."

He was right, of course; you can't *injure* the nonorganic and viruses can't cause nonorganic *illness.* So the counselor quipped: "Your problem, then, must be the result of some unknown nonorganic cause affecting a nonorganic part of you that has caused a mysterious nonorganic illness."

"Right," he agreed in all seriousness, missing the point entirely. "You have understood exactly."

Roger's real difficulty was blind faith in the expert. The expert had explained the problem in expert terms (jargon) and had classified the problem with a psychiatric label. He was not responsible for his problem; after all, he *was sick!* He said, "I don't feel guilty at all about not working; I am sick and I can't do anything about it." He was sick, so he was not responsible. He said, "Other people have made me ill." His mother was sitting in the room. The counselor asked: "Have you and your psychiatrist discovered yet *who* did it to you?" He hedged nervously, glancing at her. It was obvious that he had been taught to blame his parents. He said, "I talk to my psychiatrist about such matters. I don't want to get into that question here; you wouldn't understand!"[15]

This case illustrates in an extraordinary manner the problem with the approach we have called Expert Knowledge. If man is not responsible but has a mental illness caused by others, then Paul's exhortation to work (or you should not eat) falls upon deaf ears. Much present-day welfarism stems from erroneous Freudian assumptions.

Behaviorism

Now, let us take a look at another approach that also fits into the category of Expert Knowledge. B. F. Skinner and the behavior modification school provide the other most prominent example today. The behaviorists claim to be committed to the use of nothing but empirical scientific knowledge."[16] This commitment is in many respects quite

---

15. Roger's problem was iatrogenic (treatment-engendered). Experience confirms the fact that psychiatrists and other counselors often have contributed (at least) dimensions to the problems of counselees. Counselors must be aware of this possibility and be prepared (when possible) to meet it. Akhilananda reports a different sort of case. The young man in question was led astray by psychoanalysis: "It was the interpretation given to him by the psychiatrists that ruined this man. He became frightened when he was led to think that he was still clinging to childhood or boyhood habits and ways of life." Swami Akhilananda, *Mental Health and Hindu Psychology* (Boston: Branden Press, 1951), p. 95.

16. Skinner's patron saints are Francis Bacon and J. B. Watson. The strong

different from that of the armchair (or couchside) theorist. Skinner does not sit back, feet up, analyzing dreams; he goes into the lab and experiments with pigeons and mice. In his popular book, *Beyond Freedom and Dignity*, he reiterates the dream of a utopian Walden II, where science will produce a problem-free society. War will be dissolved, as well as other social problems, by the application of scientific analysis to the control of human behavior.

According to Skinner, it is time to demythologize psychology. For too long mythical concepts like mind, attitudes, freedom, dignity, etc., have impeded progress. A truly scientific analysis of man acknowledges the existence only of what can be observed and measured, namely, *behavior*. There is nothing else. Man is an animal, the highest yet in existence. Organic evolution is the dynamic behind man; the goal is survival and natural selection is the process. Skinner's main concern is about the herd. Quite simply, then, man is the product of his environment. He has been created by it, is dependent upon it, and if we knew all of the contingencies (some day, perhaps soon, we shall), we would see that he is strictly determined by it. He is not free in any sense of that term. All this may be translated into Freudian terms and amounts to saying about the same thing. Whereas Freud sees the counselee as not responsible but holds *others* responsible (poor socialization is the problem), Skinner would say that man is not responsible because a determined animal cannot be held accountable (the *environment* is the cause of human behavior). For Skinner, even to speak of responsibility is nonsense. The Freudian solution to problems is to analyze the counselee to determine who did what to him and, on the basis of the findings, resocialize him. The Skinnerian solution is to discover scientifically the contingencies related to the "poor" (all value judgments are part of the mythology) behavior, and on the basis of the data rearrange the environmental contingencies so as to reprogram the counselee's responses. This is done by the use of rewards and aversive controls.

Of course, it takes the scientific expert to manipulate the man and

dependence of Skinner upon the latter may be seen by reading the (excellent) refutation of Watsonian behaviorism, "Does the Behaviorist Have a Mind?" by William Hallock Johnson, in *The Princeton Theological Review*, vol. 25, January, 1927, no. 1, pp. 40-58. The article is quite timely as a trenchant reply not only to Watson, but also years later to Skinner. Modern advances have been largely in technology; certainly not in fundamental philosophy.

his environment. The expert may teach (train) him how to use operant conditioning. The maze and the man-sized Skinner box and all that it takes to construct these require a high degree of expertise. Indeed, Skinner would like to see not only counseling, but government, education, etc. (every phase of human activity), controlled by a small group of technocrats. This is his solution to the world's problems.

There is an element of truth also poorly reflected by Skinnerianism. The environment is of great influence upon man. It is true that making changes in the environment may be useful in counseling. Reward and punishment are biblical concepts; the Bible is replete with exhortations and laws that depend upon the reward/punishment dynamic. However, to say that is a far cry from accepting Skinnerian presuppositions or methods.

When Dobson, for instance, recommends strictly behavioristic methods for child raising *in the name of Christianity*, he badly confuses important distinctions and erases lines that forever must be drawn clearly.[17] His near total capitulation to behaviorism is couched in Christian terms but really introduces an equally godless system into the Christian home while purporting to be a Christian reaction to permissiveness. In Dobson's methods there is no place for nouthetic confrontation.[18] Reward and punishment are prominent (particularly the former), and the need for structure is emphasized. But Dobson's approach is cold and godless. It centers upon manipulation but says nothing of biblical confrontation.

---

17. Cf. James Dobson, *Dare to Discipline* (Wheaton: Tyndale House, 1970). See *The Big Umbrella*, pp. 130, 131.

18. Ephesians 6:4 insists not only upon structured discipline with teeth ("nurture"), but also nouthetic confrontation ("and admonition"). Cf. *Christian Living in the Home*, pp. 103 ff. Those who advocate control by manipulation fail to recognize the place in biblical thought devoted to bringing the child to faith in Christ and then leading him to interiorize the Word of God as his Standard. Personal conviction seems to have been forgotten or ignored. Others seem to think that physical means of discipline will do all that is necessary. Yet Proverbs 29:15 agrees with Ephesians 6:4 when it couples together the "rod *and* reproof." The latter word means "verbal discussion" of the problem.

Strict adherence to Skinnerian training would, were it possible (fortunately, man as the image-bearer of God reacts negatively to such treatment), train a man to *live like an animal.* He would always act to *avoid* suffering and to *gain* pleasure. This is strictly an amoral view of life contrary to Christian decision making (Hebrews 11:24-26). If not animal behavior, criminal behavior results: avoid all trouble; get what immediate satisfactions are available. Only redemption and conformity to a Standard (God's Word) can train up a moral man who is pleasing to God.

Conspicuously absent in such child discipline is the use of the Scriptures, conversion, repentance, the work of the Holy Spirit, and sanctification. Ephesians 6:4 emphasizes, in contrast, *both* discipline (by reward and punishment) and nouthetic confrontation (the "nurture *and* admonition of the Lord" A.V.).[19] Biblical persuasion, conviction, and personal commitment are ignored. They must not be.

While there is an *element* of truth reflected in Skinnerianism (the need for a disciplined reward/punishment structure), again this appears only as a dim distortion of the balanced biblical position. The image of God in man as a created being (man is not viewed as the product of environmental evolutionary selection) is the basic presupposition upon which the biblical approach is based. This presupposition is diametrically opposed to Skinnerian notions of man merely as an animal. Christians, therefore, will use other methods appropriate to this important presupposition. They may not manipulate persons as Skinner (or Dobson) recommends. Reward and punishment of men who bear the image of God (including true righteousness, knowledge, and holiness) is reward and punishment within the context of responsibility toward God, based upon the law of God as the Standard and conditioned by God's eternal reward/punishment structure. Man is held responsible and capable of dignity because in Christ he may reflect the divine image.

There is, of course, a side of man that is similar to an animal. Men and animals live in the same environment, breath the same air, and share many bodily functions. But it is his relationship to God, sustained through language, conscience, etc., that marks him out as different and makes a tremendous cleavage between man and everything else in his environment.

Man is as worthless as any other animal on Skinnerian presuppositions. He may be used at will, therefore, by the experts. Indeed, behaviorists tell us that they can make about any sort of man that they wish, starting with genetic manipulation and then setting up the desired environmental contingencies. If they have their way, men will be bred

---

19. Here Skinnerianism must not be thought of merely as deficient, needing an additional element. It is deficient *because* it is based upon the wrong presuppositions. Skinnerian behaviorism cannot be improved by *adding* nouthetic confrontation. Reward and aversive control are themselves conceived of in a non-Christian manner as part of the evolutionary process of selecting and training an animal.

by herds like cattle.[20] The only fly in the ointment is this: when you get two Skinnerians together to decide what kind of sausage they want to come out of the meat grinder, they can't. There is no value, no standard; all is relative. Christians alone can say *what* a man should be, for they alone have that Standard in God's written and living Word.

Common Knowledge

Rogerianism

Now take a look at the second category, the *Common Knowledge* approach. Again consider a couple of prominent examples. To begin with, there is Carl Rogers.[21] Quite contrary to the idea of the necessity of the expert, Rogers would contend that there is no need for an expert at all. That is one reason why so many ministers and social workers have seized upon the Rogerian methodology. It is simple, easy to learn, runs little risk, and is so immediately usable. Its broad acceptance has been encouraged by all kinds of people. Haim Ginott teaches it in a modified popular form to parents; Seward Hiltner to ministers. The expert might do better than others, but almost anyone can become something of an expert in time.[22]

Rogerian theory (and therapy) is based upon the idea that all men have adequate knowledge and resources to handle their problems. That, naturally, offers an optimistic outlook for counselors. Even the counselee himself has such knowledge. The basic assumption is that persons with unresolved problems simply have not been living up to their own potential. Latent within them lie the solutions to all of their problems. They have the potential to do right. As a matter of fact, Rogers believes that at his core man is good, not evil. Adequate resources are there, built in. The task is to plug these in; to release the power.[23]

The therapist (or counselee) shares time with a client in order to help him to help himself. The therapist is a catalyst. He assists him

---

20. Presumably, those who do not conform to the standards of those in control will be eliminated. Cf. Philip Edgecomb Hughes, *The Control of Human Life* (Philadelphia: Presbyterian and Reformed Publishing Co., 1971).

21. Cf. the section on Rogerianism in *Competent to Counsel*, pp. 78-100.

22. Cf. Charles F. Kemp, *Learning About Pastoral Care* (Nashville: Abingdon Press, 1970), p. 112.

23. Michael Beldoch writes: "The human potential movement believes that man is essentially good and needs only the proper climate and soil in which to bloom." *The Intellectual Digest*, October 1971, p. 87.

much as a midwife does (to use B. F. Skinner's figure) to deliver the solution. The counselee, by the process, himself is able to come up with the answers. Since the resources to solve problems are there in the counselee, there is no necessity for expert advice from the outside. The difficulty was an inside problem to begin with and may be solved from the inside as well. No authoritative Standard from the outside may be imposed upon the counselee. No authoritative Word may be spoken by the counselor as a representative of the Framer of that Standard. A preacher is not needed; *indeed* he is not.[24] Instead, a counselor evokes from the counselee all of the answers that lie down there inside. If he looks at his problems long enough and clearly enough, and if he feels deeply enough about them, he can solve them on his own. The counselor, therefore, becomes a wall or mirror off of which the counselee's own resources are bounced or reflected back to himself. By this reflective process the counselee at length comes to see the dimensions of the problem and what the solution to the problem really is. The counselee's words are rephrased, sharpened, or repeated in similar but different words to help him clarify his own thoughts. Rogerians believe in the Common Knowledge approach because of its fundamental commitment to the idea that every man has the resources in himself.[25] There is, then, a basic belief in the goodness and autonomy of man. God is not needed (in fact is considered an Intruder) by Rogerian counselors.

There is an element of truth reflected by what Rogers does. The element of truth is in his *reaction* to the expert who considers man not responsible for his behavior. Rogers wants a responsible man; yet he has failed to postulate a responsible man by declaring man independent of God. When man is not responsible to God and is only held responsible to himself, responsibility is swallowed up by anarchy. Man is totally responsible before God. Christians believe that God is sovereign and works His will in man; yet man must use his divinely appointed human agency under the providence of God. Nevertheless, in the use of human

---

24. Cf. the author's review of Harold I. Haas, *Pastoral Counseling with People in Distress* (St. Louis: Concordia Publishing House, 1970), in which Haas distinguishes between the pastor as pastor and the pastor as counselor and shows that on a Rogerian basis a minister must cease to be a pastor whenever he acts as a counselor. *Westminster Theological Journal*, May 1971, pp. 253-255.

25. The later Rogers, who espoused the Encounter and Sensitivity training approaches, which are essentially "lay" movements, is altogether consistent with this presupposition.

agency, Christians recognize their utter dependence upon God's resources. God alone can regenerate him, instruct him, and empower him by His Spirit through the Scriptures.

Man is responsible, but he is responsible to use those valid means directed and provided by God. Among these is the help of directive counselors using nouthetic confrontation. Human personality is not violated by the program and plan of God. God makes resources beyond the counselee available in His Word by His Spirit through the various channels of grace (help).

So much for the element of truth. Man does have resources that he may tap, but they certainly are not all within himself. The idea that God is not necessary, the Spirit is not necessary, the Scriptures are not necessary, the help of other Christians with gifts that have been given for the mutual edification of the whole church is not necessary stems directly from Rogerian anthropology. His concept of man fully boxed and packaged with all of the resources in himself can lead to no other conclusion. His approach, therefore, must be rejected.

O. Hobart Mowrer

Now let's look at the views of Mowrer, who also fits into the category of Common Knowledge. Mowrer sees the problem somewhat differently. Instead of the failure to live up to one's potential as the root difficulty, he thinks that man's problems stem from bad behavior. Bad behavior for Mowrer means behavior that hurts other people, the kind of behavior that brings one into head-on clashes with other persons in society. When he does such things, man feels guilty, since he fails to measure up to his own standards. What he needs to learn is how to confess his guilt and make restitution and atonement for his "sins" (meaning horizontal offenses against another person[26]). Mowrer uses words like religion, sin, and guilt, but he drains them of biblical meaning and then fills them with humanistic content. Christians must become aware of this fact. When Mowrer talks about bad behavior, for instance, he does not mean behavior that violates the law of God. He has no concept of rebellion against a holy God or of sin against *Him*. Bad behavior means merely, "I've hurt another individual."

---

26. Mowrer does not believe in sin against God, since he does not believe in the existence of a personal God.

Mowrer recently has begun to move toward a modified type of Encounter group. Bodily contact and "reaching out" to touch another are involved. More expression of emotion is being encouraged. This is a marked change from Mowrer's past practice. What further developments will occur in the days ahead are as yet uncertain.

Mowrer believes that bad behavior (the violation of one's conscience usually by wronging another person) is the reason why one feels guilty. He sees this as genuine guilt, not false guilt. Guilt may be removed by confessing one's wrong to the offended person and engaging in restitution for atonement. Confession, restitution, and atonement, remember, are strictly horizontal; they have dimensions only on the level of man to man. Atonement is not through Christ (with Bonhoeffer, Mowrer calls Christian grace "cheap grace"); it is achieved by the suffering of confession and restitution.

But because he has no Savior, Mowrer is like the priest that stands daily ministering the same sacrifice that can never take away sin. He must continue to make atonement after atonement. Sin, as such, is never forgiven; only sins. Consequently, counselees can never be satisfied and have peace about sin. Mowrer knows nothing of the one sacrifice for all time, of the once-for-all sacrifice of the cross, after which Christ *sat down*. His work was full, final, and complete, but Mowrer's Integrity Groups are unaware of the fact.[27] Mowrer, the secular priest, stands daily making atonement. He can never be seated. Mowrer's own personal unrest and that of his counselees grows from this fact. For him there are certain resources in the counselee himself, and there are resources in other people too. He needs forgiveness from others; they need forgiveness from him. Thus Mowrer, in harmony with Rogers, sees the potential to solve problems within man himself, but in contrast to Rogers finds the resources in the *group*, not in the individual alone.

Mowrer used to call his Common Knowledge approach Integrity Therapy; but now he has shaken off the last remnant of the medical model, at present referring to the movement under the name Integrity Groups. The constant, "Integrity," stresses the need for integrity with oneself and one another. It involves honesty and openness and willing confession when needed. Openness (which is painful and involves atonement) also leads the counselor to share his own sinful experiences

---

27. Cf. Hebrews 7:27; 9:25; 10:1, 3, 11-14, 18.

with counselees. Mowrer calls this "telling one's story." It is very painful for Mowrer to tell his story,[28] but he believes suffering pain helps to take away the feeling of guilt.

Mowrer's method works something like that of the fellow who hit his head against the wall because it felt so good when he stopped. That is not intended humorously; it is tragic. Mowrer's every-day unending efforts to atone do not satisfy. There is no atonement in them. The attempt is really quite pathetic. People who have "graduated" from his groups often hang around the edges of the group. They revisit. They seem to be searching for something. One said, "I think there must be something more." They have gotten over a couple of life's humps through the group. They have gone back to spouses or made restitution for embezzling, but something is lacking. There is something missing, something hollow, so they keep coming back, hanging around hoping to find it. The taste of change has served only to whet their appetite for *real* change. But Mowrer fails to offer God's change to them. What they lack, and do not know it, is true forgiveness once and for all through the only sufficient atonement, the death of Jesus Christ. They lack the radical change that the Bible calls the new birth.

According to Mowrer, the group holds the answers; they must be shared. All have some answers and, therefore, all can help another in some way. Together, pooling resources, all can be helped more significantly than alone. Through the group one can get back into community with others.

There is some reflection of the truth in Mowrer, dimly perceived. God made us social creatures; we need one another. "It is not good for man to be alone"; therefore we must not forsake the "assembling of ourselves together." When we come together it should be for mutual edification, "provoking one another to love and good works," and to "encourage one another."[29] But self-atoning Integrity Groups can never be that; true society exists only among the redeemed community of God—the Church of Jesus Christ.

Group Therapy, Encounter Groups, T Groups, Sensitivity Groups, or whatever you wish to call them (the names are slippery and indefinite)

---

28. Mowrer feels such a need to do so that he has even done this in print: cf. O. Hobart Mowrer, *Abnormal Reactions or Actions* (Dubuque: Wm. C. Brown Co., 1966).

29. Genesis 2:18; Hebrews 10:24, 25.

all seem to have a do-it-yourself approach.[30] The expert may help get things moving, but by the group process, which is a here-and-now do-it-yourselves effort, one learns to shed his hangups and inhibitions and becomes truly free. With Rogers, the counselee does it himself with a small assist from a wall-like counselor off of whom he bounces his own ideas. With Mowrer, he does it himself along with others who are doing it themselves and who will put the pressure on him to do it, and do-it-yourself, their way.

In other do-it-yourself Common Knowledge groups you find a mixture of Mowrer-like activities, as well as all sorts of other things. It is impossible here to survey these groups.[31] It is possible only to mention a few of the problems Christians encounter in such gatherings. Any particular group may have one, more, or all of the following characteristics. One common idea is since counselees got into trouble by maladaptive behavior *in society*, they must get back into community to solve their problems. The Group is supposed to provide the best kind of society in which to make one's reentry. A number of people with maladaptive behavior get together to hammer out between them the right answers to life's problems. They then may feel safe to go out from the group and make it in ordinary society. Since in many of these groups self-help and do-it-yourself are significant themes, the basic idea becomes, let's get together and *share*. Much is shared; "openness" is usually a key word. Often openness means that a cutting-up session will emerge. "We're going to be open" and "We're going to cut each other up" are nearly synonymous phrases for some. One member of the group may begin:

"For a long while I've been wanting to get a lot of things off of my chest. My hangup is that I've really never been open with other people. I have never told people what I really think. I never told my boss what I think of him; I've never told my wife what I think of her, but here in this group I'm going to start telling people what I think and then maybe I can go back and tell my boss and my wife. At least here I'm going to start." (He'll probably never get to his wife; he might get to his boss.)

---

30. Cf. "Group Therapy—or Slander?" *The Big Umbrella*, pp. 237-246.
31. For enlightening descriptions of many of the principal groups, cf. Jane Howard, *Please Touch* (New York: Dell Publishing Co., Inc., 1971). For viewpoints of various practicing group leaders see Arthur Burton, *Encounter* (San Francisco: Jossey-Bass Publishers, 1970).

In the group he begins to tell people what he really thinks of them, systematically taking them apart joint by joint, beginning with the ears. For his own (selfish) benefit, he abuses another person. There is nothing Christian about that. (Rather, on this point read carefully Romans 15: 1, 2, 3; Philippians 2:1-7). He systematically unlaces other members of the group; by the end of the session their stuffing is all over the room. Then it is their turn to go to work on him. Soon there is stuffing everywhere. That is one kind of group, a cutting-up group (if you want to call it by an accurate name that nobody uses).

There are other kinds of groups, for example the Can-You-Top-This? group. In it counselees share experiences with each other. One member tells about his sexual conquests and then the next says, "Yes, but you should hear about mine." Oh, they usually don't quite put it in that language, but that is what the session amounts to. One person, leaving such a group, remarked, "That was better than an X-rated movie!"

Then there are still other sorts of groups. They are careful not to be so gross. In one type, the members meet to talk about other people. The group may not define its goals that way. Nothing at all may be said about talking about *other people*; the group may be advertised as a confession group or a problem-solving group. But before long that is the way things begin to shape up.

Let's say that a group of Christian college students are sitting around in a group therapy session to "confess" or "share" or "become more open." Before you know it, they are talking about their parents. "I've got a lot of hangups; I think a lot of them go back to my home life. Let me tell you about the way that my father . . . ," says one guy. "Yea, me too. *My problem* is that my parents just don't know what's going on in society any more; why just last month my mother. . . ." And so it goes. Another and then another gets on the bandwagon, and before you know it the parents of each family have been ripped to shreds in what can turn out to be a defaming or slander session. Have the members of this group "honored" their fathers and mothers?

Or maybe a group of wives meets for discussion of common problems, but soon they are working over their husbands. A group of Christians from a church may go to work on the pastor or the elders of the church. Instead of talking about themselves and their own problems, sinful men tend to turn on others who are not present, who supposedly are the source of their difficulties. Blameshifting is so easy; after all, it has such a long history—it goes back to the Garden. A person's personal relationship to the counselee is discussed publicly without any knowledge of the fact on his part and without any opportunity for him to straighten out misunderstandings or balance off unfair judgments. His name and his actions are being discussed in an intimate way by a group of people who know nothing about him and have no right to know anything about him. Often the discussion is instigated by a bitter, resentful person who, according to Matthew 18, should have gone directly to the husband or parent or pastor to seek reconciliation if he felt that way.

Now, not all groups are wrong; not all groups are involved in these abuses. Christians must develop the use of the group form properly according to biblical norms. I have tried to point out the dangers of *many* groups today, but groups *per se* are not wrong. There is an element of truth dimly reflected by many of the ideas current among the members of these groups. For instance, we must all operate in groups; we can't avoid them. You were probably involved in more than one group today. There are groups at home (the family is a group), at church (itself a group), at the youth society (a powerful group), etc. But there must be rules and limitations for groups. There are biblical norms for groups.[32] One of these norms says that Christians must not talk negatively to other people about those who are not in the group. Instead, they are instructed to speak *privately* about their differences to these individuals themselves. Matthew 18:15-17 is quite clear on the point.[33]

Groups are essential for the assimilation of new converts, for study, for sharing good things, for mutual encouragement, for instruction, and for many other biblically legitimate purposes. It is fine for a group of Christian women to get together to talk about their own inadequacies as mothers and to swap ideas about how to become better mothers. But that is quite different from these same wives getting together to talk down their husbands. Such groups as the former must be diligent always not to allow the discussion to deteriorate.

---

32. Cf. I Corinthians 12-14, where Paul carefully orders the activities of the church as a group.

33. Cf. also James 4:11: "Do not speak against one another, brethren." The word *Katalaleo* means to "slander" or "defame" someone. It had the meaning of speaking against someone behind his back.

Divine Knowledge

There is no need to say much under this head, since in a sense the whole book is concerned with this question. A Christian must start with a Christian foundation and build upon it a Christian methodology that rests upon and is consistent with that foundation. In the common grace of God, unbelievers stumble over aspects of truth in God's creation. They always distort these by their sin and from their non-Christian stance toward life. But *from the vantage point of his biblical foundation* the Christian counselor may take note of, evaluate, and reclaim the truth dimly reflected by the unbeliever so long as he does so in a manner consistent with biblical principles and methodology. He may not become eclectic, however. That means that he may not start the other way around. He may not begin pragmatically by gathering together every method that looks like it might work, whether it involves a couch or a mirror or a room large enough for a group.[34]

Constructing a biblical methodology takes critical care; it is going to take much time and much effort to build that foundation adequately. No one has a foundation and methodology that is totally scriptural. Such work has only been begun. My foundation surely has planks that are rotten and some that are missing. The reader must watch where he walks. There may be planks that have been nailed in backwards or upside down. But of one thing I am certain: there are a number of biblical planks that are solidly nailed down. At present I am measuring and sawing others. But in order to get them nailed all of the way across, other Christians must also lay hold of the hammers and nails and help. On a foundation of biblical presuppositions, there must be built a fuller methodology that grows out of them and that is appropriate to them at every point. The

---

34. When Bruce Narramore writes: "By combining the practical insights of modern psychology with the lasting truths of the Bible, we have a solid and balanced approach to the problems of the modern parent" (*Help! I'm a Parent*. Grand Rapids: Zondervan Publishing House, 1972, p. 7), he expresses an eclectic viewpoint. The Bible does not need to be "balanced" off by modern psychology. Nor may it be "combined" with psychology to construct a balanced approach. God sets forth *His* approach in the Scriptures. The principles of His approach are plainly revealed in His Word. *On the basis of* these principles (not *in combination with* Rogerian, Freudian, or Skinnerian principles), he may discover that some aspect of non-Christian methodology in some way may remind, illustrate, or amplify a biblical principle. But the principle must be scriptural. From a biblical foundation, upon which a house of biblical methodology has been constructed, a Christian counselor may view the surrounding landscape. But he must not construct his foundation or house out of any non-Christian materials.

methodology must be oriented biblically and remain within the framework of scriptural principles. When you have constructed a platform like that, then you are able to stand upon it, look around at what is happening elsewhere, and you can pick and choose and adapt from that perspective whatever nuggets that an unbeliever (in the common grace of God) has unearthed.

But that is quite a different viewpoint from that of the eclectic, who begins with the premise that there are no basic biblical foundational and structural materials from which to frame up a biblical system. The eclectic pragmatically attempts to take the best of everything and glue it together in a patchwork. That we may not do as Christians, because instead of saying that nobody has anything, we must say that God has given us *everything*. This is the distinctive fact about the Divine Knowledge approach. The Scriptures plainly declare: "His divine power has granted us *everything* pertaining to life and Godliness" (II Peter 1:3); note: everything.

There is another significant passage that even more strongly emphasizes this truth: II Timothy 3:15-17. These verses are well known for their teaching about the inspiration of the Bible. They really do not discuss the question of inspiration directly. Inspiration is mentioned only in passing, because that isn't the main point of the passage. That makes their teaching about inspiration all the more powerful, of course, since Paul assumes and alludes to the doctrine and sees no need for discussing it. Divine inspiration was clearly an undisputed presupposition of the early church upon which other points could be based (as here). Such casual references make this certain.

Paul's main purpose was to speak of the *use* of the Scriptures. Paul says that *since* God breathed the Scriptures, they are *therefore* useful; he did not put it the other way around (i.e., that they are useful, therefore inspired). God breathed forth the Scriptures as His Word. The term "inspired" means *God breathed*. The holy writings are as much His Word as if God had spoken them physically and audibly by means of breath.

Since the Scriptures are God's revelation to man, they are useful (or profitable) to the minister[35] *to equip him for* teaching, reproof, correc-

---

35. "That the man of God may be equipped" (vs. 17). In his letters to Timothy, Paul addresses Timothy as a "man of God" in lieu of his office as minister: I Timothy 6:11. Cf. also the usage of this phrase in II Kings 1:9, 11, 13; 4:7, 9,

tion, and discipline in the way of righteousness. The whole process of counseling, plus the resources and methodology to be used, is either stated or implied in this passage. Structuring a person by disciplined training to walk in the path of righteousness is preceded by three important counseling activities, all of which involve the use of the holy Scriptures.

To begin with, Paul asserts that the Scriptures are holy (or unique[36]). Because they are peculiarly or uniquely God's, they possess a unique power, the power to lead unconverted sinners to salvation through faith in Christ. Then, for those who have experienced this salvation, they have the power to do four things: (1) *teach* (i.e., set the norms for faith and life); (2) *reprove* (i.e., rebuke erring Christians effectively so that the rebuke brings a conviction of wrong[37]); (3) *correct (epanor-*

16, etc. A series of four lectures entitled, "The Use of the Scriptures in Counseling," to be delivered as the Griffith Thomas Lectures at Dallas Theological Seminary in the fall of 1973 is under preparation. Those lectures are scheduled first for publication in *Bibliotheca Sacra*, and then in a revised and enlarged form will be published (D.V.) as a book within the next two years. For this reason, discussion of this vital subject will be held to a minimum in the present volume.

36. The unusual term *hieros*, translated "holy," designates "that which is peculiarly associated with God." Thus the Scriptures are not *merely* set apart (*hagios*), but *especially* so. They are specially, uniquely His as no other writings can be said to be.

37. *Elegmon* is a legal term meaning more than rebuke. It is used of the successful prosecution of a case to the *conviction* of the guilty party. Cf. John 16:8. The Word of God not only informs the Christian's conscience, but also becomes the Spirit's sword to bring conviction by means of the conscience. Conscience is the God-given ability to evaluate one's own actions (Romans 2:15) and respond emotionally to that evaluation. Conscience (*suneidesis*, "a knowing together") is viewed functionally as self-evaluation in three ways in Scripture: (1) As the *capacity* for self-judgment (as in Romans 2:15); the ability to evaluate and, therefore, excuse or accuse oneself. (2) As the *rule* or standard by which the evaluation is made. (Cf. Romans 14 and I Corinthians 8, esp. vss. 10, 12.) Some consciences are "weak," i.e., poorly informed. The Scriptures are to be internalized into the heart (written upon the heart) as the rule of conscience by which one evaluates his own attitudes and behavior. (3) As the *effects* of the evaluation. This is the emphasis in those passages in which one is said to have a "good" or "clear" (or by contrast, "bad") conscience (e.g., I Timothy 1:5, 19; 3:9; II Timothy 1:3; Hebrews 13:18; I Peter 3:16, 21). Pleasant or unpleasant physiological responses (visceral and otherwise) are activated as the result. Cf. Proverbs 20:9, 27 (T.E.V.). The three aspects of conscience are analogous to the three steps in the process of trying a case at law. Conscience, at once, is the lawyers, the jury, and the judge. Conscience argues the case (both *accusing* as the prosecuting attorney and *excusing* as the defense attorney), decides the case (as the jury) according to the law, and pronounces the verdict (as the judge) and thereby sets into motion any penalties. There is good reason, therefore, for the use of much legal termi-

thosin means to "set up straight again." After knocking us down, the Scriptures set us up again to walk in the path of righteousness. They wound, uproot, and tear down sin in our lives by reproving; they bind up, plant the seed, and build the foundation for righteousness by correcting[38]); (4) *discipline* (structured training) in *righteousness* (the Scriptures continue to work with us structuring our lives in a daily discipline toward godliness; cf. I Timothy 4:7[39]).

A Judging Activity

These four uses of the Scriptures, ministered not only by preaching but also by private proclamation in counseling (cf. Colossians 1:28), set forth plainly the four basic activities involved in biblical counseling. There is a *judging activity* (not on the faulty, sinful bases of prejudice, pride, etc., that are in view in Matthew 7:1 ff., but by the biblical norms and standards with a view toward the beneficent ends of nouthetic confrontation which always has the welfare of the counselee in view and which moves the counselor to treat him in a familial manner[40] Numerous issues today rage hotly. For example, many Christians are uncertain about whether homosexuality is a sickness or sin. The biblical Christian has no problem making judgments about this matter; the Bible calls homosexuality sin. That settles the question for him.

---

nology in the Scriptures such as "convict," etc., in conjunction with such processes. When we sin and our consciences evaluate the act or attitude as such, they next proceed to activate unpleasant visceral and other bodily responses to warn us to cease and desist and repent. God expects us to repent, confess our sins, and become reconciled to Him. Our future behavior must be changed by the Spirit to conform to the Word of God. Conscience evaluates such an actual course of action as the proper one, and eases up on the unpleasant physical responses. Taking pills, using alcohol or other drugs in order to dull pain, anesthetize the brain, or drown out memories, is one faulty solution to the problem that is widely followed today. The solution should not be handled by attacking the nervous system directly, since the unpleasant bodily sensations are not the result of an "emotional problem" (the emotions are working all too well) but rather are the result of a behavioral problem.

38. Cf. Jeremiah 1:10.

39. See also the pamphlet, *Godliness Through Discipline*. This pamphlet was designed as an aid for counselors to use in encouraging scriptural, disciplined living in counselees.

40. Judging of *motives* is forbidden ("man looks at the outward appearance, God looks at the heart," I Samuel 6:7); judging of *actions* is prescribed: "By their fruits shall you know them" (Matthew 7:15 ff.); "Judge righteous judgments" (John 7:24).

A Convicting Activity

There is also a *convicting activity*. Not every counselee says in her very first words, "I'm here because I am a murderer," as did one woman bearing the guilt of abortion. This convicting activity must be pursued whenever the counselee is either unaware of his sin or is still unrepentant. The work of using the Word to bring men to repentance is greatly neglected. Many counselees come only in order to obtain relief from the consequences of sinful life patterns; they do not think of the holy God whom they have offended by violating His will. They must be brought to conviction of *sin*, not merely to recognition of their misery. True relief, like true happiness, is always a by-product; it never may be found by seeking it directly. Every counselee, to be helped, either must come seeking "first the kingdom of God and His righteousness," or must be brought to that point by the ministry of the convicting Spirit (John 16:8) as He uses His Word.

A Changing Activity

There is a *changing activity*. The Scriptures were given not only to set forth the perfect pattern of life that was realized only in Christ, but in addition they recognize the Christian's imperfections and in an intensely practical manner make provision for his restoration. Constantly the Bible directs its attention to what to do when one falls into sin, how to break harmful habits, how to overcome failures and weaknesses, etc. Because they are so practical, the Scriptures *dwell* upon how men fail in serving God *and what may be done about this failure*. In this, they stress such things as reconciliation, restitution, putting on new patterns, etc. They not only show us our sins, but also tell us how to recoup from sin. Thus, after convicting us of sin, they set us once again upon our feet in the way of righteousness, head us in the right direction, and give us a push. This they do quite specifically. Generalizations are not enough. Counselors must learn to use the Bible practically, as it was intended to be used.[41]

---

41. Too much preaching, as well as counseling, is general and not specific. Platitudes do not change lives. It is easy enough to agree sincerely about noble goals; the problem comes in developing the proper biblical ways and means for achieving these. Counseling must center upon the *what* and the *how*. Instead, much has focused on the *why*.

A Structuring Activity

There is also a *structuring activity*. God knows that without disciplined training with teeth (*paideon*), we will continue to stray from the path of righteousness. Thus he has enjoined regular Bible study and the regular ministry of the Word so that we may be disciplined continually by it. Much more must be said about this later on.[42]

Paul then sums this up by saying that the "man of God" (the minister of the Word) is complete, thoroughly equipped for every good work. The word used is the term that described the efforts made to furnish a ship, so that no matter what exigency might be encountered on its voyage, it would be equipped to meet it. The ship owner tried to anticipate every possible problem ahead of time and rigged it out with gear calculated to meet these. Paul says, then, that there is no counseling situation for which the man of God is not adequately equipped by the Scriptures. All of the answers that he and his counselee need for pursuing the four comprehensive activities mentioned above are in the Bible. There is no need for eclecticism. This passage very plainly says that *all* that we need as the basic foundation and framework for helping others and helping ourselves has been given to us.

You, Christian counselor, have the resources. The resources are not in the outside expert, the resources are not in the counselee, nor are they in ourselves; the resources are in God. All of the resources are in God. That is the Bible's answer and, therefore, that must be the Christian's viewpoint. The God of all resources graciously has given them to us fully in His Word.

In this book are principles that deal with every problem of life. We don't know them all, of course; we don't have them all put together. One reason is because Christians haven't been working at this the way they should. Instead, there has been a tragic disposition to glue and paste all sorts of things together with the Bible. It is time that we got down to the hard business of studying God's Word in order to use the resources of divine knowledge. It is time that we all put our hearts and minds and abilities to the problem of exegeting the Scriptures, not merely academically, but pastorally. We also need to look hard at the world out there *in the light of the Bible* to discover how *biblically* these two fit together. We must know men's problems and we must find God's answers.

---

42. Cf. also *Godliness Through Discipline*, pp. 12-14.

Chapter Eleven

TECHNIQUE

Before turning from the study of presuppositions and principles basic to biblical counseling to a consideration of the practice of counseling which involves processes in which techniques must be employed, it seems necessary to take a brief look at the matter of technique itself. Christians sometimes have problems with the very idea of technique. Such difficulties are not associated with counseling alone, but also with preaching, teaching, or any other area in which the acquisition and use of skills in the development of one's gifts plays a dominant part. It is very important for Christians to understand that legitimate problems concerning technique are not really problems with technique itself; rather they arise from the use of technique *apart from the power of the Holy Spirit*. This problem most frequently appears in two forms: (1) attempting to counsel in one's own strength without the Spirit; (2) attempting to use techniques that are contrary to the principles recorded by the Spirit in the Scriptures. Some earnest Christians confuse the use of technique with the abuse of technique and, as a result, reject the study or use of technique *in toto*. This is a tragic mistake.

The Spirit does not place a premium upon sloppy and careless technique in confronting others. Skillfulness is often emphasized in the Scriptures. For example, Paul warned, "Be careful how you walk" (Ephesians 5:15); "conduct yourselves with wisdom toward outsiders. . . . Let your speech always be with grace, seasoned with salt, so that you may know how you should respond to each person" (Colossians 4:5, 6). Paul himself asked for prayer so that he might "make clear" his message "in the way that he ought to speak" (Colossians 4:4). All of these statements focus more or less upon technique, but technique properly under the control of the Spirit of God. Paul was concerned not only about the *what*, but also about the *how* (how to "walk" and "speak").

Technique is, to put it simply, *skill*.[1] Some people (erroneously)

---

1. The Greek word *Techne* (from which our word technique was derived)

equate technique with the use of gimmicks. But there is no necessary connection between gimmicks and techniques. Techniques, of course, may be gimmicky; but they are not necessarily so. All gimmicks are techniques (which simply means that they are unscriptural techniques), but not all techniques are gimmicks. The Holy Spirit works through *biblical* techniques, not through gimmicks. A biblical technique is one that is commanded in the Scriptures (cf. Colossians 4:5, 6 above), commended in the Scriptures (cf. III John 5, 6), or grows out of a scriptural principle.

There is no counseling apart from technique. You cannot avoid it; the minute you open your mouth you are using technique. Your technique in counseling may be conscious or unconscious, growing or frozen, biblical or unbiblical, etc. The only vital question to ask is whether one's technique is good (biblical) or bad (unbiblical). One thing is certain: whenever someone counsels another, he is using technique. Let us, therefore, turn our attention to the practice and process of counseling. Too frequently books on counseling have failed to consider the problem and needs of the counselor in a practical way.[2] What follows is the largest section in this book because of that fact. It is by no means exhaustive. Selectivity in the choice of materials was based largely upon the criterion of whether the problems and situations were those with which the average pastor and other Christian counselors would be familiar. That is, the more commonly occurring problems rather than the more esoteric difficulties have been emphasized.

---

means "skill" or "trade," which is the practice of a skill; cf. Acts 18:3; Revelation 18:22. Cf. also Psalm 78:72 (Berkeley).

2. In every area the crying need is for practical biblical materials that stress the "how to" of Christian life and ministry in a biblical context that is based firmly upon the Word of God. It is easy to get all sorts of persons to agree upon noble goals and ideals, but when they come to the ways and means, these same persons often fail altogether or soon part company over differences. Because it is easier to discuss abstract goals and write about pious platitudes, practical issues have been seriously neglected.

Chapter Twelve

THE LANGUAGE OF COUNSELING

Language Is Important

Language at times can be determinative; it can spell the difference between success and failure in counseling. It is with language that we think as well as talk. We use language not only to communicate with others, but also to talk to ourselves.[1] What we tell others, and especially what we say to ourselves, in time we tend to believe.[2] This is especially true when the way that we say it becomes repetitious. Words and phrases that are constantly repeated help to induce attitudes and them-

---

1. Language is a characteristic of God. God spoke and creation took place. God spoke again in the living Word, and there was a new creation. God's *Word* is recorded as the *Scriptures* (*writings* of *words*). Language is an important gift from God. By it we can discover what God requires of us and what He has done for us in Christ since we have failed to meet those requirements. Man is like God in that he too speaks. Language was given to man alone at creation and plays a large part in making man unique among God's creatures. By language, man is capable of sustaining meaningful relationships to God and other men. It made organized, interpretative thought possible. By the word of Satan man sinned. By the living and written Word of God man is saved. The idea of the word in the Scriptures is central. *Dabar,* the Hebrew term for word, carries greater weight than its English equivalent. It refers to both the word and the thing that it signifies. The power of a name is frequently mentioned in the Bible (cf. Acts 4:10, 12, 17, 18, 30). Notice also how names were changed. Peter, Abraham, Saul, and, here in Acts 4:36, Barnabas, were all renamed in order to signify facts about them as persons. Language has greater power than modern man recognizes. Its power may be performative; it shapes and thereby brings about the fact that it describes. In some instances this may be true of people who have been labeled according to psychiatric categories. Counselors, therefore, must be students of the Word and of words. They must learn to note the effect of the counselee's words upon others (inflammatory, encouraging, disparaging words; cf. Proverbs 15:1, 23; words can be missiles or medicine), as also their effect upon the counselee himself. Notice God's concern over speech in Ephesians 4:25-33. Cf. *Christian Living in the Home,* "Communication Comes First."

2. Note especially Romans 1:21b, 22, where this process seems to be in view. Cf. also Psalm 14:1 speaking to oneself in the heart may corrupt outward behavior. Proverbs 18:20 points out that we feed ourselves (not only others) on the words that we speak.

selves become a part of a mind set that may have to be broken before counseling can be effective. It is important, therefore, for a counselor to learn to recognize what counselees say *precisely,* particularly when they repeatedly use the same word or statement. Repetition in audible conversation usually indicates an underlying attitude or belief that sometimes must be dealt with before counseling can proceed. This is vital when the language that is repeated constitutes an *excuse.*

I have commented elsewhere at length on the use of the word "can't" which provides a graphic example of how a counselee may fix an unscriptural concept in his thought/action pattern so as to determine habitually the courses of action that he will take under certain circumstances.[3] A counselee may tell himself that he "can't" do this or that so often that he soon may come to believe it. The same thing may happen in a case of unrealistic fear. Until that thought itself is corrected by a more biblical evaluation of God's power, one's gifts, and the circumstances, there may be little hope of constructive biblical action.

Of course, it is neither possible nor desirable to erase all metaphor, euphemism, or other figurative language; there are valuable, legitimate, and important uses of each in counseling. Yet, the reader will notice in this book that whenever it is of importance to do so, I have tried to substitute literal language for figurative in order to remove any misunderstandings that less literal language may occasion.[4]

Let us take another example: the imprecise use of the word *tension.* It is not unusual to hear counselees blaming their actions upon the "tense situation" or speaking of the "tension between me and Mary." As an everyday nonliteral language this sort of language usage is quite permissible. But in a counseling session, when one is discussing the actual state of affairs in the counselee's life with a view to correcting it, such expressions may be highly dangerous. One can get along quite well when talking about the sun *setting* while he is lying on the beach in Santa Barbara, but it may be unwise to do so in an astronomy class. Thus in counseling, where one is attempting to understand, define, and solve problems having to do with a subject like tension, such

---

3. Cf. *Competent to Counsel,* pp. 131 ff.; see also *Christ and Your Problems.*
4. Some of the worst uses of figurative language appear in the literature of counseling and psychiatry. These have occasioned much hardship and confusion. The almost universal acceptance of the words "mental illness" as literal rather than figurative perhaps is the outstanding example. Cf. *The Big Umbrella,* pp. 39-61.

usage cannot be tolerated. The simple fact is that tension is not *in* the *situation*; nor does tension exist *between* the counselee and Mary. If this is understood as figurative language, fine; usually it is not.

If tension were in situations or between people, then in many instances nothing could be done to relieve tension; in all, the procedures for relieving tension would be quite different from those that we shall consider. Strange questions arise from taking the figurative concept literally. How does one relax a situation or the space between two persons? The faulty description of the problem can do nothing other than lead to despair if it is accepted.

Counselees must be shown that the tension they are concerned to alleviate exists only in muscles; literally, it is the description of a muscular state called contraction. Tension, therefore, is always in the counselee; not in a situation nor between him and someone else. If tension is in muscles, then the counselee knows that the solution to his problem is to learn how to control himself. When he discover's God's way of controlling muscular tension, he will be able to deal with the question of tension in hope and with personal responsibility.

To speak of tension between people or in situations instead of in one's muscles unnecessarily confuses.[5] The language is vague, imprecise, and ethereal. As a result it tends to push solutions beyond reach. To speak of tension in the muscles, however, makes the problem quite tangible. There can be no excuse for failure to handle tension when one recognizes that tension is his own bodily response to a difficult problem. Language usage, then, often can be the decisive factor in helping a counselee to solve problems God's way.

Confronting Counselees About Their Language

Whenever the metaphorical or other use of language becomes a hindrance to proper thought and action, the counselor must confront the counselee directly about the problem, explain the facts, and correct the erroneous thought and speech that lie at its base. You can see, therefore, how important that it can be to make an issue over words. Obviously counselors should not make an issue over every word or phrase that is

---

5. E.g., "Tension is observed in our interpersonal and intersocial relationships. It extends throughout society where it exists between two minds or among many minds." Swami Akhilananda, *op. cit.*, pp. 80, 81; note especially the prepositions in, between, and among.

used imprecisely. They should look, rather, for those words and ideas that express faulty attitudes, beliefs, or opinions which may impede counseling. We have already noted that these often are repeated as stock phrases and used especially as excuses.

Jesus sometimes used this method of confronting a person about his use of language. When the rich young ruler said "good master . . . ," Jesus challenged his use of the word "good." The term, in his vocabulary, had become attached to a superficial outward conformity to the law by which he was judging both himself and Christ to be good. In the challenge, Jesus showed the young ruler that (1) according to the inner meaning of God's law, he was not good and that (2) he should be prepared either to acknowledge that He (Jesus) is God or not refer to Him as good either.

Whenever counseling is hung up, it is wise to take a hard look at what is happening with language. While counseling can founder as the result of various causes, it is often good to *begin* with an inventory of the counselee's language usage. Begin to jot down what appear to be the counselee's stock words and phrases during the first interview and note whether they are used frequently thereafter. Perhaps the best clues to discovering impediments to progress may be found in the frequently reoccurring words and clichés that the counselee employs.[6] Watch especially for such possibly problematic expressions as those that

---

6. Also take note of the tendency to exaggerate or overstate. "That was a sneaky, dirty, nasty trick," says one counselee who has convinced himself that it was simply because his workaday vocabulary is rich in such terms. The counselor analyzed the accusation word for word in terms of what happened, and at the end they both agreed that the difficulty stemmed merely from a difference of opinion. As in this case, counselors must watch out not only for exaggeration, but also for the judging of motives (Matthew 7:1) which often accompanies it. Many persons have learned to use a crisis vocabulary when speaking only of minor irritations. When *everything* is described as a "tragedy," the counselor might call attention to the vocabulary: "Are all of these incidents *really* tragedies, Mrs. Greene, or could we more accurately describe most of them as, let us say, 'setbacks'?" Counselors must help counselees to learn to relate their language to reality. Exaggeration may stem from many sources: perceptual distortions, self-interest, limited experience. Persons who tend to be ingrown, shut in, self-oriented, and out of touch with others, usually will exaggerate partly because of the circumscribed environment. Unless they work at enlarging their interests and contacts, they may continue to give undue importance to small matters. When a counselor suspects that this is a problem, he may assign (as homework) the counselee the task of drawing a "map" of *his* world, noting the principal persons, places, and things located within it. The counselee may be surprised at the smallness of his interests

are listed below. They do not form an exhaustive list, but serve simply as samples of the types of excuses and fuzzy thinking that frequently are found in the language of counselees. The list also includes some responses that counselors have found effective in challenging this sort of language abuse.

Typical Counselee Remarks	*Typical Counselor Responses That May Be Used*
1. "I can't!"	1. "Do you mean can't or won't?" or, "*God* says that you *can*."
2. "I have done everything that I could."	2. "Everything? What about. . . ."
3. I've tried that but it didn't work."	3. "Did you *really* try? How many times? For how long? In what way? How consistently?" (Get the details: "precisely, what *did* you do?")
4. "I did my best."	4. "Are you sure? Tell me precisely *what* you did." or, "Remember, the *best* is what God says to do. Did you . . . ?"
5. *No one* believes me, etc."	5. "Can't you think of *one* person who does? How about some more?" or, "I believe you. . . ."
6. "I could *never* do *that*."	6. "Never is a long time. Really, how long do you suppose it might take to learn? By the way, if you think hard enough you will discover that you have learned to do a number of things that are just as hard (or harder). Take for instance. . . ."
7. "If I had the time, I'd do it."	7. "You do. We all have 24 hours each day; it all depends on how you slice the pie. Now let's work on drawing up a schedule that honors God."
8. "Don't blame me. . . ."	8. "Are you saying that you are not responsible? God says. . . ."
9. "Don't ask me. . . ."	9. "But I am asking you. Who else would know? I am sure that you know the answer. Think hard; I'll help you by asking some other related questions, and perhaps we can come up with it."

and concerns. Look too for language like this: "She makes me sick; he's a pain in the neck; I can't stomach people like that; what a headache she is!" Sometimes the usage has gone beyond the metaphor to become a reality.

Typical Counselee Remarks	*Typical Counselor Responses That May Be Used*
10. "I guess so."	10. "Are you really guessing or is that what you believe (think)?"
11. "You know how it is. . . ."	11. "No, I don't know; can you explain it more fully?"
12. "But I've *prayed* about it."	12. "Fine! Then what did you *do?*" or, "Have you prayed for help to discover what God's Word says to *do* about the problem?" or, "What, exactly, did you pray?"
13. "I'm at the end of my rope."	13. Which end? Perhaps you are beginning to uncoil your problem for the first time."
14. "I have a need to. . . ."	14. "Is it a need or only a desire? (or, habit)."
15. "I'm just one of those people who has to. . . ."	15. "Yes, I'm sure you are; but Christ wants you to become a different sort of person."
16. "That's just the way I am."	16. "Doubtless, but God says that you can be different."
17. "That is impossible."	17. "What you mean, of course, is that it is very difficult."
18. "There are all sorts of [too many] objections to doing that."	18. "Would you mind naming six or seven so that I can see what sort of things you have in mind and determine what it will take to answer them?"
19. "You can't teach an old dog new tricks."	19. "Perhaps that is true—but you are not a dog. You were created in the image and likeness of the living God! He knows you and commands you to change."
20. "It'll never work."	20. "It is God's way and it *always* works when people abandon that attitude."
21. "I'll never forgive him!"	21. "If you are a child of God, as you claim, you will. You are going to live with him for eternity; why don't you forgive him and begin to get used to it now?"
22. "I don't do anything half way, so. . . ."	22. "Are you sure? Can't you think of some things that you do? For instance, what about . . .?"
23. "Everything [one] is against me. . . ."	23. "No, you are wrong. If you are a Christian the Bible says the opposite: 'If God be for us, who can be against us?' (Romans 8:31)"
24. "How do you feel about . . .?"	24. "May I tell you what I think, or may I only discuss my emotions?"

Deadly Euphemisms

Words like "emotional problems" are euphemisms. Nobody has *emotional* problems; there is no such thing as an emotional problem. Those words are strictly euphemistic. If you have followed the evolution of the language on the chuck bag (a euphemism) in airplanes, you know what a euphemism is. The study of such terminology is a study in euphemism. The language identifying the chuck bag originally said, "For Vomiting," and probably more people did because it said so than for any other reason. The language later was changed to read: "For Air Sickness," but that wording still had powerful side effects. A later euphemism, still found on some planes, says: "For Motion Discomfort." The latest bags have either no wording at all or tic tac toe designs!

The study of words like "emotional problem," "mental illness," etc., provides another more serious study in euphemism. Usually when one complains of emotional difficulties, there is nothing wrong with his emotions (i.e., there has been no neurological, glandular, or vascular impairment).[7] When a depressed counselee says that he has an emotional problem, the counselor should tell him: "No you don't; your emotions are working very well. Look how depressed (anxious, etc.) you are. The problem is not that you have an emotional problem, as if your emotions have been disturbed or were *immature* (another euphemism), but that some other cause has triggered these unpleasant emotions. To get on top of your emotions, you must get to the bottom of the problem, and in many cases at the bottom of unpleasant emotions is sin."

Christian counselors may not euphemize when it comes to dealing with sin.[8] His problem, for instance, is not "emotional immaturity" when a

---

7. Strangely, the euphemism "emotional problem" is used to denote problems that do not have an organic base. Yet emotion is organic. For one to have an emotional problem would mean, literally, that he was suffering from some organic difficulty.

8. Typical examples of such euphemism are "alcoholism" (implying that the counselee is not responsible for the condition) rather than "drunkenness." Habitual thieves are often called "kleptomaniacs" for the same reason. (But see Ephesians 4:28). The use of technical terms like schizophrenia, kleptomania, manic-depressive, etc., is quite problematic. Such non-biblical terminology at once carries much unwanted freight and, on the other hand, tends to distort or to screen out the full weight of Christian truth. It is impossible to put the Christian new wine into many such old wineskins. Whenever the possibility of loss or addition by virtue of using old terms exists, it is probably wise either to coin new terms or employ non-technical language and circumlocutions.

counselee is following a pattern of life other than God's. The counselee's behavior is wrong; there is nothing wrong with his emotions. His conscience, i.e., his ability to make judgments about his own behavior (accuse or excuse[9]), may trigger all sorts of pleasant or unpleasant emotions it is true. Sinful behavior leads to unpleasant emotional experiences. But the way to get relief from these is not by attacking the emotions, but by changing (repenting of) the behavior. One may not repent merely for relief. He must repent because he has sinned against God. The problem is a behavioral problem, not an emotional problem.

It is unfortunate that this misleading euphemism, "emotional problem," is so frequently used by Christians. It has gained wide acceptance and is used in several forms: emotional difficulties, emotional problems, emotional immaturity, and emotional sickness.[10] Obviously emotions do not mature. One of the worst combinations that I have seen occurred in a recent publication by a Christian who is a psychiatrist. He speaks of "damaged emotions."[11]

The source of one's problems, in the instances of nonorganic difficulties about which we have been speaking, then, is not an emotional impairment or malfunction but lies *behind* the unpleasant visceral (etc.) responses that the counselee wishes to expel. These emotions are organic bodily responses that are largely involuntary and are triggered by behavior, thoughts, and attitudes.[12] The problem is not emotional but *pre-emotional*. The emotion is triggered by (1) immediate conscious

---

9. Romans 2:15.

10. What may be meant in most instances is habitual patterns of emotional response that are sinful.

11. Quentin Hyder, *The Christian's Handbook of Psychiatry* (Old Tappan: Fleming H. Revell Co.), p. 69. Hyder also speaks euphemistically of "disorders of the emotions or feelings," p. 97. Bruce Narramore writes, "This is emotionally unhealthy" and "But our emotions cry out. . . ." He also speaks of "emotional growth." *Help! I'm a Parent* (Grand Rapids: Zondervan Publishing House, 1972), pp. 18, 45. A booklet by a popular Christian who is a psychologist is entitled *Damaged Emotions*. Wesner Fallow speaks of the "reeducation" of emotions. *The Case Method in Pastoral and Lay Education* (Philadelphia: Westminster Press, 1963), p. 38.

12. The emotional is sometimes distinguished from the physical and set off against it. It is important to understand the physical nature of the emotions as bodily "sets" determined by thoughts and attitudes. Feeling is physical; it is how we perceive our bodily state at a given moment (pleasant or unpleasant). Schindler writes "an emotion, far from being an ephemeral sort of thing, is a very tangible affair that you can easily *observe* in the body." John Schindler, *How to Live 365 Days a Year* (Greenwich: Fawcett Publications, Inc., 1954), p. xiii.

thought and/or action, or (2) unconscious habit patterns that automatically release emotional responses. The solution lies not in direct attacks upon the emotions (drugs, alcohol, frontal lobotomies, etc.), but in rooting out the *cause* of the emotional response.[13] If there is specific behavior or thought that is directly associated with the undesirable emotion, then it may be dealt with concretely. If the emotional response resulted from a well-developed sinful response pattern no longer requiring conscious thought to set it in motion, then the solution lies in discovering the pattern and dehabituating the counselee through the sanctifying work of the Spirit by means of His Word. The pattern must be broken and replaced by a biblical one.

Since emotion plays such a significant role in counseling and since there is a considerable amount of confusion regarding it, it will be well to consider the language of emotion and action.

---

13. Cf. *Competent to Counsel*, pp. 93, 103.

Chapter Thirteen

THE LANGUAGE OF EMOTION AND ACTION

I have already commented on the importance of language in counseling. Perhaps nowhere in the whole field of counseling is this question more pertinent than with reference to the language of emotion and action. The terms *attitude, feeling,* and *behavior* must be distinguished. They are easily confused because at points they converge or overlap and because they are all integrally related. As they are used in this book, they may be distinguished as follows:

Feeling

The word *feeling* refers to the perception of a bodily state as pleasant or unpleasant ("I feel bad; I feel tired; I feel happy"). It is true that feelings may differ in intensity or kind, but fundamentally there are two categories into which all may be classified: good or bad. Visceral, muscular, galvanic, or other emotional responses of the body are responses to judgments made about the environment and oneself. These judgments trigger body chemistry to orient the body in a particular direction to meet a specific situation. This body orientation accounts for the feeling.

When a Rogerian, while reflecting, says, "You *feel* that such and such should be done," or "You *feel* that this and that is true, he seriously confuses words and meanings and muddies the waters.[1] Such language pollution must be combatted. Because of his fundamental feeling orien-

---

1. This language has fairly permeated society. Listen carefully to common language usage at this point to discover how prevelant the feeling motif is. In Rogers' Human Potential movement, for instance, "It is exactly this notion that feeling and expressing, rather than thinking, are the solutions to what ails man." Beldoch, *Intellectual Digest*, October, 1971, p. 87. When asking a question it is more common for many persons to say, "What do you feel we should do about . . . ?" To point out the subtleties of the language problem at this point, a counselor might reply: "May I share an idea or an opinion rather than merely emote?"

tation, he reduces thoughts, opinions, beliefs, convictions, and attitudes to feeling. We cannot follow him in this serious error.

When a counselee complains, "I feel inferior (or stupid, or inadequate)," it is important to point out to him that he is not speaking *altogether* accurately. No one *feels* inferior, stupid, or inadequate. What he is expressing is not a feeling but a judgment or attitude or conviction or belief about himself. He is saying, "I *am* inferior, stupid, or inadequate." On the basis of that judgment, he may *feel* sad or guilty or angry or embarrassed or depressed, etc. He *feels* sad (or angry, etc.) because of the conclusion that he has reached about his own behavior, attitudes, character, or capabilities. He cannot *feel* inferior because inferiority is not an emotion.

All of this has wide implications. Here it is possible to note only one or two of these. If inferiority (or stupidity—"I feel stupid," or inadequacy—"I feel inadequate") is a feeling, there is little or no hope of changing it. If it is a self-judgment about one's behavior, character, etc., that has triggered unpleasant emotions, then there is hope of changing the feelings of sadness, embarrassment, etc., by changing the behavior. If "I am inferior" is (rightly) considered a judgment, then the counselor can explore the counselee's *reasons* for this conclusion. The counselor may ask, "What reasons do you have for concluding that you are inadequate?" or perhaps even more directly, "You must have good reasons for this conclusion; tell me in what ways you have been inadequate." If the reasons are sound, the answer to the problem lies in a change within the counselee. Feelings are not so directly related to reasons as are judgments.

The problem often emerges at the level of one's assurance of salvation. Counselees may say, "But I don't feel saved." That is understandable since the conviction that one is saved is not an emotion; assurance is not a feeling. One may *feel* afraid, or sad, or angry, etc., over doubts about salvation or elated, or peaceful over assurance of salvation, but he may not *feel* saved or unsaved. The condition is not an emotional state, it is a relationship to God that affects the emotions, to be sure, but it is *not in itself* a feeling.

Distinguishing between the emotion and the conviction or judgment that triggers it is often fundamental to the solution to one's problem. In this case, assurance depends first upon the promises of God in His Word, one's dependence upon Christ (faith wrought by the Spirit's witness to that Word), and the evidences of salvation in his life. A judgment, sometimes based upon less than these biblical criteria, is made. If the criteria are poor, the judgment will be faulty and the emotional state that this self-judgment arouses will be unpleasant. For instance, take the complicated and cyclical problem of basing one's assurance upon a feeling (supposedly of salvation). The negative feeling, in the first instance, may arise from an entirely different source (lack of sleep, guilt over failures at work, etc.). If this feeling for some reason is interpreted as evidence that one is not converted, then that judgment (on the faulty basis of feeling) triggers more negative emotional responses, which give further "evidence" of one's unconverted state, *ad infinitum*.

The basic way to break through this vicious circle is to help the counselee to understand the biblical criteria for assurance and to help him to make his judgments on the basis of these.

Frequently, it is not the promises of God that are questioned, or at first even whether one has genuinely believed (although he may become entangled in that maze later on); rather, he finds that his failures in assurance stem from the lack of evidence that there is a changed life.

We have been assuming, up to this point, that the lack of assurance was not a result of a state of non-conversion, but rather originated in a true believer largely from his feeling orientation.[2] It is possible, of course, that the counselee may not be converted. This option ought always to be considered as one genuine possibility by the counselor. The counselor must take the counselee quite seriously about the matter and thoroughly investigate the possibility. He may want to suspend judgment where there is serious reason for doubt.

In most instances, after this discussion, the counselor will be wise to move directly to a consideration of the counselee's life. Usually, dealing with sinful living will—in itself—bring the answer that is desired. If he reveals a number of sinful ways of life, confesses these to God, and by the Spirit of God begins to conform to the Scriptures, often the very process *itself* brings the needed assurance. On the other hand, since the unconverted man is unable to do what God requires, in such cases counseling will founder upon the demands of the Scriptures. Rebellion, lack of ability, failure to understand the Word of God—

---

2. Ordinarily unconverted persons are not deeply concerned about the matter.

one or more of these responses almost inevitably arises from a serious attempt to conform to the inner demands of the Bible. At this point, the counselee may need to be confronted anew with the gospel.[3]

One thing is certain, the genuine feelings of salvation (i.e., those that arise out of the conviction that one is saved) will come only out of a judgment soundly based upon the scriptural basis of such assurance. That basis is *not* feeling itself; feeling is the fruit of salvation. It arises out of assurance and thus enhances it. But assurance itself has a more objective foundation.

Attitude

An *attitude* is that combination of presuppositions, beliefs, convictions, and opinions that make up one's habitual stance at any given time toward a subject, person, or act.[4] It is a mind set that strongly influences behavior.[5] In counseling, attitudes may be attacked and changed more directly than feelings, which, in most instances can be altered only indirectly through change of attitude and action (behavior). This is important, since attitudes often stand in the way of solving issues. Negative attitudes may prejudice one person against another, thus making significant communication and problem solving impossible. Sometimes attitudes that trigger bitterness, hatred, anger, or fear toward another first must be removed before such problem-solving is possible. Because of the confusion of feeling with attitude in the writings and techniques of some counselors, wrong approaches to counseling have been developed. Attitudes usually involve habits of thought; habitual ways of thinking. Change in attitudes, like changes in behavior patterns, require changes in habit that stem from the biblical discarding/acquiring (putting off/on) dynamic.

Behavior

In its narrower sense, *behavior* must be distinguished from a larger global usage that is employed by many behaviorists. Skinnerians, in

---

3. One may assume, in counseling, that the counselee's profession of faith is genuine (if it conforms to scriptural standards) until he begins to show evidence to the contrary.

4. Typical attitudes toward a problem may be discovered in the following responses: "I don't know what to do" . . . "There *is* no problem" . . . "I don't care" . . . "I can't do it" . . . "But I've never done it that way before."

5. Once a mind set develops, a whole way of life may grow out of it in which a self-propagating total misinterpretation of reality is possible.

particular, consider any and all activities of the body as behavior, even the activities or functions of nerves or glands. Such bodily functions, though closely related to attitudes and actions, have been distinguished from behavior in this book. Skinner subsumes both attitudes (*behavior* of the brain and spinal column) and feelings (*behavior* of the glands, viscera, etc.) under the word. This pan-behaviorism must be rejected since it fails to acknowledge the moral and cognitive image of God in man. The term behavior is best used to describe those activities of a whole person (not of a gland) that may be judged by the law of God. Behavior is responsible conduct. Behaviorists (with Skinner) frequently deny the concept of responsibility altogether. This denial is the direct outgrowth of what Lazarus calls the "Animal Game."[6] Skinner believes that man is only an animal; he is a complex animal, but nothing more than an animal. There is no such thing as value or dignity to man. Indeed, there is nothing more to his attitudes and actions than conditioned responses to the environment. All is behavior. The biblical concept of behavior, in contrast, is more restricted.

---

6. Arnold A. Lazarus, *Behavior Therapy and Beyond* (New York: McGraw-Hill Book Co., 1971), p. 6.

Chapter Fourteen

SIN IS THE PROBLEM

Counseling Is Warfare

Christian counselors should not need to be reminded that they have been called to labor in opposition to the world, the flesh, and the devil. Their task involves not merely a struggle with flesh and blood (that side of the problem is large enough), but also a fight against the supernatural forces of darkness (Ephesians 6:12).

Counseling, therefore, must be understood and conducted as a spiritual battle. The counselor must consider himself a soldier of Christ engaged in spiritual warfare when counseling. For that battle the "full armour of God" alone is sufficient. Unbelieving counselors not only lack such equipment, but, moreover, obviously are totally ignorant of the true nature of this situation. In fact, since they are soldiers in the army of Satan, they are on the other side and, therefore, hardly can be relied upon to free Christian counselees from Satan's grips.[1]

The enemy must be defeated in all of his varied manifestations. Counselors must be careful not to allow him to take advantage of situations (II Corinthians 2:11) or to give him an opportunity to gain ground (Ephesians 4:27). One way of guarding against such incursions by the evil one is, as Paul noted, to become aware of his tactics ("We are not ignorant of his schemes"—II Corinthians 2:11). This requires diligence in coming to a biblical knowledge and understanding of Satan's place and methods. Counselors must become cognizant of the fundamental themes of sin. These fundamental themes are apparent in the account of the first sin recorded in Genesis 3. Therefore, we shall find it necessary to

---

1. Not that God, in His amazing providence, at times does not use unsaved persons to do just that and thus "make the wrath of man to praise Him." But, as faithful Christians, *our* responsibility is to turn to *Christian* counselors and not to test the Lord (Galatians 6:1). See *The Big Umbrella*, pp. 146-155.

examine the story of the fall afresh in order to understand some of the problems that are connected with sin and its consequences.

Opting for Desire-Oriented and Motivated Life

Fundamentally, the problem of the first sin amounted to this: Adam and Eve opted for the satisfaction of desire rather than for obedience to the commandment of God. The devil appealed to "the lust of the eyes, the lust of the flesh and the pride of life" (cf. I John 2:16 with Genesis 3:6). Over against this was God's commandment: "You shall not eat." The options given to them are the same options that one faces now. They reflect two distinct moralities, two antithetical religions, and two discrete manners of life. The one says: "I shall live according to feeling"; the other: "I shall live as God says." As one counselee put it succinctly: "I hate her and I hit her!" When Adam sinned he was abandoning the commandment-oriented life of love for the feeling-oriented life of lust. There are only these two ways of life: the feeling-motivated life of sin oriented toward self, and the commandment-oriented life of holiness oriented toward God.[2]

Living according to feeling rather than God's commandment is a fundamental hindrance to godliness and is a factor with which every Christian counselor must learn to deal. It is a clever "wile" of Satan to tempt men to think that they cannot *do* what God requires because they do not *feel* like doing it, or that they must *do* what they feel like doing and cannot help themselves.

---

2. The two ways of life are diametrically opposed to one another and force one to choose between them. Throughout the day, one's life consists of many such choices. The two life styles involve patterns of lust or love. They are oriented toward and motivated by the counselee's desires or God's commandments. They acknowledge two distinct sources of authority: self or the Bible. They focus upon separate goals: temporary pleasure; eternal joy. They acknowledge two masters: Satan or God. They offer two different ways of handling life's problems: the one resorts to running, covering up, lying and blame-shifting, etc., while the other insists upon facing, confessing, speaking truth, and assuming personal responsibility. They bring about their own results: the bondage of chaos in this life and eternal loss, or the freedom of structure and eternal joy. One was the way of the so-called Enlightenment, the other the way of the Reformation. Until recently the former was present in Western culture, but the latter was the "official" stance of most of the institutions of society and of culture. A reversal is now taking place in what has been called the rise of the new morality. It is not new. What is new is that the former hedonistic way of life is newly replacing the latter as the *official* stance of the Western world.

Often the argument takes subtle forms, which at first seem plausible, even pious. For instance, a husband and wife may say, "I guess there is nothing left to our marriage—no love—no feeling—nothing," and thereby hope that the Christian counselor will concede that a divorce is allowable on other than scriptural grounds. If they can get him to agree to this, they hope that their bad consciences over what they have already determined to do may be salved. They vainly look for balm in Gilead. But, instead, the nouthetic counselor replies: "I am sorry to hear that. I guess you will have to confess your sin and learn how to love one another, then." Their reaction to this usually is sheer astonishment.

"But," they protest, "we told you that we don't feel anything for each other any more."

"I understand, but that is irrelevant; God says that you must love one another. When you learn to do so, the feelings of love will follow. Love is not feeling first; it begins with obedient living."

"What? Do you mean to say that we must try to love one another *contrary to all of our* feelings?"

"Exactly!"

"But wouldn't that be hypocrisy?"

"No, that would be obedience to God, who has commanded: 'Husbands, love your wives as Christ loved the church and gave Himself up for her' (Ephesians 5:25). Joe, God says that you are responsible to love Phyllis; love begins with the husband, whose love must reflect the love of Jesus Christ (I John 4:19)."

"Oh, I couldn't love her *that* way!"

"Well, then, start at a lower level. Christ commanded: 'Love your neighbor as yourself' (Matthew 22:39). As Paul observed, *she* is your *closest* neighbor; you have to live with her (Ephesians 5:28-31)."

"I don't think I could do that either."

"All right, then, we'll begin at the *lowest* level of all: 'Love your enemies' (Matthew 5:44)! You see, there is no escape; God *commands* love, even toward an enemy. The two of you must repent of your sin and by the help of God learn to love each other, even if you begin by loving as enemies."

"But how can I love an enemy?"

"As I said, love is not feeling *first*. Hollywood and the TV have taught us that fallacious doctrine. Christians must reject it. Love is not *getting* but rather is *giving*: 'God so *loved* the world that He *gave*

His only begotten Son' (John 3:16); 'He *loved* me and *gave* Himself for me' (Galatians 2:20); and remember also Ephesians 5:25 that I just quoted. When you learn to give of yourself—your time, your money, your interest—you will eventually *feel* what you now want. But that feeling, to be enduring, must be the fruit, not the root of love. When you invest enough of yourself in another, you will feel what you wish for him: 'Where your treasure is, there will your heart be also' (Matthew 6:21). The "heart" speaks of the whole man, including his feelings.

"Well . . . perhaps; but, it still seems hypocritical."

"No, it is *never* hypocritical to obey God. You have fallen into a trap of the devil in thinking that it is. Every morning—*contrary to my feelings* (all of which encourage me to pull the covers over my head and go back to sleep)—I get up. Does that make me a hypocrite?"

"No, I guess not."

"What *would* make me a hypocrite, then?"

"Well, I suppose if you went about bragging that you loved to get up in the morning."

"Precisely! Now, if, as the Scriptures command, you *give* in concrete ways to your enemy (a 'cup of cold water' or 'something to eat' when he is hungry or thirsty); i.e., if you care for his needs, even though at first you don't feel like it, does that make you a hypocrite?"

"Well . . . I guess not."

"What would?"

"If you *said* that you felt like doing it."

"Right again. So, you see, it is *not* hypocrisy to work at love at all. That is the lie of Satan, who wants you to rationalize your desires not to give of yourselves to one another by excusing your failure with the protest that obedience to God without feeling is hypocrisy."

Feeling-Oriented Counseling

Feeling-oriented counseling (and much current counseling is[3]) plays into the hands of Satan, who got to the first man and woman through desire.

---

3. Cf. *Competent to Counsel*, pp. 93 ff. Cf. also: " 'It is not ideas themselves which are the important factors in determining the patient's mental content or his form of behavior but the effects that are attached to his ideas.' *This is a first principle of practically every form of psychotherapy in use today* [emphasis mine]." Robert M. Goldenson, *The Encyclopedia of Human Behavior* (Garden City: Doubleday and Co., 1970), vol. I, p. 39. Even in Roman Catholicism the Rogerian feeling orientation has had a strong impact. The Rev. Michael P.

To encourage counselees to follow their feelings rather than to obey the Word of God is to side with Satan, to solidify the original problem, and to elicit the complications that come from further sinful behavior. It is to side with the problem and its causes rather than with the solution. Instead, a counselor, with Paul, must insist: "Therefore do not let sin reign in your mortal body that you should obey its lusts [desires]" (Romans 6:12). What would a feeling-oriented counselor have said to Esau (Genesis 25:27; Hebrews 12:16)?

Haim Ginott, whose clever use of Rogerian techniques has made his books on child rearing bestsellers, emphasizes feeling. He teaches parents to focus on the feelings. But, as plausible as Ginott's suggestions may seem at first, one can see that they fail whenever there is a problem to be solved. To acknowledge that "things are bad" may have its place, but to *focus* on the child's feelings can be a cop-out by which the parent tries to avoid the problem and thereby fails to teach his child how to face and solve it. Often Ginott's method leaves the child juggling options in the air.[4]

Decision Making

The two ways of life often need to be set before the counselee antithetically. One means of doing so may be to hand him a decision-making sheet to fill in.[5]

This sheet attempts to point up the antithesis between biblically based

---

Sullivan, of *Marriage Encounter*, urges husbands and wives at their retreat center "not to try and solve problems." Instead, they are to discuss their feelings toward each other, etc. "Feelings are neither right nor wrong; they just are," he said. *The Bulletin*, April, 1973, p. 16.

It must not be thought that God is opposed to pleasure and good feeling; precisely not that! At His right hand are "pleasures forevermore." But notice: the pleasures of God (1) come from Him, (2) are enduring. The issue is joined because the hedonistic way of life fails at these two points. The Source of true pleasure, its nature, and its means of acquisition are all unknown to those outside of Christ. Hedonism must be opposed because, ultimately, it destroys all possibility for lasting pleasure.

4. Ginott offers no absolute standard for decision making, since he does not base his methods of child training upon the Scriptures. Ginott dimly reflects one aspect of the truth. By emphasizing respect for the child, he nudges up against the biblical concept of the image of God in man. Yet, having approached it, he turns aside from its implications with respect to sovereignty over this world by failing to teach scriptural decision making.

5. Available from the publisher in any quantity and as part of *The Christian Counselor's Starter Packet*.

CHRISTIAN DECISION MAKING

(Read Hebrews 11:24-27 before making your decision)

Two ways to go:

COMMANDMENT ORIENTED decision making begins by asking:	DESIRE ORIENTED decision making begins by asking:
"What does *God* want?"	"What do *I* want?"
Write out your answer:	Write out your answer:
_____	_____
_____	_____
_____	_____
Opts for present suffering in order to receive long-term pleasures.	Opts for present pleasure and forgets long-term suffering.
Note both:	Note both:
_____	_____
_____	_____
_____	_____

With Moses, your decision is an opportunity to "choose Christ."
Write out your decision:

_____

_____

_____

_____

decision making and decisions made out of desire (which is so often at odds with the Scriptures).

Much more could be said about decision making. One important matter to note is an extension of the principle mentioned above. Counselees must be warned against making moves out of despair. When one is *sure* that a course of action is biblical he may move; otherwise he should never do so merely because of feeling[6] (cf. Romans 14:23). And when a decision has been made on a scriptural basis, the counselee must be urged not to waver from it when things are not going well— *no matter how he feels.* Christians make more bad decisions on the basis of some passing feeling than perhaps for any other reason (and turn from good ones for the same reason). Feelings are up and down, they have peaks and troughs. Often, feelings generated by other causes get tangled up with a decision and color one's vision. Nothing short of commandment living (often *in spite of* feelings) can keep life stable. The peaks and troughs grow larger as they are allowed to become the life motivating force;[7] however, on the other hand, they tend to flatten out as life becomes commandment oriented.

Common Themes of Sin

All of the common themes of sin grow out of the desire-oriented life. A look at Genesis 3 discloses some of the basic themes and shows that:

1. Adam and Eve sinned because they rejected the Word of God. Whether the rejection stemmed from blatant rebellion or disbelief is unimportant. All rejection of God's Word, whatever the motive, is in the last resort a rejection of God Himself.

2. This rejection led to serious consequences, both from without and from within. Outwardly, the *judgment* of God, the *expulsion* from the Garden, the *curse* of the ground, and the *souring of interpersonal relationships* between the man and his wife resulted. Within, man's *nature was corrupted*—with all of the baneful consequences that flow therefrom—and *a bad conscience* was felt in the painful emotional responses that it triggered. All of these results themselves became occasions for more sin. The *intertwining complexities of tangled living* began to be experienced. Sin brought complications to life.[8]

---

6. Cf. *The Big Umbrella*, p. 90.
7. So that some even enter what has been called a manic-depressive cycle.
8. Sometimes Christian counselors are faulted with the argument: "But it is

3. Man began to *run*, to *hide* and *avoid*, to *cover up*. The wicked flees when no man pursues. In a thousand ways counselees still do the same. The materials from which they weave their garments may be more sophisticated, but the Christian counselor knows to *look for the fig leaves*. He also sees innumerable *patterns of avoidance*. He may hide behind intellectualism rather than trees; but unless smitten by repentance he hides. Christian counselors must know how to *ferret the sons of Adam out of the forests*. Men are still running from God.[9]

4. Man began to shift the blame: Adam said, "The *woman* that *you* gave me, *she*. . . ." Eve declared, "The *serpent, he*. . . ." Hardly any husband and wife whose marriage is on the rocks will be free from much *blame shifting*. They will blame one another, their circumstances, relatives, etc. Ultimately, their blame amounts to nothing less than shifting the blame to God. Christian counselors must *learn how to teach counselees to sort out the proper responsibilities each bears toward God and one another*.

These common themes of sin and the sinful attempts to avoid sin's consequences paint a despicable picture of man. He rejects God, becomes miserable before God because of guilt, runs from God, and then (to top it all) blames God for his own sin! And so often this is precisely the state in which the counselor first meets the counselee. Undoubtedly, the task of counseling sinful men is a formidable one!

Themes Expressed in Individual Styles

Beneath the styles of sin is commonality. Sin, then, in all of its dimensions, clearly is the problem with which the Christian counselor must grapple. It is the secondary dimensions—the variations on the common themes—that make counseling so difficult. While all men are born sinners and engage in the same sinful practices and dodges, each develops his own styles of sinning. The styles (combinations of sins and dodges) are peculiar to each individual; but beneath them are the common themes. It is the counselor's work to discover

---

all too simple," or "That sounds simplistic." But the answer to this is that righteousness always untangles things, makes life simpler and thus allows one properly to enjoy and appreciate the infinite varieties of life in God's amazing creation.

9. Yet at times even a reminder of this fact can be helpful to the counselee. His situation is bad, but no worse than others who, by God's grace, have found forgiveness and a new life. There are times when a counselee needs to be told "others have felt embarrassment, others have entertained sinful feelings," etc.

these commonalities beneath the individualities. How may he do so?

Let us begin by considering two cases. Madeline has developed a serious problem with headaches. There is no indication that the headaches stem from anything but tension; they are muscular in nature.[10] The headaches are real, bring about considerable discomfort and at times cause serious debilitation (inability to concentrate on work, enjoy activities, etc.).

Phyllis has problems with diarrhea from time to time.[11] At times the problem becomes so severe that she is unable to leave the house or participate in family activities. Physicians can find no organic cause for the malady.

The effects (headache and diarrhea) are quite dissimilar. Yet their cause and their results may be identical. In both of these cases the use of DPP forms[12] and the core data[13] obtained by questioning indicated that the onset of diarrhea and headaches uniformly preceded stress situations which the counselees wished to avoid. The style of "copping out" (running or avoiding) in each case was different, but the basic theme was the same. By focusing upon the cause of the difficulty (located through noting attitudes toward people and problems associated with the onset of the headaches and the diarrhea), together with an analysis of its effects or results (avoiding responsibilities, situations, or persons, etc.), a counselor was able both to detect and to handle the common problem at the root of each case.

Of course, a counselor must be careful not to find similarities where none exist. It is too easy to see in today's case the very same factors that were operative in the case so successfully handled last week. By prayer-

---

10. Persistent headaches, especially those that show increasing frequency and intensity could indicate brain tumor and should be investigated medically. Counselors always ought to be interested in whether there may be a physiological base. Tension headaches may appear as pain located at the top of the head. Edmund Jacobson, *You Must Relax* (Garden City: Blue Ribbon Books, 1946), p. 126. They may be recognized by tautness in the back of the neck. William Barry Furlong, "Headache Hunters," *Today's Health*, March, 1971, p. 69. It is important to know that "Only two percent of the severe recurring headaches have an organic basis," says Dr. Seymour Diamond, president of the American Association for the Study of Headache. Steve Maurata, "New Help for the Headache That Won't Go Away," *Family Health*, February, 1973, pp. 55. Some headaches stem from foods or viruses. *Ibid.*, p. 56.

11. Diarrhea is a frequent result of the triggering of unpleasant emotions.

12. Explained *infra*, p. 279.

13. Explained *infra*, p. 259.

ful concern, stringent care, continuous, regular reevaluation, and constant awareness of the danger, counselors may avoid this error and keep from falling into this trap. While the good counselor appreciates the possible existence of numberless variations on a theme, nevertheless he also has certain commonalities toward which to look.

As he reads his Bible, therefore, the Christian counselor will look for reoccurring themes. The various biblical lists of sins,[14] as well as the Ten Commandments, provide clear-cut data for discovering common sinful practices. In addition, again and again the counselor will see the same patterns emerging, in both biblical and modern life. He should note these and develop a growing list of problems, together with corresponding Bible passages and counseling cases from his own experience.[15]

Satan and His Associates

In order to understand the nature of the battle in which he is engaged, the counselor must study the biblical data concerning the evil one and his forces.

To begin with, he must recognize that even though it may not look like it, as a soldier of Christ he is on the winning side. The enemy has already been defeated. Christ has thoroughly routed him by His sacrificial death, bodily resurrection, and ascension to power and glory. Satan's condition, since the cross, is described as follows:

He is "bound": Mark 3:27; Luke 11:20; Revelation 20.[16]

His power is restricted and restrained: II Thessalonians 2:6 ff.

He has been rendered "powerless over believers": Hebrews 2:14.

He is defeated, disarmed, and spoiled: Colossians 2:15; Revelation 12:7 ff.; Mark 3:27.

He has "fallen" and was "thrown down": Luke 10:18; Revelation 12:9.

His kingdom has been replaced by God's: Daniel 7; Luke 11:20.

---

14. Cf. Exodus 20; Galatians 5:19-21; I Corinthians 6:9-10; Revelation 21:8; Romans 13:13; Mark 7:21-23; I Timothy 4:1-5; II Timothy 3:1-7.

15. See Reference 2, p. 453, for a form to use. The list can be kept in this volume.

16. Cf. Jay Adams, The Time Is at Hand (Nutley, N. J.: Presbyterian and Reformed Publishing Company, 1970), for a fuller discussion of this text and others listed below.

He had a short furious time of activity in the first century that has ceased: Revelation 12:12.

He was "crushed" under the foot of the early Christians: Romans 16:20.

He has lost "authority" over Christians: Colossians 1:13.

He has been "judged": John 16:11.

He cannot "touch" a Christian: I John 5:18.

His works have been destroyed: I John 3:8.

He has "nothing": John 14:30.

He must "flee" when "resisted": James 4:7.

Surely Satan is alive, but not "well, on planet earth"!

His minions, likewise, have been cast out, subject to the authority of Christians, overcome by them, bound in chains, etc. (Cf. Matthew 10–12; Mark 1:27; 6:7; Luke 9:1; 10:19; I John 4:4; Jude 6; Revelation 12:9, etc.) All in all, the data are overwhelming. These, and more passages, make it quite clear that the Christian counselor, when counseling a Christian, sets out on a task that is most hopeful, whatever the outward signs may seem to indicate. Satan truly is a defeated foe. His power over unbelievers still is great: the "whole world lies in the evil one" (I John 5:19); he can "take them captive at his will" (II Timothy 2:26). Yet this no longer is true of the believer. Thus the Christian by God's grace (help) can overcome evil and is exhorted to do so (Romans 12:21).

It was not without reason then that I wrote about demon possession in *The Big Umbrella* as follows:

> Paul said that extensive demonic activity would characterize the last days of the Old Testament era (I Timothy 4:1). It was during the period that John predicted that Satan's rage would be intensified because he had been cast down upon the earth (Revelation 12:13). There is reason to believe that this was fulfilled in the overlapping period of time dealt with in the Book of Revelation. There are good reasons also for believing that when Satan was bound (Revelation 20) and bruised (Romans 16:20) by the full coming of the kingdom that this short intervening period was curtailed. This curtailment or restraint (II Thessalonians 2) upon Satanic power and influence necessarily involved the virtual cessation of such activity by his demonic forces. This accounts for the rare incidence, if not the entire absence, of demonic possession in

modern times. It is possible, of course, that demonic activity is still in the process of being curtailed *as the gospel penetrates* new and previously untouched communities of the world.

Significantly, at the end of the millennial era (which extends from the ascension of Christ to a point shortly prior to His second coming) Satan will be released to "deceive" the Gentiles again as he did throughout the Old Testament era (cf. Revelation 20). During the present "times of the Gentiles" the empire of God has been spreading (like a stone growing into a large mountain) throughout the world so that some from every tribe, tongue and nation shall become part of His empire. Looking forward to these times Zechariah predicted that the "unclean spirits" would be removed (Zechariah 13:2, cf. NASB). The present restraint that Paul declared would be imposed upon Satan (II Thessalonians 2:1-22; n.b. vss. 9-22) prohibits wholesale "deceit" by direct demonic activity. Yet Paul, with John (Revelation 20), predicted that this restraint will be lifted just before the return of Christ, thus bringing about another brief period of intensive demonic influence (cf. also Revelation 16:14 with II Thessalonians 2:9-12 and Revelation 20:7-10) that may be characterized by renewed incidents of demonic possession. The eschatological timetable and the nature of the present millennial era adequately account for the failure of the modern church to encounter demon possession as a common daily contemporary phenomenon.[17]

and:

There is no biblical reason to think that demonic possession (or oppression) can occur in the life of a Christian. The simultaneous presence of the Holy Spirit, who dwells within every true child of God, and an "unclean spirit" is impossible. This is clear from the utter antithesis of the two noted in Mark 3:20-30. Here also (3:30) Jesus warns that it is unforgivable blasphemy to attribute the work of the Holy Spirit to a demon.

This, and the other considerations about the cessation of demonic activity mentioned above has important implications for Christian counselors. More and more frequently failure in counseling has been attributed to the fact of demon possession. In the light of biblical theological eschatology, it would seem that a heavy burden of proof belongs to the one who retreats to demon possession as the cause of bizarre behavior. Counselors, in this present era, have every reason to expect that the cause of the problems with which they will deal in counseling will be other than demonic possessions.

---

17. Jay Adams, *The Big Umbrella*, pp. 117, 118.

In more instances than one, I have seen incompetence in counseling excused by resorting to the diagnosis of possession by demons, sometimes with very damaging effects. If, for example, one's problems are the result of his own sinful behavior, and they are instead charged to possession by an evil spirit, those problems may be complicated rather than solved by efforts to cast out the demon. Not only will such efforts fail, leading often to hopelessness and despair, but they will shift the focus from the counselee's own responsibility. He will be viewed as a helpless victim rather than as a guilty sinner. The results are likely only to confirm him in his sinful life patterns, and the frustrations of counselors who are reduced to fruitless prayer and pity are likely to encourage deeper depression and even despair. It would seem vital to effective biblical counseling to presuppose that a counselee is free from such direct demonic influence in this era.[18]

Along with the wave of popular interest in the occult, Christians, influenced by their times, have become preoccupied with demonic activity. One woman, in deep concern, spoke of casting out demons from her infant child. She knew the baby had been demonized because it cried excessively! Christian counselees, of the sort who before would have become concerned about the assurance of their salvation or about having committed the unpardonable sin, now theorize about having been possessed or oppressed[19] by a demon. Like the other two excuses ("I can't be expected to live as God wishes if I'm not truly a Christian" and "If I have committed the unpardonable sin, then there is no hope for me; I might as well live as I please"), demon possession or oppression affords a ready-made cop-out from personal responsibility. ("The demon made me do it." One counselee said: "The demon reached over and pulled the car wheel.") All three stances not only allow counselees great latitude in behavior, while reducing their responsibility, but also lead to binges of self-introspection. Wallowing for any length of time in the morasses of self-absorption can virtually lead one to convince himself of the truth of what may have begun merely as a suspicion, a fear, a misrepresentation, or as a convenient excuse. In a short while, it can become a dominant theme around which the counselee builds his life. For help in dealing with counselees caught in the web of such sinful patterns, cf. the section on "Counseling Those Who Fear That They Have Committed the Unpardonable Sin" (chapter 37).

---

18. *Ibid.*, pp. 120-121.
19. For further discussion of this false distinction, see *ibid.*, pp. 119, 120.

The problem and methodology for handling this difficulty and the means of counseling those who have reached a faulty interpretation of demon possession are substantially the same.

Counselors also must recognize that:

> The weapons of our warfare are not of the flesh, but mighty by God for the destruction of fortresses. We are destroying speculations and every lofty thing raised up against the knowledge of God, and we are making every thought captive to the obedience of Christ, and we are ready to punish all disobedience, whenever your obedience is complete.

Thus, the equipment that God has given to the counselor is adequate both for evangelism (to take captives from among Satan's forces) and for edification (to punish all disobedience among such captives). There is nothing lacking. The enemy is powerful, but the mighty Counselor, under whom the Christian counselor serves, has subdued him. The words of Luther's great hymn, "A Mighty Fortress," exactly express the fact: "One little word shall fell him."

Feeling and Doing

The discussion of the counseling problem in terms of the two ways of life,[20] with their two orientations and two life motivations (desire or obedience), raises the question of the relationship of feeling to doing. I have discussed this to some extent in *Competent to Counsel* and will not repeat what I have said there. However, some additional comments may prove of interest. Perhaps the following excerpts from Ichabod Spencer will set the problem in perspective.

The following "sketch" (Spencer's word for case study) deals with the matter of feeling and behavior from the point of view of a conservative Christian. It is also a sample of one sort of pastoral counseling that was done by a Presbyterian preacher prior to the near capitulation of the Christian ministry to psychiatry. In his *Sketches* (which appeared in a First and Second Series), Spencer discussed a large variety of problems and how he handled them. There are many good

---

20. Frequently this anthesis finds expression in the Scriptures (Psalm 1; the broad and narrow road; the two masters, etc. Note especially Colossians 1:21: formally alienated and hostile in *mind* and *deeds*) and in Christian literature (cf. the *Didache*). That is why Christian counseling consists of helping the counselee to put off his "former manner of life" and to put on God's way of living (Ephesians 4).

insights in Spencer, although his work is outdated. In this sketch, among other things, Spencer rightly observed:

1. That feelings are largely involuntarily ("Your heart will not feel at your bidding").

2. There is no biblical injunction to feel ("The Bible never tells you that you must feel, but that you must repent and believe").

3. That feelings flow from behavior ("He could 'feel' when he found his father's arms around him"; "I find, if a poor creature will turn to God, in the name of Jesus, he will learn to feel as he never felt before").[21]

A careful study of this interesting sketch demonstrates (in what now seems a quaint manner) the basic dynamic that exists between feeling and doing. For more information concerning the fundamental principle that feelings flow from action and attitudes, cf. *Competent to Counsel*, especially pages 87-97.

Case by Spencer[22]

From early spring down to the autumn of the year, a very sedate and contemplative man had been accustomed to call upon me, in respect to his religious thoughts and anxieties. At first he seemed to have thoughts only, but they ripened by degrees into anxieties.[23] He began by asking about theories, or doctrines, apparently without any idea of making an application of the truth to himself. He had points of difficulty which he wished to have explained, and then he found other points; and these gradually changed in character from abstract questions to those of the application of the truth. From the first, I tried to lead him on to the personal application; but months passed away before he appeared to have much sense of his sin, or much anxiety about himself.

But he came to this; and after quite a struggle of mind, as it appeared to me to lead himself to believe in salvation by personal merit, he gave that up; he said to me, "I have become convinced that sinners are saved, not by their own goodness, but because they

---

21. On this point see *Competent to Counsel*, pp. 93 ff., etc. One may not sit waiting for the proper feelings before obeying the Word of God; he must obey regardless of how he feels. Often doing leads to proper feeling (cf. Proverbs 15:30; 17:22, T.E.V.).

22. Ichabod Spencer, *A Pastor's Sketches*, Second Series (New York: M. W. Dodd, Publisher, 1861), pp. 180-185.

23. Concern about anxiety is not of recent origin. In 1861 a Presbyterian pastor is dealing with the issue. In Matthew 6:24-34; Philippians 4:4-9; and I Peter 5:7, Christ, Paul, and Peter deal with the question.

are pardoned on account of Jesus Christ. Faith in Him is the only way for them."

After this, I had conversed with him several times, when he appeared to me to be not far from the kingdom of God; but I was often disappointed, for he would come back to me again in as much trouble and unbelief as before. Again and again I had answered all his inquiries, teaching him out of the Scriptures; had brought up to his mind all the doctrines of truth, the divine promises and directions, sin and salvation; but all in vain. He had become very solemn, and seemed to be entirely candid and really in earnest. His Bible had become his constant study; he was a man of prayer; he attended upon all our religious services with manifest interest; he appeared to have a deep sense of his sin and danger. But he had no hope in Christ.[24]

I finally said to him one evening, "I do not know, my dear sir, what more can be said to you. I have told you all that I know. Your state as a sinner lost, exposed to the righteous penalty of God's Law, and having a heart alienated from God; and the free offer of redemption by Christ; and your instant duty to repent of sin and give up the world and give God your heart; and the source of your help through the power of the Holy Spirit assured to you, if you will 'receive' Christ: all these things have become as familiar to you as household words. What more can I say? I know not what more there is to be said. I cannot read your heart. God can, and you can by His aid. Some things you have said almost made me think you a Christian, and others again have destroyed that hope. I now put it to your own heart—if you are not a Christian, what hinders you?"

He thought a moment,—said he,—

"I can't feel!"

"Why didn't you tell me this before?"

"I never thought of it before, sir."

"How do you know this hinders you?"

"I can think of nothing else. But I am sure I shall never be converted to God, if I have no more feeling than I have now. But that is my own fault. I know you cannot help me."

"No sir, I cannot; nor can you help yourself. Your heart will not feel at your bidding."[25]

"What then can I do?" said he, with much anxiety.

24. Notice the need for hope acknowledged by Spencer.
25. A crucial insight by Spencer.

"Come to Christ, now. Trust Him. Give up your darling world. 'Repent: so iniquity shall not be your ruin.' "

He seemed perplexed—annoyed—vexed; and with an accent of impatience, such as I had never witnessed in him before, he replied,

"That is impossible. I want the feeling, to bring me to that; and I can't feel!"[26]

"Hear me, sir," said I, "and heed well what I say. I have several points:

"1. The Bible never tells you that you must feel, but that you must repent and believe.[27]

"2. Your complaint that you 'can't feel," is just an excuse,[28] by which your wicked heart would justify you for not coming to Christ now.

"3. This complaint that you 'can't feel,' is the complaint of a self-righteous spirit." (He started—rose upon his feet, and stood as in amazement.)

"How is it?" said he.

"Because you look to the desired feeling to commend you to God, or to make you fit to come, or to enable you to come."[29]

"Yes, to enable me," said he.[30]

"Well, that is self-righteousness, in the shape of self-justification for not coming, or the shape of self-reliance, if you attempt to come. That is all legalism, and not the acceptance of a gracious Christianity. You cannot be saved by Law.

"4. Your complaint is the language of the most profound ignorance. To feel would do you no good. Devils feel. Lost spirits feel.

"5. Your complaint that you 'can't feel,' tends to lead you to a false religion—a religion of mere self-righteous feeling. Religion is duty."

"But, sir," said he, "there is feeling in religion."

"But, sir," said I, "there is duty in religion; and which shall come

---

26. The basic error of feeling-oriented persons is that they (wrongly) believe that they cannot or should not *do* what they first do not *feel* like doing.

27. Absolutely basic as a reply.

28. Spencer may have been a bit too harsh here; there may have been genuine misunderstanding on the part of the counselee. Yet, he knew the man and, unlike us, was in possession of many nonverbal clues.

29. The problem of all preparationists.

30. Notice, again, the fundamental error of the feeling-oriented counselee: "I must *feel* in order to *do*."

first?[31] You ought to feel: you ought to love God; and grieve that you are such a senseless sinner."

"I know I am a sinner; but I can't feel any confidence to turn to God, to draw me to Him."

"You are like the prodigal in the fifteenth of Luke, when he thought of saying to his father, 'make me as one of thy hired servants.' Poor fool! Say that, to his father? Why, the very idea is a libel on his father's heart! But he didn't think so. Poor fool! he knew no better. And you are a greater fool than he. He went home. And where he met his father, he found his heart. He could 'feel,' when he found his father's arms around him, and felt the strong beatings of his father's heart. Do as he did. Go home and you will feel, if you never felt before. You will starve where you are; your 'husks' will not save you."

As I was uttering this he hung his head, cast his eyes upon the floor, and stood like a statute of stone. I let him think. There he stood for some long minutes. Then turning suddenly to me, reaching to me his hand, says he,—

"I am very much obliged to you; good night." I let him go.

About a month afterwards I met him riding alone in his wagon, and he insisted upon my taking a seat with him, for he had "something to say" to me, and he would "drive wherever I wanted to go." I was no sooner seated in the wagon than he said to me,—

"The human heart is the greatest mystery in the world; inexplicable, contradictory to itself; it is absurd. Man is a riddle. Who would imagine that when a sinner really wishes to feel his sins more, and wishes to have the love of Christ in his heart, it is because he is not willing to give up the world. He says, (as I said to you that last night) 'I can't feel,' as an excuse for holding on to it. I found as soon as I was willing to 'go home,' as you called it, the road was plain enough."

"Were you hindered long with that want of feeling?"

"No; I never thought of it till that night. It came upon me like a flash; and then, just as I was thinking it was a good reason in my favor, you dashed it all into shivers."

"And can you 'feel' now?"

"Oh, yes; I have no trouble about that. I find, if a poor creature will turn to God, in the name of Jesus, he will learn to feel as he never felt before."

---

31. The crucial issue.

Sinners, not willing to give up the world, and wanting an excuse for their irreligion, exclaim, "I can't feel."

Spencer has put the matter into perspective. One *feels* those sensations that accompany the judgment that he is saved when he *is* saved. He *feels* those sensations that we call grief, sorrow, shame, fear, and conviction when he *is* truly repentant. Sinners always turn matters about. But the biblical rule is plain: the student *feels* that combination of sensations that we call "confidence" in taking an examination when he knows he *is prepared* for the examination. At the end of the day the man who has worked productively is tired but satisfied (Ecclesiastes 5:12: "The sleep of the working man is sweet"); at the end of a day of idleness or worry, he feels tired but dissatisfied. He must *do* that which "brings satisfaction," as we say. Whenever Martha cheated in school, she experienced the feelings that accompanied guilt, and in her case these were so strong that she threw up. The diagram that follows indicates the process.

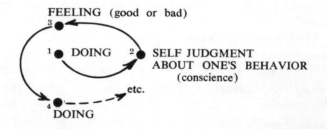

Are Feelings Important?

It is not because Christian counselors are unconcerned about human pain and suffering or because they exalt the will of intellect in man over his emotions according to some outmoded scheme or faculty psychology that they insist upon obedience to God's commandments rather than submission to one's feelings. Rather, they do so, first, because God requires this and, secondly, because they know that it is only in this manner that the proper feelings of peace and joy can be achieved.[32]

32. Christ, not Satan, gives peace and joy (John 14:27; 15:11). If men would have the abundant life both here and hereafter, they must "seek first the kingdom of God and His righteousness." Then, "all these things will be added."

Therefore, it is entirely incorrect to suppose (with some) that Christian counselors are indifferent and unsympathetic because they do not *focus* on feelings. Exactly the opposite is true. They do not *focus* on feelings simply because they care. They know that when they focus upon attitudes and actions that the proper feelings will follow. Indeed, since feelings cannot be altered permanently (apart from some surgical operations) in any other way, they *focus* upon living a new way of life, which, simply *because* men are *whole* men, means a life filled with new feelings.[33]

Responsibility and Sin

It is difficult for some to acknowledge personal sin as the root and cause of most of the day-by-day counseling problems that arise. This is particularly true in an age deeply steeped in Freudianism. As Rogerianism has taught us to put feeling first, so Freudianism has declared blame-shifting legitimate. More recently, Skinnerianism has gone on record as opposing the very concept of responsibility *per se*. If, therefore, in ordinary activities it is hard for some to see the place of personal responsibility, this becomes still harder for them whenever they consider *special* cases.

The Christian counselor must be firm at this point about his insistence upon human responsibility. In order to understand what the dimensions of such problems may be, let us consider two emotionally charged categories: temporary insanity and the influence of poor training in childhood.

Temporary Insanity

Is there such a thing as temporary insanity? When one goes berserk, is he no longer responsible for his actions? Physiological factors may lead to temporary insanity. One may go berserk from a blow on the head, from a toxic reaction to medicine, etc. For two days a child completely lost his senses as the result of a very rare reaction to a common cough remedy. There are, then, instances of temporary insanity in which the counselee cannot be held responsible for his behavior.

---

33. Pain is real. But to focus upon it only *enlarges* it. Thinking about one's heart can give rise to palpitations; concentrating upon a spot in one's arm can cause it to ache. Focus on pain often gives occasion to the counselee to begin to use his pain to manipulate others. If the pain brings these secondary kinds of rewards (getting what one wants), the counselee's pain is likely to increase both in frequency and in intensity. Cf. John Schindler, *op. cit.*, pp. 41-43.

However, in many (probably most) situations where people speak of temporary insanity (by which they mean losing control of oneself), the circumstances are quite different. Then, the serious question of whether the person is responsible is more problematic. Does a man who uncontrollably murders another in a fit of rage bear responsibility for the act?

Perhaps an analogy will help to reach an answer. Picture a situation in which a householder has been piling oily rags in his basement for years, knowing all the while that these could cause fire. In spite of this knowledge and repeated warnings, he has continued to accumulate these rags until they are stacked thick and high in all parts of the basement. He has piled them closer and closer to the furnace. Finally, one day the rags catch fire and begin to burn. A serious fire starts in the basement that it is impossible for him to control or put out. Should he be held responsible? Would anyone seriously object that since he could not control the fire, he could not be held responsible? Of course not! Plainly he was responsible! Over a long period of time he had been laying the groundwork for the fire. To change the figure to a biblical one, eventually he reaped only what he had sown. Similarly, people who continually handle life's situations in sinful ways are stuffing the cellar with oily rags. One day when they go up in flames they cannot excuse themselves for the (often genuine) lack of control that occurs under those circumstances. Temporary insanity (of a nonorganic sort), then, cannot be separated from its causes as they are rooted in sinful behavior.

To fail to recognize responsibility in such contexts, as in any other, is to take away hope. For the counselor to recognize it is to provide the only adequate basis for counseling.[34] When the fires have been extinguished and the situation once again is under control, the counselee must face up to the effects of his actions, repent, and rectify these as fully as possible. By God's grace he also must be taught how to dispose of oily rags in the future.

The Influence of Childhood Training

"But," someone contends, "how can you hold a four-year-old responsible for the life style that he develops under the strong home

---

34. There is no hope for change apart from responsibility. Rage (uncontrolled anger), for instance, *can* be curbed. At a later point, the biblical method for handling anger will be discussed in detail. For now, refer to Proverbs 29:11.

influences of his childhood? For instance, doesn't extreme abuse by his parents disadvantage him for life?" Would not abuse cause a child so to deviate from normal living patterns that inevitably he would become abnormal? Part of the answer to the question of permanent effects of extreme child abuse doubtless lies in the *physical* (*organic*) abuses which so often affect later life. Much abuse also may occur in forms similar to the types of communist brainwashing that combine organic and psychological factors. Here too, where organic damage occurs, the effects may be lasting.

While recognizing that any discussion of childhood responsibility evokes an undue amount of emotion from some, first, nevertheless, we must be bold to assert the biblical fact that God *does* hold children responsible for sin from the very first day of their lives. "By nature" (i.e., that corrupted deposit with which they were born) they are declared to be "children of wrath" (Ephesians 2:3b). They are guilty in Adam (Romans 5). In addition, they express this sinful nature by living "in the lusts of their flesh, indulging the desires of the flesh and of the mind" (Ephesians 2:3a). The extent to which God holds a child responsible may be hard to measure, but the fact that He does so is certain. David said: "Behold, in sinful state I was born and in sin did my mother conceive me" (Psalm 51:5, Berkeley). Elsewhere he wrote: "The wicked are estranged from the womb; these who speak lies go astray from birth" (Psalm 58:3). The fact of infant mortality in a world in which God has declared, "The wages *of sin is death*," substantiates this doctrine of the moral culpability of infants before God. They are both held guilty for sin (because of Adam's sin—cf. Romans 3:23; ch. 5) and polluted by sin. Their corrupted nature expresses itself *from birth* (see passages above) in acts of actual transgression. So, there can be no doubt about it; God holds children responsible for their sin.

The question, therefore, is not *whether* the sinful life styles developed by children with sinful natures in response to sinful influences or even acts of abuse against them are wrong or not. They are. Sin is sin, whether the sinner is young or old. Nor is it a matter of whether they are responsible. Again, they are. The very fact that children are not considered to be morally neutral in the sight of God means that they may be held responsible for making whatever righteous responses that it is possible for a child to make at any given age. As unredeemed sinners, children will fail to respond *as they should*. For this they are accountable. As they grow in age, their responsibility grows as capability for response enlarges (obviously a three-month-old and a three-year-old child are able to handle life in two distinct ways). And failure to use their capabilities (speech, mobility, etc.) righteously also increases the scope of culpability for actual sin. As capabilities enlarge, not only is the capacity for obedience greater, but the capacity for sinful responses is enlarged as well. At any given point in his life, therefore, a child is held responsible for doing whatever he ought to be able to do at that age.[35] It is also true that at every given point the unconverted child will fail. His failure is nothing less than sin.

Moreover, as the responsibility of the child for his life broadens and the responsibility of his parents, guardians, and teachers narrows, he becomes more and more fully responsible, even to the extent of re-evaluating and abandoning those sinful patterns that he developed and those that largely were built into his life by others.

Christians do not accept the deterministic views of psychologists and psychiatrists, who think that early socialization or early environmental conditioning so fixes the course of his life that all of a child's future behavior is virtually determined by those forces.[36] While the Scriptures everywhere acknowledge the important place of habit and faithfully describe the hard struggle to put off old sinful ways, they also ring with the assurance that by the Word and the Spirit radical changes are possible *at any point in life* and *regardless of what one's background may have been like*. There is hope for great change in the gospel of Jesus Christ. Therefore, when a child becomes a Christian, he must be taught that much of what he has learned to do previously must be

---

35. That is to say, the child is held accountable for doing what a sinless child might have done were the fall not to have occurred. "Man's responsibility goes far beyond his ability," wrote R. B. Kuiper in an excellent clear discussion of this point, *The Bible Tells Us So* (London: The Banner of Truth Trust, 1968), p. 47. Kuiper also has interesting comments on physical and mental disabilities, pp. 48, 49.

36. Nor do they teach children to abhor and revile parents for their supposed guilt in making children what they are, as do some psychiatrists. Parents have their guilt; children theirs. Neither can fix the blame for his own failures upon the other. Because each is properly held responsible, estrangements between parents and children are not fostered. One pastor reports that a member of his church was directed by a psychiatrist to urinate on his father's grave! No biblical counselor could countenance such advice.

changed. The former sinful manner of life developed by others and by himself must be replaced by godly ways of living.

Much today is being said about prevention. Of course, godly parents from the beginning can structure ways of living that will lessen the need for later radical change in behavior. But prevention will never replace conversion and will never be able to forestall the need for reclamation, since children are born sinners, raised by sinners, and influenced by sinners. There always will be a great need for the remedial work of counseling.

One of the crucial tasks of the counselor, therefore, will be to convince counselees that in Christ there is a biblical basis for hope of significant change. The habits of the former manner of life can be altered.[37] To that important subject we must now turn our attention.

---

37. Failure to adopt this biblical position removes hope and the possibility for successful counseling. Adler's position: "We must understand that they are victims of a mistaken development whose unfortunate consequence is that their attitude toward life also is mistaken," leaves only the insipid and condescending prospect of being "very modest" in "our judgment of our fellows, and above all . . . never allow[ing] ourselves to make any *moral* judgments." Alfred Adler, *Understanding Human Nature* (New York: Greenberg, 1946), p. 159. The victim theme, dominant in much counseling, removes hope. The only answer to victimization is the appearance of an unseen benefactor. Responsibility is the only route to hope that is certain.

Chapter Fifteen

LOVE IN COUNSELING

Love Is the Goal

Love for God and one's neighbor constitutes the sum of God's requirements for the Christian. The man who loves needs no counseling. Love cements relationships between God and man and man and man. While love attracts, fear repels. When love gives, lust grabs. What love builds, hatred destroys. With love communication flourishes; with resentment it withers. Love is the ultimate answer to all the problems of living with which the Christian counselor deals. Love, therefore, is the goal.

Under this heading in *Competent to Counsel* I wrote:

> What are the goals of nouthetic counseling? In I Timothy 1:5 Paul puts it this way: "But the goal of our instruction is love from a pure heart, and a good conscience, and a sincere faith." The word "authoritative" might be added to that translation: "The goal of our authoritative instruction is love." The original word (*parangelia*) is more than simply instruction; it is instruction imposed authoritatively. The authority of God is presupposed. The purpose of preaching and counseling is to foster the love toward God and love toward one's neighbor which God commands. Jesus summed up the keeping of the whole law as love. Any notion of authority as antithetical to love is inconsistent with Scripture.

> Love is precisely man's problem, however. How can sinful man love? Since the fall, in which Adam's sin led to a guilty conscience, hypocrisy, and doubt, it has been impossible for natural men to keep their hearts pure, their consciences good, or their faith unhypocritical. All are born with a warped sinful nature that vitiates any such possibility. And yet love depends upon these very qualities. That is why Paul conditioned love upon the solution to these problems (note: "love from," i.e., "which issues from"). God's authoritative instruction through the ministry of his Word, spoken publicly (from the pulpit) or privately (in counseling), is the Holy Spirit's means of producing love in the believer.

141

The overarching purpose of preaching and counseling is God's glory. But the underneath side of that splendid rainbow is love. A simple biblical definition of love is: The fulfillment of God's commandments. Love is a responsible relationship to God and to man. Love is a relationship conditioned upon responsibility, that is, responsible observance of the commandments of God. The work of preaching and counseling, when blessed by the Holy Spirit, enables men through the gospel and God's sanctifying Word to become pure in heart, to have peaceful consciences, and to trust God sincerely. Thus the goal of nouthetic counseling is set forth plainly in the Scriptures: to bring men into loving conformity to the law of God.[1]

Must One First Love Himself?

When Christ said that the whole law could be summed up in *two* commandments (love for God and love for one's neighbor[2]), He intended to say exactly that and nothing else. Yet some Christians (with a psychologizing bent) and some psychiatrists who are Christians are not satisfied with that; they (dangerously) add a third commandment: love yourself.[3] They claim that unless one first learns to love himself properly he will never learn to love his neighbor, for Christ (quoting Leviticus 19:18) distinctly commands: "Love your neighbor *as yourself.*"

At first this argument sounds somewhat plausible. How can I love another unless I know how to love myself? If I think (wrongly) that a practice is desirable, I may wish to urge this upon my neighbor for his benefit, although it can only injure him. But all such argumentation is beside the point. The Scriptures, not one's personal experience, tell us what constitutes love to another. One cannot go wrong in loving another when he loves him in a *biblical* manner.

When Christ urged the Christian to love his neighbor *as himself*, He did not intend to say that this would necessarily entail doing for one's

---

1. *Competent to Counsel*, pp. 54, 55.
2. Cf. Matthew 22:34-40.
3. The idea has become widespread. Note the concept in such popular writings as Eugenia Price, *Find Out for Yourself* (Grand Rapids: Zondervan), pp. 28, 29; Richard Peace, *Learning to Love Ourselves* (Downers Grove: Intervarsity Press, 1970). Note also R. Lofton Hudson, "Love Yourself," in J. Allan Peterson, ed., *The Marriage Affair* (Wheaton: Tyndale House Publishers, 1971), pp. 47-49. It is always dangerous to add to God's Word; particularly is this true when considering so pivotal a question as the summary of the law.

neighbor precisely what one does for himself. Instead, His stress was (as it is also in the *first* commandment) upon the *intensity* or *devotedness* of love, the *amount* and *quality* of loving *concern* that one has for his neighbor, not upon its content. The words "as yourself" parallel exactly the phrase in the commandment to love God "with *all your heart*, etc." The stress in both falls not upon the *content* of the love (that is found in the Ten Commandments themselves), but rather upon the *fervency* and *genuineness* of it.

But beyond these considerations, the fact that Christ distinguishes but *"two* commandments" (vs. 40) is decisive. Had He intended to stress a third (particularly when one of the other two was dependent upon it)[4] He could not have done so by using the language that He employs in this passage. Such psychologizing of the passage erases its plain intent and seriously diverts its stress. This psychologizing usually leads to endless speculation about matters of "self concept," etc., that grows not out of the Scriptures, as has been alleged, but rather out of preconceived notions that have been read into the Scriptures.[5] It is incorrect and dangerous, therefore, to make a large point out of that about which Christ did not make a point at all (and, indeed, which He explicitly excluded by the limiting word *two*). This is particularly so when one is speaking about so basic a question as the summary of the very law of God.

I am prepared to move one step further and say that, except possibly as loose rhetoric, the notion that one must learn to love himself is biblically false. My objection is not simply that love of oneself as basic to love of another is not taught in Matthew 22:34-40; it is more fundamental. The concept of self-love espoused by the psychologizers of the Scriptures runs counter to the expressed principle that is repeated throughout the Bible in one form or another: that one's self-esteem and what he receives for himself is the by-product of that which he gives in love to another. "It is more blessed to give than to receive," "He who loses his life shall save it," and "Seek ye first the kingdom of God and his righteousness and all of these things shall be added to you" represent the

---

4. If obedience to the second commandment is dependent upon meeting the requirements of a third, the latter is more basic and is "greater than" the former. But see Mark 12:31b, "There is not another commandment greater than these."

5. See, for example, Harold Nelson, "Do You Love Yourself?," *Eternity*, February, 1970, p. 22, where the author erroneously equates love of self with Carl Rogers' notion of "positive self-regard."

consistent theme of the Scriptures. Self love is nowhere either commanded or commended.

The Scriptures presuppose that men already love themselves far too well. Indeed, it is that thought that is behind the words of Leviticus 19:18.[6] Men tend to disparage others and hold grudges against them (19:18). They do not do so toward themselves, but rather tend to give themselves the benefit of any doubt. And, as a matter of fact, they find it possible even to love themselves when they know (more intimately than they know it of any other) how unlovable they are. Love of oneself is a love that "covers a multitude of sins." What Jesus was saying, therefore, is that Christians must learn to have the same intense love for others that they have developed for themselves. They must learn to cover another's faults in love as they do their own. And similarly, they must learn to give others the benefit of the doubt as they give it to themselves.

The thought parallels Ephesians 5:28-29, where Paul urges husbands to *love* their wives *as* they love their own bodies. Paul does not intend to say that husbands must first *learn* how to love their own bodies before they can love their wives. Exactly not! He assumes (as does Christ) that men already love themselves. As a matter of fact, he baldly states that assumption: "No one ever hated his own flesh, but nourishes and cherishes it." The two passages belong to the same category of arguments. Christ says, in effect, do good for your neighbor (or wife) with the same devotion and zeal that you exhibit in doing good for yourself. Paul says love your wife as you love your own body.

What of One's Self-Concept?[7]

The man who loves God and his neighbors will not have a problem with his "self-concept" (what he thinks of himself). He will be a humbly

---

6. Note, for instance, the contrast to "hating" one's brother (vs. 17).

7. Discussions of the "self" sometimes boggle the minds of counselees. They become all wrapped up in questions like, "What is my *real* self? Is it the inner one or the outer one? Who am I? What is the real me?" Beldoch puts it this way: "It is as if they think there is another self just hiding there in the bushes of social facade; a quick psychic rake, and 'Voilá!' the timid one is revealed." *Intellectual Digest*, October, 1971, p. 88. Apart from the organic, chemically induced problems of bodily perception that may cause one to feel as if he is separated from his body, such talk is nonsense. It is not biblical. The *real* self is the one that you and God know that you are: "It is your own self that you see in your heart" (Proverbs 27:19b, T.E.V.).

grateful man who will praise God for the work of the Holy Spirit within him. He will be thankful that he has been chosen and enabled to exhibit the Spirit's fruit of love in his life.

Notions of the importance of a good self-concept, identity, and self-esteem are widespread today. Theorists, who misunderstand the biblical way of Christ, are perpetually insisting that one cannot love others until first he has come to love himself. His self-image must be adequate before he can reach out to others. Thus, much modern counseling focuses upon the building of a good self-image as the prerequisite for all else:

> A realistic self-evaluation and a full measure of self-acceptance and self-esteem are regarded as foundation stones of healthy adjustment.[8]

Thus Erikson interprets the Reformation in terms of Luther's "Identity Crisis." Personality tests have been designed

> to determine how the individual views himself—that is, the pattern of attitudes he entertains or assumes concerning his values, goals, abilities and personal worth.[9]

And everywhere one turns today, even in Christian circles,[10] he hears of the need for more "ego strength."

How should the Christian counselor view such matters? First, for a man to live peacefully, he *must* find the only identity in this life that has worth: that of the *child of God*. When he knows that he has been regenerated by the Spirit of God, is a member of the family of God, is forgiven of all iniquity, counted as righteous as Jesus Christ through identification with Him, and destined for an eternal inheritance in the presence of God, that is identity enough for any man! Such identity has been given freely to those who are in Christ (cf. I John 3:1: "See how great a love the Father has bestowed upon us, that we should be called the'children of God; and we are"). The Holy Spirit has been

---

8. Robert M. Goldenson, *The Encyclopedia of Human Behavior*, vol. II, *op. cit.*, p. 1180. A realistic self-evaluation is good but impossible for those who do not have the Bible for their yardstick. Self-acceptance is possible only in Christ, in whom God accepts forgiven sinners. Yet a realistic self-evaluation can lead only to non-acceptance of oneself and the determination that he must repent and be changed.

9. *Ibid.*

10. Cf. Frank Cheavens, *Creative Parenthood* (Waco: Word Books, 1971), p. 58.

given to secure that identity: "Do not grieve the Holy Spirit of God, by whom you are sealed for the day of redemption" (Ephesians 4:30). A seal secured and identified. For the Christian, the identity crisis is over. In Christ, who is his wisdom, his righteousness, his power, and his sanctification (cf. I Corinthians 1:30), he has all of the ego strength that he needs. Indeed, with Paul, he may declare: "I can do all things through Him who strengthens me" (Philippians 4:13).

But what of the "not yet" of the Christian's life that in sanctification needs to be conformed to the "already?" Two things may be said. First, in sanctification one does not seek more personal ego strength. As a branch, he receives all of his strength from the Vine. It is true that he grows stronger and more confident as he grows by grace; but his confidence is not in himself. The self-concept of the believer focuses not upon what he in himself is, but upon what in Christ he has become: "Consider yourselves to be dead to sin, but alive to God in Christ Jesus" (Romans 6:11). This is something totally foreign to the thinking of psychiatrists. They cannot imagine one finding his self-worth in Another. An analysis of this Christian concept can lead unbelieving theorists, who are blind to Christian realities (I Corinthians 2), only to the conclusion that the Christian doctrine of self-concept is unhealthy. The Christian considers himself entirely unworthy apart from Christ; indeed, worthy of *death* (as Romans 6:11 puts it). All of his worth and self-esteem resides in his relationship to Another. He is *entirely* dependent upon Christ for such worth. Unbelieving analysts could only conclude that this teaching (1) is unhealthy because it stresses worthlessness leading to repentance on the part of the sinner, and (2) is unhealthy because it makes the Christian a totally *dependent* person.[11] Christians know better, but would not attempt to explain the biblical rationale to those without eyes to see or ears to hear.

Secondly, the Christian does not seek self-worth as an end because he knows that such a search is hopeless. Instead, he knows that this, like all personal gain, is a *by-product*: "Seek first the kingdom of God and His righteousness and all these things will be added to you" (Matthew 6:33).[12] Invariably, in God's order of things, it is as the catechism

---

11. As such it is diametrically opposed to Carl Rogers' stress upon personal autonomy. Cf. Rogers, *On Becoming a Person* (Boston: Houghton-Mifflin, 1961), pp. 256-258, for comments concerning the self concept.

12. Cf. also Romans 8:32.

says: when we glorify God, we *enjoy* Him forever. The Scriptures put it this way: "It is more blessed to give than to receive" (Acts 20:35).

More directly speaking to the issue at hand, Christ declared: "He who has found his life shall lose it, and he who has lost his life for my sake shall find it" (Matthew 10:39), and "For whoever wishes to save his life shall lose it; but whoever loses his life for my sake shall find it" (Matthew 16:25). Clearly the one who seeks his identity in himself or in his relationship to other men will never find that which he seeks. It may be found only by the abandonment of one's own desires and a willingness to follow Christ. *Identity* is found in Him; in letting loose of all else for His sake. One finds a satisfying identity nowhere else.

Thus, love of self is not a biblically legitimate end. One is satisfied with himself[13] only when he is in the proper relationship with Christ, having a clear conscience before God and men.[14]

The Counselor's Approach

This chapter has laid an importance upon understanding that God does not require a man to love himself or possess a high self-concept before he can love God or his neighbor. Why? Is this merely an internecine battle among some theologians and some Christian psychologists? No. Although the issue bursts with theological significance, that is not primarily why space has been given to it here. Rather, the present discussion grows out of (1) a proper interpretation of the Scriptures and (2) the cruciality of the proper understanding of the matter for the Christian counselor.

Counselors who have psychologized the Scriptures on this point invariably find themselves getting nowhere. Such counselors seek to find ways to strengthen the egos of the counselees but fail to do so. Much time and energy is wasted on this futile endeavor. It is as fruitless as the pursuit of happiness, which one never finds when he seeks it. Exactly like happiness, self-satisfaction comes only as a by-product. By recognizing this biblical principle and acting in accordance with it, hours of counseling time can be saved. There is neither need nor biblical warrant for trying to alter self-images directly or for building up self-

---

13. Never *finally* so in this life since we never achieve perfection here.
14. Conscience is that evaluative ability that causes one's body to react in sensations that we interpret as satisfaction or dissatisfaction. It can trigger feelings of guilt, shame, embarrassment, sorrow, remorse, and their opposites.

esteem in the counselee. Nor is it possible. Instead, counselors may move *directly* to the next step, and deal with repentance.[15]

Repentance, as we have seen, always culminates in behavior change. Here is the crux of the issue. Those who try to build ego strength, attempt to give a new sense of identity or endeavor to sweeten the counselee's self-concept, operate on the assumption that he is able to *do* what God requires apart from such a change. And, in addition, they assume that the self-image can be changed without changing the self. Yet, they can offer neither biblical precept nor example for these assumptions. Surely, therefore, they will discover no scriptural directions for reaching these goals.

The Bible, contrary to the presuppositions of the psychologizers, insists upon the opposite procedure: one must obey God regardless of his self-image. He is not excused by pleading that he does not possess the ego strength to obey. *Only* by obedience can he achieve any sort of inner satisfaction at all. If one says that he "feels" inadequate, it is probably because he is! He does not need to be convinced that he isn't in order to do adequate things; he must begin to do them if he wishes to feel adequate.[16]

Rather than ego strength leading to righteous behavior, righteous behavior is the sole source from which one may derive a satisfying self-concept. But since righteous behavior always involves seeking *first* the kingdom of God and His righteousness (never *in order to* get things added at the end), the danger of the latent hedonism wrapped up in the contrary view is avoided.

Once righteous behavior leads to satisfaction, the latter does *encourage* the counselee to further obedience. But the place to break in is at the point of obedience. Not only is this approach to the problem scriptural,[17] but one can see the rationale behind it, since it is vain merely to *tell* a counselee that he must bolster his self-image when you

---

15. "Acceptance" is the opposite of repentance. We are accepted and accept other believers only *in Christ* (Romans 12–14).

16. Remember, counselees do not really "feel" inadequate. They may *feel* sad, depressed, unhappy, guilty, ashamed, etc., but when they say they feel inadequate, they mean that they have *judged* themselves to *be* inadequate. It is unwise to minimize such negative self-judgments. Counselors always should think through the implications of phrases: e.g., "I'm not confident" often means, "I am one in whom confidence cannot be put." "I have a headache" often means, "A headache has me" (but sometimes a counselee may actually *have* it, for his own ends!).

17. Cf. *Competent to Counsel*, pp. 93 ff.

offer him *no concrete reasons or means* for doing so. On the other hand, the obedient Christian has a clear conscience based upon righteous living from which the sense of satisfaction may arise. It is foolish (not to speak of the discouragement that it fosters) to urge counselees to work directly on the development of a different self-image. They cannot do so success-fully apart from becoming a different self. One's concept of himself emerges from what he is. In Christ there is always strength to obey; where does one acquire the power (or right) to change his self-image apart from obedience?

"But what of the child who has been berated time and again by his parents; who has been told in a hundred ways that he is worthless; who is constantly criticized and condemned?" The principle does not change but remains the same. If he believes what he is told, then that is what he is—a weak person dependent upon others for self-evaluation. And, that is one way in which the counselor must help him to change. So long as he does not, he *rightly* views himself as a weak person who does not know how to respond properly to the abuses of others. Granted that either this or rebellion is the most likely response of a sinful child to such treatment; grant even that it will occur 100 percent of the time. That still neither excuses nor helps him as a child or as the blame-shifting adult that (unless he is changed) he will become. Somewhere in the course of his life he must be confronted about his wrong responses, counseled about God's way of handling abuse, and helped to do so. He cannot go through life successfully by blaming others for his poor behavior.

The earlier the child can be confronted, the better—for all con-cerned. That is why the greatest sympathy and the strongest help that a counselor (whether he be a Christian school teacher, a youth worker, a pastor, etc.) can give to a child is to focus not upon what others have done or are doing to him (probably nothing immediate can be done about that), but upon what God expects him to do in response.[18] There-in lies the hope for change that at once will honor God and (as a by-product) change his self-concept.

What Is Love, After All?

The Hollywood and *Playboy* views of love, marriage, and non-marriage permeate our society. These philosophies quickly get down

---

18. Passages in Romans 12 and I Peter are especially helpful for such counsel.

into homes in a thousand ways. Hollywood, ever since its beginning, has taught a pagan philosophy of love. The philosophy is that love *happens.* Love is not something to work at; it just happens. Love comes full blown from the head of Aphrodite. It's the kind of thing that just is or isn't. It isn't something that you develop, it isn't something that grows, it isn't something that you work hard to achieve, it isn't a thinking thing, and it certainly isn't something that you can *will.* It is something that happens. And when it happens, it happens in such a way that you know that it has happened! It bowls you over; you hear music, see wonderful lights, or have a near psychedelic experience. Such love at first seems wonderful, but what happens when the happening no longer happens? What happens when the happening is over? What happens when the sounds grow cacophonous and the colors turn to gray? What happens when feeling dies, the embers grow cold, and the lights go out? What happens to a Hollywood-type marriage based on feeling when the parties begin to experience the fluctuating character of feeling? What happens when one or the other begins to have growing *feelings* for someone else? When something begins to happen with the secretary down at work, when something begins to happen with the man next door; is that the signal for a change? If love is happening, what else should you expect when the happenings change? In the *Playboy* philosophy, love is getting; it means getting what one can out of another person, using the other person as an object for love. It means grasping and holding and satisfying oneself by using another.[19] And when he is through with that person, well fine, she's been used . . . up. That's it. When there is no more nectar in the flower, the bee must flit to the next, and the next, and then to the one after that. Hollywood has taught this, too, not only by film but also by the way in which so many of the stars themselves have been notorious flower flitters. If mom is to dress like the stars, style her hair like the stars, and make up her face like the stars, why shouldn't she also hitch her marriage to a star?

Madison Avenue similarly pressures us in other ways. Advertising has its own code of ethics that underlies all of its marketing practices. You may read about it in a book by Ernest Dichter, *The Strategy of*

---

19. *Playboy* emphasizes sex, of course; but the basic philosophy extends into all human relationships. The life of self and desire orientation is based upon the sinful proposition that it is more blessed to receive than to give.

Desire.[20] Much advertising is rooted in the philosophy of hedonism. Motivational research people, like Dichter, have been saying that we ought to become out-and-out hedonists. Dichter thinks that it would be desirable to accept this philosophy candidly, and openly pursue pleasure as the goal of life. But he realizes that hedonism is still a rather bitter pill for many people to swallow openly, so he disguises it *thinly*; just enough to help "justify" the pursuit of pleasure. Then he and his ilk unstintingly pour hedonistic values into the ears, the eyes, the nostrils, and through every other gate. It inundates us in magazines, on billboards, over the television, and in newspapers. Everywhere one turns, Madison Avenue is at him again and again with this hedonistic view of life.

Corresponding to the two basic philosophies of life, then, hedonism and biblical theism, are two views of love. Everyone, of course, is *for* love. The hippies are for love, the situation ethicists are for love, the followers of Hari Krishna are for love, Christians are for love. But it is true of love, as it is of heaven, that "everybody talks about it ain't got it."

What, then, is biblical love?

Paul is clear about what it is. Love is giving—giving of oneself to another. It is not getting, as the world says today. It is not feeling and desire; it is not something over which one has no control. It is something that one does for another. No one loves in the abstract. Love is an attitude that issues forth in something that actually, tangibly happens. Notice Christ loved the church and *gave Himself* for her (Ephesians 5:25). John 3:16 says, "God so loved the world that he *gave* his only begotten Son." In Galatians 2:20 we read, "He loved me and *gave* himself for me." "If your enemy hungers, *give* him something to eat. If your enemy thirsts, *give* him something to drink. *Do good* to those who despitefully use you." Love is not first a feeling, but rather a giving of oneself to another. Feelings follow.

Hollywood has distorted love, the television screen distorts it, musical records distort it. Everywhere today, love is considered a happening. It

---

20. Ernest Dichter, *The Strategy of Desire* (Garden City: Doubleday, 1960). Note how Dichter's view fits the desire-oriented life. He advocates a sales approach suited to appeal to sinful persons whom he recognizes (rightly) are motivated by desire and feeling. He wants at length to legitimize hedonism; until that time he will provide a thin coat of rationalization with which to cover it. Dichter's sales approach is of a piece with Satan's approach to Eve in the Garden.

just happens. "I couldn't help it," said the young man who had gotten himself and his girl into trouble in the back seat of the automobile. "I couldn't help it." He is *feeling* oriented, but not *love* oriented. He is *desire* motivated, but not *love* motivated. True love is always under control. It is commanded. Christ commands, "Love your enemies." You can't sit around whomping up a good feeling for your enemies. It doesn't come that way. But if you *give* an enemy something to eat or *give* him something to drink, soon something begins to happen to your feelings. When you invest yourself in another, you begin to feel differently toward him. Where your treasure is, there will your heart be also. Feelings must be based upon something solid. The feelings that develop out of giving are genuine and lasting. But feelings as the base of love are fickle. When such spurious love happens, what happens when the happening stops happening? Feelings are not dependable; they are up one day, down the next. Feelings are not always under control, but true love is. The Bible *commands*, "Love the Lord your God with all your heart, mind, body, soul, and strength; love your neighbor as yourself; and love your enemies."

Where there is no love in a home, it is the husband's fault. Principally the responsibility for love in the home falls not on the wife (she should show love, of course), but on the husband. The husband must love his wife *as Jesus Christ loves* His church. Listen to I John 4:19: "We love" (that is, *the church*; remember, the wife reflects the church); "We love [the church loves] because he [Jesus Christ] first loved us." That is how love for Christ began. It was not because the church was so loving and lovable that Jesus just couldn't help but love her; but rather, while we were enemies, while we were sinners, while we were rebellious, vile, and loathsome creatures in His sight, Jesus first loved us—and gave His life for us! He looked on us with love in spite of it all, and determined to set His love on us. He elected us in love for us, apart from anything in us that would commend us to Him.

If love has grown cold in a family, the counselor should encourage the husband to do something about it. He must urge him to emulate the love of Jesus Christ for His church, stressing his responsibility to initiate love. He must not allow him to plead, "I can't love her because she doesn't love me." Instead, he might respond, "Jesus loved us when we had no love for Him. You are the head of your home. If there is little or no love in that home, it is your fault. God holds you responsible to introduce love. At least your love can be shown. You must begin by *giving*. You must give your time, your interest, your money, yourself. Let's plan now to do something specific (concrete) for your wife each day this week. It is possible that your wife will fail to return your love, no matter how much you give. But, regardless, there can be love in that home. Your love for her can permeate all. If your home is cold and sterile, you have the prime responsibility to change the situation. The wife, in Ephesians 5, is not told to love her husband; she is told to submit. The husband is told to love his wife. You have a difficult job. But to honor and reflect Christ's love you must not fail."

The fact that the husband is responsible for maintaining love in the home doesn't excuse the wife from loving. If her husband doesn't love her, counselors must say, "Nevertheless you must show love for him."

Traditionally, counselors have found I Corinthians 13 the clearest explication of what the responsible relationship of one to another called love is like. Here are particularizations of love that are invaluable to all counseling. Every counselor should familiarize himself fully with the varied possible applications of each function of love that Paul noted. He should know how to point out to a jealous husband (or wife) that love demands change. Instead, he must learn how to teach the one partner to give to the other the benefit of all doubts. To those who lose their tempers and are easily angered, there are several important words in verses 4, 5, 7. Selfishness is excluded (vs. 5), etc.

The great difference between the Old and New Testament periods with respect to love is that in Christ there has been a living, breathing, sinless, perfect example of what the love that God requires means. That is why John says that God's old commandment to love is new (cf. I John 2:7 with John 13:34). He has *demonstrated* His love in Jesus Christ and called upon His disciples to love as He did (see also Philippians 2; Ephesians 4:32; 5:25).

Love, therefore, may be *commanded* (Luke 6:27 ff.; Ephesians 5:25) and *taught* (Titus 2:3-4). Love does not come naturally, it must be learned.[21] But since it is the fruit of the Spirit, Christians may be sure that it will take the work of God's Spirit in their lives to learn to love. The Spirit works through prayerful obedience to the Scriptures.

---

21. Love is concrete, not abstract. It means ministering to others as Christ did when He washed the disciples' feet. It means giving a cup of cold water to an enemy if he thirsts. Because it is concrete, love can be learned.

Chapter Sixteen

SUPPORT, SYMPATHY, AND EMPATHY

Modern Ideas

Akin to modern concepts of love are the equally untenable ideas about support, empathy, and sympathy held by many counselors. The notion that pastoral counseling (particularly in dealing with persons having any serious problems) ought to be supportive is widely held.[1] Yet, this view as it is popularly expounded is antithetical to all that the Bible says about change. The word "support" as used by counselors and psychiatrists fails to express a biblical concept. Giving comfort, encouragement, instruction, and all of the specific things that a pastoral counselor should do in time of grief, for example, are much more than mere support—just standing by.[2] Struggling over the problem itself and helping the counselee to come to grips with it in biblical terms and helping him to solve it God's way is what is needed rather than support. Even a casual study of the Bible should reveal this fact.

Nevertheless, the pastoral role is frequently conceived of as primarily supportive. Biblically speaking, a pastor's counseling activities extend far beyond mere support. Support is not enough. Moreover, it is necessary to take issue with the modern psychological *concept* of support itself. If by support one means encouragement to continue in following the Word of God, consolation, and the like, there can be no difficulty with the idea; there is much in the Scriptures to stimulate a pastor to

---

1. For instance, Gary Collins writes: "The church leader, especially the pastor, often finds himself giving support and encouragement in times of need." People that he calls "psychological cripples," such as alcoholics, are supposed to be in special need of support. Gary Collins, *Effective Counseling* (Carol Stream: Creation House, 1972), p. 55. Quentin Hyder, in his book, *The Christian's Handbook of Psychiatry, op. cit.*, sees support as a temporarily "valuable technique." Fortunately he speaks of it with qualification and suggests that it has limited goals.
2. Cf. "Grief As a Counseling Opportunity," *The Big Umbrella, op. cit.*, pp. 63-94.

engage in such activities.[3] But that is not what modern writers have in mind when they use the term. Instead, they think of support as a passive, non-active *presence* of the counselor, who by his presence accepts and shows empathy.[4] For instance, Carroll Wise wrote:

The frequent question of pastors, what do you say to persons in such-and-such a situation?, should be changed to, what can I be to persons in such a situation?[5]

Elsewhere Wise explained:

By support we do not mean an attempt to get at her feelings or to interpret her feelings. Rather, he should let her talk as she wishes.

He should listen without trying to reflect feelings or interpret them. in this listening he can give her an assurance of his interest and his encouragement without committing himself as to whether or not he believes her ideas in regard to her husband are true.[6]

Earl H. Furgeson put it this way:

What this boy clearly needs is pastoral support and psychiatric care. . . . The young man needs the support of his pastor before, during and after treatment; but treatment, in this case belongs to the psychiatrist.[7]

The article on support in *The Encyclopedia of Human Behavior* de-

---

3. Yet, "support," even in this non-technical sense, is neither passive nor non-directive. Encouragement or comfort may involve instruction, challenge, and even admonition (cf. I Thessalonians 4:13, 18; Hebrews 10:24, 25; 12:12, 13). A counselor thus may *support* a counselee who is actively engaged in solving his problems God's way, but he may not support either failure to do so in the past or in the present. God's "support" is active: "The Lord supports all those who fall, *and lifts up* all those bowed down" (Psalm 145:14, Berkeley).

4. Daniel Day Williams says that "acceptance is not a passive taking in of another's problems, but a deliberate and constructive act of self-identification." *The Minister and the Care of Souls* (New York: Harper and Brothers, Pub., 1961), p. 77. For further comments on *acceptance* cf. *Competent to Counsel*, pp. 83 ff. Akin to the idea of acceptance is the concept of support as "consensual validation." This means agreement of others (counselor, members of a therapy group, etc.) with the counselee in support of a viewpoint that has been condemned by a superior, society, etc. Cf. Michael F. Hastings, "Pastoral Counseling for Ego-support," *Medical Bulletin of the U. S. Army, Europe*, vol. 28, no. 10, October, 1971, pp. 287, 288. Interestingly, this study shows the counselee's identification of support with acceptance or consensus.

5. Carroll A. Wise, *The Meaning of Pastoral Care* (New York: Harper and Row, 1966), p. 76.

6. Carroll A. Wise, Cryer, and Vayhinger, *Casebook in Pastoral Counseling* New York: Abingdon Press, 1962), p. 195.

7. *Ibid.*, pp. 198, 199.

fines support as "treatment aimed at *reinforcing existing defenses* and alleviating distress through techniques that operate on a conscious level [emphasis mine]."[8] Wise stresses the counselor's passiveness, Furgeson his helplessness, and the *Encyclopedia* article his intended (or implicit) approval of the present response patterns of the counselee.

Not a Biblical Concept

The Bible knows nothing of support as conceived by such modern writers. It is safe to say that such support is an unbiblical concept and, therefore, also proper to conclude that the activity (so defined) either fails to lend genuine support to counselees or ends up supporting sinful attitudes and activities. Even minimal reflection should indicate how far the psychiatric idea strays from the scriptural ideal.

First, Christian counselors must never support sinful behavior.[9] If a counselee has failed to handle a problem God's way, what he needs is not support for his faulty responses (or non-responses), but rather nouthetic confrontation. In nouthetic confrontation the counselor points out the biblical principles and through kindly, concerned conference seeks to bring the counselee to repentance, faith, and hope. It aims at *change*. Whenever the Spirit so blesses His Word, the counselee may then not only abandon his faulty and counter-productive methods of handling life's problems, but also turn to God's solutions instead. Whatever else a counselor does, at all costs he must avoid every suggestion that he is lending support to ways of handling life that do not originate with God. He simply may not by support "reinforce existing defenses," if these are contrary to scriptural injunctions.

Secondly, support is harmful in that it not only acknowledges but also approves of the failure of the counselee to handle his problems. Offering support suggests that there are no better answers to the counselee's problems than those which he himself has discovered even though they

---

8. Robert M. Goldenson, *The Encyclopedia of Human Behavior*, vol. II (Garden City: Doubleday and Company, 1970), p. 1281. Here, support again is viewed as agreement (consensus or acceptance) since its effect is reinforcement of an existing response pattern.

9. Contrary to some protestations, psychotherapists do define acceptance in ways that indicate approval of sinful behavior. Cf. the following: "His attitude is respectful, accepting, nonevaluative, noncondemning, noncriticizing. . . . Hans H. Strupp, *Psychotherapy: Clinical, Research & Theoretical Issues* (New York: Jason Aronson, Inc., 1973), p. 38.

may be manifestly unsuccessful. Such a realization probably was what led him to seek help. But, in short, support is not help. No help is extended. Indeed, support is offered *in the place of* help. It is an alternative to help. Because this is so, the Christian must recognize that support offered instead of *direction* from the Word of God represents Christ as a helpless Savior who has no better solutions than the counselee to life's problems.

Thirdly, there is no evidence in the Scriptures that a minister of the Word should stand by passively "being" but neither *doing* nor *saying*. Can you picture a passive Savior or a passive Apostle Paul?

A Christian school teacher had been giving support (as she said) to Violet, a teen-age girl in one of her classes who (allegedly) was suffering from the difficulties of a bad home situation. This girl often came to school depressed and deeply resentful. The teacher frequently allowed her to unload and get it off her chest. The teacher thought standing by as a friend would help. But one obvious difficulty with this approach is that it suggests that the student's sinful behavioral responses to bad treatment at home were acceptable. The support encouraged, participated in, and thus strongly condoned rather than challenging her sin. The teacher unwittingly encouraged as she supported self-pity and resentment in the student. Support, as Hastings observes, leads to "consensual validation" (i.e., agreement with the views and/or behavior of the counselee). This is what the *Encyclopedia* called reinforcing existing defenses.

The teacher also failed to see that she was destroying her student's hope. Although meaning well, the sympathy she expressed in the absence of all advice, rebuke, or direction, communicated but one thing to the pupil: "You are doing the best that you can in a bad situation, and I have no better course of action to suggest." Christ, the teacher unwittingly taught her, is unable to help you; you must continue to grow discouraged and resentful. This behavior by the teacher did not really support the child in any positive way; rather it tended to destroy her hope. As a matter of fact, what Violet needed most was to be shown her own sin in responding with despair and bitterness. Such a challenge to (rather than support of) the counselee's faulty behavior brings hope —it suggests the possibility of and demands a *change* in the situation and indicates that God is not helpless. Perhaps she could not alter the behavior of others in the home, but Violet herself could change *radically*.

Changes in Violet also inevitably would lead to *some* changes in the home. Repentance would lead Violet to learn and develop new Christian responses to wrongdoing. Any lesser help is unchristian.

Support Is Harmful

Support, as it is conceived by those who do not understand the biblical approach, harms rather than helps because it is not biblical. Support suggests hopelessness; it indicates to counselees that the counselor is buffaloed by the problem; the message communicated is: "I know there is no answer to your need, but I love you and will try to suffer through it with you." But support, so understood, is impossible for a counselor who believes God's promises. Take, for instance, I Corinthians 10:13:[10]

> No test has overtaken you but such as is common to man. God is faithful who will not allow you to be tested beyond that which you are able to bear, but (together with the test) will make a way of escape in order that you may be able to bear it.

Passages mentioned earlier, such as II Timothy 3:17:

> . . . that the man of God may be adequate, fully equipped for every good work,

And II Peter 1:3:

> His divine power has granted to us everything pertaining to life and godliness,

plainly indicate that God never leaves the Christian without access to adequate resources. God, by His Word and Spirit, has provided help sufficient to enable the believer both to "will and to do" what must be done in every circumstance of life. If, therefore, a counselee is *not* performing as God requires, the blame for his failure lies on his own shoulders. He cannot blame God or the circumstances. Support, therefore, is an unbiblical denial of the power and promises of God.

What of Sympathy and Empathy?

But what of sympathy and empathy? Does not support show em-

---

10. For further discussion of this verse, see *Christ and Your Problems, op. cit.*

pathy? Not really. One cannot begin to empathize with another until he comes to grips with the other person's problem. It is one thing to stand by (support) as another suffers and struggles, assuring him that you care; it is quite another to roll up your sleeves and pitch in alongside of him. You may best show empathy for a motorist with a stalled engine by giving him a push, not by uttering assuring words that you "understand" or "feel" his plight.[11] Indeed, when you do something concrete to help him, you do not have to assure him; he knows that you care. In counseling the same is true. Love in the Scriptures, we have seen, is always active, never passive.[12] Attestations that "I care" are unnecessary when the counselee sees his counselor struggling to analyze the circumstances by helping him to find the scriptural solutions to his problems. It is questionable whether one who passively stands by to support ever becomes more than that—a bystander—despite his *too* frequent and *too* loud protestations to the contrary. The words of James seem to be not altogether inappropriate:

> If a brother or sister is without clothing and in need of daily food, and one of you *says* to them "Go in peace, be warmed and filled," and yet you do not *give* them what is necessary for their body, what use is that?[13] [emphases mine].

As in other areas of life, so too in counseling, "faith without works is dead." Support as defined and practiced by many counselors is dead. And unfortunately, as a result, what it so often says to counselees is that the counselor's God is dead.

---

11. Empathy comes *only* from entering into the problem so that it becomes one's own: "Your joy is your own; your bitterness is your own. No one can share them with you" (Proverbs 14:10, T.E.V.). It is properly expressed, therefore, in helpful action and communicated through active involvement. It may not be sought (and found) directly as an end in itself, but rather must be viewed as a by-product. In Hans Knight's article, "A New Hospital Focus: Helping to Ease the Burden of the Dying," the Rev. Lynwood Swanson is quoted as saying, "I felt what you said. . . . I shared it with you." Knight says, "He didn't talk about religion and the mercy of God. If he ever prayed, the time wasn't now." *The Bulletin*, April 1, 1973, pp. 1, 10. The only real way to help a dying man is to share the gospel of Christ!

12. Cf., for example, passages previously mentioned: "God so loved the world that he *gave* . . ." (John 3:16); "He loved me and *gave* himself for me" (Galatians 2:20); "Christ . . . loved the church and *gave* Himself up for her" (Ephesians 5:25); "If your enemy . . . is thirsty, *give* him a drink" (Romans 15:20).

13. James 2:15, 16.

The story of the good Samaritan (Luke 10) puts it plainly. The Samaritan not only "felt compassion" (vs. 33) over the man who fell among thieves, but acted in accordance with that compassion (vss. 34, 35). Jesus made the point: "Which of these three do you think *proved* to be a neighbor?" (vs. 36). The answer could only be: "The one who *showed* mercy to him" (vs. 37).

The biblical response to problems is change; no lesser and insipid goals are acceptable. To that matter we must, therefore, turn.

Chapter Seventeen

THE MOTIVATION FOR CHANGE

Motivation is so often lacking in counselees. Loss of hope, lack of patience, and the sheer difficulty of making changes leads to such a lack. Sinful failures of all sorts contribute to the problem. The Christian counselor, therefore, in order to effect change, must become familiar with biblical concepts of motivation.

Be What You Are

Basic to the New Testament concept of motivation is the task of becoming what you are. In a real sense we are not merely human *beings*, but also human *becomings*. The Christian life is not static; it is a life of change. The Christian is a pilgrim and a stranger who is on the move. He is travelling to the heavenly city. He has not yet arrived. Change is of the essence to his sanctification, which is the process of putting off sinful ways of life and putting on godly ones. But such change is difficult; it is not easy to "say no to self" (putting off) and "yes" to Jesus (putting on).[1] This denial of self (lit. "saying no to" one's own ways that one may "follow" Christ's) is described as "taking up the cross." The cross was an instrument of death. Sanctification requires the daily crucifixion of one's own desires. That is hard. Paul described this struggle for growth in Romans 7:14-25. While victories in the struggle are possible through Christ (vs. 25), they do not come easily or apart from daily battles involving just such self-sacrifice.

All change is hard, and there must be powerful motivation to achieve it. Since change comes only gradually and through patient endurance, there must be hope.[2] To what source of motivation may the counselor

1. Matthew 16:24.
2. In the Scriptures *hope* always means confident expectation; never a "hope-so" attitude. Strupp writes: "What makes the therapist's task so enormously difficult is the patient's tenacious unconscious opposition to unlearning inappropriate patterns and learning new, less conflictual ones. The fundamental problem . . . is the search for optimal procedures to effect lasting modifications of the patient's personality structure." *Op cit.*, p. 36. The Christian hope is that in Christ's Word,

turn to give the counselee hope and to move him to take and maintain biblical action?

Ultimately, the counselee must be pointed to Christ. Because of Christ and His "mercies," every believer may be urged to holy living (cf. Romans 12:1). But, more specifically, is there any way in which those redemptive mercies particularly may be pressed home to a Christian counselee?

The answer to this question is found in Ephesians 4:1 ff. and in the parallel passage in Colossians. Following a remarkable three-chapter discussion of Christ's mercies to His own in planning and providing redemption for them, Paul makes the transition to the second half of the epistle in which he urged believers to Christian living with these words:

I, therefore, the prisoner of the Lord, entreat you to walk in a manner worthy of the calling with which you have been called.

Paul's argument is clear. Because of his high calling in Christ, the believer must live differently. He must live a life consistent with that to which he has been called, and that life is a life that reflects Christ's life. In Colossians 3:8-12, Paul puts it this way: since in Christ (by virtue of your representative union with Him in which he perfectly fulfilled all of God's law for you) you have already "put aside" your old way of life and have "put on" a new one pleasing to God, you must now in actual fact begin to do so as well. That is to say, you must become (in your day-by-day living) what you are (in Christ).[3]

The high calling of the Christian, conferred upon him in Christ by which he is to reckon himself dead to sin but alive to God,[4] is itself a powerful motivation to holy living. Putting on the uniform is itself a potent factor that the Holy Spirit uses to bring about change. Consider the following analogy: when a minister is ordained and the weight of the office of a bishop[5] is laid upon him, that fact in itself acts powerfully to

---

those "optimal procedures" may be found. For those who have trusted and followed that Word, the "search" is over.

3. Cf. vss. 8-10, "put aside . . . since you laid aside."

4. Romans 6:11.

5. *Episcopos*: "overseer." The words *bishop* and *elder* are used in the Scriptures to refer to the same man (cf. Acts 20:17, 28, the "elders" are called *episcopoi*, which means, "bishops" or "overseers"; Titus 1:5, 7, the words "elder" and "bishop" again are used interchangeably). Elder ("mature") speaks of the pastor's *qualifications*; bishop ("overseer") speaks of his *work*.

alter his life. It is *then* that he first begins to live like a minister. The fact of his position and the burden of his responsibilities continually influence his living from day to day. Similarly, the Scriptures urge the believer to *be* what God has *declared* him to be in Christ.

Implications for Counseling

Counselors, like the Apostle Paul, must hold before counselees both the possibilities and the challenges of the Christian life: "Even so consider yourselves to be dead to sin, but alive to God in Christ Jesus" (Romans 6:11). When one evaluates himself as he is evaluated by God (considers himself dead to sin and alive to God), both hope and a sense of the potential for dramatic change should well up within. He sees that he is no longer enslaved to sin. In Christ he has died to that old life of slavery and risen to a new life that he may live for God (Romans 6:9, 10). Part of the counselor's task is to help Christian counselees who are discouraged and defeated to *see who they are*. They must help counselees to look upon themselves as God sees them: now perfect and risen to newness of life in Christ. They must bring to bear upon them the divine logic which argues:

> We have been buried with Him through baptism into death, in order that as Christ was raised from the dead through the glory of the Father, so too we might walk in newness of life" (Romans 6:4).

The counselor will find it necessary not only to reassure Christians that the possibility of change is great, but also from time to time he may find it necessary to challenge the reality of the faith of a counselee who steadfastly denies such a possibility. Genuine Christians at length will recognize the possibilities for radical change in Christ; spurious Christians cannot.

Paul's exhortations to be what you are have meaning and potential only to those who already are what they may be. Only those who legitimately can "consider" themselves dead to sin, alive to God, risen with Christ and "in Christ" know what they must become. Moreover, only such persons, who by virtue of their relationship to the living Christ (who in the person of the Holy Spirit indwells them), have the power to become what they are. That is why evangelism is a prerequisite to the counseling of unbelievers.

It is wrong to think of the present imperfect existence as the more real situation and the perfect record that we have in Christ merely as the ideal toward which we must grow. Perfection (if either) is more real for the Christian than imperfection, since the ultimate proper and eternal state of every Christian will be a state of perfection. There can be no uncertainty about this since the eternal sinlessness of every believer has been secured by the work of God in Christ and the Spirit. The present imperfections are unnatural and temporary. They are, therefore, in this sense less real than the eternal perfection obtained in Christ since, unlike that perfection, inevitably they will pass away. That which is imperfect and sinful, indeed, already is passing away;[6] ultimately it must give way completely to that which is perfect.

To deny that the eternal is less real is not to deny the reality of the present situation; both are real for the Christian, but *in this life* he lives a unique sort of life—a life lived in light of the certainty of the future reality which has been secured for him by His Lord. The problem in counseling is to bring Christian counselees to full recognition of the glorious reality of the eternal inheritance. The present, as a result, will be strongly conditioned by the future. This great hope and assurance provides a foundational motivation to make the present approximate the reality of the future.

Reward/Punishment

The mercies of God have been manifested in the high calling of the Christian who bears the name of Christ and who by virtue of his union with Christ has become a risen son of the living God. That should stand as high motivation in counseling. All counselors should explore and utilize the many implications of the fact. But in His loving mercy the Father also has determined to motivate His children by means of rewards and punishments.

Consider the familiar area of child discipline as an example.[7] It is well known that in the book of Proverbs God commands the use of the "rod." Without question this is the most humane form of punishment. Administered quickly, in close proximity to the offense, corporal punishment allows the parent and child to become reconciled immediately thereafter. Punishments that linger on ("You may not ride your bike for a week") are more like torture; they go on and on. The

---

6. I Corinthians 7:21b.
7. For further comments in detail, cf. "Discipline With Dignity," *Christian Living in the Home, op. cit.*

child is stretched on a rack. He is "in the dog house"; the parents must remain "on the outs" with him. The rod gets it over with rapidly and efficiently and provides for ready reconciliation.[8]

On the other hand, Christian parents have been too slow to recognize the importance of the reward (or incentive). This should not have been true of Christians. God Himself, in instituting the children's commandment ("Honor your father and your mother"), appended to it the promise of a reward: "that your days may be long upon the land which the Lord your God gives you." While it is true that the promise also implies a threat ("Don't, and you may not live long"), nevertheless the statement is to be regarded primarily from its positive side. This is clear from Paul's observation in Ephesians 6:2, where he calls attention to the fact that this is "the first commandment with a *promise*."

Since God teaches by His own example that children should be motivated not by punishment alone, but also by hope of reward, Christian parents should take up the clue.

Some parents, who seem to think that they know more than God, immediately object to any use of reward as a motivating factor. "Bribery!" they call it. The Christian counselor must point out to them that they *may* be right about the charge in *some* instances. Rewards may be used wrongly to reward a child for doing that which he is able and ought to do already and which in no way indicates achievement. Rewards, *as bribes*, always must be rejected. But rewards *as incentives*, rewards as goals to reach in attaining desired ends, are part and parcel of every society and actually inhere in the very fabric of life.[9] Rewards come in hundreds of forms: the man who perseveres through perspiration in mowing the grass at length has the satisfaction (reward) of view-

---

8. God chastises His people (Hebrews 12:4-11). While the rod may be viewed as basic, it is important not to *confine* discipline to the use of the rod. Ordinarily *both* the rod and rebuke are to be used (Proverbs 29:15; cf. also Ephesians 6:4, where discipline and nouthetic confrontation also are used jointly). Cf. Proverbs 17:10 for an instance of discipline by rebuke *over against* the use of the rod: "An intelligent man learns more from one rebuke than a fool learns from being beaten a hundred times" (T.E.V.). Cf. also Isaiah 66:4: "So I will choose their punishments and I will bring on them what they dread."

9. A woman who always was late getting ready to go anywhere, and who wanted to change, practiced getting dressed on time for three successive nights. The fourth night in a row her husband promised to take her out for the evening. Both were pleased that they went out exactly four nights after the counseling session! This short-term incentive helped her to realize the important goal of responsible living.

ing a neatly trimmed lawn; the child who does his homework faithfully has not only the immediate rewards that come from the teacher's approval each day, but also the ultimate pleasures that accrue to those who pass a course with good grades. Rewards, tangible and intangible, are a part of the structure of life. God rewards (Hebrews 11:6[10]); even the faithful preaching of the gospel is rewarded (I Corinthians 3:8, 14). Just because rewards may be abused is no reason for *rejecting* their use. The concept of reward is biblical.[11]

How may one distinguish between the proper use and the abuse of reward? One good rule of thumb for counselors to share with dubious counselees is the rewards should be given for genuine *achievement*, not for doing what one already has learned to do. As an example of reward that motivates to achievement consider the following:

"Bill, I will buy you the new trumpet that you want when you have demonstrated that you have learned to practice the used one regularly without having to be reminded and your teacher tells me that you are making steady progress."

As an example of the abuse of reward, consider this:

"Mary, if you and Tom get home on time from your next five dates, I'll buy you the dress you wanted."[12]

It is important for the counselor to note the difference between the biblical view of reward/punishment in motivation and the Skinnerian (or behavioristic) view. With Skinnerians, rewards and aversive controls (punishments) are used as environmental manipulations to *train* a child (or adult) in the way that one trains a dog or a rat. There is no essential difference in method or purpose. There is, first, no place

---

10. Lit., "God is a reward-giver" (*misthapodotes*). If God is a rewarder, so may we be.

11. The word "reward" occurs 101 times (in the A.V.). Cf. such passages as: Romans 14:12; I Corinthians 3:14; 9:16-27; II Corinthians 5:10; Philippians 4:1; I Thessalonians 2:14; II Timothy 4:8; James 1:12; I Peter 5:4; Revelation 2:10; 3:11. Note also how a passage like Hebrews 13 stresses the interplay of both reward/punishment as motivation factors (cf. vss. 2, 3, 4, 5, 11, 14, 16, 17, 18, 22). Cf. the great significance of reward in Hebrews 12:2, where the writer explains that "For the joy set before Him [Jesus] endured the cross" (the best authorities agree that *anti* should be translated "for" rather than "instead of").

12. The reward/punishment dynamic may be built into doing daily chores. At the Rehobeth Mission Christian Boarding School in New Mexico, the girls work in the laundry one hour per day (Monday through Friday). What is not done by Friday accumulates and then has to be done on Saturday, when the girls otherwise would be free to play. There is seldom anything but play on Saturday.

for personal confrontation with the Word of God; secondly, no opportunity either for persuasion from that Word or encouragement to rely upon the power of the Holy Spirit to effect the needed changes; thirdly, there is no scale of value by which to weigh or measure relative rewards/punishments on an ultimate basis, etc. Taking the last point, one finds that the difference between behavioristic manipulation which is based on short-term rewards and punishments and the Christian concept is as great as day and night. Christians view the whole in the light of the *eternal* reward/punishment situation as it has been revealed in the Scriptures. The Christian must take a Hebrews 11 viewpoint on the present life. Rewards/punishments today, therefore, are conditioned and highly colored by the eternal reward/punishment structure.

Other Means of Motivation

Moreover, reward/punishment should not be the *only* (perhaps not even the primary) motivational factor in one's life. As we have noted already, the "mercies of Christ" exhibited in redemption and the high calling of the believer stand side by side with rewards and punishments as motivating factors. Others, presently, may be mentioned. The Christian counselor, therefore, is not *limited* in his motivational repertoire, as is the behaviorist.

In addition to the three motivational factors above, consider Peter's Words:

1. "Submit yourselves for the Lord's sake . . ." (I Peter 2:13).
2. ". . . for the sake of conscience toward God . . ." (I Peter 2:19).
3. ". . . suffer for the sake of righteousness . . ." (I Peter 3:14).

These passages all seem to appeal to something *more* than reward or punishment. They go beyond and seem to stress that there is a greater (not necessarily higher) consideration by which a Christian may be motivated. The counselor may appeal to the Christian to live righteously not merely for fear of loss or in anticipation of gain, not only because of what Christ has done for him and what he has become, but *beyond* that, simply to please God—for "His Name's sake." This seems to have been Paul's thinking when he wrote:

> Wherefore it is necessary to be in subjection, not only because of wrath, but also for conscience sake (Romans 13:5).

and also when he advised slaves:

> Obey those who are your masters on earth, not with external service,

as those who please men, but with sincerity of heart, fearing the Lord. . . . It is the Lord Christ whom you serve" (Colossians 3: 22-24).

While Paul, like Peter, urged the love of God and the honor of His Name upon the Christian as a motive, he *never* disparaged other motivational factors.[13] He did not say, "You must cease obeying out of fear of wrath" in Romans 13:5. Rather, he included punishment as a *legitimate* factor, but not necessarily the sole motivating factor. While adding another ("for conscience sake"), he was careful not to do away with the former. When stressing the high calling of serving the *Lord* Christ, he *also* holds out the promised reward of the inheritance. The two clearly are not incompatible. The Christian counselor, then will follow biblical precepts and example by utilizing all legitimate forms of motivation. He is not limited to one alone as are those who adhere to unbiblical schemes.

It may be well to add to the discussion one more means of motivating (this additional item by no means exhausts the biblical motivational possibilities). *Modeling*, or encouragement by example, provides a rich source of motivational appeal. The argument goes this way: "If *he* can . . . so can I." That is the basic appeal in such passages as I Corinthians 10:13.[14] The model motivates from the point of view of feasibility.[15]

Because of the interrelatedness of all behaviors, the personal model becomes an important motivational factor. The model is a *whole* person. What he does, he does as a whole man acting in a life context. In the behavior of the model, therefore, one can *see* how the particular practice that is being enjoined can be done *in life*.[16]

In discussion, it is helpful to analyze a practice. But such analysis usually involves a certain amount of abstraction. This is often necessary in order to understand the practice. Yet a given behavior, par-

---

13. It is important to note that even in Colossians 3:22-24 he does stress reward too: "knowing that from the Lord you will receive the reward of the inheritance" (vs. 24). Reward in the Scriptures is never considered a low motive. At the end of his life Paul was looking toward his reward (II Timothy 4:8). The heroes of faith were motivated strongly by reward (Hebrews 11:6, 10, 26).

14. Cf. *Christ and Your Problems, op. cit.*

15. Cf. also Hebrews 13:7, 8.

16. Cf. remarks on disciplining and modeling in *Competent to Counsel*, pp. 177 ff., 257 ff., and *The Big Umbrella*, pp. 249 ff.

ticularly if it involves a measure of skill, can be put into practice only when another sees it *done*. Thus the relating of an experience by a counselor (the model can be an actor in a well-told story), or the assignment to observe another who is achieving this in his life (in premarital counseling an elder may visit a young couple to conduct family devotions with them), or the playing of a role (as practice in a counseling session[17]) with a counselee may make all of the difference in motivating him. When the feasibility of the how-to can be demonstrated, counselees will be much more likely to respond.

Choosing the Motivational Method

How does a counselor decide which motivational methodology to use in a given case? The answer is twofold. First, he does not always need to decide between the various ways and means of motivating counselees. That is to say, one option does not necessarily exclude others. *All* biblical means may be used and, as we have just seen, more than one means may be used in conjunction with the very same appeal. A careful study of Hebrews 13 discloses a powerful multifactored approach to motivation.[18] Secondly, when he selects one or more of the biblical means in preference to others, the counselor may do so from the following considerations:

a. If the data have disclosed one means to have been most productive for motivating the counselee in the past, probably he should opt for this. The likelihood is that such means once again may become the prime spring of motivation. Of course, they must be biblically legitimate.

b. The counselor should encourage the counselee to consider additional reasons for acting whenever necessary.

c. Motivation that is self-oriented or humanistic must be challenged and changed to that which is other-oriented (for the sake of God's Name and the welfare of one's neighbor).[19] This change may demand a confrontation leading toward repentance. Fear changed to love (I John 4:18) is a good example.

---

17. Cf. *Competent to Counsel*, pp. 110 ff., 178.

18. Cf. especially vss. 2, 3, 4, 5, 11, 14, 16, 17, 18, 19, 22. Note how both positive and negative motives are interspersed.

19. All secondary or short-term goals, however, clearly must be conditioned by the ultimate goal of honoring God. His glory, as the end product of all proximate objectives, ever must be held before the counselee.

Motivation in counseling cannot be avoided. It can only be ignored. To ignore it is either to motivate poorly and ignorantly or to motivate in biblically unethical ways. Either result makes a Christian counselor culpable. For further discussion of this important matter (especially in relation to the ethics of motivation), see my *Pulpit Speech*, pp. 81-97.

Chapter Eighteen

EFFECTING BIBLICAL CHANGE

Change: The Goal

Biblical change is the goal of counseling. But change is hard. Joel Nederhood pointedly refers to the title of an article by Amitai Etzioni entitled, "Human Beings Are Not So Easy to Change After All." In this article Etzioni cites the failures "to bring children of disadvantaged backgrounds up to standard," . . . "indicates that driver's training has reduced accident rates somewhat, but [only at the cost of] $88,000 for every life saved," and other similar information.[1] Jeremiah pointed out the difficulty of breaking into an established life pattern when he quipped:

> Can the Ethiopian change his skin
> Or the leopard his spots?
> Then you also can do good
> Who are *accustomed to* do evil [emphasis mine].[2]

Calvin, in his commentary, observes that this passage has been interpreted wrongly as referring to the sinful nature with which men are born. The interpretation still is common. Instead, he insists, it should be understood as a description of "the habit that is contracted by long practice." Careful attention to the exegesis of the passage shows that Calvin is right. Jeremiah, elsewhere, makes the same point in another way:

> I spoke to you in your prosperity;
> But you said, "I will not listen!"
> This has been your practice from your youth,
> That you have not obeyed my voice (Jeremiah 22:21).

Change Is Hard

Counselors must be realistic about the work to which they have been

---

1. Joel Nederhood, 'The Irresistible Force and Immovable Objects," *The Radio Pulpit*, vol. 17, no. 10, October, 1972, pp. 31, 32.
2. Jeremiah 13:23. "Accustomed" is literally "learned in evil."

called. While in Christ there is a genuine basis for hope of change, as we have seen, this change is hard. Children, who have "learned" to slam doors have a hard time relearning the process of closing them;[3] young marrieds must make many adjustments of their former habits to construct a third way of life that will be different from their two backgrounds;[4] older persons upon losing a life partner discover change inevitable but not easy.

Change, then, is necessary, but change is hard. One of the major reasons why Christians founder is because they are either unwilling to make changes or do not know how to make the changes that God requires of them in order to meet the vicissitudes of life.

Counselors should not be surprised, then, when counselees protest, "I'll never change" or "I guess that's just the way I am" or words to that effect. Counselees *continually* confuse learned behavior patterns with inherited nature (*phusis*). Counselors may take it *as a rule* that any quality of life, attitude of mind, or activity that God requires of man may be acquired through the Lord Jesus Christ. Thus, whenever a counselee protests, "But I just don't have patience," and means by those words, "That's the way that I was born and nothing can be done about it," the counselor must protest and insist that patience can be acquired, since the Scriptures list it as the fruit of the Spirit.

While it is true, for instance, that not all of the *gifts* of the Spirit may be acquired by all Christians, for He distributes them to whomever He wills and in the quantities that He sees fit (I Corinthians 12:4-11; Ephesians 4:7), all of the items in Galatians 5 that are said to be His *fruit* are available to every Christian.

Changing the Past

Some persons focus on the past. So long as they do, change will not be possible, since no one can change the past. It is not the past that needs to be dealt with; actually the past no longer exists. It is

---

3. Incidentally, easy-to-give reminders that *follow* the slam are less effective as help than the more difficult (because it requires action rather than reaction) method of reminding just as the child is *about to go through* the door.

4. See *Christian Living in the Home* for help in this matter. As every parent knows, it may take a concerted effort to break even small habits like biting fingernails, tipping back a chair, etc.

not his *past* that needs changing; it is the counselee *himself as he now is* who must change.[5] Counselors must help the counselee to refocus from the past to its effects upon the present. They must explain that the past is present in the life patterns of the counselee himself and in the present effects of past activities. Just as those who focus on the future (which does not exist) in worry do not change,[6] so too those who expend their energies and concern upon the past (which does not exist) find that they are unable to make the required adjustments.

The past can be dealt with only in the present by forgiveness, rectification, reconciliation, and other changes that must be made today. Counselors, then, must not allow themselves to become ensnared by the web of fretting, guilt, self-pity, discouragement, and regrets in which some counselees have become entangled. If they too get caught up in the tangles of the "what might have beens," they will be unable to help their counselees to free themselves.

Rather, the task of the Christian counselor is to call for repentance, which is a call for *change*—a change of mind leading to a change of life.[7] Repentance differs from mere sorrow over the past. Sorrow may *accompany* true repentance but never must be *identified* with it. Esau was sorry over the ultimate consequences of his sin, but not truly repentant (Hebrews 12:16, 17). On the other hand, "Sorrow that is according to the will of God produces a repentance without regret" (II Corinthians 7:10). In true repentance the Holy Spirit always effects change. Paul described this when he said that he preached to the Gentiles in the hope that they "should repent and turn to God, performing deeds appropriate to the repentance" (Acts 26:20). Thus the true counselor calls the counselee not to dwell upon the past, but instead to deal with the present guilt and other effects of the past now, so that the past may be forgiven and buried and, "forgetting the past," the counselee may be helped to "reach forward to what lies ahead" (Philippians 3:13, 14).

---

5. Also it is frequently important to observe that when a counselee complains that *he* would be different if the *situation* were different, the literal truth is that the only sure way to change the situation is for him to change his behavior in it (e.g., I Peter 3:1 ff.). When counselees change their behavior, the change leads to a change (1) in the situation, (2) in attitudes, (3) in others.

6. Cf. *What to Do About Worry.*

7. *Metanoia* literally means "an after thought."

Changing Present Patterns from the Past

Perhaps the past is present with the counselee most plainly in his personality, attitudes, and life style. Personality is the sum total of all that one is by nature and nurture ([1] *phusis*, i.e., inherited nature and [2] acquired habits). While the *phusis* is genetic and largely unchangeable, one may radically change the ways in which he uses his nature. Temperament, for instance, may be attributable to a given trait (there may well be in Tom inherited traits of persistence). But how this temperament develops and is used (on the one hand Tom may develop these traits as stubbornness, hardheadedness, etc., while on the other hand, the Spirit of God may develop them into patience and endurance) is his responsibility before God. So then, the counselee is responsible *in this way* even for the *phusis* (inherited nature).

It is vital for counselors to come to grips with this issue since *so many* counselees maintain (as an excuse, out of discouragement, or merely false views of responsibility) that they (or others) cannot do anything about their attitudes or behavior "because that is just the way that I am."[8] For example, one counselee thought that the way his son sat was hereditary. Another parent wrongly attributed voice intonations to nature. Both were learned, imitated behaviors. Often counselees need clear instruction in this matter before a program for change can be effected.

In summary, then, the counselor himself must believe and steadfastly maintain that change is possible in Christ. He must insist that every change that God requires of any Christian is possible. Age is no insuperable hindrance, heredity cannot remove responsibility, and the presence of a well-cultivated life style is not too formidable for the grace of God. The Scriptures give the needed hope, directions, and goals, the Holy Spirit provides the power, and Christian discipline is the method.

Changing Life Patterns

In considering the past, we have seen how life styles and patterns set by habit may become so much a part of one's personality and behavior that he may confuse them with hereditary traits. Indeed, our phrase "second nature" is an expression of the problem. Counselees

---

8. Counselors may counter by replying, "I do not dispute the fact that that is the way that you are, but by the grace of God that is *not* the way that you *need* to be for the rest of life. Indeed, in some way God can change you *today*."

may, as Jeremiah put it, become fully "accustomed to" sinful ways of life, so much so that (in one sense) they are comfortable with them. They have learned to perform sinful acts with ease, often unconsciously. When it comes to changing such patterns, counselors who are unaware of biblical methods often *think* that they have effected change but find that in time the old patterns emerge again. How can they be sure that change will become permanent rather than temporary?

Failure to Effect Changes That Stick

The repetitive pattern of sin-confession-forgiveness, sin-confession-forgiveness, that is so well known to counselors as well as to counselees, probably accounts for as much discouragement and failure in counseling as any other factor. Why do counseling resolutions, following the style of the traditional New Year's resolution, so often fall so flat? Why is change so frequently temporary? And . . . what (if anything) can be done about the problem?

Well, let us answer by asking another question (actually the first line in a child's joke):

"When is a door not a door?"

You know the answer, of course:

"When it is ajar!"

Now I did not tell this joke for its humor value (which is doubtful), but because it can become a useful paradigm for the discussion that follows. Let's ask and answer the question again, with a slight change:

Q. "When is a door not a door?"

A. "When it is something else."

In thinking about change, the biblical data indicate just *that*— change takes place not merely when certain *changes* occur, but only when there has been a *change*. The change of an activity is not the same as the change of a person. The former may involve actions sporadically or temporarily sustained by certain conditions; the latter involves a pattern developed as part of the fabric of the person's life that brings about those actions in spite of conditions.

Let us take an example or two and clarify this concept. Ask the question once more with blanks:

"When is a .... not a ....?"

The blanks may be filled in with the counselee's problem. For instance they may read:

Q. "When is a liar not a liar?" or

Q. "When is a thief not a thief?"

What are the answers? Should they read as follows:

A. "When he stops lying";

A. "When he stops stealing"?

No, precisely not. There is no assurance whatever that a thief who is not stealing has ceased being a thief. All that the cessation of stealing indicates is that *for the moment* or *at present* he is not stealing. Perhaps all that this means is that it is strategically not wise for him to steal at this time. Or it may mean that he has made a good resolution to stop; yet what he will do when he finds himself under economic pressure is another matter. In other words, since thieves do not steal at all times, liars do not always lie, and drunks are not always drunk, cessation of these activities is (in itself) no indication that there has been a permanent change. Indeed, if that is *all* that has taken place, the Christian counselor must conclude that changes, not change, have occurred, and with confidence he may predict the future failure to which I have alluded in the opening paragraph of this chapter.

What then is wrong with the answers given above? Simply this, they do not conform to the paradigm that the revised answer in the joke sets forth:

A. "When it (he) is *something else.*"

Dehabituation and Rehabituation

Let us consider the biblical base for this framework and the scriptural principles that underlie these assertions. In Ephesians 4, Paul deals directly with the problem of change. As we have noted elsewhere, he is discussing the need for walking in new working relationships between Christians; unity is essential. But that requires a change in lives. But unlike some present-day conservative ministers, Paul not only exhorts, he explains *how* change can be effected.

We shall skip over the early part of the chapter and begin with verse 17, in which he stresses the necessity for such a change:

This I say therefore, and affirm together with the Lord, that you walk no longer as the Gentiles walk. . . .

That is as strong an imperative as he could have laid upon his reader. The words "and affirm together with the Lord" underline the need, strengthen the emphasis, and show that there is no question about the matter. The exhortation is to change: "walk *no longer* as the Gentiles walk." "You *once* did, when you were a Gentile (i.e., heathen, unbeliever), but now that you have become a Christian, your walk (manner of daily activities; life style) must change."

Do not fail to note how plainly Paul speaks of more than the cessation of some objectionable actions; he calls for a change in the "manner of life" (cf. vs. 22). Paul calls for genuine change; change in the person. Not merely in his actions. There is hope in that—God expects His children to change. If so, such change must be *possible*; if so, He who commands also must have provided the *ways and means.*

Again, we shall pass over verses 17b-21 with only a comment or two. What Paul describes in those verses as the Gentile style of life amounts to the description of a life that is focused upon self; what we have called the desire-oriented and motivated life. This comes to the surface especially in 19b: (they "have given themselves over to sensuality, for the practice of every kind of impurity with greediness," and in verse 22, in accordance with "deceitful lusts." Notice that the change contemplated is directed toward *a way of life*, not merely toward some of the activities involved in such living. Paul speaks of it as a "walk" (vs. 17), as a "practiced" way to which they have "given themselves over" (vs. 19), as a "former manner of life" (or as the Berkeley Version has it, "previous habits") and as "the old man" (vs. 22). In describing the change, it is as if one must become a "new man" (vs. 24), one that has been renewed in "mind" (vs. 23), in "righteousness," and in "holiness" (vs. 24). A man like Jesus Christ. These changes issue, he says, "from the truth" (vs. 24b). The change is a change in the man; he is renewed by changing his entire life style. The new style must conform to the image of Christ so that in his new manner of life the Christian truly reflects God. Nothing less will do.

This is the setting for the "how to" which is described in verses 22-24 that is vital for every counselor to understand. The key fact here is that Paul does not only say "put off" the old man (i.e., the old life style), but also says "put on" the new man (i.e., the Christian life style).

Change is a two-factored process. These two factors always must be present in order to effect genuine change. Putting off will not be permanent without putting on. Putting on is hypocritical as well as temporary, unless it is accompanied by putting off.

Let us return, then, to the liar and to the thief. Ask again,

Q. "When is a liar not a liar?"

A. "When he is something else."

Very good, but *what* else? When he *stops* lying what must he *start* doing? By what does the Bible say that lying must be replaced? (That is the kind of question that counselors continually should be asking and answering.) Well, what does Paul say? Look at verse 25:

> Therefore [he is now applying the principles of change] laying aside falsehood [putting off], speak truth, each one of you with his neighbor, for we are members of one another [putting on].

There you have it.

Q. "When is a liar not a liar?"

A. "When he has become a truth teller."

Unless he has been "reprogrammed" or rehabituated, when the chips are down, when he is tired, sick, or under great pressure, a counselee's good resolves and temporary cessation of lying will not last. He will revert to his former manner of life because he is still programmed to do so. The old sinful habit patterns have not been replaced by new ones. Until that occurs, he will remain vulnerable to sinful reversion. Dehabituation is possible only by achieving rehabituation. The counselee must be repackaged. New patterns of response must become dominant. It is to these instead that he must learn to turn habitually under life stresses.

Let's do it once again:

Q. "When is a thief not a thief?"

When he stops stealing? No. Look at verse 28:

> Let him who steals steal no longer [putting off] but rather let him labor, performing with his own hands what is good, in order that he may have something to share with him who has need [putting on].

A thief is still a thief if he only has stopped stealing. He is simply a thief who *at the moment* is not stealing. Under pressure, he is likely to revert. But if after repentance he gets a job, works hard at earning his money honestly, and learns the blessings of giving, he is no longer a thief. A thief is not a thief when he has become a hard-working man who gives. He becomes dehabituated to stealing only when he becomes rehabituated to hard working and sharing.

All through the Scriptures, the two-factored process appears. In this chapter, for instance, notice what Paul says about anger (vss. 26, 27):

put off: resentment (holding anger in);

put on: dealing with problems daily (letting anger motivate to biblical solutions).

Consider his words about speech (vs. 29):

put off: unwholesome words that cut up others;

put on: words that build up another.

He advocates in place of the nasty verbal or physical expression of "bitterness, wrath, anger, clamor, slander and malice," tender-hearted forgiveness (vss. 31, 32).

The two factors occur in Peter:

Not returning evil for evil or insult for insult / but giving a blessing instead (I Peter 3:9);

and in John:

Beloved do not imitate that which is evil / but that which is good (III John 11);

in Hebrews:

Not forsaking our own assembling together as is the habit of some / but encouraging one another (Hebrews 10:25);

and scores of other places.[9] The works of the flesh must be replaced by the fruit of the Spirit (Galatians 5). The way of the ungodly must give way to the way of the righteous (Psalm 1).

The discipling method of Christ,[10] in which the disciple must become *like his master* (Luke 6:40), involves the two-factored process:

If anyone wishes to come after Me, let him deny himself, and take up his cross [put off] and follow Me [put on] (Matthew 16:24).

The new life style of Christ's disciple is acquired by dying to self (putting self to death on the cross) and / living to God (following Christ). It was begun by turning *from* idols / *to* the living and true God (I Thessalonians 1:9). Sanctification continues as the believer daily turns *from* sin / *to* righteousness.[11]

---

9. Cf. as examples I Peter 1:14, 15; 2:11, 12; 3:9; 4:2; 5:2; 5:3, 5, 6; Romans 12:16, 21; 13:12; 14:17; 15:1-2; Galatians 5:16, 19 ff., 22 ff.; 6:3, 4, 8. The counselor should compose his own working list of put-offs and put-ons for use in counseling. Cf. Ref. 3, p. 457.

10. Cf. *The Big Umbrella*, pp. 249 ff.

11. A beetle lies on its back, helplessly kicking its feet in the air. What sort of change does it need? "It needs to be turned over," you reply. Very well, we shall do so. There, all seems right again. He can move and . . . wait! Look at

Breaking and Establishing Habits

A way or manner of life is a *habitual* way of living. God gave man a marvelous capacity that we call *habit*. Whenever one does something long enough, it becomes a part of him. Counselors must remember that their counselees (as well as themselves) are fully endowed with this capacity. Sometimes, however, counselors must point out the dynamic of habit to their counselees. When they do so they may need to stress the fact that habits are *hard* to change because we have become comfortable with them, and because they have become unconscious responses. One counselor puts it this way: "Fred, let's take an example: did you put your left or right shoe on first when you got up today? Ah, it took you a minute to answer that, didn't it? Maybe you don't even know yet. You don't think about where to begin any more; you just *do* it. You don't consciously say to yourself, 'Now, I'm going to put my shoes on this morning; I shall begin with the right foot.' You don't think about that at all. You just do it without thinking about it. You just get up and unconsciously do what you have done hundreds of other mornings. You probably don't know which arm you put into a shirt first, or hundreds of other details. We no longer find it necessary to think about details. That is the capacity that God gave to us. Take another example: think of the first time that you sat behind an automobile wheel. What a frightening experience that was. There you sat, thinking, 'Here is a wheel (it looked about ten times bigger than it was), and here is a gear shift, here is a complex instrument panel and foot pedals down below. I have to learn how to use and to coordnate all of these! And at the same time I must look out for stripes painted down the middle of the road, and signs along the roadway, and pedestrians and automobiles, and . . . How will I ever do it?' Can you remember back to that time? But now —*now* what do you do? At midnight, on a moonless night, you slide into the car seat as someone else slips into the seat beside you. Deftly you insert the key into the slot without scarring the dashboard, turn on the motor, shift the gears, depress the gas pedal, back out of the driveway into the street and start down the road, all the while arguing some abstruse point of Calvinism! What an amazing feat that is when you think about it! Well, just think about it. You have learned to perform

what is happening! He is trying to go up the same incline again. Oops! Sure enough, he has rolled over on his back again. Turning him right side up is not enough—he must learn to change his life course as well.

highly complex behavior unconsciously. Think of what Brooks Robinson and Willie Mays have learned to do *in the same way*. How did you learn? How did they? By practice, *disciplined* practice. You drove the car long enough that driving has become a part of you. It has become second nature to you. That is what Paul was talking to Timothy about when he wrote 'discipline yourself for godliness' (I Timothy 4:7). That is how one establishes a life style and lives according to it—by habit."

The writer of Hebrews (Hebrews 5:13 ff.) speaks clearly about this matter. There he is upbraiding the Hebrew Christians because, although they had received so much teaching of God's Word, yet they had not profited from it. The reason was that they had not *used* it. Consequently, when they ought to have become teachers they still needed to be taught. He says that everyone "who partakes only of milk is *not accustomed* to the word of righteousness, for he is a baby" (vs. 13). He continues: "But solid food (meat and potatoes) is for the mature who *because of practice* (because they have done it so often) have their senses *trained* to discern between good and evil." There it is. The practice of godliness leads to the life of godliness. It makes godliness "natural." If you *practice* what God tells you to do, the obedient life will become a part of you. There is no simple, quick, easy way to instant godliness.[12]

"But," you protest, "I don't seem to be able to do it." The protest is invalid. You already have. You have practiced and learned *something*; you have developed some unconscious patterns. As a sinful human being bent toward sin, you have practiced sinful practices so that they have become a part of you, just as they have become a part of all of us. There is no question that the habit capacity is there. The problem is that it has been used for the wrong purposes. The capacity of habit works both ways. It operates in either direction. You can't avoid habitual living, because this is the way that God made you. He gave you the ability to live a life that does not demand conscious thought about every action or response. It is a great blessing that God

---

12. E. J. Young has helpful words about *learning* a new way of life in his comments on Isaiah 1:10-17. The picture there is putting off (vs. 16) and putting on (vs. 17) by learning. He says "the people needed to be taught. To do well was something new to them, something that had to be learned. . . . The nation is to become skilled in doing well, just as at present it is skilled in doing evil." E. J. Young, *The New International Commentary: The Book of Isaiah*, vol. I, (Grand Rapids: Wm. B. Eerdmans Publishing Co., 1972), p. 73.

made you this way. It would be unbearable if every time you did anything you found it necessary to think consciously about it. Imagine yourself each morning saying, "Now, let's see, how do I brush my teeth? First, I have to get the toothpaste tube and roll it from the bottom, etc., etc." It is a great benefit that you don't have to consciously think about everything that you do, or you probably would not get to breakfast by midnight.

But practice itself is indifferent; it can work either for you or against you, as a blessing or as a curse, depending upon *what* you have practiced. It is what you feed into your life that matters—just like the data fed into a computer. A computer is no better than the data with which it operates. The end product is good or bad according to the raw material provided for it. That is just like habit capability. In II Peter 2:14, Peter speaks about people whose hearts are *"trained* in greed." Trained is the same word that Paul used (*gymnazo*), the word from which *gymnastics* comes. A heart that has been *exercised* in greed is one that has faithfully practiced greed so that greediness has become natural. Without consciously thinking about it, such a person "automatically" behaves greedily in various situations where the temptation is present.

Since God has made counselees with the capacity for living according to habit, counselors must reckon with habit when seeking to help counselees change. They must help them consciously to take a hard look at their life styles. They must help them to become conscious of life patterns by carefully examining their unconscious responses. The unconscious must again become conscious. As they become aware of life patterns, they must evaluate them by the Word of God. What the counselee learned to do as a child he may be continuing to do as an adult. Pattern by pattern the counselor must help him to analyze and determine whether it has developed from practice in doing God's will or whether it has developed as a sinful response. There is only one way to become a godly person, to orient one's life toward godliness, and that means pattern by pattern. The old sinful ways, as they are discovered, must be replaced by new patterns from God's Word. That is the meaning of disciplined living. Discipline first requires self-examination, then it means crucifixion of the old sinful ways (saying "no" daily), and lastly, it entails practice in following Jesus Christ in new ways by the guidance and strength that the Holy Spirit provides through His Word.

The biblical way to godliness is not easy or simple, but it is the solid way.

A counselee wondered whether this sort of change was possible. He asked, "Can a fifty-year-old man change?" He was deadly serious. There sat a forty-two-year-old counselor thinking, "Will it be only eight more years before I am canned and refrigerated?!" So the counselor told him about yo-yos. "Recently the yo-yo craze returned. As a forty-two-year-old (at that time) I vividly remember the original glorious age of the yo-yo from my boyhood. Back in those days the Duncan Yo-Yo Company had a much better advertising campaign and, incidentally, a much better yo-yo. Today, they offer a plastic model with a metal rod in the center. The steel rod does not provide enough friction for the string, and causes slippage. The old yo-yos had a wooden rod and were wooden themselves. Duncan also used to sponsor corner drugstore yo-yo contests. Down to every drugstore came a factory representative. He showed you all of the latest tricks: around the world, eating spaghetti, rocking the baby in the cradle, walking the dog, etc. If you practiced hard enough, you could learn to throw the yo-yo out or down, or up or around; you could spin it over your head, under one leg—almost anywhere you wished.

"I had forgotten all about yo-yos until about a year ago, when one day one of my children came home with yo-yos. But he didn't know what to do with them! Here was my son operating a yo-yo like a girl! 'Horrors!' I thought, 'he doesn't know what to do with a yo-yo. There are no factory representatives any more; there is nobody to teach him. I can't have him doing that to a yo-yo; I guess I'll have to show him myself.' Now, I hadn't touched a yo-yo for a hundred and fifty years at least. So I picked the thing up and showed him how to tie a slip knot that would stay on the finger. (He didn't know *what* finger to put it on.) So I put it on, and after hefting it a time or two spun it downward with force . . . and it slept. Well, his eyes grew as large as dinnerplates. He didn't even know it could sleep. I practiced several times to get the feel of this new, inferior, plastic-and-metal product. Soon the old patterns began to come back. Even with that inferior product it wasn't long before I was doing all of the old tricks that I used to be able to do. I grew ten feet tall with the kids! It took only a few attempts, and the old acquired skills returned."

Then the counselor continued, "You ask, 'How can a fifty-year-old man change? Can this really be for *you*? Can *you* really be different?

Can you *at this late date in life* make a change and start to live a life that really will be godly?' I answer, positively! When I was ten years old I learned how to yo-yo, and now many years later I was able to pick up a yo-yo and found that the old skills were still with me. The question, you see, is not whether a fifty-year-old man can change; the real question is, can *anybody* change once he has learned something habitually? When I was only ten years old, I learned a skill that I haven't forgotten, even though I haven't used a yo-yo since. Perhaps you haven't ridden a bike for years, yet you know that you *could* do so. It probably wouldn't take you five minutes to get the feel of it again. It would come right back to you. The question, then, is not whether a fifty-year-old man can learn new ways; the question is can *anyone*—even a ten-year-old—change once he has learned a wrong practice? When a practice has become so much a part of a child that it lasts without reinforcement for over thirty years, can even *he* change? The answer is that all change is hard, but every change God requires is possible. By the grace of God, you can change."

When the counselor undertakes this task, he knows that he and the counselee do not have to do it alone. He may assure the counselee, "It is God who works in you" (Philippians 2:13). All holiness, all right-eousness, all godliness is the "fruit of the Spirit" (Galatians 5:22, 23). It takes nothing less than the power of the Spirit to replace sinful habits with righteous ones, for a ten-year-old or a fifty-year-old. God never said that once a person reaches forty or fifty or eighty that he is incapable of change. Look what Abraham did as an old man. Look at the tre-mendous changes that God demanded of him in old age. If anything, age and the *experience in change* that it brings should help, as we have observed already under the discussion of *hope*. The Holy Spirit can change any Christian, and does.

Christians never should fear change. They must believe in change so long as the change is oriented toward godliness. The Christian life is a life of continual change. In the Scriptures it is called a "walk," not a rest. They never may say (in this life), "I have finally made it." They must not think, "There is nothing more to learn from God's Word, nothing more to put into practice tomorrow, no more skills to develop, no more sins to be dealt with." When Christ said, "take up your cross daily and follow me" (Luke 9:23), He put an end to all such thinking. He represented the Christian life as a daily struggle to change. The counselee can change if the Spirit of God dwells within him. Of course, if He does not, there is no such hope.

Counselors must recognize that too many Christians *give up*. They want the change too soon. What they really want is change without the daily struggle. Sometimes they give up when they are on the very threshold of success. They stop before receiving. It usually takes at least three weeks of proper daily effort for one to feel comfortable in performing a new practice. And it takes about three more weeks to make the practice part of oneself. Yet, many Christians do not continue even for three days. If they do not receive instant success, they get discouraged. They want what they want now, and if they don't get it now, they quit.

Often counselees need encouragement. Using examples like that which follows may help.[13] The counselor may say, "Think about this problem for a moment. Remember when you learned how to ice skate? What happened the first time that you went out on the ice? You know what happened. Zip bang! You got a wet bottom. That's what happened every time that you got up and tried again. Nobody ever learns to skate without falling at first. You had a decision to make as you sat there freezing: 'Am I going to continue this, or should I give up the whole idea of learning to ice skate?' Perhaps you did quit after the first or second failure and have never learned since. A lot of people make that decision right then and there. They do not consider learning to skate worth the embarrassment, awkwardness, trouble, and fear that it usually entails. But others go on in spite of it all. They get up, brush off, and start out again; zip bang! zip bang! zip bang! zip bang! then, . . . zzzzzzip bang. Something has begun to happen. Before you know it, you are going zzzzzzzzip bang, zzzzzzzzzzzzzzzzzzzip bang, and then zzzzzzz. . . . If you practice long enough, you will no longer have a problem with skating; instead, you will be concerned about how to get the puck into the net. There comes a point at which an activity *begins* to, and then *does*, become a part of you, but only when you stay with it long enough."

Perhaps the counselee fails at first to change a habit. Maybe every time that he has tried, as far as he is concerned, he went zip bang!

---

13. Much of the present material is replicated in the writer's pamphlet, *Godliness Through Discipline*, which was designed to be used in counseling to reinforce the counselor's efforts.

Suppose he *did* get a wet bottom. Was that a good reason to give up? Certainly not; that is simply part of learning to skate (or witness, or love). Suppose he has found it difficult to read the Scriptures and pray daily; that was reason for working harder; not for quitting.

Possibly he failed to keep short-term goals in view. He may need to say, "Today I shall do this, then this week that, and then in three weeks the other." If he skates every day for three weeks in a row, he will probably become a skater. If he really wants to be godly, he must stay out on the ice. He must not let the wet bottoms discourage him. If he is willing to get wet, he is soon going to get a lot of zzzzzzzzzips and a lot less bangs! Sooner than he may think.

Week after week, counselors encounter one outstanding failure among Christians: a lack of what the Bible calls "endurance." Perhaps endurance is the key to godliness through discipline. No one learns to ice skate, to use a yo-yo, to button shirts, or to drive an automobile unless he persists long enough to do so. He learns by enduring in spite of failures, through the embarrassments, until the desired behavior becomes a part of him. He trains himself by practice to do what he wants to learn to do. God says the same is true about godliness.

All of the stress that the Bible puts upon human effort must not be misunderstood; we are talking about grace-motivated effort, not the work of the flesh. It is not effort apart from the Holy Spirit that produces godliness. Rather, it is through the power of the Holy Spirit alone that one can endure. Of his own effort, a man may persist in learning to skate, but he will not persist in the pursuit of godliness. A Christian does *good works* because the Spirit first works in him.

Now the work of the Spirit is not mystical. The Holy Spirit's activity often has been viewed in a confused and confusing manner. There is no reason for such confusion. The Holy Spirit Himself has plainly told us how He works. He says *in* the Scriptures that He ordinarily works *through* the Scriptures. The Bible is the Holy Spirit's book. He inspired it. He moved its authors to write every wonderful word that one reads there. This is His book; the sharp tool by which He accomplishes His work. He did not produce the book only to say that it could be laid aside and forgotten in the process. Godliness does not come by osmosis. Human ideas and efforts will never produce it. There is no easier path to godliness. It always requires the prayerful study and obedient practice of the Word of God.

The Spirit took pains to raise up men and mold those men to fitly write His book. Under His good providence they developed the vocabularies and styles in the kinds of life situations that He required. Thus they could write a book of exactly the sort that He wanted to meet our needs. He was careful to assure that not one false word was penned; in His book there are no errors. It is wholly true and inerrant; it is the dependable Word of God. After going to all of that trouble, one must not think he will zap instant holiness apart from the Bible. He doesn't work that way. The Spirit works through His Word; that is how He works. So to help a counselee to discipline himself toward godliness, a counselor must insist upon the regular study of God's Word as an essential factor.

It is by willing, prayerful, and persistent obedience to the requirements of the Scriptures that godly patterns are developed and come to be a part of us.[14] When we read about them we must then ask God by His grace to help us live accordingly. He has given the Holy Spirit to us for this purpose. The word *grace* has several meanings in the Bible, one of which is *help*. The Holy Spirit gives help when His people read His Word and then step out by faith to do as He says. He does not promise to strengthen unless they do so; the power often comes *in the doing*.

In II Timothy 3:17, Paul mentions four things that the Scriptures do for the believer. First, they *teach* what God requires. Secondly, they *convict* of sin by revealing how one has fallen short of those requirements. Thirdly, they *"set us up straight again."* Lastly, they *train* or *discipline* in righteousness. This fourth benefit of the Bible means a structured training in doing righteousness. Using the Bible every day disciplines. Disciplined, biblically structured living is what is needed.

Structure alone brings freedom. Discipline brings liberty. People have been brainwashed into thinking the opposite. They think freedom and liberty come only by throwing over structure and discipline.

Liberty comes through law, not apart from it. When is a train most free? Is it when it goes bouncing across the field off the track? No. It is free only when it is confined (if you will) to the track. Then it runs smoothly and efficiently, because that was the way its maker intended it to run. It needs to be on the track, structured by the track, to run

---

14. How Christians doing counseling expect to effect God's changes apart from the use of God's Word is hard to understand. Counselors, therefore, must always insist upon establishing the habit of daily Bible study.

properly. Counselees need to be on the track. God's track is found in God's Word. In God's round world the counselee cannot lead a square life happily; he always will get the corners knocked off. There is a structure necessary for the commandment-oriented and motivated life; that structure is found in the Bible. Conforming to that structure by the grace of God enables Christians to change, to put off sin, put on righteousness, and thus to become godly men.

This, then, is the counselor's biblical answer: regularly read the Scriptures, prayerfully do as they say, according to schedule, regardless of how you feel.

That last factor points to what is perhaps the biggest problem of all. Counselees give up because they don't *feel* like doing something again. Counselors must tell their counselees: "You probably didn't *feel* like getting up this morning. But you had to do so in spite of how you felt. After you were up and around awhile you began to feel different, and you were glad you *acted against your feelings*. From that first decision on, the rest of the day is filled with similar decisions that must be made on the basis of obedience to God rather than capitulation to contrary feelings."

There is much that people do not feel like doing. But there are only two ways to live. These two ways of life reflect two kinds of religion and two kinds of morality. One religion and life and morality says, "I will live according to feelings." The other says, "I will live as God says." When man sinned he was abandoning the commandment-oriented life of love for the feeling-oriented life of lust. There are only two kinds of life, the feeling-motivated life of sin oriented toward self, and the commandment-motivated life of holiness oriented toward godliness. Living according to feeling is the greatest hindrance to godliness that we face. Godly, commandment-oriented living comes only from biblical structure and discipline.

We have seen, therefore, that breaking a habit is a two-sided enterprise that requires regular, structured, endurance in putting off and putting on. Dehabituation is *more* than that; it also involves rehabituation. When a counselee turns his back upon his old ways, at the same time he must turn to face God's new ones. If he does not, what he turns to face instead may be equally as bad or worse. If the new way is vague and indefinite, he may vacillate from one thing to another, becoming confused and exasperated rather than developing new biblical ways of living. The process, then, should be clear both to the counselor and, through him, to the counselee.

The following form may be used to establish plainly the twofold nature of biblical change for the counselee.[15]

Change . . .

is a two-factored process

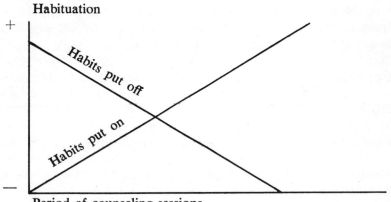

Habituation

+

Habits put off

Habits put on

−

Period of counseling sessions

Dehabituation   Rehabituation
(List habits to put off:)   (List habits to put on:)

_____   _____

_____   _____

_____   _____

_____   _____

_____   _____

_____   _____

_____   _____

Figure 2

15. Form available in the Christian Counselor's Starter Packet, or in any quantity from the publisher.

Counselees, in conjunction with their counselors, early should identify and list sinful habit patterns in the left-hand column that God in the Scriptures says must be put off. The corresponding biblical patterns to be put on should be listed in the right-hand column. Early identification of these can clarify the work that needs to be done and keeps everyone on the track.[16]

We have seen that a counselee is no longer a thief when he "puts on" the righteous way of life that accords with honesty in getting gain. That is to say that he does not cease to be a thief when he stops stealing. If his whole way of life is still programmed toward stealing, he is still—*in character*—a thief even though (at the moment) he may not be stealing. He has not become dehabituated because he has not been rehabituated. If he does not become reprogrammed by the Word and the Spirit, when the pressures of life grow heavy he will react to them according to the only habit patterns that he knows. That is why Paul insists not only that he must steal no more, but also that he must learn a new way of life that consists of (1) toiling with his hands to earn money and (2) giving to the poor. Until he has developed a life characterized by toil and giving, he is still *charactologically* a thief.[17]

The reversion to character will be more than a mere temporary reversion in some instances. In cases that counselors see, it may involve discouragement, heartache, and many times other negative factors that make it even more difficult for the counselee to change. The situation, at times, may seem to entail conditions similar to those that existed when the unclean spirit returned to the cleaned-up house along with seven others (Matthew 12:45). So the key to change is to recognize the double-faced nature of the process. We must now consider *how* this change may be brought about.

---

16. There is always the danger of identifying problems and solutions too quickly. Counselors should feel free to revise and change forms as necessary. If they find that this is happening often in many of their cases, however, they should learn to reach such decisions at a later point.

17. Though, of course, he may be a forgiven thief.

Chapter Nineteen

ELEMENTS OF DEHABITUATION AND REHABITUATION

Let us suppose that the counselee has made a basic commitment to change and that he understands the need both to put off and to put on; what comes next? That is to say, exactly *how* does one go about dehabituating and rehabituating a counselee? One way to look at this problem is to think of the steps or elements involved in the processes.

There are at least seven separately definable elements involved in biblical change. These cannot be viewed merely as successive steps, since most of them must be introduced into the counseling process and pursued simultaneously. The elements are as follows:

1. Becoming aware of the Practice (pattern) that must be dehabituated (put off);
2. Discovering the biblical alternative;
3. Structuring the whole situation for change;
4. Breaking links in the chain of sin;
5. Getting help from others;
6. Stressing the whole relationship to Christ;
7. Practicing the new pattern.

Becoming Aware of Patterns

The three most fundamental problems with a habit are summed up by saying that the habitual practice has become "second nature." That means:

(1) The counselee has become *comfortable* with the practice. He no longer feels awkward or wooden while performing.

(2) The counselee *automatically* responds to certain given situations (or stimuli) in a habitual way.

(3) The counselee engages in the practice (or at least begins to do so) *without conscious thought* or decision.

191

Thus, it is important to the counselee to become fully aware of the nature, the frequency, and the occasion(s) for any practice. Unless he knows exactly *what* he is doing, he will not know how to correct the practice. If, for example, he thinks that a particular facial expression conveys the message of love and concern whereas many people read it instead to mean boredom and lack of interest, *this fact* clearly needs to be established for the counselee. In addition to the *fact* itself, the counselee will need to be able to identify the facial expression visually and kinesthetically. When it occurs, he will need *someone* (counselee, wife, friend) at first to call attention to it so that he may take stock of and learn to identify the expression exactly. Whether the practice consists of something as simple as a facial expression, or a tone of voice, or whether it has to do with an attitude or a particular behavior, the counselee will need to be *sure* that he knows precisely what it is that must be replaced. Often he will need the help of another to identify the practice.

The help of another also may assist him (at least in the early stages of his efforts) to learn of the frequency with which he engages in the practice. Often he will be unaware of this matter, usually thinking that it is far less of a problem than it is. Because the practice has become unconscious, without enlisting another to remind him regularly the counselee may not even recognize most occurrences. The frequency of occurrences also can be ascertained by the faithful use of a DPP form.[1]

Discovering frequency of occurrence is important for several reasons. First, to learn how much more frequently one daydreams or engages in self-pity rather than doing his daily chores usually becomes a high motivating factor in seeking to change. Secondly, determining frequency helps one to determine the nature of the difficulty that he seeks to overcome; only *then* does he become aware of the severity (or lack of it) of the matter. Thus it can be placed in proper perspective and priority. Thirdly, frequency of occurrence allows one to determine whether or not he is involved in a life-dominating practice (about which we shall have more to say later on in the chapter), and whether, therefore, the elimination of the practice also will require the strengthening of many or most of the *other* areas of his life. If the pattern has affected each of

---

1. See *infra*, p. 279.

these areas and they in turn affect it, other patterns may have to be dealt with simultaneously. Lastly, he must become aware of the occasions that trigger the practice. Unless he does so, he will never be able to take the third step: breaking the chain of reactions at its first link.

The help of others who are involved, plus the careful use of a DPP sheet are two very useful adjuncts to assist one in becoming conscious of the circumstances under which he engages in the sinful practice that must be put off. The DPP, by structuring the counselee to record, let us say, outbursts of temper and their occasions on a morning, afternoon, and evening basis, not only helps to make him aware of the true frequency of the problem, but also gives him a handle on whether it is always in response to a particular stimulus that he loses his temper, whether the pattern extends to two or three sorts of stimuli, or whether it is generalized to any sort of frustration or inconvenience in life. If he knows that it is particularized the counselor will help to structure one sort of program to solve problems. If generalized, he will need to structure differently. Temper always relating to the presence of a particular neighbor, for instance, may (through questioning) lead to the discovery of jealousy and fear that the counselee's husband may be romantically interested in her. Obviously, that particularized problem must be solved in a different way from that of the counselee who is irritable with anyone under any circumstance about anything that keeps him from getting his way. The first instance calls for work in interpersonal relationships between one husband and wife, whereas the second calls for repentance from pride and selfishness leading to the practice of humility and to engaging in a ministry to others. Biting fingernails and drunkenness are of a different character, since the effects of the latter tend to dominate all of one's life (social, economic, family, health, etc.), while the former does not. But the study of triggering circumstances may be of equal importance in discovering how to deal with both. If the DPP shows that self-pity sessions invariably lead to hitting the bottle and that arguments just as surely lead to nail biting, then, in principle, the solution to each problem may be the same.

Thus, the first vital element in the dehabituation/rehabituation process is awareness by both the counselor and counselee of the exact nature, frequency of occurrence, and the associated occasions for the attitude or behavior pattern that must be put off. The use of DPP forms and reminders by others is often helpful in bringing about such awareness.[2]

Discovering the Biblical Alternative

We have seen that scriptural change is a two-factored process that requires putting on new patterns in place of old ones. Since much already has been made of this point, little needs to be said here. Counselors must gain some skill, however, in helping counselees to locate biblical alternatives. Elsewhere I have suggested that the counselor use Reference 3 to build his own list of most-used verses.

Yet, verses themselves are not all that is required. Counselors also must develop the ability to translate the principles of the Scriptures into concrete applications to specific life situations. One pastor, in discussing this matter, explained how he had countered a bad habit of murmuring by replacing it with prayerful thanksgiving. He said that he had developed the baneful habit of complaining in the words "O great!" whenever things did not go his way. He knew this was wrong because he believed Romans 8:28. So, he determined to add three words to his complaint that transformed it into praise and helped to change his attitude toward the providence of God. Instead, he determined to say:

"O great . . . is thy faithfulness!"

The name of a boat in Pensacola, Florida, was *Insteadov*. Presumably the owners determined that, rather than spend time or money on other things, they would purchase this boat. This is the counselor's task to know (and increasingly become familiar with) the biblical "insteadovs." There is a proper practice, pattern, or habit to replace every improper one. Counselors must read the Scriptures with an eye ever alert for passages that indicate the proper alternatives. It might be helpful to use a counseling Bible in which these are marked. One way to do so is to use a slash (/) to divide the put-off from the put-on as follows:[3]

> Do not swear, either by heaven or by earth or with any other oath; / but let your yes be yes, and your no, no (James 5:12).

---

2. Often awareness, itself, is an adequate deterrent. Counselees, in keeping the DPP record, frequently report that the task led to a marked decrease in the undesirable behavior.

3. Others prefer plus (+) and minus (—) markings. Whatever scheme he adopts, the counselor will discover that the discipline of searching and marking will greatly alert him to the biblical alternatives.

How blessed is the man who does not walk in the counsel of the wicked, nor stand in the path of sinners, nor sit in the seat of scoffers / but his delight is in the law of the Lord, and in His law he meditates day and night (Psalm 1:1-2).

Structuring for Change

Structure often is essential for effecting the twofold change that we are discussing. Structure helps both in putting off and in putting on. When a counselee prays in faith for change, his faith should extend to works that are consistent with his prayer. If he prays for deliverance from a smoking habit, he should stop buying cigarettes. If he wants to overcome an impure thought life, he must burn the girlie magazines. If he wishes to get rid of a bad temper, he should abandon the company of others with a similar problem (Proverbs 14:7; 22:24, 25).[4] Thus the structure of one's activities, surroundings, and associations should be consistent with and aid his avowed desire to put off a sinful practice.

Equally important, since change is two-factored, he must structure for the new practice that he wishes to develop. If he wishes to learn to keep problems current rather than allow resentments to build up, he should appoint a time each day for settling matters with other members of the family. If he is seeking to develop regular habits of Bible study and prayer, he should schedule time for them and, if necessary, even post a reminder in a place where he will see it daily. If he wishes to make new Christian friends who can act as positive models for behavior, he must join a conservative Christian congregation and regularly attend its services. Thus, one must rearrange his environment, associates, schedules, activities, or whatever other impediments in his life that might become an occasion for sin so that these, instead, become facilitators in learning God's new way of life.

What this means, then, is that he must structure for the removal of impediments to the new life and the addition of facilitators, as well as the addition of impediments to the old ways and the removal of their facilitators. The following sheet used at C.C.E.C. helps to pinpoint such factors:

Breaking Links in the Chain of Sin

Many counselees think of change only in terms of changing the

---

4. Cf. also I Corinthians 15:33.

IMPEDIMENTS AND FACILITATORS[5]	
To the Former Sinful Ways	**To the New Holy Ways**
I M P E D I M E N T S	Add:	Remove:
F A C I L I T A T O R S	Remove:	Add:

5. Form available in *The Christian Counselor's Starter Packet*, or available in any quantities from the publisher.

full-blown problem. When they think that way, they become discouraged. A woman may picture herself virtually out of control, yelling and screaming at her children. However, that point was reached *not all at once*; it came in stages. While even at its most spectacular point it is possible to get control over anger, it is much easier to break the earliest link in the chain of events (or steps) that led to this point. That is why it helps for counselors to break down an activity into its steps or stages or links.[6] When the Scriptures speak of self-control, they sometimes have this very idea in mind:

> The beginning of strife is like letting out water, so abandon the quarrel before it breaks out (Proverbs 17:14);

and

> A gentle answer turns away wrath, but a harsh word stirs up anger (Proverbs 15:1);

and

> A fool always loses his temper. But a wise man holds it back (Proverbs 29:11).

There are always *at least* two points at which one can stop an action:
1. at the point of resistance;
2. at the point of restraint.

Resistance

Man's brain enables him to *delay* his responses and *choose* a course of action. Animals without brains respond immediately by reflex. Man, made in God's image as a responsible creature, is not like that. Because of this fact, there is the possibility of *resistance* to and the *rejection* of sinful courses of action. When Jesus was faced with the three temptations at the mountain, in each instance He entertained the *thought* of the wrong action in His mind, but in holiness He *rejected* each suggestion, citing the biblical reason for the rejection.

Jesus, by breaking the first link, was able to avoid forging a chain

---

6. Thus, if a DPP form is used, one can identify the triggering factor(s). Knowedge of these will aid not only in restructuring, but also in resisting. If a woman finds it harder to control her temper during her monthly periods, she can keep accurate records and plan (as much as possible) to avoid stressful activities during that time (e.g., that is not the time during which to invite the relatives to spend a week).

of sin. It was because He knew God's will in the Scriptures that He was able to resist the wrong decision and choose the right one. This process is known biblically as resistance: "Resist the devil and he will flee from you" (James 4:7). Part of the counselor's task, therefore, is to help the counselee to learn the will of God in the Scriptures, with reference to the tests that he has handled wrongly in the past. Even Jesus relied upon the Scriptures for His strength. The Spirit was with Him, but the Spirit did not work mystically. Rather, He used His Word to fortify Christ against temptation. This learning is not merely intellectual, but must become experiential as well (cf. Colossians 1: 9-10). When one's faculties by reason of practice have been trained to discern between good and evil (Hebrews 5:14), he will be able to make good biblical choices and, thus, break the chain of sin at its earliest link. The goal, therefore, is biblical *action*, not sinful *reaction*; control by the Scriptures, not by the situation.

Consider Phyllis. Phyllis wanted to break the sinful habit of clamming up whenever she disliked something that Bratt, her husband, said or did. She realized that this led to self-pity, resentment, and sometimes ended in depressions. Her counselor suggested: "Phyllis, you must not allow this destructive process, this chain reaction, to get started. Let's work on *nipping it in the bud*. You must learn to resist the temptation God's way." Together they studied Epesians 4, Colossians 3, and other passages in which her problem is dealt with and concluded that God says that she would have to learn to *confront her husband helpfully* about issues instead of clamming up (cf. Ephesians 4:25, 29). Both Phyllis and Bratt agreed to begin working on the problem. Whenever Phyllis began to feel like clamming up, she was instructed to say to him immediately: "Bratt, I'm tempted to clam up, but I must not allow the sun to go down on my anger; will you hold a conference with me *now*?" He agreed to do so and promised to help her deal with the issue then and there. And if, in fact, Phyllis began to clam up without doing so, Bratt himself was to call a conference *at the earliest moment*.

Often, breaking the destructive patterns that accelerate sin involves the structuring and development of new responses of this sort. Proverbs 15:1, "A soft answer turns away wrath," for instance, suggests this. Here is a typical downward *reaction* pattern of the husband and wife who fail to follow this biblical injunction:

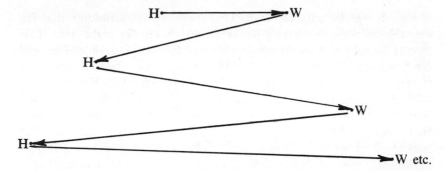

As each adds fuel to the argument, the relationship deteriorates, the gap between them widens, and the whole situation plunges into hopelessness. It is a pattern of wrath encouraging wrath. Proverbs 15:1, instead, encourages the pacification of wrath by a soft (rather than an equally hard) response:[7]

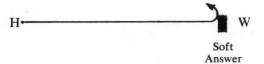

Soft
Answer

Restraint

While resistance is the desirable response that every counselee must learn and develop, since it alone will keep him from sin, counselors nevertheless must teach him what to do whenever he *fails* to resist temptation. It is then that restraint comes into view. The counselee will not always succeed in rejecting the sinful response. Sometimes, before he realizes what is happening,[8] anger toward another leading

7. Cf. also Proverbs 26:21. The same dynamic is true in talebearing (and receiving) as the close conjunction of Proverbs 26:20 and 26:21 indicates. Gossip takes two to flourish. When presented with gossip and slander, the potential recipient must learn to refuse to listen. One way is for the recipient to suggest: "This looks too serious, Mary, for you to tell me; I think you should see Sue herself about this matter." See also Hendricksen's excellent comments on *sophronizo* in Titus 2:4, where he notes the stress in the Word upon "curbing" as a necessary factor in Christian training. Wm. Hendricksen, *Commentary on I–II Timothy and Titus* (Grand Rapids: Baker Book House, 1957), p. 380.
8. Remember, a prominent feature of habit patterns is the essentially unconscious way in which one begins to respond to a given situation. Consequently, though he is responsible for it, yet he may often find himself going beyond the

to vicious thoughts of revenge will begin to burn brightly within. Only *then* he may realize that in his heart hatred is welling up. What can he do? Well, even if he has sinned in heart, by no means is it necessary to allow this sin to run its full course into outward expression as well. It can be *restrained* and checked so that the Christian counselee can gain the self-control which the Spirit develops in believers.[9] It is just by such testings that this self-control often is developed as one "practices" it (II Peter 1:10b).

How does such restraint work? What does it mean in practical contexts? Consider the following:

> When there are many words, transgression is unavoidable, but he who restrains his lips is wise (Proverbs 10:19; cf. also 21:23; 13:3).

and

> He who restrains his words has knowledge, and he who has a cool spirit is a man of understanding (Proverbs 17:26; cf. James 1:19).

and

> The heart of the righteous ponders how to answer, but the mouth of the wicked pours out evil things (Proverbs 15:28).

Thought before action or speech is an essential element in the restraint of evil. If he cannot speak coolly, he must wait until he cools down to do so. Pondering *how* to answer also is important.

If one has sinned in his heart, first he should ask God's forgiveness; then, having done so he may seek His help in meeting the situation biblically. The very time that this takes often is used by God to cool hot passion.

Take another example. Jane's problem is self-pity. Before recognizing that she has been doing so, she awakens to the fact that she has drifted into a blue funk. She suddenly recognizes that she is becoming depressed, sulking, and growing bitter. What can she do at this point?

Asaph found himself in a similar situation which he describes in the

---

initial point of resistance, and having sinned in heart *before* becoming conscious of his sinful behavior.

9. In Galatians 5:23, the last mentioned fruit of the Spirit is self-control. Peter speaks of this quality in his second epistle (II Peter 1:6) as an important addition to knowledge. He also stresses the practical importance of self-control as a help for the Christian in becoming useful and fruitful (1:8) and warns that bad consequences follow when one lacks it (1:9). It is also a necessary qualification in an elder. (Titus 1:8).

73rd Psalm. He says, "My steps had almost slipped." He was on the verge of some strong outward sinful expression of his inner sinful ruminations (cf. vs. 16). Envy and self-pity had almost gotten the better of him (vs. 22). But by the teaching given in the house of God (vss. 17 ff.), he was able to combat this problem. God's "counsel" (vs. 24) guided him out of the problem and would keep him from it in days to come. David's advice is similar:

> Fret not yourself because of evildoers. . . .
> Trust in the Lord and do good. . . .
> Fret not yourself, it leads only to evildoing (Psalm 37:1, 3, 8).

Clearly, again the answer is to turn to the Word of God as quickly as one becomes aware of the fact that he has slipped into sinful thoughts and attitudes. Usually it is the emotions that these stir up that make him aware of it. That Word both convicts of wrong (which must be confessed to God) and then guides in the proper response. Whatever the problem, there is a biblical response to it. In the Scriptures he will look for the biblical alternative. *Restraint* means, then, recognition of sin, seeking forgiveness for it, and obtaining help to discontinue it. It involves doing what God says rather than allowing the wrong to break out into outward manifestation. Instead of sinful action he must put into practice his proper responsibilities at the moment. Instead of self-pity, this may mean self-sacrifice. In place of revengeful thoughts, this may mean seeking ways to do good for another. Instead of sitting and worrying about what *might* happen tomorrow, this may mean getting up and getting to work on today's responsibilities. The self-centered man who makes mountains out of molehills because of his great concern even over the smallest matters pertaining to himself,[10] may need to turn to ways in which he may center his concern on others (cf. Philippians 2).

In conclusion, it is important to recognize that there are at least two points at which to break the chain of sin: (1) to prevent it, or, once begun, (2) to curtail it. The more frequently one prevents sin, the less frequently he will need to curtail it; and the more frequently he curtails it, the sooner he will be able to prevent it altogether.

---

10. So-called *perfectionism* is often no more than intense pride. In other cases it may be diversionary, redirecting others away from an area of sinful failure. Such intensive demands upon others (especially when they involve suspicion of others) may indicate the presence of sin of the very sort suspected in another.

Getting Help from Another

Change, we have insisted, is difficult; it is difficult for a fifty-year-old man, and it is difficult for a child. Once a pattern has become a habit, it has become almost a part of one's nature. As we say, it has become *second nature*. Habits are a blessing or a curse, depending upon *what* the habit is. We are blessed by not having to think about what to do every morning when we brush our teeth or button our shirts. We now perform these daily procedures automatically (i.e., without thinking consciously about how to do them), because they have become habitual to us. So too, *without thinking* we respond in temper, clam up, internalize resentments, etc., according to the sinful living patterns that we have developed. We all know the curse of such habits.

A child at first must be reminded to pick up his socks when he removes them at night if he is to learn this good habit. When he begins to do so on his own, words of appreciation spur him on. So, too, when adults attempt to replace a sinful response by a biblical one that is pleasing to God, they often need reminders and encouragement. Christian adults sometimes think such help is beneath them. Usually those who fail to accept available help (from a friend, family member, etc.) end up poorly. Often pride is behind the objection. Two verses are helpful at this point: I Corinthians 10:12—"Let him who thinks he stands take heed lest he fall," and Proverbs 16:18—"Pride goes before destruction and a haughty spirit before a fall." The Scriptures continually *stress* the need for mutual help. A good exercise for any counselor is to study the use of the words "one another"in the New Testament. For starters, he can refer the counselee to Hebrews 10:24, 25.

Mary had developed the habit of interrupting her husband whenever he was talking on the telephone. She wanted to break this habit which had led to frequent quarrels between them. But she found that she needed help, since she found herself still interrupting before she realized it. Peter, her husband, devised a sign that he kept in a desk drawer near the phone. Whenever he was using the telephone, he pulled out the sign and set it conspicuously upon the desk (see top of following page). It was not long before Mary had overcome the habit. Cooperation on the part of her husband had, in a few weeks, enabled her to solve a problem that had caused irritation and difficulty between them for many years.

> **Please do not interrupt.**
>
> **Remember honey,**
>
> **You are working on this problem.**
>
> **Thanx!**

Such help usually is readily available to any persons who truly are anxious to find effective solutions to their problems. Christians everywhere are exhorted to help one another. No one who knows Christ and wants to "put off" the "old man" with his temper, lust, lying, etc., need go without help. If he is willing to state his purpose and request help, he will find it among the people of God.

People who quarrel viciously over squeezing toothpaste tubes in the middle, turning lights on or off, leaving closet doors open after using them, etc., give evidence of several facts:

1. Their problem is probably bigger than the particular issue (or issues) over which they are quarreling. The intensity of the emotion is far greater than that which is appropriate to the issue *per se*. Usually there is a host of other problems dammed up behind it exerting the emotional pressure. Resentment and bitterness often are revealed by inappropriate amounts of emotion attached to an otherwise minor issue.

2. They are not seeking solutions to problems; they are concerned about making points, proving themselves right and the other wrong, etc. Wherever people truly seek solutions and turn their energies to such efforts, like Peter and Mary they are able to devise ways and means of helping one another. Change *then* comes quickly. Counselors always must be aware of the fact, then, that *seeming* cooperation may not always be genuine cooperation and help. It will not become such unless the *relationship* has been dealt with before tackling the *issue*.

People do not look for solutions to personal conflicts when they have not yet repented of their sins. They must be brought to repentance before God for their unforgiving attitudes and led to seek reconciliation. Repentance leads to "fruit" which is fitting or appropriate. It is out of repentance (lit., "a change of mind") that changed living develops. Repentant persons readily accept all the help that they can get.

Often counselors need to instruct well-meaning but poorly informed persons about *how* to help another. For instance, if the person is overly sympathetic (i.e., not truly sympathetic in the deepest sense) and allows the counselee to get away with failure without pointing it out to him, he really harms rather than helps. To be safe, it is wise for counselors to state *exactly what sort of help* needs to be given, *who* might best be enlisted to give help, and *how* he may give it.[11] This may involve noting possible pitfalls in giving help. It may entail both warning against these and instructing the helper how to avoid them. It may necessitate the writing out of specific instructions. Help is important, but it is even more important that what is done *helps* rather than aggravates. Nagging does not help; reminding does. Appreciation helps; minimizing or false assurances do not. Counselors will discover that time spent making sure about help is time well spent and, in the long run, time saved. It is important, in checking upon homework, to check out the way in which promised help actually was given. Here again it is mandatory to get specific information. (Ask, how often? How consistently? When? In what ways? etc.)

Stressing the Whole Relationship to Christ

To Avoid Gimmicks

Since so much time in counseling (rightly) must be spent in detailing the concrete and specific changes and aspects of changes that must be made, counselees may tend to focus upon the change and forget the more basic fact that this all has to do with pleasing God and living for the honor of His Son, Jesus Christ. The forest easily can be neglected in caring for the tree. Counselors thereby must never allow techniques to become gimmicks.

How can this evil be avoided? To begin with, counselors can warn against the danger. Often, they will find themselves saying (for example), "Fred, you must not want to make this change chiefly to get your wife back; you must do it because God says so, *whether Myrtle returns or not*."

But in addition to warnings, certain measures can be taken. (1) Whenever extended counseling is in order, the counselor should discuss not merely the particular problem presented, but the counselee's *whole* life. He is a whole person, and to some extent (more or less) the problem

---

11. Cf. *Competent to Counsel* for more information on enlisting others to help, pp. 241-247.

will relate to other areas of life. (2) Regular Bible reading, prayer, and fellowship with the people of God should be encouraged. The regular discipline of Bible study, prayer and fellowship, and ministry in the church is essential to all growth and forms not only the proper ground upon which specific tasks can be handled, but also provides for the regular sustenance necessary for healthy Christian livng. Moreover, whenever these proper activities are carried on, regularly, all areas of the life are strengthened, and the particular area that is in focus during counseling does not balloon out of proportion. Too often life can be built around problem-solving. Too often counselees can focus upon themselves and become morbidly and idolatrously introspective, rather than center their concerns about Christ. Insistence upon regular attention to these vital elements in strengthening the whole man in his proper perspective to God and his neighbor, therefore, is essential. Counselors who fail to emphasize the need for them may wonder why counseling itself can also become an occasion for failure and furthering failure.

It is wise, therefore, early in counseling (the first or second session) to pay attention to these matters. Raise the question (the P.D.I. does this automatically prior to the first session) and take time to explain the need for regularity in these questions. Early homework often consists of assignments to begin daily morning Bible reading and prayer and/or to attend the worship services of a conservative Reformed church. Sometimes devotional guides, like *Today*, are distributed to counselees.[12] Often a Scripture portion (the Gospel of John for non-Christians or the book of Proverbs for believers; "begin reading with chapter ten") may be handed out with profit.

Prayer and Bible reading *in the morning* is encouraged to stress the practical use of the Scriptures in life. The counselor suggests: "If you read a portion each morning and determine what change God intends to effect in you by it, you can carry that thought with you throughout the day and prayerfully seek to live accordingly." This means that if the counselee reads: "return a blessing for evil," he should then ask God to help him to do so during that day at home, school, or work.

To Handle Life-Dominating Problems

It is of special importance to counselors to recognize that focus upon

---

12. Publication of the *Back to God Hour*. Copies may be obtained by writing to 10858 South Michigan Avenue, Chicago, Illinois 60628.

"*the* problem" to the exclusion of or diminished attention to the rest of the counselee's life patterns easly can result in counseling failure. This is particularly true whenever the counselor is dealing with a counselee who has been involved in a life-dominating problem. A typical example of a life-dominating problem is what James referred to when he spoke of the doubter who is a "double minded man," "unstable *in all his ways*" (James 1:8). He is not to be trusted in any area of life. Nor can his problem be handled *merely* by dealing with doubt. It cuts a wide swath across every area of his life (cf. also James 2:10; 3:2, 5, 16; 4:8; 5:14-16).

To some extent, all problems affect all of the man, since he is a *whole* person. Also, all aspects of his life have effects upon *the* problem that he presents. But this point is of particular significance when dealing with certain problems that tend to affect (and are affected by) every area of one's life. These are the sorts of life styles that Paul singles out in I Corinthians 5:11; 6:9, 10, and that John mentions in Revelation 22:15. When a man (as a man; as a whole person) can be labeled fairly as a *drunkard, homosexual*, a *drug addict*, etc., he has a life-dominating problem. He is no longer merely a man, but the Bible speaks of him as a certain kind of man (drunkard; liar; double minded, etc.); i.e., a man characterized by or dominated by the particular problem that gives him his name. The Bible labels those with life-dominating problems.

Since all of his life is affected by (and affects the problem), the man with a life-dominating problem finds that all of his life must come under review in counseling. All areas of his life will need alteration. A drunkard develops sinful patterns of family relations, irresponsibility toward his job, church, neighbors, etc. His health usually is affected as well. Total restructuring, therefore, is necessary. Drunkenness leads to bad family relationships; on the other hand, trouble in family relationships may be the occasion for the drunkard to run to the bottle. A life-dominating problem, thus, is one that is fed circularly in a vicious circle.

Whenever a counselee's problem turns out to be one large, life-dominating sin, like homosexuality, erroneously he may think that he has only one problem to solve. He even may become impatient with a counselor who attempts to look at other aspects of his life. "Why don't you get to *the* problem? Why all of this extraneous concern about family relationships, work, health?" he may ask. But in such cases, the problem cannot help but affect every other aspect of his life. Its effects doubtless have bled over into social life, married life, work, physical and financial matters. Whenever he has problems at work, he seeks out his homosexual companions for some immediate gratification. When he resorts to homosexual sin, the guilt adversely affects his work. *The* problem and problems in every area tend to feed one another. Structured, or disciplined, living is living that conforms to God's commandments. Living a life of love is the goal. But life like this requires full structuring of the whole person. Clients and counselors alike should be satisfied with nothing less than the goal of total structuring according to God's law.

The following chart shows the problem and points to God's solution.

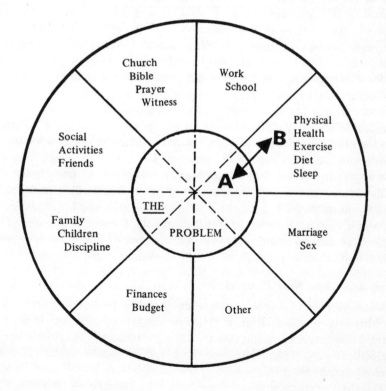

Figure 3

Total restructuring means dealing with *the* problem in relationship to all areas of life. The problem affects (and is affected by) all areas, and whenever all areas are in proper relationship to God, the dotted lines become solid lines and *the* problem dissolves. Arrow A-B indicates the way in which each affects the other. Drunkenness, e.g., leads to poor health. Poor health, in turn, may discourage and lead to hitting the bottle.

Of course, not only life-dominating sins lead to the need for total life counseling. For a discussion of how patterns of general irresponsibility can produce the same effects as life-dominating sins, cf. *Competent to Counsel*, pp. 153-156.

Total counseling takes seriously the commandment to be "filled with the Spirit" (Ephesians 5:18). In the context, the phrase is set over against a life-dominating sin: drunkenness ("Do not get drunk with wine . . . but be filled with the Spirit"). As that which must replace such sins, the apostle commands, "be filled with" (let your life be dominated and controlled by) the Spirit. To be "filled with" fear, or joy, or sorrow in the Scriptures means to be so affected by these that they dominate and control all of one's life.

Total structuring in counseling, then, is the attempt to take this commandment seriously. The counselor's task is to encourage the counselee to seek God's dominance in *all* of his life in place of the life-dominating sin. Focus upon *the* sin or *the* problem alone is insufficient. Another way to put it is to see that *the* problem is not *drinking*, but *drunkenness* a life style affecting one's whole way of life). That which must be put on in such instances is a new way of life across the board, the particulars of which can be discovered only by making a total evaluation of the counselee's life style and replacing in every area of life all of those sinful activities that were geared into the life-dominating sin.

Practicing the New Pattern

Patterns do not develop automatically. They become a part of one's life through practice. Jotham "became mighty because he ordered his ways before the Lord his God" (II Chronicles 27:6). *Ordered* or *established* ways (Berkeley) are the result of such practice. Holiness does not come instantaneously.

Why is it that counselees often fail in the attempt to become holy? They *want* the right thing; yet so rarely achieve it. Of course, there may be many reasons for this. At the bottom of it all is sin. But here let us single out one major reason (perhaps *the* major reason) why the gears don't mesh as they should. What is the problem? There is no such thing as instant godliness. Today there is instant pudding, instant coffee, instant houses shipped on trucks, instant everything. And counselees want instant godliness as well. They want somebody to give them three easy steps to godliness that they can take next Friday and be godly. They want counselors to speak magic words, sprinkle wiffle dust on them, or wave their Bibles over them to effect instant change. The trouble is, godliness doesn't come that way.

The Bible is very plain about how godliness does come. Paul wrote about godliness to Timothy. In his first letter to that budding young minister, he said, in contrast to all of the ways that will fail (mentioned in the first part of the verse), "Timothy, you must *discipline yourself* for the purpose of godliness" (I Timothy 4:7). Discipline is the secret of godliness.

The word discipline has disappeared from minds, mouths, and pulpits in our culture. Modern American society hardly knows what discipline means. Yet, apart from discipline, there is no other way to attain godliness; discipline is God's path to godliness. The counselor, therefore, must learn how to help the counselee to discipline himself for the purpose of godliness.

The first thing to notice is that there is no option about being godly. Counselees must be persuaded of this fact. Paul's words constitute a divine command to discipline ourselves for that purpose. God intends for His children to be godly. In other places He commands the very same thing. He says, for example, "Be holy as I am holy," and "Be perfect as I am perfect." It is certain that we will never reach perfection in this life (I John 1:8), but perfect godliness is the goal toward which every believer must discipline himself and toward which he must move every day. This means becoming more like God Himself each day. The godly man leads a life that reflects God. Godliness is the goal of the Christian life; he must be shown how to please God by being, thinking, doing, saying, and feeling what God wishes.

Notice God says that believers must discipline themselves "for the purpose of (or, literally, *toward*) godliness." The original means "to be *oriented toward* godliness." One's whole life ought to be disciplined (i.e., structured, set up, organized, and running day by day) toward the

goal of godliness. Everything that happens should be used to contribute something toward reaching that goal. Monday through Saturday.
not Sunday only, the counselee must be shown how to move toward the
goal, one step, or two steps, or ten steps further down the road. He
will become that much more like God only because of what he has done
and thought and said each day.

When life is oriented toward (or focused upon) godliness, the goal
will come into mind constantly. The counselor will instruct the counselee to think at work, at home, or in school, "I am to reflect God
in this project." There are times, of course, when he is discouraged or
gets tired or becomes upset that he will lose sight of the goal. He may
even rebel against the idea. But if he is a genuine believer in Christ, the
well will never run dry; down in his heart the desire trickles back, and
he will find himself saying, "That is what I want." It is true that the
believer "hungers and thirsts after righteousness." Counselors, therefore, must not give up too quickly.

When Paul wrote, "You are a new creature; all things have become
new," this is one thing that he had in mind: the Holy Spirit already has
oriented believers toward God and His holiness, putting a new focus on
all of life. But that does not automatically make them godly. Because of
the work of Christ, they have been *counted* perfect in God's sight, but in
actuality are still far from the goal. Yet, the new life in Christ is *oriented*
toward godliness; that is why at times the believer aches for it.

The problem is that although basically the orientation is new, many
day-by-day practices have not yet been oriented toward godliness. The
"old man" (old ways of living) is still an unwelcome companion. One
reason why the counselee's good resolves have not been more fully
realized may be that he has never learned how to *discipline* himself for
godliness. It is the counselor's task to urge and help him to do so.

"How may I discipline myself?" he may ask insistently. First the
counselor must indicate that the word *discipline* clearly shows that godliness cannot be zapped. It cannot be whipped up like instant pudding.
Godliness doesn't come that way. Discipline means *work*; it means
sustained daily effort. The word Paul used is the one from which the
English words "gymnastics" and "gymnasium" have been derived. It
is a term related to athletics. An athlete becomes an expert only by
years of hard practice. There are no instant athletes. It takes years of
regular practice to achieve athletic skills.

No erstwhile weight lifter, for example, says, "Here is a very heavy weight. I have never lifted weights before, but that looks like the largest one. I'll try to press it." He is likely to break his back. He can't do it that way. He must start out with a small weight the first week, then gradually over the months and years add heavier and heavier ones. He must work up to the heaviest one. Nor does he decide, "This week I'll lift weights for five hours on Friday and then I'll forget about it for the next six weeks." Athletes practice regularly, usually every day for at least a short period of time. They work daily, day after day, until what they are doing becomes "natural" (i.e., second nature) to them.

That is what an athlete does. And that is exactly what is involved in the word that Paul used here. Continued daily effort is an essential element of Christian *discipline*.

Discipline, so conceived, is something that the Christian church lacks in our time. It is high time, therefore, that counselors recognize that God requires discipline by constant practice in obeying His revealed will and thus exercise (train) their counselees toward godliness.

Practically speaking, what does this involve? In Luke 9:23, Jesus commands His disciples: "Take up your cross *daily*," *denying* the self. He does not mean denying oneself *something*. There is no idea of doing penance in this. "For Lent I'll stop chewing gum," says the penitent. This is exactly *not* what is in view. Rather, Jesus insisted that Christians must deny *the self* within them. By the self, He meant the old desires, the old ways, the old practices, the old habit patterns that were acquired before conversion. They became so much a part of day-by-day practice that *they* became second nature. Men were born sinners, but it took practice to develop each man's particular style of sinning. The counselee's old life was disciplined toward ungodliness. That is why Paul says that he must daily deny (literally say "no" to) the self.

The need for daily denial of the self indicates the presence of a day-by-day battle inside of the Christian. He must "take up the cross" as an instrument of death upon which to crucify the self every day. Taking up the cross we have seen doesn't mean carrying some heavy burden. It is not enduring a trial ("I guess my cross is my wife"). No, that isn't what is in view. Taking up the cross means going to the place of death. It means putting to death the old life patterns of the old man.

But that is not enough. We have seen that whenever God says "put off" He also says "put on." On the positive side, each day one also must seek to "follow" Jesus Christ. That is what it means to discipline oneself for godliness. It means to continue to say "no" to self and to say "yes" to Christ every day until one by one each of the old habitual ways is replaced by a new one. It means that by daily endeavor to follow God's Son, one finds at length that doing so is more "natural" than not doing so. The Holy Spirit thus enables a believer to put off the old man and put on the new man.

The new ways reflect the true righteousness and holiness that is in Jesus Christ. The image of God was ruined by the fall, but by this process of sanctification bit by bit it begins to show up in the Christian's life as it originally did in Adam's life. That is what discipline toward godliness is all about. Godliness in the final analysis is becoming, by His grace, like God once again.

There is no question that much counseling fails because of the neglect of discipline. In II Timothy 3:16 the counselor must not miss the fact that Paul says the Scriptures not only provide that which is necessary for teaching what God requires, all that is needed to *convict* a counselee of his sin, and the essential help to *correct* him, but also that which will enable him to *train* the counselee *in righteousness*. It is not enough to know what God requires, that one has failed to meet those requirements, and how to recoup when he does so. It is of the greatest importance to learn to live in such a way that he does not continually fall back into those old ways again. Training in righteousness, therefore, must not be neglected.

Cases of Change

Now, how does all of this work out in practice? How may these principles be applied in specific cases? The two similar cases that follow illustrate some of the simplest fundamentals of biblical change. Hopefully, precisely because of their simplicity, the principles will stand out most clearly.[13]

The Case of Bill and the Traffic Light

Almost as soon as he learned to drive, Bill discovered that he began

---

13. Cases, dealing with other particular problems, appear later in their appropriate places.

to have mixed feelings about driving. While he enjoyed driving on the open roads, whenever he was forced to drive in traffic he suffered from extreme tension and headaches. This was found to be true particularly in those areas in which there are many successive unsynchronized traffic signals. Early in his driving experience Bill developed the bad habit of trying to beat red lights. Whenever he failed, he would sit impatiently waiting for the light to change, tensely stiff-arming the wheel and holding it with a vise-like grip. He would rock the car back and forth on hills or inch forward on levels, urging the light to turn green. In recent years he had begun to talk to the lights, telling them off for their failure to cooperate with him; where another driver in front of him did not respond instantly to a change of light, Bill would make his disgust audible for blocks, not only by yelling at him, but also by blowing his horn condemningly. At length Bill so learned to hate traffic lights that, it made no difference whether they were red or green, he would begin to become tense and angry (often without even recognizing why) whenever driving in an area with many such signals.

Bill finally became acutely aware of the need to do something about the driving problem when he moved from the country into an urban area. Ever since the move, driving had grown very distasteful and the tension and headaches were becoming a daily occurrence. He now regularly arrived at work nervous and tense; when he came home at night he was almost always irritable and upset. Interpersonal relations were suffering on both fronts. It was then that he came for help. In about five weeks he had not only conquered the problem, but in addition he had learned to enjoy drivng in traffic and (in particular) to look forward to red traffic lights. How was this accomplished?

The procedure was as follows: first, in counseling Bill determined to change his feelings about stop lights, since his attitude and behavior were unbecoming to a Christian. He became truly repentant over the problem; that made him willing to change. His counselor encouraged him not only to stop his impatience but also to use stop lights for a good purpose. Instead of considering them to be barriers, together they decided to ask God to turn them into blessings. Rather than becoming tense and worked up over each red light, he determined to look on them as relaxation breaks in his driving routine for which he should give God thanks. He was to learn to look forward to stop lights as an opportunity to take time out from driving, to thank God for it, let his hands drop loosely into his lap, lean back, smile, and relax. He posted on the dashboard a card containing these words:

Remember . . .

At

Relaxation Breaks

Thank God,

Smile & Relax!

At first, Bill frequently caught himself slipping into the old patterns, but each time the card reminded him. So instead, he prayed, gave thanks and then leaned back. Soon relaxation became the rule rather than the exception. In almost no time, urban driving became not merely tolerable, but a distinct pleasure, with traffic lights giving the most satisfaction of all.

Many other variations on this theme are possible. Instead of yelling at poor drivers and working up one's blood pressure over their lack of consideration or mistakes, such incidents may be turned to profit by learning to look on them as *opportunities* to practice defensive driving techniques and show Christian courtesy, love, and concern. The key to each is the recognition that a sinful habit pattern not only must be broken and eliminated, but that it also must be *replaced* by a proper (biblical) response. Indeed, the only way to eliminate a habitual response to an inevitably recurring circumstance, we have seen, is to replace it by another. Bill could not simply cease reacting to stop lights; he had to develop a *new response*, since a response could not be avoided. Denial alone does not extinguish a bad response pattern. If instead Bill had opted for the non-Christian process of negative affirmation, he might have practiced saying under his breath, "I will not become upset with traffic lights." But the chances are that soon he may have heard himself repeating those words in *anger*. It would not have been long before he would have abandoned the practice as futile. Something more than denial was needed.

The Case of Benjamin and the Toll Booth

For Benjamin every toll booth had become a hated reminder of the high cost of living (and he had to use toll roads going to and from work each day). No matter how jovial he had felt in the morning as he started out from home, a feeling of despair and distress always overtook him as soon as he sighted the toll booth. As a Christian he knew that this was wrong. Like Bill, he overcame this by prayer and the consequent determination that by the grace of God he would turn every toll booth into a high point in his daily driving experiences. In a short while, instead of frowning, he learned to look forward to toll booths. How did he do it?

Instead of concentrating on the money that he paid out at the booth, Ben determined instead to become interested in the persons to whom he paid it. In no time at all, he learned to enjoy every pleasant brief exchange with the only human being to whom he had the opportunity to speak while driving. He became well acquainted with two or three of the officers who manned the booth and particularly enjoyed their cheery responses. He pictured the many hundreds of persons who passed through those same gates impersonally with not a single thought about the human being who received their coins and tokens. He soon gained a genuine sense of compassion for the toll gate officers and was delighted when they responded with surprise and evident appreciation to his daily greetings. Each day he thought more and more about those guards, what he could say briefly, and how he might witness to them. He even prayed for them as he approached the booth. It was not long before the initial picture had been reversed entirely. At this point Benjamin has not yet witnessed to those men, but he is currently looking for just the right tract or pamphlet that he can leave in their hands as an opener. What a difference!

Summary

The instructive facts in these two cases are (1) that rapid radical change is possible when a counselee becomes aware of his sin, repents, and determines to change. (2) A new proper activity, deliberately substituted for a faulty one by disciplined practice speeded up the change and made it permanent. There was not merely a putting off but also a putting on. Traffic signals and toll booths still were encountered regularly, but the *way in which* Bill and Benjamin learned to handle lights and booths was exactly the opposite. (3) Because they *acted* differently toward the problem, they soon began to *feel* differently about it. It is doubtful whether they merely could have determined to change their feelings without substituting a new approach for the old. That is one reason why God insists upon positive action (put on) as well as the negative (put off). (4) Change required discipline. They continued until the new practice became automatic, Once the change had occurred, the "natural" (comfortable, unconscious) response to a light or to a toll booth was pleasant. The change in feelings (as it usually is) was an indication that a permanent change in the life pattern had been effected.

Chapter Twenty

GETTING STARTED

Advertise

How does a young pastor begin his counseling ministry? Assuming that his convictions are biblical, his background and training are adequate, and his qualifications are sufficient, the first thing that the pastor must do is to *advertise*. It is unfortunate that this is necessary, but because many pastors have avoided their counseling responsibilities or have shown themselves to be so incompetent, congregations do not know what to expect from a new man unless he lets them know. A young man, because of his youth, also may find that a period of waiting is inevitable.[1] Young or old, unless he is well known beforehand, a new pastor may find that there will be a waiting period before serious counseling begins. During this period, the congregation will be sizing him up. Members of the congregation may want to take a hard look at his maturity, balance, and understanding of the Scriptures, as well as his ways with people, before approaching him for counsel. This initial precaution is not only normal, but good (cf. I Timothy 4:12b). However, if after a reasonable length of time there still is no counseling to speak of, something is wrong and *must* be rectified. What one may not conclude from the failure of members to seek counseling, is that in this world of sin with its sad consequences he has happened upon a congregation of saints who are just a shade away from glorification.

Let us return to *advertising*, then. By advertising, I mean that the pastor not only must be an example, but he must let his people know that he is willing and able to help them. He may do this directly or indirectly. Since the latter is more desirable than the former, let us consider the indirect approach first.

Indirect advertising (and I confess that I am using the word with some

---

1. He should not allow any man to "despise" his youth (I Timothy 4:12). He may best counteract this common tendency (as Paul says) by demonstrating through his own prudent, godly living aided by timely, helpful preaching that he is capable of handling life's problems God's way.

reservation because of the poor connotations that have gathered about it) at first may be done largely through preaching. Whenever a preacher's choice of subjects, his practical application of the Scriptures, and his use of bell-ringing illustrations ring true to a congregation, he usually will find that (unless there is a special problem) people will begin to turn to him for help. What makes a sermon ring true? Above all else, the sermon that has the ring of authenticity about it is one that meets human needs with the Word of God at the level where people themselves are grappling with them. It brings the abstract down into the concrete. Listeners vibrate responsively to such sermons. After hearing a sermon like that, one does not merely go away with new information. He says to himself: "He knows me; he knows the problems that I am facing." Illustrations drawn from experiences that are typical of the everyday life and struggles of the congregation are of the greatest importance.

When the members of the congregation are convinced that the pastor is on their track, they will seek him out. After he has actually helped a few people overcome their problems God's way, the word will get out. Then people will come, often in droves. The need for advertising, thankfully, may be short-lived in such cases. Satisfied counselees will from that time do the pastor's advertising for him![2]

If there is inordinate hesitancy on the part of the members of a particular congregation to seek counsel in response to indirect advertising, it may be because of special circumstances in that congregation which contribute to the reticence. Perhaps there has been a history of failure in counseling on the part of previous pastors. They easily could have destroyed confidence by foolish or simply ineffective counseling practices. Possibly scandalous leaks of information took place. Perhaps indiscreet advances were made by a previous pastor toward a female member of the congregation. Conceivably group counseling of a sort that adopts unbiblical principles was practiced.[3] Who can begin to

---

2. Cf., in this regard, Mark 3:10; 7:36; Luke 5:14, 15. In such cases it may be necessary to train elders to share in the work of counseling.

3. Cf. *The Big Umbrella*, *op. cit.*, "Group Therapy—or Slander?" for a discussion of some of these abuses of group processes, pp. 237-246. In any case, whenever a pastor discovers that wrong has been done (in counseling or otherwise), he should seek to discover whether the wrong has been righted. If it has not, it is possible that God's blessing upon that congregation may be withheld until the wrong has been dealt with. Cf. Revelation 2-3 for Christ's concern about the spiritual conditions of whole congregations.

enumerate the various ways in which a congregation might have become
wary of or disillusioned about pastoral counseling? What does one do
in such circumstances to change this situation? How can he show that
we must not stop eating food altogether because some food is poisoned?

There are several things that he can do. First, he can patiently wait
and pray. God may send him a counseling case in spite of the former
difficulties. When persons are desperate, they will throw reservation
and caution to the winds. It is altogether possible that rendering sufficient pastoral help in such a case might lead to a breakthrough that
will release the logjam. Or, a case or two from outside of the congregation may give counseling its necessary momentum.

Secondly, the pastor can begin to advertise more *directly*. In the
church paper he can write a series of articles discussing typical problems that God's people face and disclose his own desire to help through
pastoral counseling. If he is able to show authentic understanding of
common needs and offer genuine help, his series may pay off. He even
may wish to discuss the place of counseling in the ministry of the
Christian pastor, referring to Colossians 1:28, Acts 20:31, etc. These
passages, in particular, indicate the need of *every* Christian at some
time or other for personal counseling.[4]

An advertising campaign may end in a complete failure, may evoke
comments about the particular prejudices toward or fears about counseling that have developed in this congregation, or it may be convincing. If the second result is forthcoming, the campaign will have
afforded the opportunity to discover and correct any misunderstandings
about counseling that may have arisen. It may unearth the information
that is needed to alleviate the fears or erase the prejudice. If the first
result (failure) is the outcome of the advertising campaign, then the
pastor must take other measures.[5]

---

4. For further discussion of this important point read *The Big Umbrella*, "You
Are Your Brother's Counselor," pp. 123-156.

5. Of course, throughout this discussion I am assuming that the pastor himself is not the cause of the problem. He ought carefully to consider whether
anything in the brief ministry already could have turned off the congregation.
If he suspects that he may in some way be at fault, he should go to his elders,
level with them about his problem, and ask them to level with him about what
they may know concerning it. He may also use his board of elders to discover
whether there are other reasons that may have made the congregation leary of
counseling.

Another way to elicit some response from a congregation is to announce a series of messages concerning topics that are likely to encourage those who are having difficulties to seek help. The pastor may mention that he will be particularly interested in conferring privately about any matters in these messages that may have occasioned some question or pointed out some need. This point may be stressed in the weekly bulletin during the period in which the messages are being delivered. A series on the family, or marriage, or Christian personal relations, or communication in the home, or biblical child discipline, etc., if carefully developed with clear scriptural principles concretely applied to live problems, may be the catalyst for counseling. But, let me stress, this series *must* be preached and applied to lives *at the level where the members of the congregation live.* That is likely to do the job. If, however, the series is abstract, he may do more harm than good. The congregation may conclude that he is an ivory tower theorist who could never help them, since he seems to know nothing of life as it is really lived.

How to Stimulate Counseling

Many other things may be done to encourage counseling. I cannot list them all here; biblical creativity, calculated to meet the individual situation, is needed anyway. Let me, therefore, make only this concluding suggestion. At the door each Sunday people have the bad habit of mentioning numerous things to the pastor as they leave. Some pastors become annoyed at this habit, but they might think twice instead. The practice, bad as it is, can be turned to advantage. It affords an excellent opportunity to begin to structure counseling sessions as a natural and assumed fact from the beginning of one's ministry. Suppose that when he is leaving church, Bill says to you: "Pastor, there is something that I'd like to talk to you about." Immediately the pastor should whip out his appointment book, find the earliest likely open space, and with pencil poised reply, "Fine, Bill, can you drop by the study on your way home from work at 4:30 Tuesday?" The new pastor must not be too quick to suggest discussing the matter on the phone. He should not offer to pay him a visit. Rather, he should *assume*, from the first week, that members of the congregation will want to discuss matters in the privacy of the study. Even if Bill's problem is not large and requires no more than one visit, the pastor will already have begun to acclimate him to the idea of coming to the study to discuss matters. After two or three profitable visits about such less serious matters, it will be easier and very natural for Bill to come about a more personal problem. Indeed, the lesser matter often turns into a discussion of a greater one in the friendly, quiet, and helpful atmosphere of the pastor's study. If the pastor becomes study oriented in his own thinking and acting, most of his people will become study oriented too. If the matter is too trivial to warrant Bill's visit and can be settled on the phone, let Bill say so. There is no harm done by making the suggestion. Besides, at the very least, a little bit more indirect advertising that later may pay off with Bill or someone else has been done.

No pastor may conclude on the basis of the New Testament and the Christian doctrine of sin as it is set forth in the Scriptures that any congregation is free from problems. Rather, he must assume that many unsolved problems exist among the members of his congregation. Massive amounts of biblical teaching about sin in the believer's life and the need for change are too clear to be misunderstood. If a pastor is not consulted frequently by many in his congregation, he may be sure that it is not because they do not need it. Therefore, the failure should concern him, and in one way or another, he must make it his business to discover what stands in their way. By the grace of God he then must do everything possible to rectify the situation. Somehow he must stir the pot so that the beans rise to the surface.

Counseling Center or Study?

Sometimes pastors complain that if they operated out of a counseling center rather than in a pastoral context they would have many more advantages for doing counseling. Take it from one who has done both that the opposite is true. The pastor has more going for him than the counselor in a center. The center lacks much and can be a very artificial situation. Perhaps you are wondering how I can say this and may even doubt that I can substantiate the claim. Well, let me try.

By comparison with those who counsel in a pastoral context, the center counselor's resources are pitifully meagre. To begin with, the counselor in the center knows no particulars about the counselee beforehand. It is true that he knows much in general, as I have said earlier. But almost all of the specific information that is gathered about him must be obtained rapidly from him and others close to him for the first time as he comes for counseling under conditions of stress. The judgments that a center counselor makes cannot grow out of long association with and close observation of the counselee in many life contexts. Such judgments are bound to lack some depth and maturity. Sometimes one of the problems that looms largest for the center counselor is obtaining an accurate picture of the counselee. This he does, in part, by making and holding tentative conclusions. These he continually subjects to revaluation and to revision as newer and better information becomes available. First impressions frequently may be wrong. Pastors, on the other hand, know much detail beforehand from various sources, the most important of which may be from personal observation and relationship. Consequently, the pastor may concentrate immediately on the new data that occasioned the counseling session. He does not have to spend precious minutes or hours sizing up the counselee and making preliminary judgments and revised judgments about his personality, etc.[6] The center counselor must allocate a significant proportion of his time to this activity, along with the examination of the data that pertain to the issue. Thus the pastor has a decided advantage that enables him to speed up counseling immeasurably. It is possible for this one factor to reduce the total number of sessions by as many as three or four.

"Wait a minute," you say, "knowing the person is not always an advantage. You can form incorrect judgments about the counselee over a long period of time that may hurt the session, and what about the problem of knowing him *too* well?" I wish to reserve any discussion of the second objection for a few paragraphs. Let me simply say with reference to the first that any good pastor is always reevaluating. A man who forms a prejudicial opinion about another and steadfastly adheres to it, in spite of evidence to the contrary, lacks a necessary ingredient for exercising good pastoral care. This kind of man not only makes a poor counselor; he also will be a poor pastor in general. If flexibility and movement are required of the center counselor, the same is required of the pastoral counselor as well. The great difference between the two is that the pastoral counselor initially has so much more

---

6. Of course, he must always be prepared to reevaluate; indeed the information that he is about to receive in counseling may make a great difference. Previous conclusions about members should be subject to revision.

information of various sorts upon which to base not only his judgments, but also upon which to base his reevaluations.[7]

The center counselor learns much in a hurried way. He cannot learn all that he should like to know in the time allotted to him; nor can he ever learn enough to make altogether accurate judgments. Some of his judgments almost always will be approximate rather than right on the nose. The center counselor sees the person only in trouble. He has not seen him in peace, in joy, in feverish excitement; he knows him only as a counselee. He can make only rough generalizations about how he relates to many of the other significant areas of his life, what kind of responsibility he has shown in the local church, etc. But before the counselee enters his study, the pastor already is in possession of most of these data.

Again, the center counselor must build confidence *de novo*, as well as learn to know the counselee as a person. In other words, it is not only the pastor who knows much already, but the counselee knows a great deal more about his counselor as well. He already has some confidence in the pastor, or he would not have come to him for help. He will not need to waste time with initial thrusts and parries in order to take the measure of his counselor. The pastoral counselor, in contrast, usually does not need to work on the problem of confidence during the early sessions as the center counselor often does. All of the pastor's time *from the outset* can be devoted to a consideration of the problem that occasioned the session. This is perhaps the greatest advantage that he has. Good pastors, because they have already established a good relationship with the members of their flock, may zero in on the issue immediately rather than spend large portions of the counseling time working on interpersonal relationships.[8]

Obviously in terms of beginning information the pastor has the ad-

---

7. Pastors should always be studying and trying to understand every member of the congregation. Such study begins when he arrives on the scene, not when the counselee turns up in the counseling room.

8. Of course, pastors often are called upon to operate virtually as center counselors in this respect when persons from outside of the congregation seek their help. The amount of time allotted to working on rapport has been over emphasized by feeling-oriented counselors. Rapport is best established as a by-product, not by seeking it *directly*. In the biblical, businesslike way that the counselor goes about conducting the counseling session, by his advice, and through the concerned effort that he puts forth in attempting to understand and take initial steps to solve the problem, he best gains rapport.

vantage over the nonpastoral counselor. Yet that is not all, by any means. Consider this significant fact: there is little or no teeth in the counseling that is done in a center. At times the best that the center counselor can do is to say, "If you don't mean business, there are other people waiting who would like to have your place." But that certainly is not adequate. In our center, we always attempt to involve the pastor or congregation whenever the situation seems to warrant it, as for example in the case of church discipline. But the pastor has the power and opportunities of church discipline *immediately* available from the outset to back up his counseling. We maintain our center in Hatboro for instructional purposes: to train pastors to do counseling rather than to encourage them to refer the members of their congregations[9] to others for counseling. Under these circumstances, we do the best that we can within our limitations. Of necessity we find that in the course of instruction we must translate what we do into pastoral terms. As we do so, repeatedly the superiority of the pastoral situation stands out in contrast.

After all is said and done, it is only the pastor who is fully equipped to get the job done. He can do all that we do at the center better; and much more. He has the resources. These include, first, available immediate knowledge of the counselee on a broad spectrum of levels. He has the power and help of church discipline. He may solicit the aid of the elders and he may utilize the reconciling fellowship of the whole covenant community to which the counselee belongs in a multitude of ways.[10] The last fact which I have just mentioned is quite significant. The pastor also has the opportunity to shape and organize this community into an effective pastoral force as he preaches, guides, and ministers to all of its members. Here is a virtually untapped source of enormous potential.

---

9. When a pastor refers people to our center, we urge him to take our pastor's training course. When he does, we get no more referrals from him—that is the way that we want it to be! Our center exists to eliminate the need for its existence.

10. I do not pretend to do more here than mention suggestively some of the ways in which the local congregation may help the pastoral counselor in his counseling ministry. To begin with, various existing classes, study groups, or activities of the church program may be used as aids in developing and maintaining specific patterns in the life of the counselee. Individuals with specific resources could be called upon to share the benefits of their gifts. For example, a husband and wife could invite to dinner counselees who need to learn how to conduct family worship in their home and demonstrate how they do it.

If a counselee refuses to do God's will, the best that the center counselor can do is to dismiss him or, in necessary situations, inform his pastor. But the pastor himself may say, "John, you are under the care of this congregation through its board of elders. They must answer to God for you and give an account of their care over you (Hebrews 13:17). You must obey the authority that Jesus Christ has vested in them." Thus the pastor can bring to bear all of the legitimate blessings and pressures of congregational care upon the counselee in the counseling context of the church.

When a member makes a profession of faith and becomes a communicant member of a congregation, he usually promises (in these or similar words) "to submit in the Lord to the government of the church" and, in case he "is found delinquent in doctrine or life, to heed its discipline." He makes such a commitment before God and the congregation. The commitment may not be looked upon lightly. It is the necessary backdrop for much counseling; without it some cases cannot be pursued successfully. So it is in the role of the pastor alone that *full-orbed* counseling is possible. In a center counseling can never be more than partial.

What About Counseling Intimate Friends?

"But," you may object, "if I listen to the intimate details of the problems of my parishioners, I shall lose them as friends and possibly as members." The objection that one can be too close is understandable.[11] Yet, it is invalid. It is easier sometimes (*if* counseling is viewed from this perspective alone) to counsel a perfect stranger with whom there has been no previous contact and with whom there will be no future contact. Possibly, too, it is easier for the counselee. Yet, it is part of the problem of every Christian to learn how to handle just such interpersonal relationships. This very fact is one of the prime reasons why counselees find it necessary to seek counseling! If the counselor fails to deal with the issue himself, how can he expect to be able to help the counselee to overcome the difficulties connected with close interpersonal relations?

---

11. I freely confess that the hardest counseling I do is when my friends or fellow-presbyters seek me out; I always begin with fear and trembling. Yet I have been able to retain such friendships and strengthen such relationships almost without exception.

Part of what the counselee must be made to understand is that all Christians have problems and that all Christians at times need one another's help.[12] They must learn to accept counsel gratefully as God's provision for their lives and not to enter into the relationship grudgingly. The pastor must be willing to take on the challenge of this admittedly difficult task. Otherwise he will be in no position to urge his counselees to handle hard interpersonal relationships.

The pastor who really wishes to be a *pastor* (i.e., a shepherd) must learn how to become *deeply involved* in the lives of his sheep; it cannot be otherwise. He must learn to "rejoice with those who rejoice and to weep with those who weep."[13] In the picture of the good Shepherd in John 10:3-5 it is precisely the *closeness* of the relationship of Shepherd to sheep that is emphasized. Members and friends are not lost, but rather ties are strengthened by the intimacy of counseling when the sheep know that their help comes from one who loves them enough that he would give his life (if necessary) for them. *Closeness binds together when it is genuine.* When the sheep know that the shepherd feels and is struggling with their problems, they respond positively. Counseling out of love is clearly distinguishable from professional prying and scientific experimentation.

Such understanding of a pastor's deep concern ordinarily does not grow out of his verbal assurances that this is so, but rather from the (sometimes unconscious) apprehension of the fact. Sheep *know* the love of a shepherd when they have been *helped* significantly by him; i.e., when he has genuinely *ministered* to them in their need. A shepherd who over a period of time has frequently helped them to solve their lesser problems God's way does not need to tell them that he cares. Nor do sheep want to alienate the counselor who has become such a valuable friend to them. The fear of losing sheep is more of a fear than a reality.

Perhaps the fact that many of those whom we have counseled over the years at the center keep up contact (sending a note, a picture of a new baby, an announcement of a wedding, etc.) may be reassuring. That they have been drawn close even in that brief, less personal situa-

---

12. Cf. *The Big Umbrella*, "You Are Your Brother's Counselor," pp. 123-156.
13. Romans 12:15; cf. also II Corinthians 11:29: "Who is weak without my being weak; who is led into sin without my intense concern?" These words plainly express pastoral concern and reveal Paul's pastoral heart.

tion rather than alienated by the counselor/counselee relationship itself seems evident.

The truth is that biblical counseling cements relationships; it does not impair them.[14] A counselor occasionally will lose a "friend" or member through counseling because that person refused to assume his responsibilities toward God; this must be regretted but cannot be helped. However, this occurrence will be the exception. If, on the other hand, he consistently drives others away from him, it is safe to conclude that his counseling falls short of the biblical norm. He has somehow failed as a *shepherd*. The problem is not closeness, but failure as a shepherd and/or counselor.

Perhaps the failure in such a case stems precisely from a lack of the nouthetic elements in counseling. The counselor may hesitate to use the Word of God. The Book is *powerful*; sharper than a two-edged sword! He may flinch from necessary confrontation. He may know what needs to be said and done and shrinks from the task. Or the pastor may not really have the welfare of the counselee at heart. He may simply be "doing his (fearful, humanistic, or distasteful) job." Attitudes like these are readily sensed by all concerned. Doubtless they are at the heart of much alienation. Again, whenever a counselor enters into counseling with so much apprehension over losing the member or friend that he allows fear to dominate the situation, he runs the risk of alienating the counselee thereby. His feeling of apprehension may be misinterpreted by the counselee as a lack of concern. Or if the counselor becomes ineffective by allowing fear to inhibit him from entering into areas of life that may be crucial to a solution of the problem, or leads to the trimming of his sails, he may drive off the counselee. Vacillation will hurt not only in counseling, but it also may become a source of irritation in the future relationship. If a counselor finds himself hung up over this problem, his only recourse is to repent, ask God for strength, explain to the counselee what the problem has been, seek his forgiveness, and then get back to work, this time on the right basis.[15]

---

14. Speaking the truth to one another enables members of the body to function more closely together and becomes the means for closer relationships (cf. Ephesians 4:25). The Scriptures are clear on the point. Therein should lie the counselor's real confidence.

15. It does not hurt to be forthright about the problem from the outset. Then the counselee is in a position to interpret the counselor's struggle more accurately.

It is at once both the glory and the hazard of shepherding that the counselor must know his sheep intimately in order to help them. "Then there is a hazard?" Of course, but the ministry and the whole Christian life is hazardous. Whoever said it would be otherwise?

Let it not be thought, incidentally, that relationships with pastors sour and members are lost only from intimacy. Every counselor who ministers to the needs of the sheep who wander astray from another sheepfold where they have failed to receive such help, knows the acute disappointment and bitterness expressed by people who have weighed their pastors and found them wanting. Sometimes, of course, it becomes the pastor's duty to urge them to return and be reconciled to their pastors.[16] If the truth were known, members and friends are lost more often (I suspect) by failure to deal directly and definitively with the problems of one's parishioners than by counseling them biblically. This failure may stem from many causes: incompetence, fear, a faulty counseling philosophy, etc. But whatever the cause, you may be sure that God will direct and bless the shepherd who attempts to shepherd his flock according to His Word.

The First Session

The first session is particularly important. Basic trends are set; initial attitudes and decisions, as well as relationships, are formed by both the counselor and his counselees. The notes that a counselor takes in the first session (and perhaps the next) usually will vary from those that follow. They will be much more copious, containing mainly (1) detailed factual data, (2) initial tentative hunches or conclusions, (3) a full agenda of areas yet to be explored, and (4) many quotations. A look at such notes perhaps best explains much of what should happen during this session.

Beyond such data gathering, the counselor will want to accomplish several things:

1. He will want to establish his leadership in the counseling context and elicit commitment from the counselee.

2. He will want to center counseling upon Jesus Christ and His Word from the outset.

---

16. Sometimes it is important to request that the former pastor come for counseling too so that the problems between them may be solved.

3. He will want to determine (if possible) whether the counselee is a Christian. If there is serious doubt, he will want to (1) present the gospel or (2) set up conditions that will lead to such a presentation as soon as possible.

4. He will want to establish regular Bible reading and prayer if it does not exist already.

5. He will want to give hope. Much has been said already about this.

6. He will want to solve some initial problems,[17] or take initial steps to do so.

7. He will want to focus on solutions to *some* problems.

8. He will want to assign homework designed to bring early success and relief growing out of biblical action.

9. He will want to work on enlisting whatever help is possible and necessary from others and get procedures under way for encouraging other involved parties to come.

10. He will want to determine what the main problem(s) is (are) if possible.

The counselor's task in proportioning the session among these purposes is difficult, since he may find that in order to do some, he must neglect others. Priorities in each case must rule. If, for instance, hope is the most vital need, perhaps one-half of the session (or more) must be devoted to it.

The *tendency* for inexperienced counselors will be to spend the entire time in data gathering. This often is a serious mistake that is easy to fall into. The most *comfortable* way *for the counselor* to become acquainted in the first session is to be relatively passive, spending most of his time asking questions and listening to the counselee's story. Yet, often that can be the least productive thing to do. When what is needed

---

17. These will often be small, but important. Big changes in attitude can arise from small changes in action. Even small efforts can *reverse* trends and set new patterns. *All* first sessions, without fail, should include the assignment of homework, no matter how small the assignment may be. A warring husband and wife (now repentant), for instance, can be given the assignment to spend the week doing all that they can *for* one another. Each can keep a record of all of the kindly efforts that he or she has noticed (to bring in) and also express appreciation whenever something is done. If nothing else, these first attempts at expressing love concretely can reverse a past sinful trend.

is hope, telling the story again will not do. Counselors must not fall into the temptation to retreat into data gathering alone.[18]

Data gathering is essential but is the one thing most easily postponed. If a disproportionate amount of time must be spent on something else and the counselor has failed to gather all of the data that he wished, he may readily recoup by asking (as a homework assignment) for the rest to be written out briefly for the next session.

Attention must be paid, therefore, to the most crucial matters at hand. These may be

Repentance
Hope giving
Data gathering
Agenda determining and renegotiating
Problem solving (especially in crisis situations)
Commitment to counseling
Evangelism
Explaining how to get a husband/wife to come, or explaining any one of a number of things
Forgiveness seeking and/or granting.

Yet, in almost every instance, while placing the stress where it is needed, the good counselor will do many things in the first session.

Sometimes the counselor will find it necessary to tell the counselee that there is much yet to be done, even explaining what he would like to have done, had there been more time. Laying out the agenda for the next session in this way often (1) encourages the counselee to return; (2) encourages the counselee to see that there is much more to be done; (3) encourages the counselee to see that the counselor (a) has a plan and program, (b) moves thoroughly, not rushing things through in order to get them done, (c) cares enough to explain what he is doing when and why.

Use of the agenda column on the weekly counseling record enables the counselor and the counselee to carry over "unfinished business" to future sessions. If he lets the counselee know that he is putting such items on his agenda, the counselee will (1) appreciate note taking and (2) feel more confident and at ease about proceeding at the counselor's

---

18. The failure leads to the problem of beginning with a talk-only session (see *infra*, "Homework." Also, Jay Adams, "Talk Is Not Cheap," *Nouthetic Confrontation*, vol. 1, no. 3, Winter, 1973, p. 2. This article is quoted intact *infra*, chapter 22.

pace rather than trying to get every item discussed before he forgets it.

At times the counselor will place items on the agenda because, as he plainly says, "You are not ready to deal with this issue until first you have solved these other problems," to which he then turns.

Counselors should take extra care about starting well, since the first session is crucial. Yet, even failures in the first session can be made up in later ones. But it is important, nevertheless, to get off to a good start.

Chapter Twenty-one

GOALS AND TERMINAL DATES

Early Morning Fog

In spite of all that he knows about counseling, including such matters as his adoption of basic biblical presuppositions, his awareness of biblically based methods and techniques, and his understanding of the counseling process, the counselor may find that the beginnings of a new series of counseling sessions sometimes resembles driving in the fog.

When you drive in fog, you may be sure of your destination, you may have mapped out correctly all of the turns, you may know the turnpike exits, you may understand precisely where you intend to go and how to get there. And yet, as you drive along, because of the fog you can see only a short distance ahead of you. Anticipated landmarks may visibly appear so suddenly as you move along, that you may actually run past your turns or exits before you realize it. Then just as suddenly the fog may lift, enabling you to see for miles ahead and gain a view of the whole picture, with all of its interrelationships plainly visible.

During the early morning fog of counseling, though it may be difficult to see it, if the counselor follows biblical principles and methods, by faith he must believe that nonetheless he is moving on the right roads and heading in the right direction. Yet driving (counseling) in a fog is harder work, demands every ounce of concentration, and requires the fullest and best attention. As the fog begins to lift and the problem as a whole becomes clearer, the intensive efforts that are required in the earlier stages of counseling can be relaxed somewhat. Not that one ever may give less than his best, but the best now actually may require less effort, allowing the counselee to do more and more of the work himself. Driving always must be done carefully, but driving in the fog requires the special qualities of assurance, extra care and attention, and patience. One must watch for every available clue. Too many counselors give up before the sun burns off the fog. The counselor must learn to trust God's promises and on the basis of these move confidently and cautiously ahead. The fog will lift. Clear-cut goals and objectives are essential to sustaining one during the early minutes or hours of counseling.

Setting Goals and Objectives

The counselor should set up goals and objectives. He may begin by assuring the counselee: "There is no reason why this problem can't be solved. All problems can be solved when they are solved God's way. We shall expect to see genuine change soon; in fact, there is no reason why we should not see *some* change today."[1]

The counselor must set goals for himself and for the counselee. These goals are not negotiated between the two and agreed upon after compromise; goals must be determined by the Word of God. Goals are very important. The counselor who aims at nothing usually hits it. When working with believers, counselors should *expect* to see substantial changes in the situation.[2] This is part of the Christian counselor's hope. Moreover change should take place *soon*. God speaks in such terms. For instance, in one urgent matter He says: "Reject a factious man *after a first* and *second* nouthetic confrontation [emphasis mine]." God does not expect counseling to continue indefinitely in such cases before disciplinary action is taken. If factious persons are allowed to continue their activities, an entire congregation may be destroyed. When such a man shows no positive response to the Scriptures, disciplinary action is necessary. But when counselees actively cooperate, as a rule of thumb the counselor may expect that by the sixth week the major issues all ought to be out on the table. By that time a plan for dealing with most of these will have been devised, the situation should be reversed, and there should be some evident progress.

Checking Up on Failure

If the counselor finds that this is not true, he should try to discover

---

1. Nowhere does the Bible say that one must wait for change. Jesus did not ask people to wait. He expected and effected change right away. Not everything, of course, but *something* can be changed as the result of *every* session, including the first. There is a solution to every unsolved problem; this is the Christian conviction that emerges from I Corinthians 10:13 and II Timothy 3:16, 17. The solution may not be found in an alteration of the circumstances, but rather may be discovered in new biblical ways of relating to them. One change always possible is a change in the counselee.

2. With unbelievers they must not expect to see significant change apart from the gospel.

what is keeping the counseling from progressing. He might ask himself such questions as the following: What is wrong? Do I really know? Am I doing an adequate job? If not, how (specifically) have I failed? Has the counselee truly been cooperating? Does he have hope? Are both of us failing? What are the facts in this case? Do I have them all? Have I omitted any area? What has happened so far? Where have we been heading? Are my goals clear? Look over *every* aspect of counseling carefully. Examine the homework that was given. Was it concrete enough? Was it done well? Fully? Was the counselee held responsible to do it, or was he allowed to develop a pattern of half-hearted performance? Also examine data: are all of the *specific* facts needed available? Ask yourself: have I been seeking to discover and solve problems God's way, or have I simply spent time listening? Have I focused each session at its conclusion upon God's solutions, or did I allow the session to end without doing so? Have I agreed with the counselee that the situation is hopeless, or have I insisted that God has an answer to the problem? Have I failed to call sin "sin"? Have I worked in generalities or with concrete specifics?

Certainly by eight or ten weeks counseling ought to be well on its way toward reaching solutions to specific problems. One reason for setting goals, then, is in order to evaluate progress.

Counselors also ought to think in terms of terminal dates so that they may talk that way to counselees. Of course, there is never a terminal date for a pastor in the sense that he may cease his shepherding care. But there should be goals for getting specific problems solved.

If the counselor sets up counseling sessions in general, he will get general results. But if he sets them up to handle specific problems, he will get specific results. Life is lived and change occurs in the concrete. If for example, a husband and wife say that their marriage is falling apart and that they are at the point of getting a divorce, the counselor is forced to be specific. First he must handle the matter of the contemplated divorce, convincing them that God will not allow this for believers and assuring them that God can make their marriage over anew. Then he must turn to the specific problems that threaten the marriage. Thus, it is vital for the counselor to be able to set forth his objectives clearly at the outset and at each subsequent point of a new departure.

Objectives, then, are of two sorts: general and specific. General objectives guide and direct the overall counseling. When counseling

believers, there are but three major objectives; the first is basic and ultimate, the other two contributory to it: (1) to honor God; (2) to
strengthen Christ's church; and (3) to benefit the counselee by building
him up in the faith. When an unbeliever enters the picture, to these the
general goal of evangelism must be added as a prerequisite.[3]

Specific goals should answer the question: "What, in particular, do
I wish to do for this counselee (what now at this point; what later on)?"
These goals may be several in number and may need to be revised and
restated as counseling proceeds. New data may force reevaluation.
Yet, some specific goals always should be in the mind of the counselor.
Probably when getting started he would be wise to write out on the
counseling record each specific goal or objective in one sentence. In
this way he will keep on the track and not allow himself to be diverted
from his main concerns.[4]

General Goals and Procedures for the Weekly Counseling Session

Three basic elements that ordinarily should be a part of every session
are: (1) the handling of transitional matters; (2) the discovery and
discussion of new data; and (3) the commitment of the counselee to
new biblical beliefs, decisions, and/or behavior.

Transitional Matters

"Transitional matters" refers to what, on the agenda of a business
meeting, might be called *unfinished business*. Ordinarily a session opens
with the counselor requesting the counselee to hand him his homework
assignment book. The assignments, how the counselee did them, and the
results then are reviewed. Assignments from the past week are discussed, together with their implications, any new complications that may
have arisen, and all new data that may be forthcoming. This unfinished
business forms the transitional continuity between the present and
past sessions.

The counselor ordinarily seeks to discuss transitional matters thoroughly but crisply so that he may move on to further probing and discussion and then, finally, to a commitment to new progress for Jesus

3. Cf. *The Big Umbrella*, "Evangelism and Counseling," for a fuller discussion
of this subject.
4. Such specific goals never should become straitjackets. They must be revised
and restated whenever the data indicate that a new problem has come into focus
or an old one has taken on new dimensions. At the conclusion of counseling, one
may check out each goal to see if it has been attained.

Christ. If no complications arise in connection with this discussion of homework, usually he may move on to new material in five or ten minutes. It is unwise for him to go ahead, however, if the homework poses serious problems. These problems usually take two forms: (1) failure to accomplish homework, or (2) complications that have arisen from doing what was required. In most cases it is important to take the time to resolve any problems, questions, or complications that may have arisen, then and there. This usually involves homework that has not been done. However, in some instances, as for example, when it is questionable whether the issue of incompleted assignments ought to be joined and the battle fought on the spot, it may be better for the counselor to suggest that, with reference to a particular assignment, he and the counselee have reached a temporary impasse. He may discuss his displeasure, assure the counselee of the importance of fulfilling the particular assignment, but acknowledge his willingness to shelve the matter *temporarily*, and reluctantly turn to another matter for the time being. The counselor's attitude in all of this ought to be hopeful, assuming that the counselee at length will agree to do what has been requested. In this spirit he simply moves on. Ordinarily, a move of this sort ought not be made *unless the counselee already has shown progress in fulfilling other assignments*. It certainly is *not* the way to *begin* counseling; to give in on the first or second assignment (or both) is to put the counselee in the driver's seat and will hinder future counseling.[5] How he handles this problem can make all the difference between success and failure. Giving in on early assignments almost inevitably sets a pattern for failure in counseling.

Since this is so, it is important to make most early assignments simple, clear, easy, and achievable, so that such impasses will not occur until patterns of cooperation and success in changing have been established. Often early success not only forestalls, but actually helps to remove such impediments to progress. Many important assignments are simple so that this is easy to do.[6]

---

5. Of course, if the counselee can show the counselor that he is asking him to do that for which there is no biblical warrant, or that the assignment really was too large or advanced, the counselor should be willing to *change* the assignment (not give in on it) so that it does conform to the Scriptures and is feasible. In such cases, he should simply commend the counselee for his objection and move ahead.

6. Cf. *infra*, pp. 318-320, for examples of typical assignments.

Whenever the counselor knows that he must assign a task that is likely to meet with resistance or failure, it is wise to assign as well one or two other more easily achievable tasks in which there is likely to be success. These should be genuine tasks, not merely *busy* work. It is good to keep progress going between all sessions, no matter how small that progress may be. These additional tasks may help to bolster one's hope, even when otherwise there is clear-cut failure.[7]

Of course, it is never wise to obscure an issue by adding other assignments to it when it is necessary for a counselor to join that issue with the counselee. In such instances, the counselee may focus upon these ancillary assignments and take so much time to do them that he may use them as an *excuse* for failing to do the controversial assignment.

The Discovery and Discussion of New Data

Transitional matters at times may provide much of the new material that may comprise the bulk of the counseling session. Counselors will jot down on the agenda column of their *Weekly Counseling Record Sheets* items that need further discussion as the counselee reports about the results of his work during the week. Hardly ever is there a session when there is *nothing* more that needs to be said about the homework assignment, even if it is simply to commend the counselee for his work and to underscore the biblical reason behind his success. Sometimes it is important to summarize and/or explain more fully what happened and why there were good results in order to solidify and consolidate the gains of the week.

In addition to transitional materials, the counselor may wish to probe areas that have not yet been explored. More must be said about this matter at another place under the heading of "Data Gathering," but it will be important to consider data gathering before, at least to the extent of noting the two fundamental approaches that are available.

Flexibility

It is necessary to develop specific goals for each counseling session. Frequently these will be determined from data acquired at previous

---

7. Remember Proverbs 13:12: "Hope drawn out makes the heart sick, but a longing come true is a tree of life" (Berkeley). There are times when it is necessary to allow time for something to develop or jell, so that the counselor will wish to space out sessions, perhaps scheduling the next session for two, three, or even four weeks.

sessions. The counselor should enter every session with specific goals in view and with an agenda that also allows for the addition or alteration of goals as the session progresses. That is to say, he must allow for and plan on a certain amount of flexibility within the basic framework and within the overall goals of counseling.

As a counselor begins a session, he ought to progress according to the general and specific goals that he has in mind. His characteristic opening, as he asks for the homework book and reads the first assignment, might be: "Well, how did this work out?" The reply that he receives may, in large measure, determine whether his predetermined but tentative specific goals for this session can all be reached. Suppose that he receives a very negative reply indicating that the homework assignment was not done (perhaps not even attempted): "I didn't go to see the teacher about my grades." If the counselor's specific goals for the present session were to build on and go beyond a conference with a mathematics teacher in which the counselee was to confess his failure to work hard in class and to seek help in catching up, he will find that this reply requires him to scrap this goal at least for the time being. He will need to focus instead upon the failure and what to do about it (for help about how to do this, see "Homework," p. 294). Obviously then, flexibility is essential to progress.

When such changes of the specific purpose for a counseling session are made, the change of purposes always should be clear to the counselor and sometimes made clear to the counselee: "Today I wanted to do such and such, but your failure to accomplish your assignment from last week will hold us back." Noting such facts can (1) help motivate, (2) explain why progress is forestalled, (3) give hope, and (4) place the responsibility where it belongs.

Again, purposes may change for other reasons, not only when failure has been introduced into the session. Greater progress than was expected ("Oh, you did *that* on your own—fine, I was planning to get to that today"[8]), new significant data ("My wife was involved in an automobile accident last Thursday"), new insights into problems, the jelling of two or three seemingly separate strands of thought or activity into an

---

8. In such cases, seek concrete information in specific detail to be sure that the counselee did *exactly* what he should have done. Faulty attempts to do right things otherwise can lead to serious problems and deep discouragement.

unexpected conclusion, all these—and who knows how many other factors—may demand the change of plans and purposes.

What is the use of planning, then, if it is subject to such change? That is a fair question. The counselor who plans is still in direction and control of the interview; the one who does not loses control altogether. If, on the one hand, plans must be scrapped or changed, on the other hand it is rare that they will be discarded totally. They possibly may be of use at a later point. They may, in modified form, become the groundwork for other plans. Secondly, unless there is plan and purpose, there is nothing specific to change. It is only the man with a plan who can change.

If counseling from start to finish is without structure, if there are no goals and objectives, there is no way to gauge progress in either thought or action. One cannot even conclude that he was *wrong* about his earlier conclusions unless he *had* some to begin with. There can be no significant changes in the progress of counseling, because there has been no progress. In other words, flexibility differs from chaos in that the flexible counselor *has* plans and purposes to revise or scrap, and *has* new ones to develop or introduce; the chaotic counselor has neither. Without plan and purpose there is no way to begin, to proceed, to make progress, to determine where one is or to know when to close.

Let us turn, then, to a consideration of:

Adaptation to Counselees

"Do you treat everyone the same way?" Of course not. Jesus dealt with every man differently; and yet in another sense He treated them all alike. Christ Himself is the one solution to every man's problems, but each one must come to know Him *individually.* Paul adapted himself to various sorts of persons but presented the same message to all. He became "all things to all men" (I Corinthians 9:22) in order that he might win men of every sort. What is true of adaptation in evangelism is true also in counseling.[9]

"What are you going to do about this fine *Christian* wife of mine?" asked Fred sarcastically in his opening words. "She's packed her bags and says that she's going home to mother," Fred shouted through the re-

---

9. Cf. *The Big Umbrella,* "Evangelism in Counseling," pp. 95-112, for an even more direct correlation of the two.

ceiver in explanation. "Fred, put her on the phone, will you please?" the pastor replied. "Yes?" Margaret said gruffly. "Margaret, you are not going to leave Fred! Paul says in I Corinthians 7 that you can't, even though Fred is unsaved. God has an answer to your problem, and we will find it. This is no way to win Fred. But perhaps in His providence God may use even this fiasco to do so. Now, unpack those bags the second you hang up, and then the two of you get over here to my study as quickly as you can; I must leave to conduct a funeral within the hour."

When they arrived, the pastor did not try to evangelize Fred. He was not in the mood to listen to the gospel, and the pastor did not have the time to present the message to him adequately anyhow. In the brief, tense first session the pastor had but one immediate goal: to extract a promise from Fred and Margaret to allow him to counsel with them regularly over the next few weeks. Finally he received this promise when he was able to get an assurance from Margaret that she would abandon the idea of leaving. At that point, he left for the funeral, after setting the time for the first formal counseling session for later that evening. This informal session was a success for evangelism and for counseling; it was not a failure. When they met that night the conditions for confronting Fred were much more favorable.

Jesus Himself did not confront any two people in identical ways. In John 3 He spoke quite directly to Nicodemus on their very first encounter about his need for personal regeneration. Indeed, His approach doubtless may seem too abrupt to some who think that there is but one (usually step-by-step) approach to use with everyone. Nicodemus came as a represenative of the Pharisees ("a man from the Pharisees"), but Jesus spoke to him about his personal need. Nicodemus inquired about Christ's ability to perform miracles; Jesus spoke instead about his inability to enter into the kingdom of God. It was truly an abrupt approach. Yet, in the very next chapter Jesus confronts the Samaritan woman in an entirely different manner. He first speaks of wells and ropes and buckets, of hills and husbands, of water and life. He *gradually* led her to Himself. First she saw Him as a teacher, then as a prophet and finally as the Messiah. In John 9 he first made clay to give hope to the man born blind. The blind man thought: "If only I could wash away my blindness as I can wash this clay off eyelids!" Then Jesus said, "go wash." He did and returned seeing. That was all—nothing more at that meeting. The man went home. Under pressure of excommunication he steadfastly maintained that all that had occurred was the healing ("This one thing I know"). Later, Jesus found him and told him about the blindness of men's hearts and what He can do to open the eyes of the soul. No two instances are alike.

In counseling, as in all human contacts, the counselor must learn adaptability. This means that he must learn how to handle different sorts of persons under all kinds of circumstances. Yet, there are no unique problems; and all men alike, by virtue of the original creation of Adam in God's image, share enough in common to make at least some rough generalizations about what to look for and how to approach persons in counseling.

Chapter Twenty-two

THE COMMITMENT OF THE COUNSELEE

It is never adequate merely to talk about problems. All talk in counseling must be oriented toward biblical solutions. That is why it is essential to direct the entire session toward its climax—the commitment of the counselee to his homework task(s) for the next week.

After some new understanding of information that calls for action, following a scriptural discussion that has concluded in work to be done, or as the result of some other form of breakthrough, the counselor should write out the assignment, explain it to the counselee, seek his commitment to accomplish it by God's grace, and, having done so, conclude the session with prayer.[1] This is the point toward which the entire session should have been moving.[2]

Naturally, during the session several topics may come up for discussion. Each discussion may be concluded by the writing out of an assignment at the time. At the end of the session, the counselor may wish to reread and review *all* of the assignments before offering the final prayer. He also may care to interrelate these to one another in the summary, showing, whenever possible, how the various tasks are a part of a whole and how pursuing them in a particular order (if important) may be of significance ("Frankly, Bill, I don't see how you can begin

---

1. Usually, to avoid after-discussion (which almost always is counter productive), the counselor arises after the closing prayer, extends his hand to the counselees as they arise, and bids them farewell as he moves to open the door.

2. The commitment begins first by the agreement of the counselee(s) to meet regularly at a specific time in the pastor's study. Often the pastor may need (or in some cases *choose*) to schedule sessions at hours that *cost*. But when a counselee must take time off from work, school, etc. (as he does to go to the dentist, the psychiatrist, or the physician), he (1) shows genuine commitment; (2) he often is more highly motivated thereby; (3) he respects the counselor and counseling session more fully (what is free sometimes is considered cheap). Counselors will use ripened judgment about *choosing* to put counselees in this predicament. Sometimes the pressures of time will necessitate it; sometimes at the initial session (or so) it will be necessary before a more convenient hour opens up.

to talk to Mary about this until you first have come to a recognition of your sin against God and in repentance seek His forgiveness"). He may need to show how one assignment depends upon another and how the latter, therefore, carries a peculiar urgency and priority ("John, when you have totaled your financial assets and liabilities, *then* you and Joan can begin to make out the budget and determine what is a necessity and what is not").

It is important to orient the entire counseling session toward commitment to biblical change as its climax. This change may be a change of knowledge, belief, or action. Almost always the former two will lead to the latter. That is why it is vital to consider the problem of talk in counseling. To some, counsel consists of talk for its own sake. Talk, to them, is considered beneficial in and of itself. I have already questioned the accuracy of this analysis. Instead, there is good evidence to establish the view that talk which is not oriented toward and does not issue in biblical solutions to problems is one of the most destructive forces of all.

Is Talk Therapeutic?

Clyde Narramore has missed the most important fact about talk in the discussion of this subject in his book, *The Psychology of Counseling*.[3] Narramore sees talk as "therapeutic." It is seen as useful for clarification, for release, and as therapy in and of itself. This understanding of talk in the counseling situation may lead to dangerously destructive consequences. There is no biblical reason for regarding talk as valuable *per se*. Nor does the Bible recommend mere talk as a valuable tool merely for purposes of clarification or for the release of feeling. Indeed, there are strong biblical warnings against any such notion.[4] Narramore's position tends to encourage counselors to adopt a very superficial concept of counseling.

Because talk, *per se*, often may bring relief, he seems to have concluded that it is, therefore, therapeutic. Yet, because this conclusion is based upon an improper understanding of the situation, it is both super-

---

3. Clyde Narramore, *The Psychology of Counseling* (Grand Rapids: Zondervan Publishing Co., 1960), pp. 44, 45.

4. Cf. Ezekiel 33:3-33; James 1:22, 23; Luke 10:36, 37. Note also Paul's contrast between naked talk and power (I Corinthians 4:20). This distinction cuts through all Christian ministry, including counseling. Cf. also Proverbs 14:23, "In all toil there is profit, but mere talk leads only to want."

ficial and misleading. It is true that talk about problems may bring relief. But this relief frequently is temporary.[5] After a short time, however, such talk may give rise to far more serious problems.[6] Narramore fails to see that talk alone usually does not *reduce*, but rather normally *enlarges* the counselee's problem. In this connection read Proverbs 14:23 and Ecclesiastes 5:7 (cf. the Living Bible).

Talk, in and of itself, usually does little more than raise the issue afresh for the counselee. In the process, it is true, he may find temporary relief. For five minutes, five hours, or even five days he may feel

---

5. Beldoch, reporting in *The Intellectual Digest*, October, 1971, pp. 85-88, observes that Encounter Groups stress "feeling and expressing" in an anti-intellectual manner. But, he suggests, "feeling alone robbed man of his most unique [*sic*] attribute [thinking]." He continues: "The movement is dishonest in that it attempts to reduce the inevitably complex and ongoing struggle of life to a mindless and momentary discharge of feeling" which leads to keen "disappointment that follows precisely from the lack of such results." The feeling/talk only orientation always disappoints those who have serious problems.

6. The contrast between talking (to oneself or others) and doing can be illustrated in terms of the flow of hope and discouragement experienced by a counselor in the course of a series of counseling sessions.

Talk Only	*Talk/Doing*
1. Counselor runs into difficulty	1. Counselor runs into difficulty
2. Counselor feels discouraged	2. Counselor feels discouraged
3. Counselor discusses discouragement with wife (ventilates feelings)	3. Counselor discusses how to solve problem biblically with another counselor as they search Scriptures.
4. Counselor feels better	4. Counselor feels better
5. Counselor feels worse as he approaches next session (has no new plan and knows it)	5. Counselor feels apprehensive as he approaches next session (yet has new plan and knows it)
6. Counselor broods and prays, yet feelings get lower	6. Counselor plans and prays; feelings level out
7. Counselor dreads next session	7. Counselor anxious to try new plan
8. Counselor fails in next session (not in mood to counsel; has no new way to go; communicates negativism to counselee)	8. Counselor successful (confident in mood; new plan succeeds)
9. Counselor's feelings are lower still; abandons case (or counseling)	9. Counselor's feelings rise; anxious to pursue case to end (and take on other cases)

better for having gotten the matter off his chest. But abruptly, sometime thereafter, he comes to his senses and recognizes that in it all he
has accomplished nothing with all of his talk. The problem is still
with him (perhaps the situation has even deteriorated), by means of the
discussion he has come to a new appreciation of the difficulties that he
faces (which in and of itself hardly is encouraging), and it seems apparent to him that now he must conclude that there is little or no hope
for a solution, since the "counselor" offered no solution. Indeed, if he
did anything, the counselor *enlarged* the counselee's problem (and subsequent despair) by "clarifying" the situation; before he never saw so
clearly all of the ramifications of his dilemma. Talk, *per se*, thus becomes little more than a ripping off of the scab and a poking about in
the bloody wound. It may infect the sore, but it is hardly "therapeutic"![7]

The following article, reechoing but amplifying the above, appeared
in the third edition of *Nouthetic Confrontation*.[8]

Four Fatal Failures

The present article is the first in a series entitled "Four Fatal
Failures." Counselors not only must avoid these common failures,
but when they occur also must know what to do to correct the
situation. In contrast to each failure, there is an important counseling principle to observe.

Nouthetic confrontation (*nouthesia*) involves talk; all counseling
does. No one who counsels, whatever his viewpoint, therefore,
wants to minimize the importance of talk. Even Freudians and
Rogerians see talk as the basic stuff of counseling. Yet their talk
in psychoanalysis and in reflexive counseling largely flows in the
wrong direction and, therefore, has little to do with what the Bible
calls "counsel" (sharing God's Word with another). But, unfortunately, the idea is abroad that a form of counseling that depends
upon talk—*mere* talk—can be helpful and (at worst) can do no
harm. The assumption that the use of talk alone is adequate for
counseling is not biblical. As a corollary, you may be sure that mere
talk in counseling *will* do harm.

"But," you may object, "talk in counseling often brings relief. Take
for instance, Haim Ginott's idea of talking about the feeling. Don't

---

7. On this subject, cf. *The Big Umbrella*, pp. 92, 93, 201, 202.
8. A paper edited by the Rev. John Bettler and published by the Christian
Counseling and Educational Foundation, with which the author is associated.
Subscriptions to this paper may be made by writing to the editor, c/o 424 Annan-
dale Avenue, Glen Ellyn, Illinois 60137.

you think that helps?" No, it does not help. The serious fallacy in this approach is that it settles for the *temporary* relief that comes from talking about a problem. Yet, such talk fails entirely, since it focuses upon the problem *only* and not upon the solution. Talking to a psychiatrist, to Mom, or to a cronie on the phone about your problems does relieve you of the immediate pressures and stresses that bother you. But it does no more for you. Five minutes, five hours or five days later you are aware that the problem is still with you, that nothing has been done about it and that all that the talk did for you was to let you get it off your chest for awhile.

Indeed, talk may do serious harm. Temporary relief, whether gained from tranquilizers, home brew or talk can take the pressure off *exactly* when the counselee needs to face the issue. Stress and pressure often are indicative of the seriousness of a situation and the need for decision and action. Talk that focuses only upon the problem—gaining insight, clarifying, etc., dangerously may forestall decisive action.

Moreover, talk that focuses upon problems only may lead to suicide. Let us assume that Bill has already tried all that he knows to do to solve his problem and that, instead, his solutions have led him into a blind corner. He comes hoping for help in determining what to do; he has come to you as a Christian counselor seeking God's solution. Suppose you talk about his problem and, indeed, do help him to see more clearly what its dimensions are, then—leave him dangling. He may receive temporary relief (even commenting about how much better he feels—watch out for this; feeling that is solidly founded grows out of the genuine hope that grows from discovering God's solution) and think that he has been helped. Doubtless it will come as quite a shock to learn that two days later Bill made an attempt upon his life. It should not.

What happened? Bill went home feeling better; the lid had been lifted from the pressure cooker while taking a look at what is bubbling inside. But the lid was replaced and the pressure mounted once again. "Why?" Because the counselor successfully analyzed Bill's problem and gave him fuller insight into his problem; that is why.

"How could that have hurt?" In at least three ways: he put the lid on but did not turn off the heat. Let's change the metaphor and look at the difficulty in another way. First, when Bill's counselor ripped off the scab and poked his finger around in the bloody wound (as he discussed the problem), he did *not* do what the surgeon does who hurts *in order to heal*. True, the counselor *thought* the hurt would heal. But *how could it?* All he did was probe the wound, thus making it sorer. Unlike the surgeon, his action itself did not remove the cancer. This raised all the old problems afresh *in all their hopelessness*. Secondly, because the counselor failed to offer any biblical solution (or even a first step toward it) to the problem, Bill concluded that there was none. Since the counselor was a Christian, Bill (rightly) expected him to present God's solution. When he did not, Bill concluded (wrongly) that God had no solution to the problem. Thirdly, because the counselor was able to give Bill greater insight into his problem, he enlarged it for him (i.e., he had even greater reason for concern). When he came to his senses the next day, Bill realized that all that they had done was talk about the problem—nothing had been done to solve it. Yet, one thing had happened: whereas Bill had thought the problem was bad, now that he and the counselor had analyzed it, he saw all sorts of new aspects to the problem that had gone unnoticed before. Previously the problem had looked large; now it appeared enormous—so huge that Bill decided there was no hope.

Obviously, then, the talk cure is not so innocuous as some may think. Talk is not always cheap; it can cost the counselee his life! The Christian counselor must talk, but not *only* talk in counseling. When he does, he takes away hope, misrepresents God and runs the danger of setting the stage for suicide.

Talk must be combined with biblical action. Nothing less than talk that focuses not upon problems, but rather upon God's solutions is adequate. No one ever left Jesus Christ the same. Of everyone who met him, He demanded change. It does not take months or even weeks to change. While the new *patterns* (that constitute a new "manner of life"—Ephesians 4:22) take time to establish, the first changes (or at least the first steps toward such changes) can be taken right away. Every counselee may (indeed must) change after each session. That is why, as the the conclusion of *every* session, the counselor should lead the counselee to an understanding of God's Scriptural solution to the problem (or at least to some aspect of it). Together, they should agree upon a biblical plan of action and close the session with the counselee prayerfully going forth in obedience to the will of God to take specific, concrete steps to change the situation.

Talk then; talk all that you must, but let your talk move within every session from man's problems to God's solutions.

One counselor keeps the following slogan under the glass on his desk as a reminder:

NEVER TALK ABOUT PROBLEMS—
ALWAYS TALK THEM THROUGH TO GOD'S SOLUTIONS!

Since it is important to help counselees to reach God's solutions, counselors not only must know the Word of God *thoroughly* and *how to use it practically*, but they also must learn how to discover the facts about the problems to which they must find biblical solutions. This requires an understanding of the important process of data gathering.

Chapter Twenty-three

IS THERE A PROBLEM?

First, before turning to a consideration of data gathering, let us consider the situation that the counselor sometimes faces when only *one* party recognizes that there is a problem. This, in effect, is the first significant datum uncovered. Now and then every counselor will run into the situation where, let us say, Phyllis virtually has dragged Howard, her husband, into the counseling room. She explains what she considers to be a serious difficulty between them (it hardly matters for our present discussion *what* the particular issue might be). When she is finished, the counselor may turn to Howard and say, "Could you fill me in on this a bit more from where you sit, Howard?" He may receive in response what (after hearing Phyllis' tale of woe) can only seem to him to be an incredible reply such as,

"I appreciate your interest, pastor, and I know that Phyllis gets upset now and then, but I don't think there is any real problem at all."

"You don't see any problem?"

"No, Pastor; as a matter of fact, I only came here to satisfy her. There is no need for counseling. I hope you will help her see this."

"But Howard," the counselor might continue, "Phyllis says that she is not sure that you love her any more; that seems as if it merits some investigation, don't you think?"

"No, Pastor, I don't think so; I love Phyllis and she knows it. There is no real problem."

"Do you still doubt his love, Phyllis?"

"Yes, I do, pastor; nothing in our marriage is right. I think unless we get things straightened out soon, we will be heading for sheer disaster."

At this point some counselors might become perplexed as to what to do next. One way of proceeding is as follows. The pastor might explain:

"Obviously each of you presents a widely different view of how your marriage is faring. Phyllis, you see the possibility of imminent disaster, whereas, Howard, you are convinced that there is nothing wrong

249

enough to call for counseling. Would you like to hear a third opinion?"

Phyllis: "Yes, what do you think?"

Howard: "Sure, go ahead, but I don't know what there is to talk about."

"Well, I am not sure about how large your other problems might be, and I don't know whether you love Phyllis or not, Howard (it will take a little more discussion to get into those matters), but one thing is crystal clear to me—you *do* have a problem, and it is an extremely dangerous one; but it has not been mentioned by either of you."

Phyllis and *Howard*: "What is it?"

The Pastor: "You have a serious *communication* problem. If the two of you cannot discuss and resolve together the question of whether the marriage is on the rocks, your marriage is suffering from a *serious* communication breakdown. I don't know whether that is the *only* problem or not,[1] but that it is a problem of proportions large enough to cry out for counseling seems evident to me. I suggest that we begin right there and see what happens."[2]

What can lead to such disparity of judgment? Sometimes one party (often the man, as in this case), out of pride, fear, embarrassment, etc., will try to avoid counseling, even though he knows full well that there are serious unresolved problems. Usually you can "trap" him into doing what he knows that he needs to do by using the approach suggested.

At other times, however, there are honest differences of opinions. If a husband (or wife) is very insensitive to the needs of the other, he (or she) can genuinely believe that no problem exists even up until the eleventh hour. This might happen especially if Howard grew up in a home where his mother and father argued and fought constantly, and this format was for them a way of life. Yet they never thought of breaking up.

---

1. Usually it is not. Poor communication will lead to other problems stemming from misunderstandings, etc. On the other hand, when other problems continue unresolved, they almost always lead (in addition) to a break in communication. Probably *both* difficulties are true in this case, and the one has been feeding the other in a downward cyclical spiral. (Cf. *Competent to Counsel*, pp. 144-148.)

2. In this case, the pastor will be likely to assign Phyllis and Howard the task of compiling a list of problems between them, at a conference, for homework. Unfortunately, superficial counseling fails to see the real seriousness of communication problems in marriage. Michael Sullivan, Augustinian priest who heads up the Philadelphia Marriage Encounter program in the Roman Catholic Church, says, "If you have a good marriage *or just a communication problem*, come [emphasis mine]. "Priest Tunes Couples into Great Marriages," *The Sunday Bulletin*, April 1, 1973, sec. 1, p. 16.

If Phyllis, on the other hand, grew up in a home where a public or heated argument was the sign of impending disaster, she and Howard could easily read the same event in opposite ways. Their real problem in such a case would be that they have never recognized this fact and resolved it. The two have not worked out a third and better way of life. Both still might be trying to live according to past patterns that are no longer applicable (usually this will be true in more areas than this one; therefore, before counseling is completed, probing extensively in all areas is indicated). In each of these instances, counseling is necessary.

It is vital to distinguish between the type of situations just described and others in which there are really no large problems at all. Rarely will persons who have relatively few problems seek out a counselor; in most instances such people lead happy, fruitful Christian lives, enjoying their families and engrossed in the work of the Lord, and the furthest idea from their minds is the notion that they might need counseling. Individuals like this may continue to rejoice so long as they remember the Scripture: "Let him who thinks that he stands take heed lest he fall" (I Corinthians 10:12).

Counsel or Counseling?

Yet every once in a while persons who are making it become concerned (perhaps needlessly) about some matter. Perhaps it is finances, it may be a matter concerning the spiritual growth of their children, etc. Or, they may have fallen into some sin or problem from which they find it difficult to extricate themselves. In such instances, *counsel* is necessary, but often the need for extensive *counseling* is not. Perhaps one or two sessions, or even a brief word of counsel, will be all that is necessary. That word of encouragement, the reminder of what God requires or the lovingly kind rebuke was just what was needed. Basically, because of the fundamental life set and because of the firm commitment to the Word of God, this sort of counselee almost immediately will respond to counsel. There is no need to extend *counsel* to a process of *counseling* in such cases. Indeed, to do so is to stand in the way of true repentance and growth in the counselee. Prayer, following up the brief session or two, and a word of inquiry in passing ("Everything still going well, Wilson?") now and then is what is indicated. Counsellors must be sure not to enlarge problems for counselees, finding difficulties where none exist.

Chapter Twenty-four

TWO BASIC APPROACHES

Approaches to data gathering in counseling may follow one of two general lines: they may be (1) *extensive* or (2) *intensive.*

The Intensive Approach

First, a counselor may dolly in on one central problem *in depth*, extending its various ramifications to many or all of the other problems. This, for convenience' sake, I shall call the Intensive Approach. This approach is sometimes helpful when there are areas about which the counselee proves to be highly sensitive. Perhaps from probes in an area the counselor discovers that the counselee is hesitant or refuses to speak about certain matters. When he is reluctant to discuss a problem directly, counselors do not need to feel stymied. It is not always necessary to enter the house by the front door. Often the counselor may lead him gradually to see that the problem about which he is maintaining silence is so intimately related to another problem which he is quite anxious to consider that, in order to resolve the latter, the former must be dealt with too. Thus, frequently it is possible to reach the problems in other areas by coming through the back door. Always remember that there are at least two entrances into a problem.

In preaching, Donald Grey Barnhouse effectively used the intensive approach. For years he preached the whole Bible, ranging over all of its doctrines (not always correctly) while ostensively preaching through the book of Romans. By cross reference, by going into essential background considerations, by the development of other passages in relationship to the preaching portion in Romans, he demonstrated that the intensive method was one means for opening up that limitless expanse of the entire field of Christian truth. It should not be too difficult for counselors to translate the intensive method from the preaching context into the counseling situation.

One advantage of the intensive approach is the opportunity that it opens for obtaining early successes by making significant changes in one area. If success can be achieved quickly and significantly somewhere, not only does hope rise quickly, but the counselor can point out how, analogously, the same biblical principles that occasioned this success can be applied to other areas in the client's life. Here comments about attacking single-stranded problems first may be apropos.[1]

Perhaps you would like an example of the intensive approach. You would be interested in seeing how it may be extended to other areas. The case that follows demonstrates one way in which this may take place.

There was strong suspicion on the part of the counselor that Frank, a single male student, had been engaging in homosexual sin. It was hard for Frank to admit the fact, and he had responded negatively to initial direct, routine questions concerning homosexuality. He was afraid of the possible consequences of confessing the sin, and long ago he had learned to cover his tracks by leading a double life of lies. Although he was actually seeking help, under the pressure of fear he reverted to the one pattern that he knew so well: lying. The counselor was aware of the fact that most homosexuals are at the same time astute liars; indeed, to carry on their sin they usually find it necessary to develop the art of lying to a fine degree, often in the process becoming excellent actors. The counselor, therefore, was not convinced by the seemingly innocent response. Too many other halo data seemed to indicate otherwise. He decided, therefore, to come through the *back* door. He began a second approach to the landing field. He noticed Frank's deep remorse over a recent altercation between him and his parents. So he began to concentrate questioning and discussion upon Frank's relationship to his parents. He found fertile ground here.

Frank was anxious to be reconciled to his parents and desperately wanted help. The counselor zeroed in on the relationship. He went back to the point where the relationship had begun to turn sour, inquired about the sorts of problems that had developed, discussed the ways in which Frank had injured them, investigated what were the wrong patterns that he had developed in relating to them, and finally

---

1. Cf. pp. 448 ff. In an interesting article, "Make Your Marriage a Love Affair," Joyce Brothers makes the following correct observation: ". . . most people have no idea of the far-reaching consequences of a single change in behavior," *Reader's Digest*, March, 1973, p. 81.

moved to the argument that had occasioned his parents ordering him
out of their home. The evidence for a serious problem, yet unmentioned,
began to mount. Under careful probing, Frank could not tell a plausible
story of the break in relationships without revealing the problem of
homosexuality, which had been at the heart of his problem with his
parents. At the probing into this last question Frank balked. The
counselor knew he had hit pay dirt. The counselor explained that unless
he received all of the data he could not help him to be reconciled to his
parents. The counselor suggested, "Clearly there is some significant
information missing." Frank hesitated; he knew that it was his parents'
discovery of his homosexual practices that occasioned the separation.
He did not want to mention this fact, yet he wanted very much to be
reconciled. The counselor pressed the point: "Frank, I *must* know all
of the facts about that serious quarrel if I am going to help you. What
did you do wrong?" Now there was *greater* motivation for telling the
truth, motivation strong enough to overcome the fear. In order to learn
how to effect the reconciliation, Frank admitted the problem of homosexuality. That is one example of what is meant by using an *indirect* or
intensive approach to reach out extensively to other issues.

A counselee is a *whole* person. In some sense *everything* that he does
has some relationship to everything else in his life. Counselors should
keep this important fact in the front of their minds. It is not too difficult,
then, through practice to develop the ability to get at one issue by
means of another.

The intensive method may be useful not only to uncover suspected
data that are unattainable by more direct means, but in cases where
there is little understanding of the actual extent of the counselee's
problems or of the particular areas in which these may exist, a truly
intensive probing of one known problem with its ramifications for each
area of the counselee's life often will lead most directly to the unknown
data.

If for one reason or other the counselor can uncover only one problem
with which to begin, an intensive approach would seem to be indicated.
This is true even if the problem may seem small or insignificant. Intensive attention to that problem initially may develop at least one more
(usually, however, several will emerge). The counselor, in such instances, next may move to the second newly uncovered problem which,
when intensively probed and dealt with, probably will lead to another

or others) and so on until all of the counselee's problems have surfaced. Homework, given in conjunction with the area of intensive concentration, also will tend to point to other basic sinful patterns of failure.[2]

The Extensive Approach

In the extensive approach, the counselor uses the shotgun rather than the rifle. He sprays his shot across the whole gamut of life problems. He inquires quickly (but thoroughly) about the counselee's relationship to God, to the church, his faithfulness in Scripture reading, prayer, Christian service, witnessing. He asks about his relationship to others, to his wife (or husband), to his mother and father, and to other significant persons in his life. He inquires about his work (or school work), his physical life (exercise, diet, sleep, bodily abuse or illness, etc.), his economic welfare, his relationship to the law (taxes), etc., etc., etc. As he roves across these and other areas, he keeps a careful record of responses (recording both core and halo type data), asking questions that grow out of feedback, but never becoming bogged down in any one area. As he does so, he makes careful notes, putting on his agenda notations about all of the areas that later on he will want to investigate intensively. He especially should be aware of halo data that indicate particular sensitivity in a given area (nervous bodily responses, unusual tension, stuttering, surprise, embarrassment, regret, evasion, etc.).

Homework at this session also may be oriented toward spot checking and filling in any gaps left in the counseling session. For some, it would be helpful to assign homework such as the following:

1. "Make a list of any problem areas in your life that we failed touch on today"; or

2. "In detail note what you believe to be the most important facts about the following three areas that we discussed only briefly today:
   Sexual relations
   Parental problems
   Budget."[3]

---

2. Cf. "Homework," in chap. 28, *infra*. That is, failure to accomplish homework assignments dealing with the problem under discussion may uncover impediments to progress in areas not under discussion.

3. Such areas should be selected according to what seem to be significant core and/or halo data. Cf. pp. 257-261.

These, and other appropriate homework assignments, allow the counselor to survey the field of probable difficulties while, at the same time, enabling him to focus upon the key areas of difficulty as quickly as possible.

Thus, it must be apparent that while one or the other of these two approaches may seem better in a given case, and it may not be necessary to use more than one, the use of one in no way precludes the use of the other. The counselor will find himself swinging back and forth between the two as the drift of the session requires. However, it is important to know that there are two approaches. This is helpful when one has attempted to use one and has failed. He has by no means exhausted his resources. He may now move to the other approach. Having received success with it usually loosens up the counselee for a second (successful) attempt at the approach that failed previously.[4]

---

4. Cf. "Probing" in chapter 26 *infra*.

Chapter Twenty-five

WAYS OF GATHERING DATA

A Vital Activity

One of the techniques vital to good counseling is skill in gathering relevant data. In biblical counseling data gathering is an important activity. Unlike Rogerians, Christian counselors are deeply concerned about data.[1] They know that these are needed in order to solve the counselee's problems.

Halo Data

A counselor may gather data basically in two ways: (1) overtly and (2) covertly. Data gathering depends upon communication. One communicates primarily in two ways: non-verbally and verbally, i.e., by what kindergarten teachers call the *show* and *tell* methods. Two kinds of data in counseling that correspond roughly to these two methods may be called *core* data and *halo* data.[2] Some data are given directly by the counselee, usually by word of mouth. But other significant data may be gathered by observation.[3] Sometimes the halo data are as important as (or more important than) the core data. Halo data may be derived not only from visual and auditory cues, but also from tactile (e.g., a clammy handshake indicates anxiety or fear) or olfactory (e.g., the odor of alcohol) cues.

Perhaps the counselees before him are a husband and a wife who have come, they say, in order to find a way to make their marriage more vital. The counselor will be deeply interested in what they tell him. But if the counselor listens *only* to *what* they say, he may find

---

1. Cf. Charles F. Kemp, *op. cit.*, p. 112: "Reflection is a phrasing of the feelings or emotional content of the counselee's statement—not the factual content."
2. Arbitrary terms, used simply to distinguish data gathered in two distinct ways from two distinct but interrelated sources.
3. Cf. the case of Sylvia, pp. 25 ff. I Samuel 1:12-13 records an interesting instance of halo data misread. According to vs. 14, raising the issue clarified matters.

little to go on.[4] So far they may have presented their problem euphemistically; actually, things are very bad but they are embarrassed to say so. To listen to *what* she says to her husband, the counselor might conclude that Jane is a model, submissive wife. But if when she says, "Yes, dear," the counselor catches the sickening sweet caustic note in her voice, he knows that she has betrayed resentment and rebellion. At this point this halo datum is much more important than her words themselves.[5] She called him "dear"; that is a loving term. *How* she spoke those words disclosed an attitude so bitter that she was willing to pervert the language of love and devotion.

An observant counselor notes the way that Sam glares at his parents whenever they bring up the question of his friends. "In that area," the counselor tentatively concludes, "I suspect I shall find serious problems." He makes the notation "friends" in the agenda column of his Weekly Counseling Record,[6] and as soon as it is appropriate begins to probe the area. Nor will he fail to note that Sally seems to do everything that she can to keep her husband from raising the issue of their relationship to his mother. Whenever the subject seems to be coming up, she jumps in with both feet and tries to scatter the shot or turn the discussion to a safer subject. The halo data clearly reveal that here is another sore spot.

Every counselor must learn to look (feel, taste, smell) and listen for halo data.[7] He looks at clothing and appearance. Changes in these may provide positive or negative indices of the direction that counseling is going. He watches for signs of embarrassment, nervousness, tension,

---

4. Listening studies have shown that it takes only one-third as long to listen to and understand a sentence as it does to speak it. That means that two-thirds of the time that a counselor is listening he must either allow his mind to wander or focus upon the problem in a more total way than the way that most people listen. To avoid distraction and to use the situation to the full, he may spend the other two-thirds of the listening time (1) taking notes and (2) looking and listening for halo data. Such totally active listening procedures must be developed in order to become an adequate counselor. The good listener works hard at listening.

5. This is so because it will enable the counselor to direct his questioning more accurately toward areas that will reveal the even more significant core material. *Speech* is a good indicator of emotion: unusually high pitch and/or rapid speech, for example, are indicative of tension. For examples of halo data, cf. Proverbs 16:30 (grimacing, winking); 14:13 (nervous laughter); 15:13 (appearance). Note especially the Today's English Version.

6. For information on the W.C.R., see *infra*, p. 263.

7. More useful than Julius Fast's *Body Language* is Gerard Nierengerg and Henry Calero's *How to Read a Person Like a Book* (New York: Pocket Books, 1973).

blushes, evasion, redirections of conversation, appearance, clothing, etc. Such signs also may indicate how counseling is progressing; changes in the halo data can, at times, be the most significant indicators of progress (or regression). Halo data are often most apparent when the counselee is pondering an answer to a question or when he is listening to a third person speak. Awareness of the importance of halo data and practice in noting and using it will develop his ability to gather data more quickly.[8]

Core Data

The other form of data gathering relies primarily upon questioning. The counselor must learn how to ask questions and probe into answers that he receives in order to elicit the information that he needs to understand his problems and thus help the counselee. Such information has been called *core* data because it is usually (though not always) more substantive and more specific than halo data.

As he begins to gather core data,[9] the counselor may say something like this:

"We must work out a plan from the Scriptures that will help you to solve your problem(s) God's way. But first, I shall need detailed, accurate data to work with. As we lay out the data, we can lay out a plan."

The counselor may then turn to the last page of the P.D.I. (cf. Appendix A) and read aloud the counselee's answer to question no. 1. "What is your problem?"[10] If the counselee has written in the reply; "I

---

8. Practice is essential. There are many ways of practicing. Turning on the picture without sound on TV and trying to determine attitudes, subject matter, etc., is one useful way. In normal day-by-day conversations counselors can *begin to* notice what halo data are appropriate to what attitudes and speech content.

9. In cases where the counselor is counseling persons previously unknown to him, as for example persons who are not members of his congregation, he would be wise to have on hand copies of the P.D.I. (Appendix A) to be filled in prior to the first session (available in any quantity from the publisher). The person himself may fill in the Inventory, or, if secretarial help is available, the secretary may ask the questions and record the responses. In *all* cases, the counselee should fill in the answers to the questions on the last page *himself*. Extra copies of the last page are made available in the *Christian Counselor's Starter Packet*. They serve two purposes: (1) for use when two or more persons enter counseling together; (2) for use with members of the congregation for whom the previous pages are superfluous.

10. Sometimes it is important first to enquire about specifics mentioned on the previous pages of the P.D.I. If, for example, the counselee indicates that he has had previous counseling or is taking potent medication, the counselor first may wish to ask for further details about this.

find that I cannot seem to keep a job longer than two or three weeks," the discussion following will focus upon the data that will give the particulars that may at length disclose the sinful pattern or patterns that lie at the base of the problem. Of course, in some cases organic illness may be at the root of the matter. The counselor will ask more questions (if the counselee does not volunteer the information) that will help him to discover the source of the organic problem. If the difficulty is not organic, he will probe to see if there has been failure to work industriously, whether the counselee's incompetence and lack of skill may be the cause, or if poor interpersonal relations or reluctance to seek jobs that correspond to gifts and abilities, or past records and references (or several of these together) are at the bottom of the problem. If he discovers, let us say, that poor interpersonal relations seem to afford one possible explanation, he will then intensively probe until he discovers *what, specifically*, is the problem pattern in interpersonal relations that is causing trouble. Isolating this, at length he can develop a biblical plan to help the counselee through repentance, hope, and biblical effort to change, secure, and keep a job.

Data gathering may take several sessions and may require serious deliberation on the part of both the counselor and the counselee.[11] At times, the counselor may wish to assign homework that is designed to procure such data. Part of the homework in the case cited above might involve securing a job. Counseling then may focus upon establishing new relationships with the boss and fellow employees.[12] Reports of

---

11. In one sense, data gathering in counseling *never* ceases. The counselor continues to ask questions in *every* session to check up on and to refine his understanding of the situation, as well as to discover how well the counselee is working on the solutions to his problems.

12. In helping a counselee to obtain a job, it is helpful to point out that in the light of God's commandment to labor for six days each week, he *already has a job*: he must labor at the work at hand, namely finding a job. He should work at finding one as hard as if he were formally employed. He is employed by and working for the Lord. If he puts in a full day's work in looking for work, at the end of the day he can go to bed with that tired-but-satisfied feeling rather than that depressing tired-but-dissatisfied one. A Christian is never without a job; he must always put in a full day's work for God whatever the work may be. Even when he works for an employer, it is still the "Lord Christ" that he serves (Colossians 3:24).

Work is important to man's well being. Labor, not work, was the result of the fall. Adam was given the job of caretaker in the Garden. He also was called to "subdue the earth." Paul writes: "If anyone does not want to work, neither let

daily records to be kept concerning what occurs at work may be required.[13] This may take time. In some instances regular counseling may be discontinued until the job has been obtained. This discontinuation will be indicated whenever no significant new data seem to be forthcoming. In others, where problems may be compounded, the counselor may find it necessary to continue counseling up until the counselee gets the job in order to encourage and instruct him in obtaining work. Some personality traits may be so obvious that, while awaiting additional data that only the job itself can supply, the counselor may begin by working on these. Indeed, the counselee may not be ready to secure or hold a position until he has begun to do so.

Get the Facts

Often persons, worried and disturbed over their plight, will tell what seems at first a tragic story replete with unsolvable dilemmas. John had lost his job; he said that bills had piled up and collectors were knocking at the door. He was sure that he was in danger of losing his house, that the automobile soon might be repossessed, and, to top it all, he had become so depressed that he could not leave home to look for work. What could be done? The counselor told John that God had an answer; that there is a solution to every problem; and that all they needed to do is to *find* it and *do* as God says.

Before going further, the counselor determined to collect all significant data. He asked *specific questions*: "What, exactly, is your financial indebtedness?" John did not really know. A homework assignment to "put it all down on paper" disclosed that his financial profile was not

---

him eat" (II Thessalonians 3:10). As he points out, an idle man will tend to get into other people's business. He will be dissatisfied with himself and with everyone else. "The sleep of a working man is sweet" (Ecclesiastes 5:12). A job well done is significantly satisfying. One must use his gifts to be happy and peaceful.

In some cases the counselee will need instruction and encouragement in obtaining a job. He may need to be given specifics about how to obtain work. It is possible that at times it will be important to confer with a would-be employer about him (with his knowledge and consent, of course). This may preclude early dismissal from the job and may actually enable the counselor to enlist the employer's help in the restoration of the counselee to responsible living. Many employers are much more sympathetic and cooperative than is usually realized.

13. The *Discovering Problem Patterns* form may be found useful; see p. 280. *Lists* of sins, problems, persons with whom there are bad relations, of good things one may do for another, of one's purposes and goals, of his gifts and abilities, etc., often provide helpful homework for this purpose. cf. pp. 310, 331.

nearly as bad as John had supposed. He asked: "What, precisely, did each bill collector say?" Again, John did not remember. "Have they actually appeared at the front door?" "Well, no," John admitted, "that was just a figurative way of putting it." The assignment was given to contact each company and discover the facts.

Following through on his assignments, John discovered to his amazement that the situation was *quite* different from what he had imagined. The companies were not demanding instant payment and were willing to work out arrangements with him. The counselor asked, "What, exactly, have you done to solve the problem?" John, under questioning, admitted that he had done virtually nothing. He had wasted time and energy worrying about the problem rather than seeking a solution to it. When the counselor and he began to look into his assets in relationship to his liabilities, they saw immediately that the sale of one of John's three automobiles (a car that was not needed) would pay off the creditor who had been most pressing. And, as the climax to it all, as soon as John began to *work* on his problems, his depression lifted. As he went out to look for employment[14] (something that he had not done previously), he found that his depression disappeared and he even began to look forward to solving the problems that remained. His new outlook made him a more vital person and, therefore, more employable. Soon he had acquired a job and what had seemed to be certain calamity was averted.

John had several problems to overcome, but the largest difficulty lay in the fact that he had concluded that disaster was inevitable before the facts were in. The counselor helped John to see that until one gathers the significant data involved, he is not in a position either to evaluate or to solve his problems. John was, in part, worrying about problems that did not exist because *he did not have the facts*.

The facts, as in John's case, may throw a more encouraging light upon one's situation. They often do, since most people who worry about (rather than work on) a problem tend to enlarge the problem in their minds far beyond its actual dimensions. But even when the facts show

---

14. John was told: "You already have a job. Your job right now is to *find* one. If you spend eight hours a day, five or six days a week looking for one, you will not be depressed. At the end of each day you will be satisfied, because you will have put in a full day's work. Few people who prayerfully make it their job to obtain work fail to find it.

that a situation is every bit as serious as one had supposed (or perhaps even more grim), constructive action aimed at meeting the problems involved is impossible until their true sizes and shapes have been determined.[15]

Counselors, therefore, must search for and uncover the pertinent facts in every case.[16] Attempting to solve problems that are unclear because the facts are not yet in is the height of folly. An early assignment written in the homework book may read something like this: "GET THE FACTS ABOUT. . . ." It is often important to emphasize principles in assignments by underlining or using capital letters so that when counselees refer to the workbook in the future, they immediately will be reminded of the principle.[17]

Note Taking

When one gathers data, he should record carefully these data both for immediate help in counseling and for future reference. Some things were said about note taking in *Competent to Counsel* that there is no need to repeat.[18] In addition, it might be helpful to present here a sample of the Weekly Counseling Record[19] used at the Hatboro center and to describe its use.

---

15. The outlook grows bleak when one broods over his problems rather than taking constructive biblical action to solve them. One cannot go over the same problem again and again without distorting its shape and enlarging its size, thereby turning all the landscape into a cold, dreary gray. Encourage the counselee to work on the problem in terms of the facts; do not allow counselees to muddy the canvas by excessively retouching the picture. Self-pity is destructive.

16. Some questions that lead to obtaining facts might be: "Can you be more specific, Fran, about *how* it happened?" "Fred, do you *really* know for a fact that you are flunking math?" Another important question pinpoints time: "What were you doing about the time when this depression began?" A further question for discovering data significantly related to the presentation problem is, "What do you think about when you are upset (depressed, angry, worried)?" A follow-up question may be, "Do you focus especially upon any one or two of these matters?" In order to discover whether a practice has developed into a habit pattern ask, "How long have you been like this?" (Mark 9:21). In order to understand more thoroughly what the dimensions of the problem are, ask this: "What has brought relief?" or "At what times (places, or with whom) do you not feel so depressed?"

17. Some other principles, simply stated, might read: "Do . . . *regardless of how you feel*"; "Attack *problems*, not *people*"; "Don't talk about *problems* only; talk about *solutions*"; "When it is difficult to do, *schedule it as soon as possible*"; "Prayerful *work* is the answer to *worry*."

18. P. 204.

19. Available in the *Christian Counselor's Starter Packet*, or in any quantity from the publisher of this book.

WEEKLY COUNSELING RECORD

X. Y. Z.
Counselor's initials

Name *Dover, Ben & Eileen*   **Date** *1-1-'80*

Session No. *3*

Evaluation of Last Week's Homework
OK - on list
OK - on Conference
"Other problems" this wk. -"could
   have gone better" (Ben)
" I got a little hurt" that
"Eileen told our physician
   we were coming for
   counseling"

Drift of the Session

He rejected her sexually for
past 8 years (on & off she
slept on sofa)
    result: poor
    sexual relations
    this week

HOMO PROBLEM - "began again 9
years ago." She was in the
hospital. He had 1st bad
problem in the army. Quit
three yrs. ago "after black-
mail threat" (fear motivates)
Been going on over 17 yr.
period (on & off). "Coerced
into practice" in army
"Knows it is sin" - discussed
it as "learned sinful behavior"
Still tempted; a current problem!
Wants to stop.
   "Recently involved again
... led to present depression."

AGENDA

✓ Eph. 5
   (discussed
roles in full)

What could Eileen
be doing that she
now doesn't do?

✓ Sex problem?

✓ any homo sin on
Ben's part?

✓ Work on homo
as sin not
sickness

Check around the
circle for the
life dominating
effects.

You will be struck perhaps by the sheer simplicity of the Weekly Counseling Record. This simplicity allows for maximum flexibility.[20] In addition to the obvious weekly notations of name,[21] number of the session, etc., there are only three main areas: Homework, Drift of Session, and Agenda. In the Homework section (coming first, since it is the item with which each new session begins), the counselor records the counselee's report about his weekly assignments. Frequent failures in doing one's assignments thus are plainly flagged, the prime importance of fulfilling assignments is emphasized, and a focus is given to each session at the outset. The Drift of Session section is self-explanatory.

In order to make notes acceptable to wary counselees, it may be important to refer to them from time to time. A counselor may make a point of referring to his counseling notes if the counselee in any way seems to be disturbed by note taking (this, however, is a rare occurrence). Reference to the notes enables the counselee to view them as a useful tool. The ways in which one may refer to notes are varied. At a time when the counselee is throwing out ideas in rapid succession, the counselor may say: "Now wait a minute. I don't want to miss any of those matters; they all seem important and I would like to take them up one at a time. Let me jot them down here in my notes and then we can come back to them in order." He then begins to list them serially along the Agenda column. The counselee at this point usually becomes very helpful in note taking and appreciative of the notes so that nothing may be missed. In addition, a counselor may frequently refer to his notes from previous counseling sessions, making quotations from them,[22] reminding himself and the counselee of information gathered or decisions made, etc. The counselee thus not only comes to see the usefulness of the notes, but also what kind of material is being put down on the notes. Counselees come to understand that there is nothing mysterious or sinister about notes but that they contain important data useful to counseling itself.[23]

---

20. Much more highly structured forms were used from time to time, but at length, in order to assure maximum flexibility, they were reduced to this.

21. A pastor might be wise to use code numbers rather than name if there is the slightest chance of anyone obtaining access to his files.

22. Exact quotations of pithy words and phrases, especially of presentation problems, should be made whenever a counselor suspects they may be of value. It is better to have more of these than one needs, rather than too few.

23. On rare occasions, the counselor may say to a nervous counselee: "Would

Use of Notes

Notes, of course, are very useful to the counselor in many ways, some of which it is not necessary for the counselee to understand. Counselors will find the Agenda column especially helpful for jotting down matters that occur to him during sessions but that he must wait to raise later on. By noting these as "agenda," he does not need to bring up these matters at the moment. There is no need to interrupt the counselee or sidetrack discussion of the topic.

Often a counselor does not want to introduce an issue at a particular point because he concludes that it is too early to do so. The agenda column has been found extremely useful for all such purposes. One word of caution: the counselor must be careful always to check ($\sqrt{}$) items on the agenda when they have been discussed, so that they are not raised again later on. At the beginning of each new session he may glance over the Agenda column of the Weekly Counseling Record for the previous week and rewrite on his new agenda any items that do not have a check mark next to them. It is usually desirable to reread notes from the previous week in preparation for the next session. Rereading the notes from four or five sessions may point out trends, oblique turns of direction, contradictions, frequent repetition of data or language by the counselee, similar behavior patterns, etc., all of which may have importance.

One word concerning contradictions, changes of emphases, etc., which careful use of good notes may reveal, may be useful. It may be vital to point out such tensions in the data gathered at earlier and later sessions. *Exact* quotations often make the difference.[24] By reading these *as direct quotations*, at least with respect to the pith of a comment, a counselee can be caught in a lie,[25] reminded of a commitment, discern

---

you feel more comfortable if I took no notes on this?" Sometimes, with no comment at all, the counselor at a crucial point may sit back in his chair, lay down his pencil and notes, and simply listen. These moves may encourage a reluctant counselee to disclose some difficult data. When the latter method is followed, immediately after the interview one may supplement his notes with the missing significant data.

24. As much as possible counselors should use exact quotations of at least the pith of significant remarks by counselees. Exact language can be studied and analyzed later on as well as compared week by week, and provides a more complete case for bringing conviction of sin when necessary.

25. God often does this very thing: cf. God's quotations of exact words throughout the book of Malachi. See also Proverbs 12:13.

changes in attitude or opinion, etc. Such use of notes can enable the counselor to uncover many other significant data.

Responsibility and Data Gathering

Early in counseling sessions (usually in the first) the counselor must begin to help counselees sort out their individual responsibilities. This is one of the first things to do with the data that he collects (Early questions, in part will aim at obtaining such data). Often as he progresses in collecting data, he can fix responsibility in the process. Data gathering and responsibility fixing work hand-in-glove with one another.

Counselees frequently (usually) confuse responsibilities. Like Adam and Eve blaming each other (and God: "the *woman* that *You* gave me, *she* . . . the *serpent, he* . . ."), they will begin with the attitude that "the problem is not my fault; it is *hers* (or *his*)." This happens because sinful people tend to justify themselves by blameshifting. Ever since the Garden of Eden they have been passing the buck.[26] In the early counseling sessions, therefore, it is important to sort out the proper responsibilities: to determine who really is responsible for what. A counselor may find it necessary to stop someone abruptly and say, "Now wait a minute, you can't blame your husband for your nasty temper." Or, "Yes, you *can* live with a wife like that; you did not *have* to leave her." Or, "You *can* solve that problem with your parents; that was no excuse for going out and getting stoned." Instead, counselees must be told: "All through life people are going to continue to wrong you. If you don't learn now how to live with and respond rightly to those who are doing wrong, you will continue to be in misery for the rest of your life; and you will make other people miserable too. Now let's turn to I Peter 2:19-23 and see what God says about this matter."

---

26. Cf. *Competent to Counsel*, pp. 212 ff. Gary Collins is quite seriously in error when he declares that "the tendency to blame other people for the deficiencies and motives which are really our own" is one of several "defense mechanisms" that are "healthy reactions which all of us use at times to meet the pressures of life." Gary Collins, *The Search for Reality* (Wheaton: Key Publishers, 1969), pp. 38, 39. Collins is correct in suggesting that the tendency is universal, but that does not justify it. Rather, it demonstrates only that sin is universal. God never calls buck passing "healthy." Collins' capitulation to pagan psychological notions at this point is most deplorable. Even Moses, God's servant, fell into this blameshifting temptation: cf. Exodus 32:7 with 32:11. God calls the Israelites Moses' people whom he brought up; Moses in disgust over their sin calls them *God's* people whom *He* brought out from Egypt.

So the counselor must help counselees to sort out their responsibilities. Usually he can make no further progress until the separate responsibilities are properly fixed. Everything (repentance, direction of change, etc.) depends upon this.

That a counselee is responsible to do what God says regardless of what others may or may not do often is one of the hardest things for him to understand. Yet it is of utmost importance for the counselor to get this point across. Romans 12:18 can be of use in presenting this imperative. Some counselees have excused themselves by blaming someone else for so long a time, that they find it difficult to compare themselves to the law of God instead of comparing themselves to others. Therefore, discovering and fixing proper responsibilities is one of the first tasks that a counselor must undertake.[27] He may begin by saying:

"Now perhaps it is true that Bill did all of these things that you have mentioned, but we'll get to that in a moment. Let's talk about what *you* did in response, Jane. Nothing that Bill did gives you the right to become resentful. Your colitis is not the result of Bill's wrongs toward you, but evidently has been occasioned by the sinful way in which you have handled those wrongs. After all, Jesus did not have a colitis attack on the cross." That is the point that must be made clear to Jane. Resentment is wrong, it is sinful, and may not be excused. Her responsibility was to handle the wrongs rightly. Jesus prayed for those who crucified Him (and so did Stephen); neither became ill over another's wrongdoing.

Christ has commanded us to give a cup of cold water to our enemies; that commandment holds true even when one's enemy is his husband or parents. Jesus orderd us to do good to those who despitefully use us.

---

27. Harris is correct when he observes, "Telling a patient he must be responsible is nowhere near the same thing as his becoming responsible." Tom Harris, *op. cit.*, p. 242. Yet one must not only begin by telling the counselee that God says that he must become a responsible person; he must go back beyond that and tell him that God *already* has declared him responsible and, indeed, *now holds him responsible.* Neither Harris nor Glasser, whom he criticizes, knows what responsibility involves. Harris adopts this as his standard: "Persons are important," p. 220. Yet how does he know this; and how does he know what is truly good for persons? Glasser will turn out counselees who are responsible to society (whatever that may be in a given time and culture). Humanistic relativity in which standards finally become little more than subjective judgments is the best he can offer, because he has no divinely imposed authoritative Standard. Responsibility for Glasser is horizontal and changing; not vertical and absolute.

Counselees can be *expected* to do so if they truly are Christians. Counselors must sort out the responsibilities and never accept blameshifting.[28] When the responsibility is shifted to another, all hope ceases. There is no way to be sure that another will change. The counselee's only sure hope is in the promise of God that by grace *he himself can change*. This change is effected by the prayerful application of the Scriptures to his circumstances and his responses to them.

Gathering Legitimate Data

All of which raises a second point: counselors should not talk about others behind their backs when counseling; nor should they allow counselees to do so. Much slander goes on whenever they do, not to speak of the distorted data that this elicits. The ideal group with which to work is the involved group of people.[29] If a husband and wife are having problems, why counsel them separately? The Bible directs them to get together (Matthew 5, 18). If they fail to come together on their own, then others must become involved in order to help them. But if a husband and wife are not able (or willing) to come for counsel together, saying all sorts of things about the absent party behind his back will not help the situation. It can only do harm. That surely is not God's road to reconciliation.[30] Each counselee knows that he is not getting a fair shake when the other party talks behind his back. Such counseling foolishly arouses unnecessary suspicion and tends to drive wedges deeper.[31]

It is also important to warn against receiving "privileged information." Counselors must refuse to be placed in a position where they accept information about another behind his back that the revealer would not be willing to state in his presence. The formula with which such information is introduced usually sounds something like this:

---

28. Blame-shifting can be directed toward things and circumstances as well as toward people: "This house has given us nothing but trouble"; "I blame my blue feelings on the weather." The fact is that neither the house nor the weather can be blamed for the counselee's poor behavior or attitudes. Things and conditions are the sounding boards upon which one's sinful responses are amplified and broadcast. Occasions and things only precipitate out what is there already. Counselees allow them to trigger their cocked responses. The counselee is responsible for loading the gun and cocking it.

29. Cf. *The Big Umbrella, op. cit.*, pp. 239-246.

30. See earlier comments concerning the Reconciliation/Discipline dynamic, chapter 8.

31. Cf. *Competent to Counsel*, pp. 236-247.

"Don't let him know that I told you this, but. . . ." Counselors should break in immediately and insist that they must be allowed to relay the information to the party, stating the source, or that they cannot receive it. Often the party revealing the information needs to be persuaded first to go to the brother as Christ advised in Matthew 18. This is true when he is speaking about a personal offense to himself. In other instances, he may need to be directed to Galatians 6:1.[32] In every case it is better for all involved parties to be made aware of all information. The revealer may need to be persuaded of this by biblical evidence.[33] A counselor also may explain that until this vital information can be put on the table openly for all parties to see, nothing significant can be done to *solve* the problem.

It is not always possible to get both parties to come for counseling. So what may the counselor do if only one will come? *He must spend his time talking about the person who is there, not about the person who is not there.* This should be an inviolable rule. He may begin by commenting: "We can't do anything directly for John, Susan, because he is not here. It would not be right for us to talk about him behind his back; and it would do no good. You can pray for him, of course; if you *must* talk about him, talk to God. What we must talk about is how you can be sure that your relationship to him is right before God. Who knows, what God may use to effect change in John is significant change in you (cf. I Peter 3:1-12)!"

A couple came in to talk about their teen-age son and the problems that they were having with him. The counselor explained: "We simply must not do this. We would ruin the whole situation if we were to do that ahead of time. Beyond saying a few things about him as he figures in the situation in general, we must not talk *against* him. Let's concentrate instead upon what you have been doing as parents and see if you can discover where you may have failed. You should have brought him with you if you expected us to discuss *his* behavior. Since he was not here tonight, go home and tell him everything that took place in this session that in any way relates to him so that he will know everything that happened before he comes next week. Tell him that we told you to tell him everything, everything that I've said and everything that

---

32. Cf. *The Big Umbrella*, "You Are Your Brother's Counselor," *op. cit.*
33. Counselors may wish to refer to such passages as James 4:11; 5:9; I Peter 2:1; Proverbs 6:19; 10:18; 11:13; 20:19.

you've said and then all of you come back together." They were afraid that their son, Phil, would not come. The counselor assured them, "He is more likely to come if he knows that I refused to talk about him behind his back." Sure enough, he came with them the following week. The first thing the counselor asked him was, "Did your parents tell you everything about our last session?" He replied, "Yes, they did." Then the counselor suggested, "If you have any further questions about that session, I would be glad to answer them." The counselor reviewed the main points of the previous discussion from his notes before going on.[34] This consideration for him as a person made all the difference in the world in gaining Phil's confidence. Eventually he was successfully dealt with and reconciled to his parents.

The same fact is true of the Christian school. Is it right for Christians in imitation of public schools to have parent-teacher meetings? Would it not be more biblical to have parent-teacher-student meetings? Not only is this better because of the blame, the distortion of truth, and the behind-the-back planning that it precludes, along with the inevitable suspicion that it creates, but it is also a good idea because it is possible to fool people so much more easily when everybody that is involved is not present. If the student is there, then he cannot think or say, "Well, that isn't what my teacher says when he talks to my parents"; or, "That isn't what my parents say when they talk to my teachers." Everyone knows what everyone said; they were all there. Everybody knows all of the reasons that were given and commitments that were made. And everybody knows that everybody knows; that in itself makes a tremendous difference.

The biblical picture leads counselors to work with such groups. There are, for example, *true* confession groups, and there are *pseudo* confession groups. The true group consists of all the involved parties; all of those who are parties to the problem. The reason why this is the biblical group is because it is the only group that may operate within a reconciliation context.

Pseudo groups consist of a conglomerate of people who were not involved in the problem and who cannot properly qualify because they

---

34. Another value of notes and records; they may be used at any time to review matters with counselees or to fill in other counselees who have newly entered the sessions. When it is necessary to make a transition to another counselor, notes also prove invaluable.

cannot engage in reconciliation. Conglomerate groups legitimately may be able to swap ideas that will help each member of the group to solve his own problems, but they have no right to talk about the problems that he has with other people.

Jesus said that matters of personal offense must be taken to the involved person privately.[35] Even if one or two others at length become involved, Jesus indicated that their role is as arbiters or counselors who speak to *both* of the reconciled parties; they do not gather as a group to talk to one party behind his back. Pseudo groups do not fit into the reconciliation/discipline framework. The dynamic is missing. Neither the picture nor its frame is there. Instead, people gather to spill the beans about other persons behind their backs. When they are not there to answer objections or to set the picture straight, they cannot defend themselves. That picture is not biblical because it involves a pseudo group, not a true group. A biblical confession group consists of the people who can get down on their knees before God right then and there to settle matters. That is one fact that makes a big difference.

Counselors should bring together as many of the people who are involved as is possible. Then the data that they gather will be more likely to be accurate. As they gather data from one person, these data can be modified or qualified by another. His explanations and amplifications *often may prove to be the most valuable data of all.* Yet such data are omitted entirely from one-to-one counseling or pseudo group counseling sessions. Omissions can be altogether important.

It is essential for both parties to be present when talking about the actions of one another for the sake of accuracy. "He hit me; he hit me in the *face!*" cried Sally. "Sure, I slapped her," Philip replied, "but only to stop her from beating *herself* with her fists in a hysterical rage."[36] What a difference between the first statement alone and the whole picture! Much false information comes from working with one person alone.

---

35. Matthew 18:15.
36. Cf. such comments: Jill: "He hit me!" Brad: "Sure, because you were biting my finger to the bone." Frank: "She lectures." Barbara: "In talking to him you never have more than a one-way conversation." Gathering data about all from one side alone may deeply distort the truth. If these conversations were conducted with *both* present, think of what might have been said with the other absent! Without the corrective and qualifying presence of the other party(s), a story about another is difficult to believe.

Counseling that fails to get the full story from all involved parties nearly always goes astray.[37] A counselor may go off on an entirely wrong track, as indeed he might have in this instance had he had the information offered by Sally from her slanted and twisted viewpoint alone. By making such a statement she was trying to gain sympathy for herself while attempting to show that her husband was a cruel and harsh person. If she was willing to tell such half truths in Philip's presence, think how she might have distorted the facts about him if she were alone! Apart from the balancing data that Philip provided, the counselor easily might have gone off in an entirely different direction. The facts, instead of pointing to the cruelty of Philip, underline the problem of self-pity in Sally. The *whole* story forces the counselor to focus upon Sally's failure to handle life's problems in a Christian manner rather than upon the cruelty of her husband.

Thus it is all important in data gathering to obtain all of the essential facts and to obtain them from all of the viewpoints represented by all of the involved parties. But what is the principal method of obtaining adequate data upon which to make judgments leading to the offering of scriptural counsel and advice? The principal means for obtaining data is through asking questions, a subject to which we must now turn.[38]

---

37. Unless, of course, the counselor carefully restricts himself to effecting change in the counselee. Even then he is at a disadvantage when his information comes strictly from a single individual. Cf. Proverbs 18:13, 17.

38. Counselors also may obtain much information through the use of homework. Sometimes these data are more valuable than any other kind. More will be said of data gathering by means of homework at the appropriate place; *infra*, chap. 27.

Chapter Twenty-six

ASKING QUESTIONS

Asking questions is a vital part of data gathering. When you ask questions, ask them in the way that Christ did. Begin with the basic whats, which are the fundamental data gathering questions. In the Gospels you will notice that Jesus asks many questions. Some are rhetorical, some are for the benefit of the other person, and some are for the purpose of data gathering. On the back page of the Personal Data Inventory (Appendix A), we have summed up His basic data-oriented questions into three inquiries: (1) What is your problem? (that is, what brought you here?); (2) What have you done about it?; (3) What do you want us to do?[1]

The purpose of the first question is self-evident. Perhaps the purpose of the other two is not. Consider, then, question number two. It is very important to find out what has been done about the problem so far, since sometimes the things that counselees have done may have become more of a problem than the original problem itself. If counselees have personally complicated the original difficulty or have sought and followed advice that has, it will be important for the counselor to know this. If, for instance, a psychiatrist has blamed the counselee's problem on his father, this may have occasioned additional problems between the two of them to which the counselor also may be obliged to address himself.

---

1. Cf. *The Big Umbrella*, pp. 163-165. Notice the stress is upon *what*, not *why*. You are interested in facts, not speculation. What questions are more likely to obtain facts. These facts will help you to answer the why. Moreover, what-type questions tend to arouse less tension and hostility. Try the simple experiment of asking a friend a series of what- and a series of why-type qusetions about her choice of clothes. E.g., What is the color of your dress? What type of material is it made of? Why did you buy a dress of that color? Why is the dress made out of that material? Christ asked questions beginning with "why," but a careful study of Christ's questions reveals that these why-type questions were not data gathering questions. On the contrary, they were mostly rhetorical in nature, asked in order to put the necessary pressure on a listener to think through the implications of his behavior and/or to convict him of sin.

Often, just disabusing the counselee of psychiatric opinions and getting through layers of psychiatric jargon itself will constitute a formidable task. It is good to know ahead of time when this problem is likely to occur.

The final question, "What do you want me to do?" is also vital. The expectations that a potential counselee has may be quite different from the ones that you have. A recent study by the National Union of Christian Schools vividly demonstrated this. Students and counselors in Christian schools were asked about their expectations in school counseling. The replies were amazingly far apart. The students had one thing in mind and the counselors another. It was important for these counselors to know this.

When the counselee has a different expectation from the counselor, unless the two expectations are adjusted, they are likely to speak past each other or to work against one another. Counselors frequently must make their purposes known to the counselee at the outset.

Fred said that he came to receive "support." He explained that he meant by support sympathetically listening to him ventilate all of his problems once a week. He wanted no counsel, no assignments, etc. At the time, he was seeing a psychiatrist. The psychiatrist was located at a distance and Fred could visit him no more than once a month. So the psychiatrist had suggested to him that he might look for someone located nearer to his home to give him support between visits. When he came, therefore, Fred was ready to structure the whole situation himself. He explained how he wanted it to be and that all that he expected was support. The counselor thanked him for revealing clearly what his expectations were, but told him that he couldn't accommodate him since he must work for a larger goal. He explained also that probably what he would be saying would be quite different from what his psychiatrist had to say. He questioned whether he could support much of what he was doing or possibly the advice that he was receiving. Finally, the counselor said, "Fred, it looks like you must make a choice between going there or here; it would hardly be productive for you to try to burn the candle at both ends. You would end up injuring yourself." But Fred wouldn't buy that. His mind was set: he had come for support, and that is what he wanted. As it turned out, he really did need (physical) support. He actually walked around the office on his knees before the session was over. But he was not going to get the help that he needed from the ventilation/support program that he desired. He was in a frightful condition and needed the fuller help that the counselor was prepared to give him. But his expectations were quite different. He was willing to settle for too little.

Counselor and counselee, therefore, must reach roughly similar expectations if they are going to get anywhere. The counselor should be willing to take a week or two (whenever necessary) to negotiate the question of expectations. This problem may be called an Agenda Problem.

What to Do About Agenda Problems

Counselees frequently come to counseling with an agenda.[2] Christian counselors do the same. It is crucial to understand that the two agendas may be *quite* different. In the first session, a counselor sometimes may discover that this difference may be the one large factor which impedes real progress. If in the first session both counselor and counselee seem to be going in distinct directions, the counselor should always check on the problem of agenda. He may find, for instance, that the counselee has come only to receive answers to two or three questions and will insistently pose those questions, seeking immediate replies. This is usually the sign of a narrow agenda with highly specific objectives. Perhaps the counselor sees that the answers cannot be given in a simple yes or no fashion or in a sentence or two. He may not be able to give good advice about the matter until he has more information, some of which will give him perspective by placing the question in its context. He may know that the counselee will require far more help than he is looking for. He may detect in the counselee's life that there are many other matters involved in what the counselee has described simplistically as *the* issue.[3] He may recognize that until these other matters are clear in the mind of the counselee and until his life

---

2. In fact, *every* counselee comes with an agenda. It may not be as clearly formulated or articulated as Fred's, however.

3. At times counselees isolate one problem (usually a valid and true problem) and find it as the cause of all of their trouble. Careful questioning that does not settle for such simplistic solutions to problems that usually have more complex causes, often may reveal that the focus upon *one* problem is a form of blame-shifting. The counselee may be avoiding a more embarrassing or more difficult problem. He may wish to retain a sin that he has minimized by over-emphasizing behavior that it is less important for him to retain. In such instances, the counselor must keep tapping the wall 'til he hits all of the studs.

has become shaped up in various ways, he really is unable to understand the biblical answer to the questions that he has posed. He may see the need for breaking underlying patterns rather than simply resolving one current instance of these. The counselee may expect to meet for only one session, whereas the counselor may envision at least six or eight. It is wise for the counselor to be aware that such differences as these may occur. He should look for them at an early point in the counseling or whenever counseling seems to be impeded. One sign that usually accompanies this kind of impasse is an impatience on the part of the counselee with the regular, normal procedures of counseling. A second sign of special importance when coupled with the first is a constant reversion of the counselee to one or two themes.

Whenever a counselor suspects the existence of conflicting agendas, he will want to discover whether his suspicion is correct before he tries to go further. The counselor may get the whole matter out on the table by disclosing his own agenda and asking the counselee about his expectations.[4] He then will want to examine the differences and make clear to the counselee where they lie. Grappling with this matter enables the counselor to seek a commitment on the part of the counselee to spend the time and to make the effort that is required to bring about the changes that God commands.

Why People Come

It is important, of course, for counselors to recognize that there are situations in which a simple answer at one session is *all* that is required. It is not wise for counselors to get the attitude that all counselees who seek answers to questions must come for more than one visit. Therefore, it is important to learn to distinguish between the various problems that motivate persons to seek help. The following list, while not exhaustive, may aid.[5] It includes twenty of the most frequent reasons why persons seek counselors.

1. Advice in making simple decisions
2. Answers to troublesome questions

---

4. Use of the P.D.I. helps obtain such information from the outset. Cf. *Competent to Counsel*, pp. 200 ff.
5. This list has been duplicated in the back of the book for handy reference (cf. Reference Section 1, p. 451). Of course many of the items in this list may overlap in any given case.

3. Depression and guilt
4. Guidance in determining careers
5. Breakdowns
6. Crises
7. Failures
8. Grief
9. Bizarre behavior
10. Anxiety, worry, and fear
11. Other unpleasant feelings
12. Family and marital trouble
13. Help in resolution of conflicts with others
14. Deteriorating interpersonal relations
15. Drug and alcohol problems
16. Sexual difficulties
17. Perceptual distortions
18. Psychosomatic problems
19. Attempted suicide
20. Difficulties at work or school

It is also important to know in what areas problems are likely to lie. With specialized groups, special areas ordinarily (perhaps *usually*) contain the "hot spots." For instance, with *children* counselors should look for problems in child/parent relations, of peer group difficulties, and of teacher and school tensions. With *older children and singles*, in addition to some of the above . . . explore the possibility of sexual difficulties, dating problems, communication breakdown, trouble with life meaning, the discovery, development, and use of gifts, and school and/or work. With *older singles* look especially for resentment over failure to marry and explore objectionable habit patterns that may have become obstructions to and reduce one's marriage potential. Check up on disorganization of life schedules. With *married persons* investigate not only strains arising from the marriage itself, but from the family's relationship to in-laws, problems relating to work or homemaking, financial worries, and the discipline of children. Communication breakdown, resentment, and depression are all possibilities too. *Older persons* may suffer from loneliness, self-pity, physical aches and pains, time wastage, purposelessness, and the fear of death. *Handicapped persons* also present specialized problems. In particular, look for resentment (against God and/or others), loneliness, and self-pity. A sense of uselessness may prevail. Such persons need to be shown how to thank God for problems and how to turn their liabilities into assets by the grace of God. Often the handicapped counselee has developed patterns in which he has learned to use his handicap to manipulate others around him.

Not all of these problems are always present in each case. In some instances the special factors that characterize the individual may play no part in the problem at all. Yet, even where some other problem or problems not specifically related to age, or singleness, or marriage, etc., seem to dominate, the special problems within the category may form secondary or complicating problems (e.g., "I know why we had the argument; I'm old and useless and just in everyone's way"), and will have to be dealt with as well.

Discovering Problem Patterns

Much has been said elsewhere about the ways in which patterns may be uncovered so that they may be broken.[6] Here let it suffice to introduce a form that is frequently used with profit in counseling as a homework handout. While this "Discovering Problem Patterns" form may be found helpful, it must be viewed as secondary to the discussion, probing, questioning, and data gathering that takes place in the counseling session itself. The form usually cannot be relied upon in isolation, but rather plays its best role in backing up conclusions drawn from the data gathered in counseling sessions. Sometimes, in addition, information recorded on the form also will stimulate questions in previously unexplored areas.[7]

One fact about the D.P.P. form that should be recognized by coun-

---

6. Cf., for instance, *Competent to Counsel*, pp. 151 ff.
7. The D.P.P. is a flexible instrument. For instance, if a counselee is concerned about breaking a pattern of eating between meals, he may keep a D.P.P. to determine when he eats (or desires to). He may discover from this that eating is connected with certain situations such as (1) when watching TV, (2) when concerned about the children, (3) when under stress, (4) just before supper when hungry. Gathering such data is useful for mapping out a strategy for breaking the habit. In interpreting the D.P.P., look for recurring events (situations) or periods (time). The pattern may be geographical, chronological, interpersonal, etc. The form is available in the *Christian Counselor's Starter Packet* or in any quantity from the publisher.

DISCOVERING PROBLEM PATTERNS

Name ....

Date ....

Directions: For one week carefully list *all* events, situations or activities (good or bad) that resulted in ....[8] Circle those that occur three or more times.

	Sunday	Monday	Tuesday	Wednesday	Thursday	Friday	Saturday
Morning							
Afternoon							
Evening							

8. The blank space should be filled in with a word that describes the problem; e.g., "fear, anger, headache, panic," etc.

selors is that it is designed to show *what triggers or precipitates problems*; it does not necessarily tell *why* problems occur.[9] However, by association (e.g., on one form it looks like tiredness and hunger may be a key to temper tantrums, since they occurred about 4:30 every day), by noticing reoccurring patterns (every time he or his wife mentioned his mother, an argument followed), etc., tentative conclusions may be drawn, the validity of which can be explored by further probing and by restructuring through homework assignments.

Another very interesting fact is that the counselor may discover that over the week or two during which the counselee is carefully keeping a D.P.P. record, the incidence of outbursts of anger (or whatever he is checking) will be greatly diminished or even eliminated altogether. This is a frequent enough occurrence to point up the fact that, for some persons, merely becoming aware of and giving systematic attention to a problem is precisely what has been needed to stop the practice. In such cases, the counselor may think that he is home free. That is not true. He must continue to counsel in order to help the counselee to establish the alternate biblical response pattern, or the counselee cannot be said to have *changed* in the biblical sense of *putting on*. If he has not *replaced* the former pattern with the latter, as soon as the systematic attention ceases, the problem will reoccur.

Scheduling

Sometimes a schedule of how one spends his time may be substituted for the D.P.P. form. This schedule may be kept in a small notebook that can be carried in one's purse or pocket. A brief notation of the time should be made whenever there is a change of activity (or non-activity). This is a difficult assignment[10] and should be required only for two or

---

9. Look for special stresses, interpersonal encounters, failures to assume responsibilities, poor sleeping patterns, telephone calls, gripe sessions, brooding, and self-pity soliloquies as triggers for depression, anger, fear, etc. When parents have difficulties with small children, they must fill in the D.P.P. form themselves, since the child is too young to understand the procedure or to follow it responsibly. In such cases, parents must be urged to *watch* their children. This means to watch as they have never watched before. For what must they watch? Primarily for *patterns*; i.e., events that reoccur. It is not one-time behavior that ordinarily bothers. Children do many wrong things once, but learn soon to avoid or correct such behavior on subsequent occasions. Patterns of behavior indicate habits that form a way of life. These are of prime concern.

10. Particularly for many counselees, a goodly number of whom already

three "sample" week days and for Saturday and Sunday. Counselees who are having trouble with time usually will discover that it has been nickeled and dimed away—twenty minutes here, fifteen there, and a half an hour at a third point. Combined, these three amounts that were frittered away would provide over an hour's worth of opportunity for productive activity. When Virginia returned with a schedule of this sort, she observed: "Now I know why I am always tired." She then remarked (typically): "And I've already made some changes."

Counselees need to structure hard tasks by scheduling them. Abraham, perhaps, is the classic example. When told to sacrifice Isaac, what did he do? He determined to get up early in order to do what God had required. Before the day dawned, he set out on his mission (Genesis 22:3 says, "rising up early"). The task was hard, so he began early. He did not wait until nightfall. If he had waited, he probably would not have gone. A footnote in the Berkeley Version on Jeremiah 44:4 comments on the phrase, "rising up early" as follows: the expression indicates "special attention to get at something." That is precisely the attitude needed to handle a difficult task.

Probing

Data gathering occurs at every level. While data gathering ordinarily is a principal activity of the first several sessions, it does not cease at some subsequent point. Wise counselors always continue to acquire data right up until the final session in order to confirm, modify, or refine conclusions. There are points in counseling, however, when data gathering activity picks up momentum. One of these occurs when a counselee at the outset (or later on) is about to replace old patterns with new ones.

Counselees often must be told, "You cannot build on the rubble of the past." Whether it be in the aftermath of grief, in the wake of a "breakdown," or following any other experience serious enough to shatter one's former life style, there is often a residue of rubble from the past that needs to be cleared away before a new life, pleasing to God, can be built in its place. This activity begins also when counseling breakthroughs resulting in repentance have occurred. Rubble consists of the demolished patterns of the past that now must be replaced by

suffer from disorderly, irregular, and undisciplined living. For more on scheduling, cf. chap. 29, *infra*.

new ones. Rubble takes time and effort to clear away. When counselors take the time and expend the effort to search among the bits and pieces of a shattered past, they frequently find evidences of something else. It is this that both complicates the problem and at the same time provides the counselor with his greatest challenge and opportunity. Grief, for example, ordinarily does not exist as a simple emotion.[11] The pain,[12] occasioned by loss more often than not, is intertwined with other emotions such as fear, guilt, and resentment. Such problems complicate the situation, but at the same time their appearance must be considered opportune.

Grief involves a powerful emotional upheaval in which such complicating factors are thrown up to the surface. Only rarely can the fear, or guilt, or resentment be hidden at such a time. And what is true of grief is true also of other life-shaking experiences. A wise counselor, therefore, in the clearing of rubble, will poke around for problems as he seeks to clear the ground to make room for future construction. Probing must be done pointedly and yet lovingly. There are extremes to be avoided. When one probes, he must do so out of *evident* concern for the counselee. Probing may follow at least one of two courses: (1) it may be *systematic*; (2) it may be *symptomatic*.

When one probes *systematically*, he does so according to a preconceived plan. He knows (and has carefully listed[13]) the areas in which

---

11. I have discussed this elsewhere in more depth: cf. *The Big Umbrella*, "Grief as a Counseling Opportunity," pp. 63-94.

12. In the New Testament, the word translated grief is *lupe*, "pain." In this word, the physiological effect of the emotion is prominent, stressing the unpleasant visceral and other bodily responses to the shock of a loss that brings about life-shattering effects. True grief tears apart one's former patterns of life, as well as causes sorrow over the loss of a loved one. Grief is, therefore, a doubly painful experience.

13. A check list of general areas might be as follows: (1) *Physical*: check up on diet, exercise, illnesses or accidents, sleep (especially) and any practices that may harm the body, sexual matters; (2) *Social*: check up on general social life and activities, relationships to parents, children, neighbors, associates at work, dates, etc.; (3) *Occupational*: check up on security of job, quality of work produced, attitudes toward the task (and toward work itself), recent changes; (4) *Financial*: check up on debts incurred, financial set backs, large outlays of funds, fear of future, conflicts over funds with other members of the family; (5) *Familial*: check up on problem areas between husband and wife, communication, discipline of children, failure to live according to the biblical basics of marriage (e.g., husband/wife relationship more basic than parent/child relationship), problems with in-laws; (6) *Ecclesiastical*: attendance at church, faithfulness of service in the use of

counselees may be likely to be having trouble. He then covers these one by one. Indeed, he may ask questions extensively about each area of life in general, becoming more specific whenever he rings a bell.

Probing *symptomatically* means probing only in those areas that *seem* to be involved in the particular case at hand. The counselor looks for clues (cf. the case of Sylvia, pp. 25-28) that symptomatically seem to point to specific difficulties.

How does one decide between the two? Many factors may combine to give direction. One key factor will be the *intensity* and the *clarity* of clues. When one is reasonably sure from the clues that if he probes in a particular area he will strike pay dirt, he should do so. Indeed, if he does not, nothing has been lost; he simply moves to the next piece of pie in the circle. If he strikes oil, he has saved time and effort both for himself and for the counselee.

It is important, however, to stress the need for *both* sorts of probing in most cases. Even when one does push a live button on his first probe, later on he should check out all of the other areas as well. Just because he has discovered one problem, does not mean that it is the *only* one. As a matter of fact, the existence of one problem in itself should raise strong suspicions that there are others, especially when the problem is of long standing.[14]

Every counselor should take to heart the particular emphasis of James 1:8, in which he is instructed that "a double-minded man is unstable in *all* his ways [emphasis mine]." Many of those he counsels will have problems of vacillation. Invariably he will discover, as God says, that this problem cuts across the whole fabric of life. Nothing short of total structuring will meet his needs satisfactorily. The counselee often must be convinced of this fact. One good way to do so is to seek for an acknowledgment of a problem of vacillation on the part of the counselee first, then make a plain and direct application of James's

---

one's gifts, participation in programs (overparticipation and underparticipation), relationship to minister and members of congregation; (7) *Personal*: one's relationship to God, salvation, guilt over particular sins, Bible study (or failure to study), prayer, witnessing, life purposes, and use of gifts. These items are not intended to be exhaustive or mutually exclusive, but may be helpfully suggestive. When nouthetic counselors probe systematically, they sometimes speak of going fully around the circle (cf. *Competent to Counsel*, p. 156).

14. Cf. comments on "Total Structuring," *Competent to Counsel*, pp. 124, 152 ff., 160 ff., 170-175, 185 ff.

statement. Get him to agree that he is a vacillator; then show him what God says about vacillators. There is always the danger that counselees will settle for less than what is needed when they obtain minimal relief. Sometimes, they need to be persuaded that there is more to be accomplished. Data gathering for use in persuasion is facilitated by systematic probing. Systematic probing is *extensive*; symptomatic *intensive*.

The Kinds of Questions to Ask

Since questioning is the principal means of data gathering, it is important to note, at least briefly, what kinds of questions one may ask most profitably to discover particular types of data.[15]

First, avoid yes and no questions unless you are looking specifically for a yes or no answer. Yes and no questions waste time when gathering data. The counselor must do all of the work, must already possess the facts to which he seeks answers (in which case the questions are unnecessary), or must do a lot of guessing. Moreover, it is too easy for the counselee to evade real issues by replying with a simple yes or no. In addition, it is possible for the counselor to be misled, since the counselee's only option is either yes or no without necessary qualification. The counselee may have misunderstood the question, may mean something quite different from the counselor, etc., but neither a yes nor a no discloses that fact. The counselee's own words, his own additions or subtractions, his own halo data when conveying information, his side remarks about other possibly important data,[16] and much more are all absent from the yes or no response.

One exception to the above is when speaking with a non-communicative counselee. Sometimes, then, it will be necessary to suggest possible situations from which to choose ("Is it like . . ."). While this leads to an initial yes or no response, the choice may be followed immediately by a series of what-type questions: "What about the situation that I described seems to fit yours? What does not seem to fit? What is missing from my picture?" Whenever using this method, be careful not to weight the matter too heavily; make it easy (by your attitude and

---

15. A study of questioning by Sherlock Holmes is helpful and instructive as illustrative of some good questioning methodology. One thing that Holmes always does is to secure *detailed concrete* facts.

16. Side remarks are often crucial. Ask, "Why did he mention the side question? Does he want me to discuss it? Did he simply state it for background purposes? etc." Investigate side remarks whenever it may seem fruitful.

what you say as a preface) for the counselee to reject the suggestion. *Do not put words into his mouth.* Always check out yes answers carefully to be sure that assent was not given too readily.

Ask questions that will eliminate extraneous material. "Twenty Questions" is a game in which, by the process of elimination, one may narrow the field of answers until he can guess (with some accuracy) what the correct answer is, no matter how specific. While the counselor does not want to begin with "Is it animal, mineral, or vegetable," he might keep in mind that the same basic process of elimination can facilitate matters.

Let's look at an example. Bill has come to enquire about his life's calling. The counselor asks about his gifts and interests. One of the early questions that he wants Bill to answer is, "Do you think that you ought to be working primarily with people or with things?" The answer to this question may eliminate half of the options. This methodology is so apparent that it is unnecessary to multiply examples.

Ask questions about specifics. One of the great difficulties that we often have with counseling trainees is getting them to speak and plan concretely. Many ministers, it seems, are adroit generalizers. They speak convincingly about platitudes, but neglect the specific in terms of data gathering and the assigning of homework. The *whats* and the *how tos* are sadly neglected. But once they catch on to the fact that life is not lived in the abstract but in the concrete, immediately their ability to counsel helpfully improves immensely.

Lives are lived concretely and they are changed concretely, not abstractly. No one was ever "careless" as such. He is not careless in the abstract, in general. Nor can he change from being careless to being "careful" in the abstract. When a counselor receives an answer like, "Well, Frank is thoughtless," he should immediately jot down the word *thoughtless* on his Weekly Counseling Record and then ask: "In what ways?" He should not settle on the generalization as true unless beneath it he can list four to six examples that Frank and his wife (let us say) agree upon. The counselor has something to work with when his sheet looks something like this:

Frank: Thoughtless:

about socks—on floor at nites; also pants strewn over chair.
about person—perspiration odor; bad breath; expels gas.

about others—
—doesn't hold car door.
—comes home late at nite without phoning first.
—cuts in front of other drivers on highways.
about money—fails to keep records on check stubs.

Remember, no changes are made *abstractly*. Frank will not become careful in the abstract; he will become careful when he begins to be careful about his socks, careful about his pants, about his body odor, etc.

Many counselors fail right here. Because they fail to probe every generalization until they have at least some of the particulars upon which it is based, they really know very little more than they knew at first. Consequently, when they come to offering solutions, they can see no clear path to pursue. The counselor who will settle for nothing less than particulars will have no end of material to deal with; *his* problem will consist of having too much to handle, too many possible courses to pursue. He must learn to take samplings from each problem area that will help to set his counselee on the necessary course of change in each so that he may break past patterns and, through success with the samplings, get the hang of how to do this with the rest of the items himself.

At the end of each counseling session, a novice would be wise to read over the notes on his Weekly Counseling Record sheet to discover whether there are any unprobed generalizations or abstractions. Each of these should be written into the Agenda column for the next session to be raised afresh, this time to obtain more supporting and more specific data.

In probing for particulars, it is helpful to know what various sorts of questions will glean:

WHAT (not why[17]) is the basic data gathering question. After asking the what, follow it with:

1. *HOW?* The answer to this question gets at the mechanics of something, i.e., the *way* in which it happened.

2. *WHAT FOR?* The answer to this question is aimed at motive,

---

17. Why leads to speculation or frustration. The why questions asked by Jesus were exclusively rhetorical. By them He put pressure upon another. They may be used profitably for the *same* reason in counseling. They are usually unproductive for data gathering.

purpose, or function. It is not identical with *why,* although at first it may seem to be. *Why* implies all of the problems of the various steps of causality that so often lead into speculation and frustration. *What for* is narrower and focuses only upon intention.

3. *HOW OFTEN?* By this question the counselor seeks to discover whether an event was a practice or only one isolated incident. He asks it when he is looking for patterns.

4. *WHEN?* The answer to this question may reveal contingencies. One of the basic questions that counselees often should be asked is, "What led you to come for counseling *now?*" Often the answer to that question will uncover an important precipitating factor. It may disclose the fact that one has reached a desperation point at the culmination of many events.

Let Questions Grow Out of the Data Received

While the counselor at length will develop a set of stock questions to ask in each area of the total life situation that he uses in tapping the walls while looking for studs (e.g., "Is your sex life together suffering?" "How is your relationship with your mother-in-law?"), most of the sub-questions will grow out of the general data that he receives in reply. First, as has been pointed out, the wise counselor will ask for specific supporting data for *every* generalization. He will ask clarifying questions (e.g., "Now, just who is this Norma that you mentioned?" "Precisely *how* late did your daughter return home?" "Tell me step by step what you did"; "I didn't get your point exactly; would you run through that again?").

One of the best rules of thumb for questioning is this: counselors should simply ask the questions that they would like to ask; i.e., those that in any good ordinary conversation might be the next in line. Ask those that grow out of previous answers—with one important exception: questioning can become much more personal in counseling than in ordinary conversation. The counselee has invited the counselor into his life, asking him to become personal. Therefore, many of the questions that come to mind—even though one might hesitate to ask them under ordinary circumstances—are appropriate for counseling.[18]

There will be times when it is better to withhold a particular question,

---

18. Indeed, these are often the best. Since this involves a change in the habits of the counselor, he will find that only perseverance and time will make him feel comfortable in asking more personal questions.

however, until a more strategic point or until further pieces of data
are in.[19]

Ask Questions of Yourself

When, for whatever reason, one begins to form a faulty interpretation
of data, he may take a position and selectively interpret all subsequent
data in accordance with it to support the earlier convictions.[20] It is
wise, therefore, to reach conclusions slowly, to think as long as possible of two to three possible interpretations and to allow the data themselves to force the conclusions.[21] One way of safeguarding oneself from
making hasty false interpretations is to continue to probe oneself with:
"But what if . . . ; yet, have I fully considered . . . ; I wonder what he
meant about . . . ; do I really know all that I should about . . ." and
similar questions.

A good check at any point in counseling is to take a sheet of paper,
draw a vertical line down the center and label the two columns: "What
I Know" and "What I Need to Know." Under the first heading list
all of the significant data (in organized form) from your notes. In the
second column write out twelve to twenty questions that you could ask
at the next counseling session(s). Frequent checks and rechecks on
oneself are essential. When team counseling is done, the members of
the team may quiz one another, discuss the case in detail and question
every interpretation. In effect, a single counselor must do the same for
himself.

How to Handle Rambling Replies

First, it is important to note that counselors should be ready to handle
rambling or wandering replies. Biblical counselors maintain control of
and guide the session *at all times.* Wandering replies can waste much

---

19. But never like Harold Haas, *Pastoral Counseling with People in Distress*
(St. Louis: Concordia Publishing House, 1970), pp. 75, 96, who seems to want
information and data without asking for it.
20. Counselees will do the same. Habit in bizarre interpretations of data can
lead one to conclude that he is being followed by narcotics agents, that he is
being harassed by a sinister unknown person, or that his food is likely to be
drugged. Such persons may have been labeled schizophrenic when their real problem is the adoption of a pattern of selective interpretation of data.
21. Thinking of rival or alternate explanations is good discipline: "Yes, my
interpretation does seem correct; but suppose there were a third factor such as
significant sleep loss . . . then. . . ."

time and lead to discouragement in counseling. Because a number of counselees are prone to ramble, it is important to know what to do to avoid such time waste.

To begin with, the counselor will want to be *sure* that the reply is wandering afield. Sometimes counselees may have associated events, persons, and places in ways that at first may not be clear to the counselor. Reflection and direct questioning ("How does this relate to the question I asked?") will often clear up the difficulty and make the associative relationships discernible. Questioning also can disclose when a counselee truly is off the beaten path.

When a counselee *occasionally* wanders off the subject at hand, it may indicate that (1) he wants to change the subject (it is too hot for him); (2) he is more interested or concerned about another topic; (3) he missed the point of the question; or (4) he simply has gotten himself off the subject by following associations not relevant to the present discussion. In cases like three or four, simple repetition of the question (sometimes in other words or by using an example[22]) may solve the problem. In case of reason number one, the issue may have to be drawn. If number two is the reason for the distraction, overtly noting that the counselee's area of interest is written on the agenda, together with a promise to return to the matter in time, usually works. The counselor then may pull back to the main theme. Of course, there are times when the counselee is correct; perhaps the subject *should* be changed. Counselors always should consider this possibility.

Sometimes the rambling answer becomes the rule rather than the exception. The counselor may become aware of the fact that this in itself is an annoying *pattern* that needs to be broken. In such cases he points it out and places it on the agenda as a problem to be solved. He promises to help the counselee with this matter and works hard in every session from then on to keep the counselee on the track.

How to Handle False Data

When the counselor suspects that he has been given false data, he may need to take any one of several courses of action in response.

First, he will want to verify his own understanding of the data. He may need to ask questions by way of repetition or clarification *in order*

---

22. "What I had in mind by that was . . . ," or "What I am asking is something like those times when. . . ."

to be sure that what he suspects to be false data is not merely his own misunderstanding of the data. He may simply say: "I am not quite sure that I have everything straight; will you please tell me again who. . . ." Often a surprising response is forthcoming. The counselee, thinking that he has been tripped up by the counselor, will back up, explain again in new ways, take back former statements, or simply admit that he had falsified earlier data. You can sometimes snag a fish without even baiting the hook!

But when this does not occur, the counselor, having confirmed or altered his understanding of the data, must prepare to make the next move. If the data remain the same, the counselor may simply state the contradiction as he sees it and ask if the counselee can clear up his difficulties for him (e.g., "Well, that's what I thought you said a few minutes ago, but the reason I asked is because two weeks ago, according to my notes, you said, '................................,' and I have it here as a direct quotation. Can you help me to resolve the seeming contradiction?"). Sometimes the counselee will supply an additional piece of information which will do just that. Then, counseling will proceed swimmingly. However, excuses, backing away, unconvincing explanations, and much similar halo data may lead the counselor to the conclusion that he was correct in suspecting that he has received false data. What does he do then?

What he does may depend upon several factors: (1) *the strength of the evidence.* If his suspicion is more hunch than anything else, the counselor may go on, and on the Weekly Counseling Record make a note of the fact that he is still uncertain about the data.[23] He will probe the area further at a later time and continue to look for corroborating data that may be forthcoming. He will ask other tangential questions that obliquely help him to evaluate the data. But *in no case* on the basis of slim evidence should he draw the line on the issue. (2) *The importance of the data.* If the data seem to be trivial (e.g., exact dates that were given at two or three different times but do not match) and not *essential* to the problem, he may proceed with counseling, concluding that the counselee's memory (or, in the example, mathematical ability) has slipped a cog. There is no need to make an issue of the fact. (3) *The*

---

23. A large question mark, circled, may serve to indicate such uncertainty. Circling will distinguish this question mark from others and provide a visual cue that will allow for rapid retrieval of these data at a subsequent session.

guilt of the counselee. If the halo data indicate that the counselee is undisturbed and, *at the same time*, in this case there is no reason to believe that this comes from the searing of the conscience by repeated, longstanding patterns of lying, he may proceed with counseling.

On the other hand, when the point is central, when the possibility of lying seems strong, and when the counselee shows evidence of considerable uneasiness in defending the contradictory data, the counselor cannot proceed with counseling. The situation has forced him to deal directly with the issue.

To judge another to be a liar is a difficult thing to do. Not that judging is forbidden as some erroneously have taught (cf. *Competent to Counsel,* pp. 84-86). Yet God insists that Christians must "judge a righteous judgment" (John 7:24). This means that all judgments made about others must be made as one would want to be judged himself (Matthew 7:1-2), that, to put it in a word, the judgment in every way must accord with biblical standards. Judgments, then, must be made soberly, cautiously, and only when the evidence is overwhelming.

Counselors who understand the biblical warnings about judging another would be wise to make tentative or provisional judgments and to identify these as such. In other words, a counselor must learn how to say in clear, straightforward English that cannot be misunderstood that (1) he has serious reservations, doubts, or questions about the truth of the data as he has heard it, that (2) he is not making a judgment about the counselee himself (he recognizes that more information may explain discrepancies, that possibly the counselee himself has misunderstood what took place, etc.), but that (3) until this vital matter can be cleared up, it appears that counseling will be stalled! With this, he has tossed the ball to the counselee.

The counselee may refuse to carry the ball. He may simply punt. In some instances he may virtually sit down on the field with the ball in his lap. If this continues through the fourth down, the counselor will find himself in possession of the ball once again. What will he do then? At this point, first he may find it necessary to probe the area further in greater depth than before. He should attempt to do so *with* the counselee ("Since you can't seem to come up with a good explanation for the discrepancy, let's see what I can do to help you. Now, think back, exactly *when* did you first become depressed? Was last month *really* the first depression, or were there other episodes—ever so brief or slight—that may have slipped your mind?"). Often this further attempt at a cooperative probe is successful.

If all else fails, the problem with which the counselor is struggling should be stated plainly, together with the reasons why counseling cannot proceed until this problem is cleared up, and these should be noted on the homework assignment sheet. The homework for the week should then be designed to set the counselee to work on researching the problem. Ways and means may be suggested ("Phone the parties involved and check the data to make sure that your facts are accurate"). *Do not assign additional homework. By focusing the homework entirely upon the problem*, emphasize that counseling is stalled until this vital issue is resolved. One final word of warning: *do not bring an issue to this point unless you are* SURE *that it truly warrants such emphasis*. Often lesser matters resolve themselves when other questions are first resolved. Yet, on the other hand, there are times (frequent enough) when a counselee must be confronted about the truth of his data. He is responsible for telling the truth, and whether he is deceived or intends to deceive, in either case if he has offered false information he is responsible for this and should be held responsible.[24]

Data gathering is of the essence in counseling and occupies the larger part of the time in the earlier sessions. All that will be done later depends upon the data that have been accumulated, their sufficiency, their accuracy, their proper interpretation. Therefore, it behooves every counselor to spend much time, thought, and prayer in developing his skills and techniques for gathering data.

While data gathering does form the larger part of the counselor's activities during earlier sessions, it by no means excludes other activities, one of which becomes a vital (usually the climactic) part of every session: homework.

---

24. In Ephesians 4:25, Paul says, "Speak the truth, each one of you with his neighbor, *for we are members of one another* [italics mine.]." The reason given is important. As in all cooperative effort truth enables persons to function, so too truth is essential in the counseling effort, which is essentially a cooperative enterprise.

Chapter Twenty-seven

HELPING THROUGH HOMEWORK

Offering Initial Help Through Homework

The counselee needs help; not only *hope*. Help, however, must be real *help*. He needs help to deal with his current problems. The counselor must not only look back into the past to help him to uncover and to settle any unfinished business, but also must teach him how God wants him to handle the precipitating problem(s) that motivated him to seek counseling *at this time*. All such problems must be considered important and genuine. One principal means of offering such help is through the judicious use of homework. First, however, let us look at some problems that might (at first) seem to indicate the use of some other method.

Many counseling books warn that the counselee does not know much about what is wrong with him. So instead of listening to the content (what he says), counselors are urged to learn rather to read between the lines. They must interpret his situation for him. Either he is thought to know little about the dynamics of his problem, or he is pictured as trying to deceive. In both cases, counselors are advised not to trust the counselee. Now, of course, some people do try to deceive, but generally speaking this is not the case unless the counselee has a strong reason for doing so.[1]

More often a counselee may reveal only a part of the picture at the outset to see what the counselor is going to *do* with it.[2] He may

---

1. Such as deep guilt over an abortion, lack of motivation in coming for counseling (his wife, boss, or parents insisted), desire to hurt another, a pattern of lying, etc.

2. Sometimes he finds it very *hard* to speak. The problem is so great or his fear or embarrassment is so overwhelming that he hesitates. Whenever, in a reasonable period of time, a counselor cannot help the counselee to deliver the information, he may use homework instead. He can tell him to write out what was so hard to say and bring it back next week. Of course it is possible at times (in the session itself) to hand the counselee a pad and pencil and ask him to do

not be sure that he wants him to see the full picture until he has tested him to see what he will do with some lesser aspect of it. Now if the counselor ignores the presentation problem, minimizes it, or treats it as a wrong analysis of the situation, the counselee may never reveal the rest. Instead, it is a better policy to treat seriously every problem that is presented. The safest way to cover all of the bases is to say something like the following: "This difficulty may not be the main issue. But you have presented it as an issue, so we will begin by dealing with it. Often it is wiser to start with more simple matters. As other, larger issues may emerge, we'll take them in course. The sooner that we get to them, the better, but we shall treat every problem seriously."

Counselors must take counselees seriously. They must take them seriously enough to assign homework designed to meet the presentation problem. If the problem was wrongly set forth or there was an attempt to deceive, nothing will disclose this so readily as homework. Nothing turns people off like the psychiatric omnipotence with which some self-styled experts look down from Mt. Olympus and declare (or, what is even worse, insinuate) that the data that have been presented are all amiss. On the other hand, it is gratifying to see the usual response to handling a couple of small problems immediately. Almost invariably the counselee will suddenly drop the big one(s) right into the counselor's lap.

Frequently, counselees who have experienced failure after failure in working with psychiatrists or other counselors may wish to gain some measure of confidence before unloading all of the freight. So remember, if the counselor brushes those little presentation problems aside and tells the counselee (or even intimates) that he doesn't know what he is talking about, the counselee may never trust him with the big one. As a matter of principle, counselors should always handle small presentation problems as carefully and zealously as larger ones. That includes giving homework. So the first order of business might be to offer homework designed to help meet current difficulties ("Go right away to the teacher and square it off").

Jesus dealt with pressing presenting problems all of the time. He

---

so. Counselors must learn to use all sorts of helps in counseling. Do not hesitate to use the telephone, chalkboards, turnover charts, etc., in a session. If one party will not come, it is still possible to communicate with him by means of the telephone (conference calls for several), a tape recording or note, etc.

never *ignored* such a plea. He first healed the blind man (John 9); only later did He confront him with his greater need for spiritual sight. Think for a minute about the incident. According to Christ's directions, the blind man went and washed and came back seeing. "What happened?," his neighbors and others asked. "I don't know," he replied. "All that I know is that I was blind and a man named Jesus put clay on my eyes, instructed me to go wash and now I can see." The Pharisees interrogated him. "I don't know any more than that," he told them; "only one thing I know: once I was blind, now I can see." Well, obviously that was *all* that he knew. Jesus did not go any further at the initial contact. Later on, however, Jesus sought him out in the Temple and dealt with his deeper need for salvation. But up until that point, He dealt only with the current or presentation problem. Often that is the way counseling will go; it has to happen that way.

Sometimes the counselor must help a person to solve an initial problem involving feeling ("I feel depressed" or "I'm tired all of the time" or "I'm afraid to cross bridges"). Much erroneous advice about feeling is abroad. From the beginning (Genesis 3:6,) sinful people have acted upon their feelings and in accordance with their desires; that is one large reason why they end up in counseling sessions. Such persons inevitably get into trouble. They live according to impulse rather than according to the commandments of God. They are precisely the kind of persons who need carefully calculated homework assignments.

There are only two options: one may live a desire-oriented life or a commandment-oriented life. The first is motivated by feeling and the second by obedience to God. Sinners, because of the orientation of the sinful human heart, live according to desire rather than according to the revealed will of God. Christian counselors soon discover that nearly every counselee is deeply involved in that kind of trouble. Indeed, they count on this and design the whole of counseling to meet it. Always look for its evidences. In doing so, note especially the *vocabulary* of the desire-oriented life. When counselees freely use words like "want, like, can't and feel," the counselor can be fairly sure that the problem is present. Such people continually say, "I can't do it; I couldn't help it; I don't feel up to it; I don't like that." The protest usually will take some such form.

While agreeing that it is difficult to do what God requires, the counselor must insist that if the counselee knows Jesus Christ, he *can* and *must* do God's will *no matter how he feels.*[3] *What does matter* is what God says that he must do; nothing else. The counselor may say: "And even if you don't have the highest sort of motivation to obey tomorrow, pray about that too, but get to work doing what God says anyway. Your motivation may not have been the highest when *against your feelings* you got up this morning, but you had to do it anyhow." He may explain this way:

"You must not wait for a warm feeling before you give a cup of cold water or a piece of bread to your enemy. You do not have to act because you *feel* like it or *want* to. You must act because God says so. When the Bible says "love your enemy," that is God's command, and it must be followed by action. Love is not the silly, sticky, sentimental *feeling* that it has been made out to be. The feeling connected with love is wonderful and substantial because it is built on a solid foundation. The view that *equates* love with feeling subjects love to tides of emotion that ebb and flow. *The feeling of love is really the fruit of love.* Love has roots much deeper than feeling. Love first is the willingness to give of oneself to another, whether it be time or possessions or concern that is given. One must *give* in order to love. He must *show* love by *doing* loving acts according to the Scriptures, whether he *feels* like it or not. And if he does loving acts often enough, at length he usually begins to *feel* like doing them as well. ('Where one's treasure is, there is his heart also.') Invest yourself in another and you will feel right toward him."

Thus, initial problems concerning feeling must stress obedient behavior rather than concentrate upon the feeling itself. Concentration upon feeling can bring only temporary relief, since it involves directing one's efforts toward effects (symptoms) rather than causes. The best method for solving initial problems about feelings is to focus upon the poor behavior underlying them. Bad feelings are altered *permanently* only by permanent change of life patterns (cf. *Competent to Counsel,* pp. 93 ff.).

Concentration upon feeling usually enlarges the problem of feeling (as, for example, in stage fright[4]). Concentration of thought upon the

---

3. Cf. possible counselor responses listed under "The Language of Counseling," chap. 12.

4. Cf. Jay Adams, *Pulpit Speech* (Nutley, N. J.: Presbyterian and Reformed Publishing Co., 1971), p. 154.

heart can cause it to beat more rapidly; thinking about pains in the chest can bring on pain or increase in pain, etc.[5] Thus, concentration of discussion and thought upon unpleasant feelings tends only to enlarge the feeling problem. Movement toward corrective behavior is the solution. Therefore, persons seeking help need to be given homework designed to meet their specific needs.

Homework, as a result, is essential to all counseling, no matter what the problem may be, since at its best it is intended simply as a means for beginning and maintaining the regular practice of godliness required by Paul in I Timothy 4:7.[6] Homework, therefore, is an essential tool on the counselor's workbench. He must learn how to use it with skill.

The Professional Counselee

In the process of gathering data, a counselor may upon occasion meet the Professional Counselee. In contrast to others, he does not come seeking help; he comes to test the counselor. He has made a career of counseling. He has been to every other counselor in town and now, hearing of a new one, he has decided to match wits with him too.

There are usually some clear signs by which to identify the P.C. First, if the counselor uses the P.D.I., he has uncovered the fact that the counselee has been visiting counselors and psychiatrists on and off for some time.[7] In and of itself this is no sign that the counselee is in fact a P.C.; there are many people who have sought help earnestly for years in various places but have not found it. But together with a constellation of other signs, it shines as one bright star. The counselor will notice also that the P.C.'s speech is studded with psychiatric jargon. He knows his problem, he knows the counselor's obligations, and he will talk freely about both. Again, his *emphasis* will be upon theory rather than problems. He will want to discuss and argue principles and methods. His attitude is not likely to be that of one who is seeking help. He is too relaxed about getting things done, but quite insistent about talking about counseling. He will discuss the fine points of counseling theory or practice all day if the counselor allows him.

---

5. S. H. Kraines and E. S. Thetford, *Managing Your Mind* (New York: Macmillan Co., 1945), pp. 65, 70.
6. Cf. *Godliness Through Discipline, op. cit.*
7. Cf. Appendix A, pp. 433-435, for a sample copy of the P.D.I. (Personal Data Inventory).

In short, he wants the counselor to *talk about* counseling rather than to counsel him. He enjoys the counseling situation. He wants to take control of the session and gladly will structure proceedings, set agendas, etc. He may be highly critical of counseling methods and philosophy. On the other hand, he may be playfully cooperative. Either extreme, however, will be just that—extreme.

One thing that he will *not* do is to work seriously on his problems. It is here that the professional counselee will run aground with the biblically oriented counselor. He has the Freudian or the Rogerian or the Behaviorist in the palm of his hand from the outset—and he knows it. Free association, reflection, and behavioristic mechanics are all subject to simple manipulation by him. But it is not quite so simple for him to deal with a man who demands repentance and reconciliation. Homework assignments, therefore, like, "This week go and deal with the person who offended you," are an enigma to him. He will soon founder or balk. The nouthetic counselor will confront him about this too. Before long his true intent—to make a game of counseling—will be apparent, and he will be forced to face the truth about himself. At this point, God may bring him to repentance, and he will become a genuine counselee for the first time. Or, perhaps, he simply may drift off.

The biblical counselor will neither despise him nor despair of him, but out of sincere concern for him will insist that all counseling be serious. He will seek to win him to Christ and to help him to overcome whatever problems have led him into the foolish game that he has been playing.

Frequently, the professional counselee is a person who long ago lost hope.[8] The problem that he presents actually may be genuine. Originally he sought counseling sincerely for help. Having failed to receive an answer to his problem from several sources, he became convinced that there was little or no hope for him. Having had his hopes dashed to the ground time and again, he began to stiffarm hope, holding it at arm's length in fear. As he approached counselor after counselor, he refused to let them help him. He told himself that he still wanted help, but less and less did he act like it. Gradually, counseling became a way of life and counseling sessions became a chess game.

---

8. Cf. "Hope," chap. 6.

It is the Christian counselor's task to slice through all such barriers by the sword of the Spirit, which at once is able to give both conviction of sin and freshness of hope. One significant factor in the whole process is the use of biblical homework, to the details of which we must now turn our attention.

Chapter Twenty-eight

AN ANALYSIS OF HOMEWORK[1]

Homework should be assigned at counseling each week. This homework serves several purposes.

(1) *Regular homework assignments set a pattern for expectation of change.* By homework the counselor emphasizes that he expects the counseling sessions to amount to more than talk. From the first session homework ordinarily should be required of the counselee. Jesus constantly required change in those whom He counseled, often at the first meeting.[2] While not everything can be changed immediately, *something* can be different *from the beginning.* From the inception of counseling, therefore, the counselee should be made to understand two facts: first, that each counseling session leads toward biblical action as its natural outcome; secondly, that he is going to be challenged to perform as God's Word requires.

It is essential to begin to set this pattern from the first session on. It is a serious error to think that after many sessions of talk alone one can then readily change his procedures and begin to call for action. Counselors must recognize that they begin to establish patterns at the first session and that these are hard to change.

The following diagram (see next page) illustrates the problem with non-biblical counseling and shows the superiority of the nouthetic approach.

Small Assignments/Large Changes

When small, easy assignments are given in the earlier sessions, counselees quickly begin to learn how to solve problems God's way successfully. As a result, hope comes at an early point in the counseling.

---

1. With school children, it is wise to speak of "tasks" or "projects" rather than homework! Adults, however, seem to get the point from the word that counseling involves teaching and learning.
2. Cf. also the words of John the Baptist (Matthew 3:8; Luke 3:8, 10-14). Lowell Colston, unfortunately, puts change at the *end* of pastoral counseling. *Judgment in Pastoral Counseling* (Nashville: Abingdon Press, 1969), pp. 115 ff.

Nouthetic Approach	Session #						
	1	2	3	4	5	6	7
	TA	TA	TA	TA	TA	TA	TA

Habits of talk leading to action formed from outset. ⟶

Other Approaches	Session #						
	1	2	3	4	5	6	7
	T	T	T	T	T	T	TA

Habits of non-action formed. ⟶

Figure 4

Habit Patterns Formed by Approaches to Counseling

(T = Talk, A = Action)

Principles learned through solving single-stranded problems may be applied later to more complex ones.

Sometimes counselors, in their haste to solve the major problems, fail to recognize that it may take more than one week to gather all of the necessary data to handle those problems, and as a result they perilously may plunge ahead on the basis of inadequate facts.[3] Moreover, even when all of the pertinent facts are in, the counselee may not be ready (i.e., able and willing) to move ahead on this issue. Yet such counselors are correct in sensing the need for action from the first. It is wise, therefore, in many (perhaps most) cases to begin by tackling small, single-stranded problems first. Not only can early success (leading to hope) more easily be achieved, but the counselee can derive strength from these successes to move on to larger problems.[4] He will come to the major problems out of the joys and achievements that come from doing God's will and will approach the larger problems with a different attitude. He is likely to be less fearful, more trusting, and more confident.[5]

Beyond this, it is important to note that often small changes can have

---

3. Cf. Proverbs 18:13, 17.

4. Cf. Proverbs 13:12: "When hope is crushed, the heart is crushed, but a wish come true fills you with hope" (T.E.V.). Even if it is small, help the counselee to see one or two of his wishes come true and hope will arise.

5. Counselors must be careful to see to it that this confidence is in God and His Word; not in himself (I Corinthians 10:12 is a good verse to emphasize in this regard).

large effects. When small achievements are made, not only is the downward spiral of sin reversed, but one or more of the counselees may begin to change radically.

When, for example, a wife distrusts her husband and has given up hope in his promises to reform, almost any change is welcome. The entire attitude of such counselees has been dramatically altered over the efforts of a husband to hang up his trousers, put his socks in the dirty clothes bin, etc. In other words, it is not merely the small problem itself that may be solved, but a much larger solution also may emerge— like the change of one's attitude toward another. The successful resolution of a small problem can lead to a complete change of direction. And not only can success in handling small problems change the attitude of the counselee and others; in addition, it may mark the beginning of new forms of cooperation on the part of husbands and wives, parents and childen. Often such cooperation must be developed *before* the larger problems can be solved. One thing is certain, if they are positive, whether the effects are large or small, they always will be good.

Multiple vs. Single-Stranded Problems

We have suggested that ordinarily counselors should begin to work with single-stranded problems. It is easier to work with single-stranded problems than with the more complex, intertwined ones. Often, the single-stranded problem is the only available problem with which to begin, because the dimensions of more complex ones are not yet fully known. Because the single-stranded problem is simple, usually it can be handled more easily by counselees. Relative simplicity itself tends to make early successes possible for counselees, and this, as we noted, is vital for encouragement and hope. Since it is simple rather than complex, the single-stranded problem enables counselees more readily to see the dynamics of the problem (running away from responsibility, etc.) and the principles of Scripture involved in solving it. Seeing these dynamics and principles clearly and how they work in an actual clear-cut instance enables counselees at a later point to apply them to more complex issues. Finally, as counselees observe one another successfully working on single-stranded problems, hope is engendered not merely because solutions to personal problems are being realized, but also by the clear evidence that one's partner is hard at work. The single-stranded problem (hang up trousers; dust the living-room) is so simple, that it demands no attention *per se*. Its dimensions are specific and clear, thus enabling the counselees to *focus not on the problem itself but on their relationship to one another and upon biblical methods of solving problems*. Large changes in attitude can be achieved by small changes of direction. By all means, then, a counselor should *begin*[6] with the single-stranded problem whenever it is possible to do so.

(2) *Homework clarifies expectations*. When homework is written out, assignments cannot be as easily misunderstood or confused.[7] It must be remembered that people who come for counseling usually are emotionally excited. As a result, they tend to miss points or forget them or selectively retain only what they are anxious to hear. They may have a tendency (or desire) to misunderstand assignments. Written homework assignments keep arguments with the counselor or between counselees at a minimum. Written expectations force the counselor to be concrete, plain, and clear. Sometimes counselors (themselves) are fuzzy about assignments. Committing them to writing obligates the counselor to state the assignment in intelligible sentences.

Written assignments extend the counselor's help. During the week the assignment book becomes an important reminder of the work that is to be done. In many respects, it acts as a counselor during the period between counseling sessions.

(3) *Homework enables the counselor to do more counseling more rapidly*. Written homework speeds up counseling. Work is not confined to the counseling session alone. Indeed, work continues throughout the week.[8] Counseling does not sag, then, in between the sessions. Actually, homework emphasizes the important fact that most of the work must be done by the counselee outside of the counseling session itself. Change with respect to one's job or neighbors or relatives does not take place within the sessions themselves. The work has to

---

6. Of course counselees must not be allowed to settle for such small change when there are also multi-stranded problems to be solved. Early suggestions that this is but the beginning and that more must follow forestall this.

7. Cf. *Competent to Counsel*, pp. 195 ff., for comments regarding the homework book.

8. Sessions are ordinarily spaced one week apart as an opportune time for the counselee to live through a full seven-day cycle in the light of the counseling session. In extraordinary cases, sessions may be held more frequently. But because change takes time, in spite of counselee urging, ordinarily regular sessions ought not to be compressed too tightly against one another. At times, when there is much to be done, sessions may be spaced out to 2 or 3 weeks apart.

be done outside, and that is what the counseling assignment focuses upon.

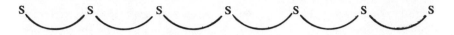

How focus upon the counseling session(s) causes a sag during the intervening periods. Approaches that emphasize the session as the magic hour tend to (1) stress the expert, (2) fail to get much done quickly, and (3) make counselees dependent upon the counselor.

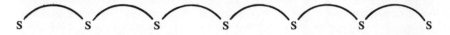

How a focus upon the week's work (1) makes the counselee's relationship to God and his neighbor (rather than to the counselor) most significant, (2) stresses life as it is lived rather than the magic hour, and (3) gets much done quickly by daily effort rather than dependence upon a one-hour weekly session.

Figure 5

Getting the Right Focus

(4) *Homework keeps counselees from becoming dependent*[9] *upon the counselor.* From the very outset *they* are required to do what God expects of them in the light of Scripture and in dependence upon the power of the Holy Spirit. The counselor does not do their work for them. He coaches them; he is a shepherd who *leads* his sheep. Yet *they* do the work. He insists that they learn to "work out their own salvation" (solution) through obedience to God and dependence upon His aid (Philippians 2:12). No matter how directive the counselor may be, when the counselee himself is required to perform during the week, dependence does not develop.[10] Homework puts the emphasis

---

9. Of course, not all dependency is wrong. All Christians are dependent upon God and upon one another. Here we are speaking of the wrong sort of dependency. A coach has respect for the person he coaches. He believes in developing the capacities of the trainee and sees his failures as "overcomeable." So does a good counselor. By means of the Word and the Spirit he sees God's potential. Neither the coach nor the counselor makes his trainee (counselee) dependent. Setting terminal goals ("ordinarily we expect to see this kind of problem solved in at most eight weeks") keeps dependency from developing.

10. Homework assignments also may be given by the counselee(s). When the counselor thinks that the counselee has begun to catch on and is successfully handling his problems, he may test his conclusions by assigning the counselee the

where it belongs—upon the counselee's responsibility to God and his neighbor. This contrasts sharply with the Expert Knowledge approach of Freud and neo-freudians.[11]

(5) *Homework enables both the counselor and the counselee to gauge progress or lack of it.* When goals are set down clearly on paper, one may turn back from week to week to see where he has come from and toward what he has been moving. Some counselees make it a habit

---

task of making his own assignments for that week. Such a transition toward the completion of counseling assures the counselor that the counselee will not become dependent. At the conclusion of the last session, before dismissing him from counseling, the counselor may write out an assignment something like this: "Give yourself written homework assignments at the beginning of each week for the next two months." The following diagram illustrates the coaching method:

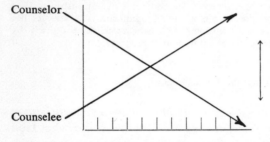

Counselor

Counselee

Counseling Sessions

Level of

directiveness and

responsibility in

problem solving

(Homework should parallel)

Coaching also involves teaching. Christian counselors, contrary to those who operate from the Expert approach, feel free to tell counselees what they are doing, why they are doing it, how they are doing it, and what their objectives are. Indeed, they often *insist* on doing so. A good bit of formal teaching, therefore, is necessary for good counseling. Most of the teaching may not come at once, when the counselee is still too deeply embedded in his troubles. He may not be ready to be taught. But when the counselor has helped him to solve a problem, he should be urged to take the time to learn exactly what happened and why. The counselor explains the biblical process. This ensures him preventively that he knows how to avoid future failure and, remedially, what God wants him to do if and when he should fail. He will know the next time what to do on his own; he will not need to depend upon the expert. Through counseling he has become more resourceful by learning what God wishes and how to use the Word of God practically. In those passages in which the word *nouthetic confrontation* appears, frequently alongside the word *teach* appears. They are two sides of one coin. That is why teaching is an important part of the Christian counselor's activities. Nouthetic counselors sometimes even use desk flip charts to teach.

11. Cf. Alger's focus upon the analytic session: "The relationship of the analyst and the patient and the complex communication between them is understood as the most crucial data in the therapy." Ian Alger, "Freedom in Analytic Therapy," *Handbook of Psychiatric Theories, op. cit.,* p. 119.

to go back and reread all previous assignments each week. The assignment book thus serves to give encouragement and hope where progress has been taking place, and it may serve also as a spur where lack of progress has occurred.

Gauging progress can be a tricky business. Sometimes counselors measure progress by comparison with other counselees. To only a small extent is this valid. But ultimately all Christian counselors must measure progress by the demands of God in the Scriptures. Yet, as one counselee moves along the path of sanctification against the backdrop of the Word of God, he may seem to be making better progress than another, when actually he is not doing as well. For instance, look at the chart below. Who seems to be making the greatest progress, counselee A, B, or C?

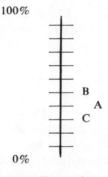

Figure 6

Life progress measured against biblical requirements

Perhaps your immediate response is B. Yet, that judgment must be changed if you look at their actual *progress* over, let us say, the past six months. Here (see next page) the progress is measured not as a snapshot, but as a moving picture during the last six months.[12] The chart, in terms of *progress*, shows that C has made the greatest strides in sanctification. B, although still at a higher points in some ways, has in others begun to slip. He has been moving in the wrong direction. A is at

---

12. Hebrews 6:1 speaks of *moving toward maturity*. The real issues in determining when one is doing so may be joined not by asking "Where is he?" but by inquiring "In what direction is he moving?" and "How far (fast) has he come?"

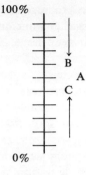

Figure 7

Life progress measured for the last six months

a standstill. But C has become a Christian, has grown immensely, and is still headed in the proper direction. There are inadequacies in representing sanctification by means of such charts, but I intend to make only one point thereby: *you cannot tell about progress by determining where a person is at the moment.* You must ask where has he come from and and in which direction is he heading?

While homework must remain chief among the means for checking progress, other factors may be joined to it in order to reinforce one's judgments. Halo data (like change for the better in appearance,[13] cheerfulness, hope, growing confidence, enthusiasm, or the opposites) give strong indications of progress. Responses to simple questions like: "Well, how did it go this week?" also are effective and should be used frequently. Yet, all such responses must be weighed carefully. If a wife, for instance, is still dubious about her husband's declared sincerity to work at making their marriage pleasing to God, she may tend to minimize his efforts. She may even find fault with solid progress when still angry or afraid. If one looks hard enough, there will be plenty to find wrong in any progress ("Yes, you did come home on time every night last week, but what about the trash?"). The counselor in such

---

13. Counselors must avoid all mention of clothing, hair styles, etc., when counseling with women *unless a change of clothing or hair style* was included as part of a homework assignment. Even then, care should be taken to be very matter-of-fact in making such assignments. Such references, apart from the homework context, may appear to be too personal and may be misinterpreted by counselees as sexual advances.

instances must emphasize the progress and not allow such minimizing ("Mary, John was not *supposed* to work on the trash this week, but he *did* follow his assignment to come home on time letter perfect. You must begin to focus on the *progress* and not water that down by stressing behavior that we have not yet begun to deal with").[14]

On the other hand, false progress may be reported by those who are too anxious to see it or who want to leave counseling sooner than they should. Whenever a counselor suspects that he is faced with this problem, he should deal with it immediately. A conversation between a counselor and his counselee may sound something like this:

Counselor: "Well, how did it go this past week?"

Counselee: "Fine; this was a *good* week."

Counselor: "I hope you're right; as a matter of fact, that surprises me somewhat. I thought you might have had a fairly rough time this past week. Tell me, what makes you say that it was a good week?"[15]

Counselee: "Well, we didn't have an argument all week long."

Counselor: "Good, but did any crises arise? Did you solve any differences together without arguing about them?"

Counselee: "No, it was a calm week. In fact, I was out of town five days on business."

The counselees were right. It *had* been a fine week, but not necessarily because they had made progress. There is no evidence of this. They merely had avoided clashes (purposely or otherwise[16]) over differences. A wise counselor will point out that, while the statement is true and it is encouraging that there were no arguments, they should not depend upon the past week for information about *progress*. There were no opportunities or tests. He may then say, "The Lord in His providence gave

---

14. Counselees may be unaware of progress because, while they are looking for a certain sort of evidence, they fail to see another sort. For instance, one wife was expecting to hear loving words from her husband which he did not utter, but failed to notice his changes in behavior (spending more time at home, talking more, watching TV less, etc.). Counselors sometimes need to point up such failures in order to encourage hope and further progress. Minimizing real progress (if allowed to stand) can deter further progress more quickly than any other factor. Counselors, therefore, must take pains to note instances of genuine progress and to discourage any minimizing of it.

15. Here the counselor zeros in on the supporting data: he wants to know the factual *basis* for the statement.

16. That is, they simply had not confronted the type of crisis situations over which they had been arguing previously. The crises were either purposely avoided or merely did not arise.

you an easy week; perhaps He was giving you a rest to handle some more difficult situations during the coming week. Now, when you run into a problem that. . . ."

(6) *Homework allows the counselor to deal with problems and patterns that develop under controlled current conditions.* As we have seen, homework can be used in several ways for data gathering. Since the counselor himself designs and assigns the homework, he sets the conditions for the present activities of the counselee. Since he himself has set the scriptural goals, prescribed the biblical methods, and circumscribed the area in which the work must be done, he is able to detect precisely what problems remain, where difficulties originate, and when achievements have been made. When the counselee fails to do his work properly, the counselor can see clearly what caused the failure. In other words, his analysis of the counselee's patterns of living is not dependent upon the counselee's report alone, but this report may be tested by current situations as well.

When the counselor himself has structured the situation, not only can he learn a great deal from the homework report, but he is also able to gain added assurance about his analysis of the counselee's problems. For example, if several conferences have been assigned, but real progress is stymied because one member of the household continues to clam up during them, there can be no question that this behavior is currently going on. That they were having this problem with communication in the past might have been uncertain if the facts were dependent solely upon reports and interpretations of the counselees. That the problem still persisted might be doubtful. The response to current homework, however, shows that the pattern is a live one.

Forms, such as the Problem-Solution Sheet that follows, also may be used to help determine current behavioral patterns.
Another is the Discovering Problem Patterns form, which has been discussed previously under "Data Gathering." Both of these may be assigned for use during the week in order to discover sinful behavior patterns. Remember also the value of making lists[17] and schedules. These homework procedures are illustrative of but a few that have been useful in counseling.

---

17. Lists of one's own sins ("First take the log out of your own eye"), then of another's, lists of areas of strengths, lists of gifts, abilities, and skills, and lists of specific ways to please another are the most common lists used. cf. pp. 261, 331.

PROBLEM-SOLUTION SHEET[18]

What Happened	What I Did	What I Should Have Done	What I Must Do Now
Problem (describe)	My Response (describe)	Biblical Response (cite and explain references)	Describe the steps that must be taken to rectify matters
Problem (describe)	My Response (describe)	Biblical Response (cite and explain references)	Describe the steps that must be taken to rectify matters
Problem (describe)	My Response (describe)	Biblical Response (cite and explain references)	Describe the steps that must be taken to rectify matters

Figure 8

Problem-Solution Form

---

18. Available in the *Christian Counselor's Starter Packet* or in any quantity from the publisher.

Homework Helps the Counselor

A counselor who makes it a practice to assign homework at each session discovers that this practice regulates and disciplines his counseling. More than any other procedure, it tends to keep him on the right track. In one sense, therefore, the homework is most valuable to the counselee in that it helps the counselor to do his work properly. In addition to what already has been said, it is important to note how homework helps the counselor.

To begin with, assigning weekly homework keeps before the counselor the goal of each session: biblical action that the counselee should take to solve some problem or some aspect of a problem. It disciplines him, therefore, by forcing him to talk to the counselee not only about problems, but also about solutions. Homework helps to prevent sessions in which nothing but counter-productive talk about the problem occurs.[19]

Homework places a demand upon the counselor to think about solutions in terms of biblical patterns of living; it drives him to the Scriptures. Homework assignments necessitate thinking about the practical implications of biblical principles. Thus the counselor feels an obligation to be concrete rather than abstract in the consideration of problems. Effective homework is always specific and concrete; it is related to life at the level on which it is lived. Generalizations, applicable to many other situations, can be understood best after the concrete solution to one specific problem has been reached.

Finally, homework gives to the counselor a natural, ready-made starting point for the next session that brings continuity to the counseling as a whole. One session is thereby logically and integrally related to the next and grows naturally out of the former one. Counselors find that they move easily from one session to the next by opening the actual session (after preliminary greetings) with words like: "May I have your homework book (assignment book) please? Thank you. Now, let's see . . . what did you do about . . .?"[20]

At the end of the counseling a personalized workbook has been de-

---

19. The counselor is forced to focus upon solutions and progress.

20. Whenever counselees report on their homework in written form (lists, schedules, etc.), request them to read the material to you. When he reads, (1) there will be no problem of deciphering illegible handwriting, and (2) the counselor will be free to take notes on the report (the counselor will want to file some of these reports in his own folder, but many he will need to return to the counselee for future reference).

veloped. This workbook (assignment book with forms, etc.) is placed in the possesion of the counselee. This personalized homework book gives the counselee something to carry with him when he leaves counseling. The counselor tells him to preserve this book as a help to which he may refer in times of future difficulty.

One of the factors that is of importance is the question of *future failure*. How future failure is handled will be determined largely by what the person has learned to do during counseling sessions. The record of what he has learned is in the homework book. Sometimes he needs just the sort of reminder that a written personalized notebook gives. The homework assignment book, then, is a very helpful adjunct to prevent the need for future counseling.

Failure to Do Assignments

If a counselee fails to do his homework assignment, the counselor may respond in at least two ways. First, he may ask, "Was the assignment not completed because there was lack of motivation?" If this is so, then the session may be focused upon the lack. Perhaps the counselor failed to give hope at the previous session. Possibly the counselee sees roadblocks and obstacles that he thinks must be removed. At times, when asked, he will frankly admit that he does not care or is not sure that it is worthwhile to make the effort. The counselor will make a genuine attempt to motivate him according to biblical promises and warnings. Often this will involve strong exhortation and sometimes clearcut rebuke. One counselor said to a counselee, "If you had a wedding or a funeral to attend, you'd find a way to get there, wouldn't you? This is equally important or more so."[21] He also may encourage him by helping him to achieve some early success through biblical action. Showing him that problems can be solved God's way thus removes one serious obstacle: the widespread idea that the Bible is impractical.

Sometimes, however, the counselor must refuse to continue counseling when homework has not been completed. He might find it necessary instead to say, "All right, we shall cancel the first half of this session today. Go into the other room and get to work on your list right now, and come back in a half hour with what you have done. Then we'll take that time to evaluate your assignment." By cancelling all or part of

---

21. Tom Tyson. Church discipline may be necessary in instances of contumacy.

a session in this way, the counselor makes it clear that progress must be made before he will move ahead. He shows that he means business when he gives an assignment and that he is going to insist upon a responsible relationship in the counseling situation. In this way, the counselor insures success for the counselee and places the responsibility for possible failure where it belongs. He will not allow spiritless, unsuccessful counseling sessions to occur.

There may come a time when assignments are so often neglected, two, three, or four weeks in a row in spite of all attempts to understand why and to motivate the counselee, so that the counselor must dismiss the counselee until he is prepared to work.[22]

Secondly, there may be times when the counselee could not do his assignment because he did not know how. Perhaps he and/or the counselor had overestimated his ability to carry out a certain assignment. Possibly the counselor did not write out the assignment clearly enough or in sufficient detail.[23] Often the very fact of assigning a task will raise new, important issues that emerge from a discussion of what hindered the counselee from doing his assignment. Discussion of the question of incompleted homework uncovers new problems more quickly than any other. The counselor, then, should not necessarily be discouraged by the fact that an assignment has not been completed. Rather, he will be wise to develop ways of *using* this situation to everyone's advantage.

In order to make the most of the circumstance, a counselor may find it fruitful to trace step by step the attempts that were made to carry out the assignment in order to discover exactly where the failure occurred. As he reviews the day, week, or other period of time very carefully, often in the process many other wrong patterns of living will emerge. He will be wise to list these in his agenda column and at an appropriate point consider them one by one.

Sometimes by discovering precisely what it was that hindered the counselee from completing the assignment, the counselor will find

---

22. In some instances, the failure to act may lead the counselor to embark upon the course of disciplinary action described in Matthew 18, or to encourage one of the involved parties to do so.

23. For children, assignments must be spelled out. The counselor cannot tell him to make the bed; he must have the parents demonstrate what they mean by a "made bed" and what each step in the process involves. The word "clean" means something quite different to a seven-year-old boy and a seven-year-old girl.

himself face to face with the major problem pattern in the counselee's life.

Counselors will want to distinguish carefully, however, between obstacles that hindered the counselee and straightforward unwillingness on his part to do the work. Usually the two can be distinguished by discovering whether or not the counselee made a real attempt to carry out the assignment. And that can be determined by the step-by-step analysis mentioned above.

When unwillingness to carry out the assignment seems to be the problem, the counselor may find it helpful to ask himself (and perhaps the counselee) the following questions: (1) Has forgiveness truly been requested and extended between all parties involved?[24] Very often the reason why other assignments are carried out perfunctorily is because the husband and wife or the parents and child may not really *care* enough to do the assignment. If forgiveness has not truly been requested or extended, then there is no sense in trying to go any further until this matter is resolved. That needs to come first before the willingness and enthusiasm that is requisite to putting forth genuine effort can be expected.

(2) The counselor also may ask, "Is there hope?" Often lack of hope will lead to lack of effort. Without hope, counselees tend to give up too easily. Enduring, persevering effort issues from hope. Faith leads to work, love to labor, but perseverance comes only when hope is added (cf. I Thessalonians 1:3). If hope is lacking, the counselee may have a "what's the use?" attitude.[25]

(3) Is the counselee a genuine Christian? Unwillingness may stem from this most fundamental problem. An unbeliever cannot be expected to be willing to do God's will.[26]

(4) Is the counselee immobilized by fear? Worry or fear can seriously block the expenditure of effort. Effort that should be used to solve problems rather may be drained by fear or worry. Fear needs to be dealt with. It must be discussed in terms of the encouragement and

---

24. Any party involved (or all) may be the cause of the problem. Previous claims of forgiveness also may need to be reexamined. There should be "fruit" appropriate to repentance. This fruit necessarily will involve a willingness to be reconciled.

25. Cf. chap. 6 for help in giving hope from the Word of God.

26. Cf. *The Big Umbrella*, "Evangelism in Counseling."

hope that comes from the Scriptures as the Holy Spirit works through them to bring love toward God and the fear of God that eliminates all other fears. However, it is important to recognize that fear cannot be eliminated by talk alone. It is precisely by *doing* God's will in *faith* that rests upon the promises of Scripture that fear may be displaced. While the homework may need to be redirected temporarily to deal more directly with the fear, the counselor must remember that he will not be able to alleviate fear apart from but (rather) through homework.[27]

Recouping

Sometimes counselees become discouraged when they try and fail to do their homework or when they have been making some progress, then slip back into the old sinful patterns once again. Counselors must be ready and prepared to meet this situation and should expect to be called upon to do so frequently. It is the counselor's job to help the counselee to recoup, i.e., to deal with the failure and to help him to turn the failure experience into a blessing and asset. He can most readily do both of these things by: (1) calling the sin "sin." Again, at this point, as much damage is done by minimizing as perhaps by any other mistake that a counselor can make. The counselee knows that the failure was serious. If the counselor treats it as anything less, the counselee may wonder whether the hope that he offers is appropriate to the real situation and, therefore, whether his help can really do the job. But if, while on the one hand acknowledging the setback as nothing less than an extremely serious offense, he still holds out hope on the other, the counselee is much more likely to have another go at it. (2) Assuring the counselee that in the providence of God, who can make even the wrath of man to praise him, this setback can be turned into a step forward. This best can be accomplished by careful analysis (again perhaps by step-by-step probing) of what went wrong. Having ascertained the facts, a defensive plan may be drawn up for handling the next episode God's way ("You lost your temper, you say, because you allowed it to build up *before* you said that you were annoyed. Remember, the next time you will do two things as you *begin* to feel hot around the collar: (1) utter a brief prayer asking God to help in controlling your temper, (2) tell your wife *immediately*, before you reach

---

27. Cf. pp. 413 ff. for further help in handling fear.

the boiling stage, that you are becoming angry. Then, Patricia, remember you and Clarence should take time to walk slowly to the conference table, sit down, read Ephesians 4:25-32, and talk it through to a biblical solution. If either of you forgets, remember, the one who remembers is to go to the table alone, sit down, and wait for the other as a reminder. That will keep you from getting into an argument over going to the table and will show willingness to talk the matter over as a Christian"). Thus, losses can be turned to gains by enabling the counselor and counselee to pinpoint the weak areas that need reinforcing, and by giving a strong incentive to do so.

Of course, although it goes without saying, perhaps I'd better: recouping first consists of confession of sin to God, righting wrongs with any others, and *then* plugging the holes for the future. That is to say, recouping equals repentance plus its appropriate fruits.

It is also important to remember that exhaustion, lack of sleep, and physical sickness can be the occasion for setbacks, as well as pride, letting up on one's efforts, etc. Check out such seemingly obvious, but sometimes overlooked, contributing factors.

These four questions are not intended to be exhaustive, but perhaps they point to the most frequently encountered causes of unwillingness. Thus, assigning of homework from the first session on enables a counselor to discover quickly (1) who is willing and able to do God's will, (2) who is willing but unable to do so (and what impediments stand in the way), and (3) who is unwilling.

Perhaps one final problem sometimes encountered in counseling needs to be mentioned. If the counselee fails to do his assignments, it may be because he seeks counseling principally for the counseling sessions themselves and not for the counsel. When he merely wants to talk (he obviously enjoys the sessions but is unwilling to work), sometimes he may be motivated to work by suggesting: "Let's see if you need more time to do your assignments, since you don't seem to be getting them done. We'll space out your sessions to give you more time. I'll see you in three weeks." Or, as an alternate, "Call for your next appointment when you have completed your assignments." Sometimes if the counselee begins to do the work in order to schedule another appointment, he may see results that will lead to hope and a better motivation for the future.

Samples of Actual Homework Assignments[28]

(1)[29] "Write out a list of all the sins in your life (a) that have never been forgiven; (b) that you are having difficulty in overcoming." (This assignment was for a single person.)

(3) "Keep a record of when you lost your temper, over what sorts of problems, and with whom, on the D.P.P. Form."[30]

(1) "Do all of your ironing by the next session."[31]

(2) "Write a letter to John and ask his forgiveness, assuming that you first have come to repentance for your sin against him and have sought forgiveness from God."

(3) "Keep an accurate record of the amount of uninterrupted sleep that you get during the next week. Carefully note any breaks in sleep, listing time and length of break."

(7) "When you go home tonight, write out your own homework assignments for the next week; then *do* them. Be sure that they deal with concrete problems."

(3) "Together, observing the conference table rules listed on the form,[32] hold three conferences this week. Work out biblical solutions to six problems on the list (three from each column). Choose six of the easiest problems. Remember, agreeing on the problems is part of the assignment. If you are unable to solve any of these problems, simply note (in writing) what it was that stopped you. Put all solutions agreed upon in writing."

(3) "Fill in the C. of C.[33] together. *DO* NOT PUT IT INTO PRACTICE THIS WEEK. Bring in the C. of C. next week so that we can go over it together to make suggestions if necessary."

(2) "Read *together* Ephesians 5:22-33 and be prepared to discuss the husband and wife relationship at the next session. Write out any

---

28. These assignments are given singly. An actual assignment sheet usually contains several such assignments.

29. The number in the parentheses indicates the week (session) on which the assignment was given.

30. D.P.P. stands for "Discovering Problem Patterns"; cf. p. 279.

31. The previous two samples were primarily data gathering assignments, although they had indirect effects upon performance as well. This assignment is a performance assignment. But the effects and the way in which it is carried out also will produce additional data.

32. *Infra*, p. 321.

33. C. of C. stands for "Code of Conduct." Cf. *Competent to Counsel*, pp. 188 ff.

questions that arose during your reading or subsequent discussion. In the light of Ephesians 5 and I John 4:19, try to determine who is primarily responsible for introducing love into a home."

(2) "Make all of the meals this week, NO MATTER HOW YOU FEEL."[34]

(4) "Make a list of places you might go and things that you could do *together*; do at least one *this* week!"

(6) "Together play a game of chess this week, remembering that it is not chess, but husband/wife relationships about which we are concerned."

(1) "As the head of the house, begin to conduct family devotions as we outlined, using the devotional guide provided."

(6) "List any reasons why you think we have not seen more change in the situation by now. Be specific. The following questions *might* be of help: (a) Do I really care enough to try? (b) Do I see any hope? (c) Am I still resentful? (d) Is there some other pertinent information I have not yet disclosed?"

(2) "Continue to look for a job this week. Remember, you *do* have an eight-hour-per-day job—finding one!"

(4) "Whenever you feel your temper rising, do two things: (a) ask God for help; (b) tell Mary you are getting angry and call a conference. Together sit down and go to work on the problem, observing all of the rules for conferring."

(2) "Make a list of small but noticeable ways in which you can please Bill, and do one thing each day this week. Start tonight by putting candles on the table."

(5) "The last two weeks were good ones; don't become overconfident this week (I Corinthians 10:12) or slacken your efforts. Push all the harder on solving problems. Finish up on as many of the items on the list as you can this week."

(1) "Write a letter (do not see them personally) to *everyone* with whom you have been using drugs. Tell them you are dry and intend to stay dry and that you are going to have to avoid them in order to avoid temptation. Read I Corinthians 15:33 in the modern translation that I gave you."

(7) "Decide this week whether you want to do your homework or

---

34. In the case of a depressed woman.

not. There is no sense wasting anyone's time. If there is some problem standing in the way of progress, I will be glad to help you solve it, if you will only tell me what it is. If you are not ready to work, please cancel your appointment by Friday."

(3) "Make a list of priorities. Which of these is of highest priority in God's sight: attending meetings, keeping the house in order, personal relationships?"

(4) "Make a schedule that you believe is honoring to God, finding time for all that God would have you do. What are you now doing that must be eliminated? What can you do more efficiently? What must be added to your week's activities? If you run into problems, note these in writing and we shall discuss them next week."

Chapter Twenty-nine

WAYS OF USING HOMEWORK

Using the Conference Table

In *Competent to Counsel* I wrote as follows concerning the conference table:

"One practical method of helping clients achieve the goals of Ephesians 4 is to encourage them to set up a conference table. Families are directed to sit down at the table (preferably one that is not frequently used for other purposes[1]) each evening and confer about their problems. A table is important for several reasons. Tables tend to draw persons together. Writing can be done easily at a table. The time it takes to get to the table may be important for cooling tempers (cf. Proverbs 15:28; 14:17, 29), and it is harder to walk away from a discussion when the parties are seated. The table soon will become a symbol of hope, a place where previous problems have been solved successfully.

"Few persons who come for counseling have been in the habit of solving interpersonal proplems *daily*.[2] That is one reason why they are having difficulty. People who have been nursing grudges and building up resentments for a long time find concrete structure helpful in changing old patterns and establishing new ones. Commitments to biblical response patterns are aided by structure erected to insure the discipline required to establish them. Setting aside a definite period of time toward the end of every day for the members of the family to meet together and talk over the day's problems seems to be one of the most realistic ways of resolving difficulties that have arisen.

"In instituting the conference table, as in the establishment of any new habit, regularity is most important. It is preferable to meet at the

---

1. Some families set up a game table each evening for the purpose.
2. Christ represented Christian growth as a daily enterprise: "take up your cross *daily*" (Luke 9:23).

same table and, if possible, at the same time every day. A student who regularly studies at the same desk finds after a short while that the act of sitting down tends to put him in the proper mood for study. Students who sometimes study at the desk and at other times lie on the bed make the task unnecessarily difficult for themselves. Not only do they fail to associate any one place with studying (and lose the benefits of mood-setting through proper association), but, on the contrary, they engage in counter-productive activity since beds are associated with sleeping. Lying on the bed automatically tends to produce the attitudes of sleep, which are certainly not conducive to study. The student who refuses to do anything but study at his desk can reinforce the study mood-association if when he finds his mind wandering or starts day-dreaming, he gets up immediately so that none of these things becomes associated with that desk. Likewise, the conference table should become *the place where the family meets to solve problems by Christian communication.*[3] They should never allow anything else (particularly argu-

---

3. Communication that gets across what one wants to get across or receives the response that one seeks is not necessarily the only kind of *successful* communication. Often we confuse the two. We must be careful to notice that through *successful* communication one may (1) communicate unintended messages, or (2) bring about an undesired response. The first is exemplified by the public speaker who expresses interest in a topic or in a person, but by his whole demeanor communicates disinterest and lack of concern. The message that he *successfully* communicates is not what he says, but rather that he is a hypocrite. Stephen's sermon (Acts 7) is a good example of the second. Stephen communicated well, but the response was not faith. The failure was not on the part of the sender *or* on the part of the receiver (*as receiver*). The failure to obtain the desired results stemmed from factors quite apart from the communication process itself (prejudice, hypocrisy, etc.). The problem was not a problem in communication. Stephen's sermon was a piece of highly successful communication (viewed only *as communication*). In God's providence he successfully communicated God's witness against the unbelieving religious leaders.

It is important, therefore, not to *overemphasize* the place of poor communication as the cause of poor human relations. While faulty communication (inability to communicate clearly, vividly, interestingly, memorably) is a widespread source of difficulty and confusion, it does not account for all difficulties. It is possible, however, that all serious relational problems do—sooner or later—become *complicated* by problems in communication. These problems, counselors must remember, *may* include successful but *unintended* communication. If this is true, then communication may be the first problem with which the counselor must grapple, not because it is the basic or most serious problem, but rather because it has become the major impediment to solving other problems. Until communication is restored, other problems cannot be cleared up, since communication is one essential tool that God uses to repair poor relations.

ing and sharp words) at the table. After a period of time (usually three or more weeks), they will find that simply sitting down automatically helps bring about a proper frame of mind for discussion.

"The rules for the conference table must be kept simple. The father calls the conference, and in general, as head of the home, is in charge of the meeting.[4] Mother often acts as recorder or secretary, and does any writing necessary. The conference is opened and closed with prayer. The Bible is studied during the conference to discover God's will concerning the questions before the conferees.

"At this table everybody *begins* to discuss the problems of the day in terms of his own responses to them (first mentioning and then setting right his own failures; thereby preempting possible accusations by others around the table). He begins by telling the others how he has wrongly responded to them, if he has been jealous, how he has felt bitter, how he has acted spitefully, etc. He may also mention wrongs done toward others outside the home and may seek advice and help on how best to deal with them. He admits his own sins first and asks for forgiveness and for help. The request for help is important for the avoidance of similar problems in the future. The family should discuss the problems and make suggestions for keeping such temptations to sin from arising in the future. Frequently, means for direct daily help can be devised and specific persons can be assigned tasks to be carried out. As one begins to talk about himself and directs attention to his own failures, fears, and sins, communication opens up. If he had begun by confronting someone else at the table about what he had done wrong, a clash might have resulted, blocking significant communication. But when one begins to talk about himself (the same person that the other person is already quite anxious to talk about), he opens communication on the same wave length. Both parties are looking in the same direction and focused on the faults of the same person.[5] When one begins by discussing his own problems, others often respond by doing the same. Conditions have been structured so that everyone finds it easier to talk about himself.

"When members of a family begin to confess sins to one another,

---

4. One of the most prevalent problems in marriage is a reversal of the roles of husband and wife. Counselors must not only deal with this matter directly, but should take every opportunity to structure the proper relationship. Cf. "Loving Leadership," chap. 7 in *Christian Living in the Home.*

5. Cf. diagram in *The Big Umbrella*, p. 210.

they also find that they can ask for and receive the help they need. Without such communication little help can be given. They discover that confession and forgiveness allows them to shift the focus from persons to problems. Getting rid of the personality aspect of the problem allows the family to move on to discuss solutions to the problem itself.

"If during the conference someone forgets the rules, feelings start to run high and he begins to argue, something must be done. Communication can break down even at the conference table. One simple means of solving this problem is to adopt a prearranged signal. The minute that anyone at the table recognizes that something is going wrong, he stands up. He does not say a word; he simply rises quietly in his place. This is a signal which has been prearranged to notify everyone at the table that, in the opinion of one member, someone has stopped conferring; someone has reverted to pre-Christian attitudes and patterns. Whenever anyone stands up the other participants recognize that one of them may have transgressed the rules of Christian behavior found in Ephesians 4. If one who is seated finds himself in the wrong, or even misinterpreted as violating the rules of the conference table (it doesn't matter which), he immediately should say something like this, 'All right, I understand what you are saying. Please sit down, let's talk about the problem instead of arguing and getting upset.' If he thinks he has violated the rules, he will want to apologize.

"The conference table does not exist in order to tell others off. After each one handles his own failures, he raises other issues that have arisen during the day. He speaks the truth, but always in love (verse 15), and always with the intention of helping. All this may seem unnatural and difficult at first. In fact it may seem foolish to go through such proceedings. And yet, most activities that now seem perfectly natural were awkward at first. Clients are reminded of how foolish they felt the first time they tried to ice skate, ride a bike or drive a car. There was nothing 'natural' about that. It doesn't take very long to establish a habit (and soon the unnatural feeling vanishes) by regular consistent daily repetition. Whenever one learns to drive a car, he at first feels awkward and foolish and wonders how he can ever learn to coordinate his eyes, hands and feet. Yet in a few months after he has been driving, he can slip into his seat in pitch darkness while debating an abstruse point of theology and without conscious thought slide the key into its slot without a scratch on the dashboard. Three or more weeks of regular effort at the conference table ought to make conferring quite natural. The structure needs to be framed up only until the concrete firms up.[6]

"Husbands and wives who have had difficulty in sexual intercourse often discover that many of their problems in bed at night stem from difficulties during the day which have never been resolved. A nightly conference table, at which they settle problems that have bothered them during the day, frequently makes a great difference in their sexual relationship. One young couple that had had serious problems in sexual relations wrote:

> "We have learned a new habit. We never let the sun go down on anger. . . . The conference table was a wedge which opened up discussion and brought us closer and closer together. Gradually our sex life improved until it reached a point of almost unbelievable success.

"Counseling often reveals the existence of a communication breakdown. Nouthetic counseling, in which all of the involved parties are usually counseled together, enables clients to reestablish communication (or establish communication for the first time) in the counseling session itself. One memorable case might be mentioned. The family consisted of three teen-age children, two boys and a girl, and of course the parents. The parents originally came with the oldest boy with whom they said they had lost all communication. The counselors discovered that there never had been any significant communication in the parent-child relationship. They explained the principles behind the conference table. But the parents doubted whether any such conference was possible, and questioned its value. In order to demonstrate the value and feasibility of the conference table, the counselors began to open and moderate discussion between the parents and their child right on the spot. The interaction which occurred was so significant that one astounded parent said, 'I never knew that my boy believed that,' and the other said, 'Well, I'm amazed to hear what he has to say, too.' The discussion proceeded so well that the counselors soon sat back and listened. After a while they sent the family home to continue conferring. About an

---

6. The principle applies in many areas. One highly successful twelfth grade teacher (and there aren't many around) put it this way: "I crack down hard during the first part of the year until the patterns are established, then I can let up along the way; the same kind of pressure will not be necessary throughout."

hour later the phone rang, and the mother was on the line. She said, " 'We're still sitting around our conference table having a good discussion. The only problem is that our daughter now wants to get in on this discussion and she doesn't know the rules. Will you please explain them to her?' The daughter was instructed over the phone and the whole family has been talking ever since."

The following form, included in *The Christian Counselor's Starter Packet*, is used:

SETTING UP A CONFERENCE TABLE

PLACE

Agree upon an area in which daily conferences may be held without interruption. Choose a table, preferably one that is not used frequently for other purposes. Hold all conferences there. If problems arise elsewhere, whenever possible wait until you reach home to discuss them—at the conference table, of course. The first week read Ephesians 4:17-32 each night before conferring.

Place ....

Time ....

PURPOSE

The conference table is a place to confer, not to argue. Begin by talking about yourself—your sins and failures—and settle all such matters first by asking forgiveness. Ask also for help (cf. Matthew 7:4-5).

Speak all the truth in love. Do not allow any concern to be carried over into the next day. Not all problems can be solved at one sitting. You may find it necessary to make up an agenda and schedule out the work over a period of time according to priorities. Direct all your energies toward defeating the problem, not toward the other person. Your goal is to reach biblical solutions, so always have Bibles on the table *and use them*. It helps to record the results of your work on paper. Open and close conferences with prayer. When you need help, reread Ephesians 4:25-32.

PROCEDURES

If any conferee argues, "clams up" or does anything other than confer at the table, the others must rise and stand quietly. This prearranged signal means, "In my opinion we've stopped conferring." Whether he was right or wrong in this judgment does not matter and ought not to be discussed at the moment. The person seated should then indicate his willingness to confer, and invite others to be seated again.

Sometimes estranged husbands and wives must be called upon to begin rapprochement by use of a *protoconference* which becomes the basis for later conferences of the type that has just been described. They are asked, possibly following the first session, to hold a series of conferences (as many as necessary, but at least three[7]), during which they are to seek to accomplish one thing and *one thing only*: to compose (together) a *his-and-her-list* of all of the specific ways in which they know that they have failed each other as husband and wife. The counselor says something like this: "This small list of seventy-five to one hundred items should be very concrete. It should include such entries as, 'I forget to send my wife anniversary cards; I do not hold the car door for her' and 'I serve my husband cold meals; I nag him terribly.' Of course, do not hesitate to include larger items such as, 'I don't love him any more.' Notice that you are to *begin* by 'taking the log out of your own eye'—i.e., by concentrating first on your own sins and failures. The first session (at least) should be confined *entirely* to a consideration of such matters. Only when you have both *exhausted* this rich lode of ore should you begin to work on one another's failings. When each of you has put down all that you can think of concerning himself, draw a line beneath the two columns on the page and then supplement each other's columns with items that you think the other party omitted and should have included. If you have done a good job, the items above the line ought to outnumber those below the line at least two to one. Now, let me give you a few precautions about making this list, some information about its purpose, effects, and use, and some directions about how to do it most effectively.

"First, *do not* debate, discuss, or argue about any items that are placed on the list. Do not try to solve any of the problems on the list. You have one assignment only: to make the list. Even if the other party shows that he (or she) has grossly misunderstood your motives or actions, *do not* discuss the fact. Wait for that until the next counseling session or two when we can take up these matters together under controlled conditions. One thing you will be learning too (as a side benefit) is patience!

---

7. Often it is necessary to agree upon the exact time (day and hour) and place for these conferences at the session, so that there can be no confusion over this matter and so that it does not become an occasion for a new dispute. *Write* these out on the assignment sheet.

"Secondly, if anyone slips and *does* become angry, argues, or clams up, don't argue about that! Instead, simply use the prearranged signal that we mentioned: stand quietly in your place, indicating that you would like to get the conference going again.

"Thirdly, it will be well for you, Tim, as head of the home, to assert that headship at the beginning by agreeing to assume the responsibility for calling the conference and seeing that it closes on time (we'll have more to say about that headship later on[8]). This week, read Ephesians 4:25-32 in a modern translation at the outset of each session to remind you both about the kind of communication that God requires of us. Also open and close the conference with prayer. Mary, you can act as secretary and do the actual writing of the list for both of you.

"Next, let me explain the importance, effects, and use of this list. This list is important because it will contain some *surprises*. You will be surprised that the other person knows as many of his faults as he (she) does. You possibly will be surprised also at the wide misunderstandings and misinterpretations that he (she) has of you. Don't argue about these, remember; instead—listen and *learn*. You may also be surprised by what to you is brand new material. Lastly, you may be surprised by your mate's priorities and the importance that he (she) places upon them.

"The lists that you compose will be of great importance to you since they will probably be the product of the first three days (or more) of united effort that you have ever made to solve your marriage problems. This is the meagre *beginning*, however, of what hopefully will become a regular practice—daily communication about problems. In time, the conference table will become a place for solving problems together. But you are not yet ready for that. This week you are only learning how to pour out the blocks; in time we shall teach you how to pick out the M, the A, the two R's, the I, etc., and then how to put them together.

"The lists are important to us all since they will become the basis for much of the work that we shall do in future sessions.[9] We shall

---

8. From the first week on, counselees can be assigned a chapter (together with its assignments) in *Christian Living in the Home*, which was designed for this purpose.

9. Occasionally the lists will show that things are not as bad as the counselees thought. One woman said the second week, "This task showed us how blessed we really are."

work on many of these items together. Eventually, when things begin to go well, on your own you will complete any work that remains on the list. In a real sense, the future of our counseling will depend upon the kind of job that you do. Therefore, don't take this assignment lightly."

Perhaps the reader wonders why it is necessary to spell out this assignment in such detail. There are a number of reasons for this. To begin with, many counselees (particularly those who have been through unsuccessful counseling previously) have lost hope and enter counseling with little or no expectations. In talk- and feeling-oriented counseling they have *accomplished* virtually nothing. Here, at the outset, they encounter something quite different—a complete program with well-defined goals, methods, and rules. This is one of the most hope-engendering factors of all. Spelling out this program in detail at the first session often is the best way to give such hope.

Beyond this, notice how the counselee sees that counseling is tied together *as an integrated program*, not merely as so many isolated un-related or freewheeling sessions. Notice how he is structured *from the outset* to take biblical action about his problems. Notice how strong pressure is exerted to start out counseling with commitment, enthusiasm, and effort. He gets the idea right off (rightly) that no assignments are trivial and that much hangs upon their fulfilments; also, that his coun-selor expects much of him, but not more than he ought to expect at any given point.

The sample list on the next page (with counselor notations) shows what kinds of items are most useful, which problems are likely to be single-stranded, and which items would be best to work on first. Circled numbers indicate items that may be used to work on as first-time assignments.

The notations on the sample list indicate counselor reactions to each item as it is read by the secretary (wife). He may simply record these in his notes, on his agenda column, or comment about these, or investi-gate at least minimally, or all of these. Some immediate verbal reaction should be forthcoming that usually indicates whether immediate or later action will be taken about each item. A good list, as you can see (and this is only an abbreviated one) can keep a counselor busy for some time. Work done on any one (or more) of these issues usually leads

A SAMPLE LIST
(abbreviated with notations)

*About what?
Ask for
specifics
(remember
can't change
abstractly)*

HIS	HER
1. I snore and this annoys my wife.	1. I do not trust Fred as I should.
Was he serious, or a bit uncooperative in making this entry?	*too general (get specifics - about what?) Too large for early sessions*
(2.) I do not lead family devotions.	2. I try to push Fred into things.
Good to work on right away.	*Get details here: What things? For what reasons?*
3. I clam up. *Work on soon (2nd or 3rd session)*	3. I nag him incessantly. *Work in combination with his # 3*
(4.) I haven't finished small jobs around house.	4. I yell at children.
Good opening assignment if you can get sub list.	*Connect with Fred's # 5.*
5. I fail to discipline children as I should. *(Again, yet specifics - then work on code of conduct)*	(5.) I do not keep the house in order. *Get specifics; these are high priority items for first assignments.*
(6.) I am inconsiderate of Barbara's feelings. *(again, in what ways? - possible first assignments if you get specifics)*	6. I am jealous. *Ask Fred straight out: "Is there any basis for this?"*
7. I work too late at nights. *Connect with Barbara's # 11*	7. I have a hard time making decisions. *Ask for 3 or 4 examples*
8. I blame things on Barbara that are my fault. *Get a half dozen examples*	8. I lose my temper. *Work on at later point. At 1st session, give her a DPP to determine what occasions it.*
9. I hardly ever express my ideas clearly or fully. *Explore in depth later on.*	(9.) I forget to tell Fred about phone messages. *good. Concrete. Work in agreed upon method for solving - Chalk-board on wall?*
10. I want things done my way or not at all. *Ask for examples.*	10. I take over leadership of home. *Will require full discussion later. Connect with Fred's # 2, 5, 7. Assign appropriate Chapters in Christian Living in the Home for both*
11. Barbara is too involved with children; doesn't care about me. *Explore in depth at some early session.*	11. Fred shows attention to other women. *Check out connection with # 1 & 6.*

to others. But, conversely, solutions reached in any one or more areas usually lead to solutions in other areas as well.[44]

Variations on the Theme

There can be many variations on the basic conference table theme. The counselor should learn to be flexible and creative in its use. For instance, if a couple should come seeking premarital counseling, several conferences may be set up to discover areas of conflict, unexplored areas of possible tension, how well they know one another, and whether they are ready for marriage. The last item is dependent upon two factors: (1) Are both parties Christians who are biblically eligible for marriage (including no complicating problems from divorce that have not yet

---

44. Many kinds of lists are useful. Here are some sample assignments for list making:

"Make a list of things for which to express appreciation to your wife."

"List at least twenty blessings of God to you this week."

"List as many ways as you can think of to put your husband first (cf. Philippians 2:3, 4)."

"Make a list of ways to please each other; then begin doing these things (cf. Romans 15:1-3), one each day."

"List all of the things that you strongly desire but cannot have." When the list appears, the counselor and counselee (1) may study which are wrong and right and why; (2) what to do to obtain worthy goals; (3) what to do if you cannot. Look for "If . . . then" excuses: e.g., "If I had a college education, then I'd teach the class; If I had a different job, then I'd have time for my family." Ask instead, "Can't you have it *another* way?" New ways to make lists will present themselves constantly. Cf. pp. 261, 310.

(12.) Barbara is too fussy about way boys cut grass.	12. He is not home enough. *get exact data on. Keep weekly schedule on hours home.*
13. She often refuses to have sexual relations. *↖ Place on agenda for later discussion and work*	13. Fred is dull and uninteresting. *Ask: "How would you like him to be?" Later assign Barbara task of describing the kind of man she would like to see him become.*
(14.) She is thoughtless. *Give examples*	14. He has given up on the marriage. *What leads you to say this?*
15. Barbara's mother meddles in our family. *- put on agenda*	

been resolved[11])? (2) Can both successfully work through inevitable difficulties to biblical solutions? The conference table may disclose such data more quickly and fully than any other means.

Conferences ought always to be encouraged during premarital counseling not only for the previously mentioned reason, but also because it is important for marriages to begin in honest communication according to the principles of Ephesians 4:25-32 that have been discussed fully elsewhere. Thus, the conference table is useful not only for diagnostic and remedial purposes, but also for preventive purposes. If more prospective husbands and wives were encouraged to work on the problems of communication from the beginning of their marriages, fewer would need instruction later on at crisis periods. Indeed, there would be fewer crises for the marriage.

Solving Other Problems Through Homework
Using Models

The analysis of many problems boils down to the fact that multi-stranded issues cannot always be untangled completely. Nor are all of the aspects of skills that need to be learned easily divisible (such as the skills necessary to effective counseling). In such instances, one of the best ways to learn to put on God's ways is to observe those who have already learned to do them. Modeling is an essential biblical method for teaching. In *Competent to Counsel* I cited, in part, the biblical evidence for this statement. In order to put it before the reader once again, let me quote some of what I wrote there:

Problem Solving Through Modeling

"In II Thessalonians 3, Paul raised the question of discipline. There were Christians in Thessalonica who, because they had heard (wrongly) that the second coming of Christ was imminent, thought they could abandon their work. They then went about as busybodies, eating and sponging off others. Paul called their conduct 'unruly' (or, literally, 'undisciplined'). Paul said, therefore,

We command you, brethren, in the name of our Lord Jesus

---

11. The divorce problem among Christians has grown immensely in recent years, and no Christian counselor can avoid it. Therefore, one's position on this matter must be thought through carefully so that he can help the many deeply confused persons who seek help about this matter.

Christ, that ye keep aloof (or withdraw) from every brother who leads an unruly life.

The word translated 'unruly,' means a disorderly kind of life, a life without order or arrangement. Inherent in the word are the ideas of being 'out of rank,' 'out of place,' or 'out of order.' Their congregation was like a column of soldiers with some marching out of step. Paul attacked the problem directly, declaring that every brother who leads an unordered life which is 'not according to the tradition which he received from us,' should be avoided. It is evident that even in that short visit at Thessalonica, Paul had thoroughly discussed the importance of leading an orderly disciplined life. When he said, 'For you yourselves know,' Paul meant, 'we taught you this; you received it as a tradition (something handed over) from us.'

"But Paul also said,

You yourselves know how you ought to follow our example: because we did not act in an undisciplined manner among you.

In that verse Paul used the same term. He said, 'We did not live a disorderly life in your midst. Therefore you ought to follow our example.' Paul frequently stressed the importance of modeling, or a good example, in learning how to structure living. The importance of showing others how to obey God's commandments through example cannot be stressed too strongly. Role play may also be one valid means of extending the principle that scriptural discipline may be taught by example. (Elsewhere role play as rehearsal has been discussed.) Thus Paul called his readers not only to remember the words that he spoke, but also to recall the kind of life that he and his associates lived among them. Often principles can be most permanently and most vividly impressed upon others by means of example. Reference to example was not something unusual for Paul. Paul frequently used his own behavior as an example for others. This is apparent in passages like the fourth chapter of Philippians. There Paul directed his readers not only to pray and concentrate upon the things that were honorable, right, pure, lovely, and of good repute, but he continued:

The things you have learned and received and heard and *seen in me*, practice these things: and the God of peace shall be with you (Philippians 4:9).

In the previous chapter of the same letter, he had already said,

> Brethren, join in following my example, and observe those who walk according to the pattern that you have in us (Philippians 3:17).

Paul considered his own life a model for new Christians. This emphasis is not limited to Philippians or to the passage in II Thessalonians; Paul also expressed the same thought in several other places. For instance, in I Corinthians 4:16 he wrote, 'I exhort you therefore, be imitators of me.'

"Paul also mentioned modeling when he said, 'You also became imitators' (I Thessalonians 1:6). The Greek term 'imitator' is the same word from which the English word 'mimic' comes. He wrote, 'You became imitators of us and of the Lord.' They learned, it seems, how to imitate the Lord by imitating what Paul was doing in imitation of the Lord. Then Paul commended them for becoming models. After they learned how to imitate Paul in imitating the Lord, they themselves became examples for others; 'You became an example to all the believers in Macedonia and in Achaia' (I Thessalonians 1:7).

"Peter similarly advised the elders of the church to which he was writing not only to 'shepherd the flock of God,' but without lording it over those allotted to their charge, to prove themselves to be 'examples to the flock' (I Peter 5:3). The word used by Peter was *tupoi* ('types'). Elders are to be types or patterns for their flocks. The idea of the model runs throughout the New Testament.[12]

"This idea of modeling also occurs in John's writings, as well as in Peter's and Paul's. In III John 11, John's words show that he assumed that imitation will take place. He says, 'Beloved, do not imitate what is evil, but what is good.' He said, in effect,

> You're going to imitate. You can't help imitating. As a child you learned to imitate, and throughout life you are going to continue to imitate others. So make your imitation consciously purposeful and be sure that you imitate that which is good.

"The influence of older children in a home clearly demonstrates the importance of example. Younger children pick up their ways of speaking, their words, their actions and their attitudes. The influence of parents is even more striking. And the influence which a counselor

---

12. Cf. I Thessalonians 1:6; Philippians 4:9; 3:17; I Corinthians 4:16; II Timothy 3:10; II Thessalonians 3:9; I Timothy 4:12; Titus 2:7; Hebrews 13:7; I Thessalonians 1:7; III John 11, etc.

exerts in counseling is an important matter, as well. Counselors in all that they do, model, implicitly. At some times they model explicitly as well.[13] And so the idea of modeling as a means of bringing about discipline is something which must receive adequate attention."

In *The Big Umbrella* I briefly analyzed the modeling as a principal teaching method of Jesus:

"Here, at the beginning, you will notice that the Lord Jesus *appoints* them as *His* students. The teacher sought out His pupils and accepted into His school only those whom He, Himself, had selected. Perhaps this principle of selectivity has too frequently been lost sight of—particularly in theological education. At their appointment, the purpose and methods that Jesus had in view, what He planned to do with these twelve disciples over the next few years and how He intended to do it, were also explained. He appointed (or chose) twelve that they might be 'with him.' That is the key word: 'with him.' You may say, 'I thought He was going to *teach* them; I thought He was going to *instruct* them. And isn't that what He did? Don't we see Jesus Christ subsequently sitting privately with His disciples explaining to them in detail what He taught the crowd in general? Do we not read of His instructing them in important truths? Don't we see Him teaching, teaching, teaching His disciples?' Yes, we do. But teaching, as many people conceive of it, is thought of very narrowly. It is often considered to be merely that contact which takes place between a teacher and his students in which the teacher imparts factual information. Certainly, that is a large portion of teaching, and *nothing* I say here (please underscore that word) should be construed to mean that I do not believe in the teaching of content. We *must* teach subject matter; indeed, much more than is taught elsewhere. But there is also much more to teaching than the teaching of content. That is why the Bible does not say that Jesus appointed twelve that He might *instruct* them. He does not say that He appointed twelve that He might send them to class. Nor does He say that He appointed twelve that they might crack the books and

---

13. "Cf. especially Christ's words in Luke 6:40b: 'Everyone after he has been fully trained, will be like his teacher.' Modeling stresses the importance of the 'with him' principle of discipleship (Mark 3:14) to which Rev. Kenneth Smith of Pittsburgh, Pa. has forcefully awakened me. Its implications for teaching as well as for counseling are sweeping. Scripture brings teaching and counseling together in one person, as indeed they should be. Note the close relationship pictured in Colossians 3:16; 1:28.

take His course. That was all a part of it, but, note, only a *part*. There
is a much larger concept in these words: 'He appointed twelve that they
might be with Him.' 'With Him!' Think of all that meant. Those
two words describe the fulness of Jesus' teaching. Such teaching is full:
rounded, balanced and complete. For the length of His ministry, the
disciples were to be with Him to learn not only what He taught them
by word of mouth, but much more.

" 'How do you know?' you say. 'Aren't you possibly reading a lot
into that phrase?' No, I don't think so, and I'll tell you why. The reason why I say that I'm not just reading my own ideas into this phrase is
because in a definitive passage, Jesus Himself gave a description of
teaching that accords exactly with this interpretation. In the sixth chapter of Luke, verse 40, He defines the pupil-teacher relationship, what
goes on in that relationship and its results. Jesus says, 'A pupil is not
above his teacher, but everyone after he has been fully taught will be
like his teacher.' Now, did you get the full import of those words?
He says, 'Everyone' who is fully taught 'will be like his teacher.' Jesus
did not say 'will *think* like his teacher.' That is part of it, but, again,
it is only part of it. Jesus said that a pupil who has been properly
(fully) taught 'will *be* like his teacher.' He will *be* like him, not just
think like him This passage helps us to understand the principles of
education underlying Jesus' appointment of the twelve to be 'with Him'
in order to send them forth to teach. He was calling them to become His
disciples (pupils) that they might be *with* Him in order to become *like*
Him so that they might teach like Him.

"But, did these principles work? Did their education really make them
'like Him'? The evidence gives a clear answer to that question. After
Jesus had risen from the dead and ascended into heaven, He sent His
Spirit back to continue His work through the Church. In Acts 4:13,
Luke gives us a view of how the enemies of the Church looked upon
the disciples (now called apostles) who were the leaders in this work:

> 'As they observed the confidence of Peter and John and under-
> stood that they were uneducated and untrained men [that is, formally
> so], they were marveling and began to recognize them as having been
> with Jesus.'

The evidence is now complete. Look at it: He appointed twelve that
they might be *with* Him. He said that a pupil, properly taught, will be

like his teacher. And in the course of time others recognized that the disciples had become, in large measure, *like Him.*"

Modeling As Homework

But, how can modeling become a factor in homework? Quite simply: by giving assignments to counselees that bring them into vital contact with other Christians who exemplify the qualities and who have acquired the skills that they need to develop. Faithful attendance at a conservative church is the basic requirement. Other assignments help too in more specific ways. Such assignments might read as follows:

> Ask an elder and his wife to come to dinner, informing them that you would like them to show you how to conduct family devotions at the close of the meal.

Or,

> Interview four Christian families in your church whose lives demonstrate their own ability to solve problems to discover how they handle differences that arise.

Or,

> Interview Mr. and Mrs. William Jones and find out how they were able to raise such obedient children. If they agree, you might even be able to sit in on one of the weekly family planning conferences that they hold.

Or,

> Sit down with an elder from your church and present a concrete problem to him. Ask him to show you how to go about using the Bible step by step in reaching God's solution to the problem.

The great value of learning from example is that *the model is a whole person.* To learn behavior in parts has its place, but to see it in operation as a *whole person* performs it is even more essential. In its parts, dissected and analyzed, behavior often becomes theoretical and impractical.

Rebuilding Trust

Something has been said about this matter elsewhere (under the discussion of forgiveness). Here, it is necessary to emphasize the important part that homework plays in the process of rebuilding trust. The visible effort displayed by the offender in becoming a new person through the grace (help) of God, coupled with the early successes achieved by concentration upon tangible, concrete changes is perhaps the most important factor of all. Usually checks should be built into the situation at the outset (a previously unfaithful husband will never fail to phone when he must work late. If the situation is still quite tense, agreement might be reached for the wife to phone *him* at work instead).

A Fresh Start

Many counselees recognize that they have undergone a vast change during the period of time that they were in counseling. To mark the freshness of the new relationship and their hopeful outlook on the future, some couples, for instance, respond quite favorably to the suggested assignment to take a second honeymoon. This can be even a mini-honeymoon over a two or three day period. Some couples have found it helpful to take along, study, and reaffirm their wedding vows during this time. This honeymoon may be assigned at the *last* counseling session or somewhere along the way in lieu of a counseling session after a turning point in the relationship.

Scheduling

A few words concerning this important matter may be helpful. God Himself works according to schedule. The *plan* of redemption included a timetable. Christ came "in the fulness of time" (Galatians 4:4); His death was predicted to the half year (Daniel 9:20-27, esp. vss. 26, 27); He Himself declared, "My time is not yet at hand" (John 7:6) and often spoke of the "hour" of (appointed time for) His death (John 12:27; 17:1, etc.). Counselees may be asked, "If God is orderly in His workings, and you were created in His image, how do you think that you can succeed by being disorderly?"

A typical scheduling assignment might read as follows: "Develop a weekly schedule in which the various essential (i.e., demanded by God's Word) elements of your life are placed on the schedule, with adequate time provided for all that God requires of you." The counselee may be told by way of explanation: "Remember, God says that you are to do *all* your work in six days. But remember also that *all* of your work includes work of different sorts; e.g., you may need to distinguish between your employment and the odd jobs around the house.[14] The six days includes both. You must find time for doing your work

---

14. Fixing doors or sleds, cutting the grass, hanging wallpaper, repairing doll furniture, etc., playing with children, legitimately is part of the six-day work. Those who work six days at their employment may need to revise their schedules or even change their jobs in order to do *"all"* their work" (Exodus 20:9).

at home. When you do, many of the problems between you and your wife may cease. This sort of work is every bit as important as the labor for which you are paid."

Sometimes counselees identify scheduling with adding tasks. However, scheduling may involve *eliminating* matters of lesser importance that get in the way of essentials. Counselors may need to help counselees to develop a list of priorities. Perhaps honest scheduling will show that time for lower priority items can be found only occasionally but not regularly. Some *meetings*, for instance, may have to be cancelled in order to find time for the family.[15] God's priorities never conflict. Conflict and confusion stem from sin, not from God.

Counselees who excuse themselves by saying that they have no time to do what God commands need to be told that they *do* have the time: "We all have the same sized pie—twenty-four hours each day. Everything depends upon how you slice it."

The record of what one *actually* does with his time that a counselee may be requested to keep over a three-day to one-week period[16] should be analyzed not only for time leakage, but also should be compared with what he *ought* to be doing. Then immediate adjustments (put it off and he will never get to it) must be made to bring the real into correspondence with the ideal. Sometimes this must be done by phasing out and phasing in. Obligations and responsibilities cannot all be dropped at once. But more frequently the needed changes will require immediate, stiffer, more decisive action (e.g., phoning the Boy Scouts and resigning as leader effective in a month).

At all costs, persons with problems of scheduling (and *many* counselees have them) must come to the place where they draw up what they believe before God to be a righteous schedule that honors Him by providing adequate and balanced time for all of those life priorities required in the Scriptures.[17]

---

15. The family should not be torn apart by church meetings. Many meetings are important for particular persons; we should not necessarily seek crowds at these meetings, but urge *only those who need* this meeting to attend.

16. What my counseling associate, George Scipione, calls a "portable schedule." A small spiral notebook carried in pocket or purse is probably most useful.

17. Including such factors as time for spouse, prayer, church, witnessing, family, work, personal cultivation, sleep, exercise, fellowship, etc. Be sure to build in fudge factors for emergencies. Leisure time, relaxation, and rest are essential. Passivities as well as activities should be included. The form that follows may be used as a homework assignment. It is a worksheet designed to help counselees to

WORKSHEET FOR SCHEDULING

Unprofitable Activities to discontinue	Profitable Activities to continue or add	Items from Column Two in order of priority

Balance in one's use of time is achieved not merely by *quantitative* adjustments; *quality* is crucial also. Two hours of quality time (rather than mere togetherness) with one's wife or child may be worth two days of other activities with them.[18]

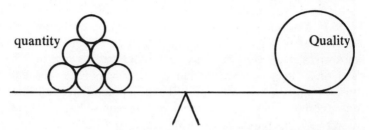

Therefore, counselees must be urged to consider scheduling balances in terms of *how much?* but also in terms of *what kind?* What one does can be of much greater significance than how long he does it. A heart-to-heart talk about a problem that lasts thirty minutes could cement a relationship for a lifetime. Five words taking less than a minute can destroy a marriage. As one joke puts it: "Too much togetherness is tearing us apart." The point of the joke for a Christian is, of course, that the counterproductive togetherness exposes the lack of a quality relationship in Christ.

Flexibility

Scheduling, contrary to what many think, is the only road to flexibility; organization is the only way to freedom. The disorganized, unscheduled person never knows, for instance, when to say yes or no. He is not free to assume a new obligation or to relinquish an old one without confusion and guilt. Since he does not know how much time is needed to do what he has already obligated himself to, he is *bound* by his ignorance. He cannot freely switch or substitute obligations as situations change, since without planning he does not know what may

distinguish between profitable and unprofitable items and to set priorities. The sheet may be obtained from the publisher and is included in *The Christian Counselor's Starter Packet.*

18. Mere togetherness can breed estrangement and alienation rather than positive results. All time together as a family should be planned time—even when the plan reads: "relaxation" or "no activities scheduled." Not only should schedules include built-in cushions (fudge factors), but also relaxation and rest periods. Leisure is important.

be swapped with what. In short, the failure to take the time to plan, arrange, organize, and schedule makes one fearful, guilty and inflexible.

Since many problems come from failing to carry on one's affairs decently and in order, it is frequently essential to help counselees to learn how to become orderly and how to schedule their lives. Counselees cannot avoid the matter. God is not a God of confusion (I Corinthians 14:33): it is such sins as jealousy and selfish ambition[19] that lead to disorder, as well as every other sort of evil (James 3:16). Disorderly housewives, husbands who have never learned to say "no" to demands upon their time, guilty Christian workers who never seem to complete projects, and persons who fail to keep appointments and meet basic life responsibilities all have one thing in common—they are living in a disorganized and confused way. Whatever the difficulties that may have led to disorderliness, the pattern itself must be met and handled as a separate problem.

God is a God of order. He has a timetable. The Scriptures speak of His plans, laid before the foundation of the world. He plans His work and then works His plan.

Christians, in restoring the image of God, must learn to put off disorder and confusion (cf. II Thessalonians 3:7, 11). This happens, of course, only when they put on proper habits of orderly thinking and living. Thus, counselors themselves must be sure that they have learned how to order their lives in a manner that pleases God. Otherwise, they hardly will know how to make proper recommendations about specifics to their counselees. The ways that counselors conduct counseling sessions (planning, keeping to scheduled commitments, insisting that the counselee do likewise, closing counseling sessions on time, giving to the counselee a written card with the time for the next appointment, etc.) reflect their own ability or inability to schedule, organize, and control the whole situation. Thus, counselors set a good or bad example for counselees. In addition, attention to such matters shows the counselee

---

19. Pastors and Christian workers who over-schedule their lives often do so out of pride and ambition. Yet nothing less than confusion of life is the result. Sleep is a vital essential that should be scheduled first. Eight hours, scheduled regularly, should be the consistent practice of every counselor and counselee if he wishes to act efficiently and not sin against his body, which for the Christian is the temple of the Holy Spirit. A good bed is a good investment; one-third of one's life is spent in it!

from the beginning what will be expected of him and, indeed, sets patterns that already have begun to structure and thus help him.

Depressed persons, lazy persons, fearful persons, persons with life-dominating problems, and those whose lives have been shattered, all usually need help either in scheduling, organizing (or reorganizing) their lives or both.

Orderliness may extend to other matters too. The condition of the house, one's financial records, and the way in which a student takes and keeps notes are just a few varied examples of quite different ways in which disorderliness can destroy effectiveness and lead to confusion and depression.

The orderly way in which a counselor (as model) organizes the data that he has gathered, draws a plan based upon scriptural principles, and proceeds to effect change all has much to say to the counselee about his problem.

Homework must stress order and scheduling whenever indicated. Where the counselee has never learned the discipline of orderliness, the homework ought to be quite specific ("Clean out the closet this week and see to it that every Monday thereafter you check it out for orderliness"; or, "Write the letter to Pat this week. Do not put off writing letters because you usually write eight to ten pages and this seems too much. Write a two-sentence letter or one no longer than one side of one page. But do it each week"). Often written schedules posted, followed, and checked up on by other members of the household are necessary.

All in all, the counselor might find that in such cases he will need to add tasks each week throughout the length of the sessions, beginning with those that are easier and ending with the more difficult ones.

Summary

Homework, then, is of the essence of good counseling. The counselor who perfects his ability to give homework soon will see the difference in his effectiveness in helping people. Learning how to give good homework, homework that is biblical, homework that is concrete, and homework that creatively fits the situation, takes time and effort, but is worth both.

Chapter Thirty

GIFTS THAT DIFFER

Gifts and Fruit of the Spirit

In counseling, the counselor must learn to distinguish (and help his counselees to distingush) between the gifts of the Spirit and the fruit of the Spirit. While the latter are fully for all, the Spirit's gifts are distributed *as* He sovereignly wills and according to the measure determined by Him (cf. Ephesians 4:7; I Corinthians 12:4-7).

Biblical Principles

In these two significant passages, at least the following factors, each of which has implications for counseling, should be noted:

1. Every Christian has gifts: "To each one of us . . ." (Ephesians 4:7; I Peter 4:10)— "each one has received a gift"
2. Gifts differ in kind, purpose, and results: "Now there are varieties of gifts . . . varieties of ministries, and . . . varieties of effects" (I Corinthians 12:4-6) and "distributing to each one individually" (I Corinthians 12:11). The saying is, "To each his own"; the biblical teaching is to each, God's own.
3. Gifts differ in measure: "according to the measure of Christ's gift" (Ephesians 4:7).
4. Individual gifts are for the benefit of all: "To each one is given . . . for the common good" (I Corinthians 12:7; cf. also vss. 14-31; I Peter 4:10)
5. All gifts are important and needed by all (cf. I Corinthians 12:14-31).
6. Gifts are distributed sovereignly by the Holy Spirit "as He wills" (I Corinthians 12:11b).

Counseling Implications

Counselors must insist just as strongly upon individual development and use of gifts as they do common growth in the fruit of the Spirit.

The implications of this biblical principle are many and varied. For instance, in scheduling, what one counselee does with his time cannot be exactly what the next counselee will do. But *both* (in common) must use their time as good stewards of the manifold and variegated grace of God. Faithfulness will mean something different for each (within the general principles of the Scriptures, of course).

Counselors will find that a vocational struggle for a counselee may boil down to this: Is he failing by trying to do what he does not have the gifts to do, or is it because he has not discovered, developed, and responsibly deployed those gifts? Or are there elements of *both* problems present? While not insisting on results that cannot be achieved, the counselor must help the counselee to discover, test, and develop his gifts so that he may try to live (not above but) according to his highest potential. Such discussions may lead to a change of job, a change of attitudes and practices[1] while continuing in the present job, or both.

While it is important for counselors not to demand what a counselee does not have the gifts to deliver, they must be equally careful not to allow the protest, "I don't have the gifts," to become a cop-out.

The biblical teaching on gifts meets all those objections of persons (elderly persons, depressed persons, suicidal persons, etc.) who have arrived at the erroneous conclusion that they are useless, have no reason for going on, etc. The biblical facts may be adduced to show that (1) no one is useless; (2) there is a niche for the counselee somewhere doing something; (3) the body of Christ is in need of his peculiar combination of gifts, and suffers for not profiting from their use, and (4) the Spirit of God knew what He was doing when He put him at this time and place in the body of Christ and gave him his peculiar gifts. While

---

1. Colossians 3:22-25 are vital verses with which to challenge those who complain about their jobs, their bosses, and, especially, lack of appreciation. They must be shown that all such complaints ultimately are against Christ, for "it is the Lord Christ whom you serve" (vs. 24). He never fails; nor does the one who serves Him well find any reason for complaint. A Christian philosophy for work is contained in these verses; wise counselors will draw it out and pointedly apply it where necessary.

A program for the discovery, development, and use of gifts is requisite for Christian counselors. Romans 12:3-7 affords the basic framework:

vs. 3—Evaluate soberly to discover God's gifts.
vss. 4-5—Recognize the function of the individual gift among the many.
vss. 6-7—Use the individual gift in practical applications by God's help.

no caviler attitude toward the counselee's problems may grow out of the assertion of these facts, they should provide hope and call him to responsibility in discovering, developing, and deploying his gifts.

Since it is the Spirit of God who sovereignly distributes gifts "as He wills," counselors will do well to use this fact not only to stamp out pride, but also all jealousy and envy that stem from the lack of gifts similar to those that others possess.[2] Also, complaints about one's own lack of abilities (if truly not present or possible) must be brought to a halt. Complaints about others not doing "as I did" at appropriate times must be countered by pointing out the variety of gifts distributed among believers.

Counselors must not push for conformity of life styles when the variety in life style stems from differing gifts. To do so is to attempt to thwart the Spirit's plans and purposes. Conformity must be replaced by complemental action, action in which one finds *his place* in the body and functions in unity with the other members of the body (cf. I Corinthians 12:14 ff.).

Each man has his gifts; that means each man has his own unique ministry or ministries (I Corinthians 12:4-6). No one can say, "There is no place where I can serve." If he has not yet found the place, he must be helped to do so. Counselees will be neither happy nor productive until they do. The counselor's task is not only to confront the counselee about his sin and help him get out from beneath its burden,

---

2. With twins the problem may take on peculiar dimensions. Because they consider it cute or clever, parents may stress the similarities between twins by dressing them identically, etc. This ordinarily is unwise. The similarities may be more imagined than real. One whose gifts may lie in another area may, therefore, attempt to live like the other in order to fulfill expectations. Wise parents will stress the fact that each twin is a *unique* person with his (or her) God-given gifts. There will be similarities, but each one has a unique combination of gifts, possessed by no one else, to fill a place in the body of Christ that *only* he (or she) can. Parents should discover, strengthen, and emphasize the unique gifts of each twin.

Twins, as well as *all* other children, need to be treated individually by parents, not merely as members of a crowd. All children need time alone (if possible every day) with each parent, even if it is brief. Parents, going to the store for a loaf of bread, for example, will be wise to take *one* child along. This gives them opportunity to be loved, heard, and cared for as the unique individuals that they truly are. Parents who address their children only as a group are missing vital opportunities for blessing. Ask youself, when is your child at his best? You know the answer: when you and he are together alone. Doesn't that tell you something?

but also to "restore" him *so that* he may carry his share of the common load (Galatians 6:1-5[3]). When he has found his proper place, functioning in the body of Christ, the counselee not only will find that his life becomes satisfying and takes on new meaning, but he will begin to become productive. Yet neither he nor another has a right to complain about the *amount* of productivity, for Paul assures us that as gifts differ and ministries differ, so too will results (effects) differ (I Corinthians 12:6: "It is God who gives the increase"). All that can be asked of a steward is faithfulness.

Summary

At many points counselors will discover the importance of helping counselees to recognize the implications of the biblical teaching concerning gifts for their lives. Largely, as we have seen, they will be concerned with these matters:

1. Helping counselees to stop trying to do what they do not have the gifts to do.

2. Helping counselees to discover, develop, and then live up to the potential that the measure of their gifts requires.

3. Helping counselees to find the proper place for the exercise of their gifts.

4. Helping counselees to use their gifts for the good of the whole body, functioning in harmony with other Christians.

5. Helping counselees to accept their gifts (not to accept themselves *as they are*) and not to complain about the Spirit's judgment in not dispensing different ones to them.

6. Helping the counselee to recognize in others when it is that their failures to live up to his expecations result from lack of gifts and, therefore, faulty expectations on his part.

Other uses will become apparent in the course of counseling, but these have been mentioned in order to stimulate the reader to think about the importance of the regulative biblical teachings on gifts for counseling.

---

3. If the reader has not studied carefully the implications of this passage for counseling, he should see *The Big Umbrella*, pp. 149-155 (esp. 151-154).

Chapter Thirty-one

HOW TO HANDLE ANGER

Anger Not Necessarily Sinful

Anger, in and of itself, is not sinful. We learn this from Paul's careful distinction between *being angry* and *sinning*: "Be angry and sin not" (Ephesians 4:26). Some well-meaning Christian counselors have failed to help others overcome anger in God's way because they do not understand this fact. Take, for instance, the following statements: "The Bible makes it clear that anger is sin and should be resolved"; "But we should not deny the bad effects of anger."[1] This is plainly not a scriptural position. The Bible teaches that "God is angry with the wicked every day" (Psalm 7:11). Much is revealed about the anger and wrath of God in the Scriptures. In I Samuel 11:6 we discover that the coming of the Holy Spirit upon Saul resulted in great anger that impelled him to carry out his work for God. And, above all else, the Word

---

1. Bruce Narramore, *Help! I'm a Parent* (Grand Rapids: Zondevan, 1972), p. 50. Narramore gives a nod to the possibility of "righteous indignation" (p. 138), but fails utterly to explain how a Christian's indignation can be righteous. Indeed, what he says about anger seems to preclude any genuine possibility for righteous anger. For example, he describes anger as a "damaging emotion" (p. 142). His whole discussion leads one to believe that in the essentially behavioristic program of child discipline which he has adopted eclectically without significant variation, there is really no place for anger. Because the Scriptures teach the possibility of righteous anger, he must recognize its validity, but he does little more than *mention* it since it does not fit the non-biblical system that he has swallowed uncritically. For him, righteous indignation becomes a kind of non-upsetting (almost non-emotional) anger. It could hardly be described as an emotion that "eats one up" (John 2:17). This is not the only place in the book where Narramore's eclecticism gets him into difficulty. It seems clear from the place that he assigns to spanking as "a last resort" (p. 107) that he really does not believe in spanking either. Yet, he *must* make some place for it since the Bible so strongly emphasizes it. One thing is certain, Narramore fails to give corporal punishment the central place that it occupies in the Scriptures. Because he *begins* with behaviorism rather than with the Scriptures, Narramore cannot present a biblical viewpoint on anger. To sum up, he can never tell the counselee *how to be angry* "and sin not."

348

of God reveals that the Lord Jesus was angry. Not only did this anger which "ate him up"[2] (John 2:17) motivate him to drive out the money changers from the house of God, but Mark informs us specifically that on another occasion Jesus turned on the Pharisees "in anger" (Mark 3:5). To call anger "damaging" or to apply James 1:20 ("the anger of man does not achieve the righteousness of God") without qualification constitutes a reckless and irresponsible use of the Scriptures that unwittingly amounts to charging Jesus with sinful action when he turned on the Pharisees. (See also later comments on the misuse of James 1:19, 20.) This is especially clear when Narramore defines sinful anger as that anger that "is conceived the minute it is directed toward another person" (p. 141). When Christ turned on the Pharisees in anger, i.e., directing His anger toward them, He sinned, according to this unbiblical conception. In contrast, E. Mansell Pattison is correct when he writes:

> Anger [in contrast to rage], however, is a very necessary and useful reaction. . . . Anger is appropriate as a communication of feeling in reaction to another's behavior.[3]

The fact is that there are no damaging or destructive emotions *per se*. Our emotional makeup is totally from God. All emotions of which He made us capable are constructive when used properly (i.e., in accordance with biblical principles). Surely the anger of the Lord Jesus did not damage His body. All emotions, however, can *become* destructive when we fail to express them in harmony with biblical limitations and structures.

Anger May Become Sinful

While Paul distinguishes between sinful and holy anger, he warns: "Be angry *and sin not*." Righteous anger can become unrighteous anger in two ways: (1) by the *ventilation* of anger; (2) by the *internalization* of anger. These two opposite extremes are known more popularly as *blowing up* and *clamming up*. When one blows up, his emotional energies are aimed and fired at someone else. When he clams up, bodily

---

2. A graphic expression for very strong feelings of anger. Nothing less could have led Him to effect the task of cleansing of the Temple. Yet the expression should not be pressed; Christ did not injure His body through anger as the expression, if pushed too far, might seem to indicate.

3. E. Mansell Pattison, "Psychology," in Robert Smith, ed., *Christ and the Modern Mind* (Downers Grove: Intervarsity Press, 1972), p. 196.

tensions are released within oneself. In both cases, the emotional energies of anger are wasted. In both they *are* used "destructively." In neither instance are they used constructively to solve problems.

Consider the following chart (fig. 9). "P" represents the problem or issue over which the counselee has become angry. N.B., the emotional energy fails to solve the problem in both instances, since it is not released in the direction of the problem but rather (a) toward others or (b) toward oneself. Both of these responses are wrong.

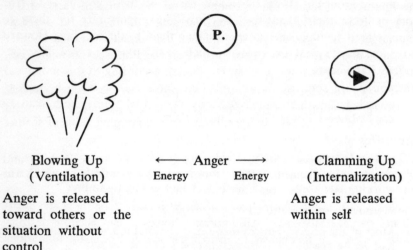

Blowing Up (Ventilation)	←—— Anger ——→ Energy Energy	Clamming Up (Internalization)
Anger is released toward others or the situation without control		Anger is released within self

Figure 9
Two Sinful Extremes

Blowing up is aimed at and principally hurts others, but it also hurts the ventilator; in firing one's gun at another, not infrequently there is a powerful recoil. Ventilation may result in the loss of friendships, often destroys the significant relationships that can be built only upon the foundation of Christian communication, and may injure one's own body.[4] While clamming up directs emotional energies destructively against one's own self, injuring his own body and making him irritable, sullen, tense, and miserable, it also hurts one's relationship to others. People who clam up are not good company. Since they "have it in for" others,

---

4. Cf. S. I. McMillan, *None of These Diseases* (Westwood: Spire Books, 1963), pp. 65-77.

they allow problems thus to come between themselves and others; that is to say—they are in an unreconciled condition.

Ventilation

There is much encouragement of the free verbal and physical expression of one's emotions, particularly of hostility, not only in the traditional psychiatric circles where such notions were born and raised, but also among their stepchildren, the group therapy, sensitivity, and encounter groups.[5] Often the major thrust of these groups is to free persons from their "hangups" by providing opportunity for them to express their feelings and by encouraging them to do so. Jane Howard provides may typical examples of such ventilation of anger. She describes one group:

> Pillows from sofas were used as props, to be beaten, struck, pounded, thrashed and abused by people who imagined them to "be" whoever it was that had made them mad.

She writes of

> A pretty woman who had been lying on a mattress, kicking and shrieking in unspecified rage. Later the woman told her son, "I was working out some angry feelings I had about Grandma."

She comments (with almost biblical insight):

> Most of the angry gestures amounted to ritual murders. Many people had to be reminded: "Remember, it's only a pillow!"[6]

---

5. Cf. L. P. Bradford, J. R. Gibb, and K. D. Benne, *T-Group Theory and Laboratory Method* (New York: John Wiley and Sons, Inc., 1964), p. 206, where the T-Group is described as providing "a situation in which anyone can attack anyone."

6. Jane Howard, *Please Touch* (New York: Dell Publishing Co., 1970), p. 150. Miss Howard concludes: "If the human potential movement had a coat of arms, the motto emblazoned on it would surely be 'STAY WITH THE FEELING,'" *ibid.*, pp. 124, 125. Cf. especially pp. 83, 84. Cf. Floyd Ruch, *Psychology and Life*, 7th ed. (Chicago: Scott, Foreman and Co., 1963), pp. 209-210, where a dummy punching bag is recommended. He writes, "Patients may regard it as the trunk or head of a person. . . . It can be made to represent the object of the patient's hostility." Such physical ventilation encourages the spirit of *murder in the heart*. Christians have been known to give similar advice with reference to hitting a golf ball. Calvert Stein has suggested the same sort of procedures for clergymen to recommend in counseling: "The counselor may invite him to punch a pillow held by the counselor, or bang down on a chair or sofa, or play a game of darts on the board on which any VIP or s.o.b. may be projected." He also suggests that the counselee, in speaking to any person who will accommodate him, may

Plainly, such expression of anger amounts to a violation of the sixth commandment and, in specified cases, of the fifth as well.

The Scriptures are explicit about such ventilation: it is sin.[7] Cf. the following passages from Proverbs (Berkeley Version):

> A fool gives full vent to his anger, but the wise man, holding it back quiets it (Proverbs 29:11).[8]

> Like a city whose wall is broken down, so is a man whose spirit is without restraint (Proverbs 25:28).

> It is prudent for a man to restrain his anger; it is his glory to overlook an offense (Proverbs 19:11).

> Have you seen a man of hasty words? There is more hope for a fool than for him (Proverbs 29:20).

> A quick-tempered man stirs up strife and a wrathful man abounds in wrong (Proverbs 29:22).

> He who is quick-tempered acts foolishly (Proverbs 14:17).

> He who is slow to anger is of great understanding, but whoever is hasty of spirit exalts folly (Proverbs 14:29).

"tell him or her off as a blankety-blank-so-and-so, using whatever language he deems proper." He even specifies certain "warm up procedures" to loosen up the aggression. Calvin Stein, "Practical Pastoral Counseling," *Handbook of Psychiatric Therapies, op. cit.,* pp. 177, 178. Behavior therapist Edward Dengrove advises: "Such patients" are to be "encouraged to shout or scream; to swear . . . to smash his [*sic*] fist into the couch or on the arm of the chair. In effect, the patient is taught to express his anger toward the authoritative figure of the therapist." He continues: "The learned freedom is carried over to real life. The patient is made happier and more capable by this character change." Edward Dengrove, "Behavior Therapy," *Handbook of Psychiatric Therapies, op. cit.,* p. 147.

7. See also *Competent to Counsel,* pp. xvii, 9-11, 24, 211 ff.

8. Many persons claim that they can't control their anger. Rarely is this true. Take, for example, the following case of Joan, who complained that she lost her temper when she became exasperated with the children and insisted that she could not control herself. The counselor inquired: "If, when venting your spleen on the children, the phone rang and you answered, wouldn't you be able to control your temper and speak civilly to a friend on the other end?" She conceded the fact. We all learn to control anger when we are embarrassed or afraid to release it. Narramore (*op. cit.*) speaks disparagingly of the control of anger and, indeed, even calls control-led anger sin (pp. 142, 145). His view of anger may be in accord with Haim Ginott (p. 49), but it hardly conforms to the scriptural position. What is controlled directly is not the emotions as such (i.e., they are not directly turned off), but as Proverbs says, they are "quieted" (29:11) when one "holds back" their *expression* rather than "venting" them. Cf. S. I. McMillan, *None of These Diseases* (Westwood: Spire Books, 1963), pp. 65-77.

A hot-tempered man stirs up strife, but one slow to anger quiets contention (Proverbs 15:18).

A man of great wrath must bear his penalty, for if you deliver him, you must do it again (Proverbs 19:19).[9]

Do not associate with one given to anger, and with a wrathful man do not keep company, lest you learn his ways and get yourself in a snare (Proverbs 22:24, 25).

No wonder James, writing also in the wisdom literature tradition, declared: "But let every one be quick to hear, slow to speak and slow to anger; for the anger of man does not achieve the righteousness of God."[10]

Internalization

I do not plan to discuss the problem of the internalization of anger here, since elsewhere I have considered this major problem to which Paul addressed himself in Ephesians 4:27 when he wrote, ". . . do not let the sun go down on your anger."[11] Anger becomes sinful not only when it is ventilated by doing a Mt. Vesuvius, complete with ash and lava, but also when one does a slow burn. Clamming up, internalizing anger, holding it in for another leads to bitterness and resentment.[12] The real question to which I wish to turn is:

How to Handle Anger Righteously

Look at the following chart. Again "P" represents the problem or issue which occasioned the anger. This diagram differs radically from the first. Here the tensions of anger are released primarily *toward the problem* rather than toward others or toward oneself. That is to say that the energies of the emotion of anger are used constructively in solving the problem—attacking it rather than people.

---

9. This verse shows the necessity for breaking the underlying patterns rather than merely handling specific crises alone.

10. James 1:19, 20. James is not thinking of all anger, but rather of that *hasty* venting of one's temper of which Proverbs speaks.

11. Cf. *Competent to Counsel*, pp. 220 ff. Deepseated resentment can lead to the most atrocious actions. Recently, radio station WOR newsman John Wingate reported about a man who made every alimony payment to his divorced wife in nickels weighing 160 pounds. There are many refinements or subheadings of the two basic categories. For instance, boredom is a form of internalized anger. Boredom is not passive, but an active rebellion against a situation in which one finds himself that he does not like but thinks he cannot change.

12. Cf. *Competent to Counsel*, p. 222, for comment on the biblical concept of "having it in for" another.

Turning anger toward the problem, however, almost always involves confronting another in anger. Yet, the *way* in which they are confronted makes the difference. They must be *confronted* to the extent that they are involved *responsibly* in the solution to the problem. They are confronted not in order to embarrass or hurt them, but to help them to move in the proper directions. The purpose for the confrontation is to help them and to solve the problem (Ephesians 4:29).

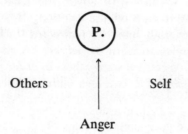

Figure 10
Using Anger God's Way

Of course, one may sin in the way that he expresses his anger toward others. When he sins, he fails to turn as Christ did toward the scribes and Pharisees. Jesus did not blow up; He did not vent His feelings in nasty words or actions. Instead, his anger motivated him to confront them about their sinful ways and thus meet the problem at hand.

One controls his anger best when he is *solution-oriented* rather than *problem-oriented*. Christians who are problem-oriented tend to talk about the problem, feel sorry for themselves, start up blameshifting operations, and focus their energies upon who is at fault. Solution-oriented Christians size up the problem, try to fix responsibilities, and then *turn as quickly as possible* toward solving the problem biblically. In the process, often they find it necessary to rebuke, but when they do so, they are able to rebuke *in love*. The rebuke, though anger-motivated, will be done *for a loving purpose* and *in a loving manner*. The energies of the emotion will be *focused* upon the solution to the problem, not upon the problem maker.

The energies of anger are wasted and used damagingly when they are directed solely toward oneself or another. Under control, anger is to be released within oneself and toward others only in ways that motivate one to confront others in a biblical manner in order to solve problems. Anger is a powerful emotion. But its power to motivate must be *used,* not *abused.*[13] This motivating power is used properly when it *drives* one to begin to rectify any wrong situation between brethren as quickly as possible. It is used biblically when it *impels* one to become reconciled to his brother immediately.

As with concern, so also with anger, the solution to sinful abuse lies not in attempting to turn off the emotion. When concern becomes fear or worry, however, it must be *redirected.*[14] The counselor must help his angry counselee to learn to *redirect* his anger.[15] Anger is not sinful, but when it is directed toward others *in order to hurt them* and/or *in uncontrolled outbursts,* it becomes sinful. When it is turned into oneself in *resentment* and *bitterness,* it becomes sinful. In either case, the counselor's task is to teach the counselee God's way of using anger: by directing all of its energies toward the solution of the issue that has arisen in order to destroy and remove any and all impediments that stand between ourselves and another.

Help Counselees to Redirect Anger

First, let us consider the problem of counselees who *blow up.* They are "hasty," they lose their temper, and they act and/or speak violently. Proverbs is plain: they must learn first to "control" or "restrain" their anger; they must become "slow to anger"; they must learn to "hold it back" and "quiet it." Counting ten (or fifty, for that matter) is quite compatible with the exhortations of Proverbs. We have seen, already, that it is possible for us to control the expression of anger under circumstances where it is advantageous to do so.[16] The counselor may begin

---

13. The strange notion that it is wrong to *act in anger* has been spread abroad in Christian circles, especially with reference to the punishment of children. Yet all of the Scriptures indicate that God, Christ, and others *act* (righteously) in (out of) anger (cf. Isaiah 63:3, 5, 6). The notion is false and comes from the confusion of sinful (hasty or resentful) anger with sinless anger. It is not wrong to act in anger, since the purpose of the emotion of anger is to motivate. Anger is a strong force that God built into man *for the purpose* of moving him to biblical action. All emotions are, *per se,* motivating forces. The only question is whether the emotion has been properly used for God's honor.

14. Cf. *What to Do About Worry.*

15. Cf. *Competent to Counsel,* pp. 228 ff.

16. Cf. n. 8, p. 352.

by pointing out that at work with the boss, with others before whom he does not wish to lose face, the counselee *has learned* how to hold his temper. This is important because it shows that whenever he deems it important enough to do so, he *can learn* to control temper. First, then, the counselee should be brought to repentance over the fact that he has not counted his wife, her husband, their children, or whoever it may be that is the brunt of the temper attack, important enough to learn to control anger against. This may involve a discussion of the whole question, including instruction about biblical priorities in life relationships.[17] The point also may raise a discussion of other matters between the parties that may indicate that there is little love lost. The counselor's agenda may grow immeasurably at this point, as all sorts of animosities and difficulties may surface. Before discussion of *how* to control anger, there must always be the *desire* to do so. If the husband (wife, child) expresses a who-cares? or a what's-the-use? attitude about the matter, it will probably be necessary to handle this attitude first. Often, husbands and wives must be brought to the point of granting forgiveness before counseling should proceed.[18]

Following any necessary discussion of God's priorities, the counselor should seek, as in handling any habit, to help the counselee to put off and to put on. He remembers that in putting off it is essential to become aware of the wrong practice, to structure the situation so as to impede the old practice, to facilitate the new one, and to seek and obtain help in doing so as it may be available. Commitment of oneself to this change before God and those involved in the problem is important. Above all, he must seek the help of God in the moment of temptation, asking God to use the structures erected and persons assisting. It is not enough, however, to put off the sin of temper by resisting and quieting one's anger; he must learn to release the anger constructively to solve the problem(s) that gave occasion for it. This is God's new way for him; in this he "puts on" a biblical way of life. The family conference table may be used as an aid at this point.[19] A code of conduct to which

---

17. Cf. Jay Adams, *Christian Living in the Home, op. cit.*, p. 26. The order of priorities in both Ephesians and Colossians is: God, spouse, parent/child, job. Frequently, those with whom we work, or study, or even pure strangers, we treat more considerately than members of our own families. In the Christian home, this wrong must be righted.

18. See earlier comments on granting forgiveness, chap. 9.

19. Cf. *Competent to Counsel*, pp. 231-236; see also pp. 264 ff.

a parent has committed himself (herself) may help.[20] Other situations may call for telling another party, according to prearranged agreements, that one is beginning to get angry.[21] This warning, given early enough, may lead to a cessation of the present type of conversation or activity upon which the anger is centered.[22] Instead, both parties might move

---

20. Cf. *Competent to Counsel*, pp. 188 ff.

21. How can the counselor direct a second party to help an angry person control his outbursts of anger? Proverbs supplies the answer: "A soft answer turns away wrath" (Proverbs 15:1). Notice God's solution carefully. He does not say silence (clamming up—nothing tends to infuriate one and inflames the issue more readily), but an "answer." The second half of the verse also excludes answering in kind (cf. also Proverbs 26:4, 5—the fool must be answered, but not in a foolish manner). The answer must be *different* in kind: a *soft* (conciliatory, non-inflammatory answer). Nothing helps more than this. A kindly, loving (soft) response like the following may help: "Honey, let's sit down at the conference table and talk it through." Proverbs 17:14 gives helpful directions too. It tells how to prevent quarrels: "The beginning of strife is like letting out water." A very small trickle, if allowed to continue to run through the hole in the dike, soon will open a large hole and the whole ocean will be in on the land. "The beginning of strife is like letting out water; so quit before the quarrel breaks out." Counselors must advise counselees: "If you don't want a quarrel to grow to larger proportions, don't let it get started in the beginning. Take immediate action to see that it does not go beyond the first nasty word." The following diagram indicates how the downward process of quarrelling enlarges. H = husband and W = wife. N.S. = the range of normal speech. The responses of each lead to larger and deteriorating responses by the other.

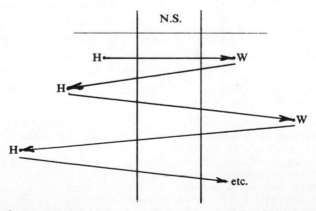

An experiment reported in the *Journal of Abnormal Psychology* (vol. 73, no. 5, 1968, p. 454) illustrated the biblical principle. The experimenter concluded: "Intense verbal aggression led to more retaliatory verbal aggression than did mild

immediately to a table where they can pray about the matter and discuss what God wants them to do about it, rather than have a fight or argument. In public situations, where such immediate discussions would be inappropriate, upon prearranged signal the two may agree to meet as soon afterward as possible. The *one* key factor is to substitute (put on) biblical action (whatever that may amount to in the specific case) that solves the problem for sinful expressions of temper.

Counselors also must learn how to help counselees to redirect anger from themselves. This problem of *clamming up* is the one to which Paul addresses himself in Ephesians 4:27. There he quotes from Psalm 4, a night time psalm, "Be angry but do not sin; do not let the sun go down on your anger." Here again the counselor must recognize that the solution to the sinful internalization of anger lies in redirecting one's wrath from within toward the problem that has arisen. Whereas he must not speak to the problem in unwholesome words that tear others apart, but instead must direct his speech to the problem that has arisen (vs. 29), and pour out his energies and words in an effort to strengthen and build up others who need aid, so too here he must keep current in

---

distraction." If, instead, a soft answer were given and a refusal to carry on the strife, the diagram might look like this:

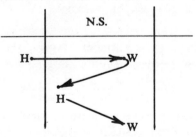

In Proverbs 15:28 is an important corollary: "The mind of the righteous ponders how to answer, but the mouth of the wicked pours out evil things." Proverbs suggests, count ten before answering, take time to think, give an answer that is not just a pouring out of immediate angry thoughts but think through a response.

22. A DPP form may help to uncover such situations. In such instances, if there has been a provocation to anger, that too must be dealt with as sin. The counselor must be careful at this point to sort out the responsibilities. While the provocation to sin (cf. Ephesians 6:4) is sinful, a provoked response is also sin. Neither party can excuse himself for the other's action. The two sins, though complementary, are distinct. Provocation does not necessarily lead to a sinful response; venting of anger does not necessarily spring from provocation.

his dealings with others. Rather than allowing matters to fester and abscess, he must settle daily all emotional issues between himself and others.[23] He may neither hold nor nurse grudges against others.

Letting the sun go down on anger is the most frequent cause of sexual disharmony in marriage. It is hard to bring all of the baggage of resentment into the bed at night and expect to have freedom of joyous sexual expression under those circumstances.

Counselors will do well to investigate thoroughly the possibility of resentment whenever counselees complain of sexual difficulties. Assuming that medical examinations have uncovered no sexual dysfunctions (these are rare), the counselor might immediately begin to probe the basic relationship between the husband and wife. As a test for resentment, he may pose questions like these: "June, when you see that Howard has left the cap off of the toothpaste tube, what do you say— 'The cap is off of the toothpaste tube' or 'That man has left the cap off again!'?" Howard, when she thoughtlessly hangs her wet nylons on all of the towels in the bathroom in order to dry them, what comes to your mind—'The nylons must be removed before I can use the towel' or 'June has been at her blasted habit again!'?" Is the emotion that is packed into your comment appropriate to the crime or is it much greater? Is the pressure far too extreme? If so, then the counselee probably has a *reservoir of resentment* behind his reaction.

Redirecting anger from oneself to the problem, from the future to today, is the solution to resentment. Again, the old ways must be put off and the new biblical patterns must be put on. The counselee may be helped to achieve this in various ways, including the institution and faithful daily use of the family conference.[24]

Anger is a problem for every Christian; sinful anger probably is involved in 90 percent of all counseling problems. Counselors, therefore,

---

23. Not *every* difference between Christians must be dealt with in this way; "love *covers* a multitude of sins" (Proverbs 10:12). Ephesians 4:27 refers to those matters that are not covered, and that, unless dealt with promptly, will be carried over into the next day. All such matters must be set to rest by reconciliation. Brethren must not remain unreconciled even for a day (cf. the element of immediacy in Matthew 5:23, 24).

24. Cf. *Competent to Counsel*, pp. 220 ff. Also see *supra*, p. 321. Here each day the problems of that day may be ironed out before its close to the accompaniment of the amount of emotion appropriate to it. To reach this point, there may have to be some hard work done to set to rest any past resentments.

should look regularly for anger as a possible root of many problems in nearly every case. Data gathering, especially in the form of asking questions should at some point focus on this area in depth. Counselors should never overlook this possible source of difficulty simply because, to the best of their knowledge, the counselee has never displayed anger publicly. There are reasons, as we have seen, why sinful anger may not surface in public contexts, yet may be the very root of the noxious weed that must be pulled. Along with the *sad* and the *bad*, counselors always ought to look for for the *mad*.[25]

In most cases of marital disruption, counselors find that it is necessary to sort out each partner's responsibilities before God. Husbands point at their wives; wives point at their husbands. Usually there is plenty to point to on both sides. But pointing at another rarely solves problems. To solve problems, husbands and wives should begin by pointing to themselves. The Scriptures say that one must take the log out of his own eye before he is able to see clearly enough to remove the splinter from another's eye (Matthew 7:3-5). That is exactly where so many go wrong. They attack one another like this:

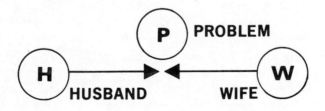

There is no communication when two people are squared off like that against one another. How may the counselor get communication started? Two people communicate when they walk and work unitedly in the same direction:

25. Cf. *The Big Umbrella*. Cf. "Grief as a Counseling Opportunity" for a discussion of the interplay of anger (the mad) with grief (the sad). The sin of adultery (the bad) has, in some instances, been committed not so much as a means of sexual gratification (particularly when the offender was an adulteress), but as a means of hurting or getting even (the mad). Cf. especially Proverbs 29:22b: ". . . and a wrathful man *abounds in* wrong." Sinful anger leads to other sins.

But how can he help them to move the arrows from the former position
to the latter? How may he turn the attack from persons toward problems? Concretely, how may a quarreling husband and wife begin to
expend their energy on solving problems God's way instead of continuing
along the same destructive course of tearing each other and their marriage apart. *That* is the question. The answer is: through the right kind
of communication. That is the only answer. They must begin by pointing both of the arrows in the same direction. Either partner may do
this by pointing first at himself:

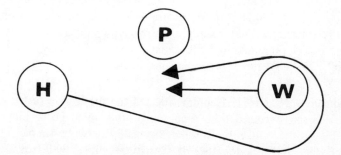

The other arrow already is pointing toward him, so all that either counselee must do is to get lined up alongside: he must be taught to look at
his own log first. For the first time in a long while the two arrows will
be pointing in the same direction. It is truly amazing how much instant
agreement comes from a person, who previously may have disagreed
concerning nearly everything, when someone says, "*I* have wronged
you." He must be taught to specify then and there and sincerely
ask for forgiveness. That is where reconciliation often must begin.
Counselees must be cautioned against taking the lid off the other

fellow's trash can before they have cleaned out their own garbage cans first. That is where communication begins.

Few things are sapping the strength of the church of Jesus Christ more than the unreconciled state of so many believers. So many Christians have matters deeply imbedded in their relationship, like iron wedges forced between themselves and other Christians. They can't walk together because they do not agree. When they should be marching side by side taking men captive for Jesus Christ, instead they are acting like an army that has been routed and scattered and whose troops in their confusion have begun fighting among themselves. Nothing drains the church of Christ of her strength so much as these unresolved problems, these loose ends among believing Christians that have never been tied up. There is no excuse for this sad condition, for the Bible does not allow for loose ends. God wants no loose ends. We have discussed the means He has provided for dealing definitively with such difficulties. Perhaps a summary reminder at this point would be appropriate.

In Matthew 5:23, 24, Jesus says that if a believer who is offering his gift at the altar remembers that he has done something to another person, he must drop the gift and go "first" (reconciliation takes precedence over worship) to be reconciled to his brother. Then he may come back and finish his offering. That example shows how important it is to get matters settled immediately. He must do so right away; he may not put it off. He must not "let the sun go down" on his wrath (Ephesians 4:26).

In Matthew 18:15-17, Jesus mentioned the other side of the picture. If someone has wronged him, then the brother must go to him to seek to win his brother and rebuild the relationship between them. Then the two can walk and talk together as Christians. Jesus will not allow unreconciled conditions to continue among believers. There is never a time when either party may sit and wait for his brother to come to him. Jesus gave no opportunity for that. It is always the obligation of each to go. In the ideal situation, if two believers have flared up over something and they both go away in a huff, when they cool down they ought to meet one another on their way to seek reconciliation. That is the way that Jesus said it ought to be.

Day by day, week by week, Christians ought to be dealing with interpersonal problems so that they do not pile up. Certainly this is

needed preeminently in the Christian home, where because the most
intimate human relationships exist sinners run into each other day by
day. Like misguided automobiles, they collide. They dent each other's
fenders, smash each other's headlights, and bang into each other in
dozens of ways. How important it is, therefore, to understand and
practice the dynamics of Christian reconciliation in the home. Matters
must be straightened out; not ignored—not even scratched fenders.

Counselors must insist that a counselee not let things go. If there is
somebody with whom he is having difficult times or who is having
difficult times with him, they must counsel him to straighten out the
matter before the day is over. Matters must be settled with God first;
then with others. Concretely, he may be advised to write that letter,
make that phone call (sometimes from the counseling room), or if possible pay that visit. Family members must be taught to settle matters
before nightfall.

Once the relationship is reestablished before God and one another, all
is not finished; it only has begun. True, the rubble of the past has been
cleared away. Now that affairs at last are on a daily, current basis,
counselees must be warned that they must never allow them to pile up
again. That means a new pattern in the relationship must be formed.
Something new must be erected upon the ground that has been cleared.
Paul wrote: "Let no unwholesome word proceed [literally, pour out]
from your mouth, but only such a word as is good for edification [or
building up] according to the need of the moment, that it may give
grace to those that hear" (Ephesians 4:29). This shows what communication must be like from now on. It is the pattern for forming the new
relationship.

What does Paul mean? He is not talking about foul language when
he speaks of unwholesome words. Of course, his statement would
include that, but it is broader. The term refers to any word that tears
down another.[26] Young people have an unfortunate expression that
closely approximates the idea: they speak about *cutting* each other *up*.
That is exactly what Paul condemns: systematically dicing and cubing
another by words.

It is not only youth, but also husbands and wives and other adults

---

26. Notice the contrast between "unwholesome words" and words that "build
up."

who use words for such purposes. Sometimes they become quite adept in such misuse of language. A couple sometimes attempts to use a counseling session to vent their spleen on each other. In one recent instance, not one word came out of either mouth without a surly, sarcastic remark about the other. Their counselor had to say to them, "That is doubtless one reason why you are here. You may do that sort of thing at home, but I will not allow you to do it here. If you continue, I will close the session." Counselors must not permit (let alone *encourage*, as some do) such a violation of God's will. The Scriptures insist that the same fountain may not produce both bitter and sweet water.[27] Christians must not take the name of the Lord Jesus Christ upon their lips and at the same time use His gift of speech to be nasty to other people.

In the Ephesians passage, Paul describes a better usage for words. Instead of pouring our energies into speech that cuts others down, he says that our words ought to build them up. When words are directed toward the *problem* rather than toward the *person*, they will build him up by helping him to solve his problems. Instead of attacking persons with words, a Christian must direct all of his energy, including his words, toward the problem, attacking it God's way.

Look at Paul's thought again: "No unwholesome word" is permissible. Instead, Christian speech involves words that "build up" the other person and that are "according to the problem that has arisen." That means that one's words must be aimed at (or concerned with) the problem. Counselees must learn to attack problems, not persons, with words.

A husband and wife came for counseling with just such a communication problem. Jan's and Chris's speech was so nasty that unless their attitudes changed, their problems could never be resolved. Their counselor knew that there are usually at least two problems involved in any human conflict. There is (1) the *issue* over which the parties differ, and there is (2) also the problem of their *attitudes and relationship* toward one another. When Chris originally phoned for an appointment he said, "I've got a problem; it is very delicate." He explained the issue that had arisen between him and his wife. This did involve a very difficult matter—one that was quite hard to settle. He said, "I've

---

27. James 3:9-12.

talked to my minister and he agrees with me. Jan talked to our physician (who is a Christian), and he agrees with her. So we can't get anywhere with either of them. The preacher suggested that I call you; but I know that you are going to take one side or the other, too, so there's no sense coming to see you." "Well," the counselor replied, "I guess there is no sense coming if you have already prejudged me; but if you are willing to come over and let me hear your problems, I want you to know that I don't intend to take anybody's side but God's. Chris mused, "Well, that sounds a little different." So Chris and Jan came. There they sat. During the first few minutes she tried to cut down everything he said, and he attempted to cut down everything that she said. The counselor quickly brought this to a halt. He said, "Look, you have been having problems because of this issue; but the issue itself isn't your major problem. You'll never settle that issue or any other until first you settle the prior problem of your attitudes toward one another. Although both of you profess to be Christians, your present attitudes certainly are un-Christian. Your pastor may have decided the issue for you and your physician may have done the same, but I don't intend to do anything of the kind. You are going to make this decision before God by yourselves. In doing so first you must be reconciled; then you are going to learn *how* to talk to one another as well. I want you to know that ordinarily we don't work with anybody longer than twelve weeks (most leave in eight weeks). I expect you to solve this problem in that time. We shall start with your relationship to God and one another. "That sounds different," said Chris in his characteristic manner.

At the time Chris and Jan were not living together. He had left her. "First," the counselor explained, "you must recognize and repent of your sin. Then you must go back together again. You can't put two people together by keeping them apart. I Corinthians 7 says that your separation is sin. To begin with, here are the things you are going to do this week. . . ." They agreed and went to work. They sought and received forgiveness from God and one another. Then they really began to work on the problem of communication. The *issue* was shelved for the time being. When other matters were cleared up and their marriage began to take shape again, then they were turned loose on the issue. Chris and Jan went to work on the problem *together*. During the weeks that followed, they had discovered how to use God's Word and their words to solve other problems God's way. Then they were turned loose on the delicate problem they had to solve. They really worked hard on this issue, and at the eleventh session they announced, "We have solved our problem." And they had! The reason why they couldn't do so before was because they did not know how to communicate as Christians should. They were using words to cut each other up; they were expending their energy by tearing each other apart. When in repentance they began to attack problems with words instead of attacking each other, they discovered the joy of researching issues biblically. Then the whole picture changed. When their *relationship* was straightened out, it was possible for the *issue* to be solved.

When counselees are of a mind to seek solutions God's way, they will find them. When they are of a mind to seek vengeance or vindication, they will not. Counselors, therefore, must always divide the *relationship* (to God and one another) from the *issues* and be sure that they do not attempt to deal with the latter until the former has been rectified. Confusing these is a significant cause of failure in counseling.[28]

Counselors must assure counselees that Christians can learn to live without bitterness, wrath, anger, clamor, slander, and malice. But they also must help them to develop and maintain attitudes of good will toward one another. In the soil of such attitudes solutions to life's problems grow thick and tall. Such attitudes can be sustained only by developing patterns of being "kind to one another, tender-hearted, forgiving one another *just* as God in Christ has forgiven." These provide the biblical alternative.[29] As the Savior did not die for lovely people but for ungodly sinners, for His enemies, for law breakers, so too Christians can learn to love one another *just as* He loved.

Love must replace anger. But counselors must remember that love at first is not feeling. Love first can be expressed and learned as giving. That is at the core of love. As the counselee gives, the feeling of love

---

28. Sometimes counselees will *claim* to have repented and to have been reconciled when they have not. A clue to true reconciliation will be their willingness to work on issues rather than on one another. Counselees who continue to argue over the past, who seek to be vindicated, whose words still sting with sarcasm *may*, of course, simply need to unlearn many of the old patterns, but *usually* indicate thereby that true repentance and reconciliation has not been effected.

29. Assignments stressing the need for forgiveness, kind and considerate deeds, etc., are essential to help the counselees *put on* these new ways of life.

will follow. To love he must learn to give of himself, of his time, of his substance, of whatever it takes to show love; for giving is fundamental to the biblical idea of love. The Scriptures say: "God so loved the world that he *gave* his only begotten Son" (John 3:16). "He loved me and *gave* Himself for me" (Galatians 2:20). "If your enemy hungers, *give* him something to eat; if your enemy thirsts, *give* him something to drink" (Romans 12:20). It is always *giving* with which love begins, and that giving should be as concrete and specific as the cup of cold water. The spirit of giving brings about a new relationship. It provides an atmosphere in which communication may grow and thrive.

Chapter Thirty-two

DEALING WITH ENVY,[1] BROODING, FRETTING, AND SELF-PITY

Envy

Joan's problem was envy. She envied everyone: her sister, her mother, other girls, and her boyfriend. It was sin, and as a Christian she knew it. She coveted the money, clothes, friends, abilities, etc., that others possessed. Consequently, she spent long hours wondering *why* she had not been blessed as other people had. Self-pity did not help. She found herself putting on the same tape and playing the same tune over and over again. As she wallowed in self-pity, her problems seemed to grow larger, her depression became heavier, and her envy escalated out of sight. What could be done?

Joan first had to acknowledge and then repent of her covetousness. But since she had developed sinful patterns and a way of life that involved envy, nothing short of the grace of God could enable her to "put off" these old ways and "put on" God's pattern of life. Her built-in habit sent her into a tailspin of depression every time that she learned of the good fortunes of a friend or noted the skilful use of another's gifts.

Joan, like many envious persons, had a potential for the appreciation of good things. She needed to learn how to discriminate, however, between appreciation and envy in order to turn from the latter to the former. Just as there is often a thin line between perseverance and

---

1. *Phthonos* is translated "envy," and denotes strong displeasure over the advantages or prosperity of others (cf. Matthew 27:18; Mark 15:10; Romans 1:29; Galatians 5:21; Philippians 1:15; I Timothy 6:4; Titus 3:3; I Peter 2:1; James 4:5). Cf. also Psalms 37, 73. Self-pity ("fretting") leads only to wrongdoing (cf. Psalm 37:8).

2. In discussions of temperament it is important to note that the basic nature (*phusis*, or genetic endowment) of one man may differ from that of another with respect to such matters. Persistence, for example, may be developed more readily by one than another. Whenever this is so, it is the result of the proper use of a temperamental trait. The *phusis* strong in persistence qualities has potential to

368

stubbornness, so there is a capacity to appreciate good things that may be sinfully distorted into lust, covetousness, or envy.[2]

Joan was helped to establish the new patterns (after repentance) by Spirit motivated works appropriate to repentance. She did three things:

1. In accordance with Philippians 2:3, 4 she began to *pray for the welfare of others*; not generally, but specifically. For instance, she prayed for the good outcome of a growing relationship between June, her roommate, and June's boyfriend, Tom. Previously Joan only had envied them and wondered why their dating relationship seemed so much better than her own. Instead she began to pray for June on every date. She loaned her a cherished necklace. Before long a close friendship grew between the two girls, and soon Joan could hardly wait for June and Tom to announce their engagement!

2. She also began to appreciate what she saw in others by *looking for good* of whatever sort she could discover in them.[3] Particularly, she was instructed in the biblical doctrine of varying gifts for the common good of believers. She began to look for God's gifts in other Christians. Instead of brooding about her own situation, in contrast, she began to thank God for what He had done in the lives of others. Thus, she began slowly to understand the meaning of Philippians 2:3, 4, Romans 15:2, 3, and Ephesians 4:7, 16 in her own experience.

3. In conjunction with these two activities she was encouraged to speak to other people about their abilities. As she expressed appreciation for their efforts and asked others how they acquired their skills, she discovered that for the most part these were learned through sustained practice, the kind of disciplined effort that she had failed to exert herself. Before, whenever she contrasted her own sad state, she always complained about others "getting all of the breaks." Now she began to see that they, more often than not, prayerfully made their own

---

develop into either the good personality trait of perseverance or the evil personality trait of stubbornness (stiffneckedness). Sinful men will, by virtue of their depravity (bent toward sin in every area of life) develop their capacities in the wrong direction until they are turned about (converted) by the Spirit of God. Counselors should look for the positive good possibilities that may be developed in Christians in place of the sinful patterns that have been learned. Often these lie parallel to one another on the other side of the "thin line," as for example *appreciation* and *envy* do.

3. Cf. I Corinthians 13:4-7.

break*throughs* by obedience to the Word of God. She concluded at
length that rather than waste more time swimming in self-pity (in which
she might eventually drown), she ought to concentrate her energies and
attention upon more productive ends. Through such profitable endeavors, by God's help, she determined to discover and develop her
gifts and abilities to the full for His glory. In the process, Joan was
transformed. The Spirit of God had turned the energies and capacities
previously used to produce the works of the flesh into the production of
fruit for His own honor. Such a transformation is what Paul contemplated when he wrote:

> Let him who steals steal no longer; but rather let him labor, per-
> forming with his own hands what is good, *in order that he may have
> something to share* with him who has need,[4]

and when he urged,

> For just as you presented your members as slaves to impurity and
> to lawlessness, resulting in *further* lawlessness, so now present your
> members as slaves to righteousness, resulting in sanctification.[5]

Thus, God in the process of sanctification as well as in providence
makes even the wrath of man to praise Him.

Brooding and Self-Pity[6]

Notice that part of Joan's problem lay in her continued brooding and
self-pity. Self-pity is always counter-productive. It consists of a concentration upon self and one's supposed "rights" and usually involves
a protest against God's providence. It is clearly a self-destructive sin.

---

4. Ephesians 4:28 (NASB).
5. Romans 6:19.
6. Self-pitying persons often cry in counseling. When women open their purses
and they virtually blossom with Kleenex, the counselor can be relatively assured
that he is dealing with a manipulative (one who *uses* crying) counselee. Of course,
tears are often real. How does a counselor best handle tears and crying? By ignoring it and plowing ahead in the discussion. Calling attention to crying by
handing out Kleenex, by saying "Go ahead and cry if it makes you feel better,"
or by stopping the flow of the discussion only intensifies it. By moving ahead
(this is a good point for the counselor to ask a probing question or make an
observation concerning *content*), he shows that tears will not be allowed to divert
attention from the subject. This is good for those whose tears are genuine (true
sympathy is best shown in counseling by doggedly seeking to find and apply
God's solutions to problems), and also provides the best response to tears of the
crocodile variety. The counselor—above all—must not allow himself to be
manipulated (by tears, or in any other way) into participation in a pity-party.

No wonder the psalmist wrote, "As for me, my feet came close to stumbling; my steps had almost slipped. For I was envious of the arrogant" (Psalm 73:2, 3). Envy, mixed with a brooding self-pity, had almost brought him to deep despair and rebellion against God. He explains: "When I pondered to understand this [the prosperity of the wicked], it was troublesome in my sight" (vs. 16). He also speaks this way: "When my heart was embittered, and I was pierced within, then I was senseless and ignorant" (vss. 21, 22).[7] Plainly, the writer only brought suffering and heartache to himself through the twin sins of self-pity and envy.

His relief came by repentance when he was instructed about the final end of the wicked in the sanctuary of God (vss. 17-21). Persons caught in the swirling vortex of envy and self-pity also need to hear the same message. Counselors will do well to turn to Psalm 73 and carefully explain the psalm to them.

In instances where forgiveness has been granted but despair and depression on the part of the forgiving individual persists, the counselor should always investigate the possibility of brooding and self-pity. Remembering that forgiveness essentially consists of the promise not to raise a matter again (to the forgiven party,[8] to others, *or to oneself*) the counselor may discover that the promise has been broken. In such cases, the forgiving party must himself seek forgiveness, and the counselor must show both how to keep the promise.

Sometimes counselees confuse brooding and self-pity with productive thinking. By calling brooding and self-pity "thinking," they seek to

---

7. In Psalm 37:8, David wrote: "Fret not yourself; it leads only to evil doing." Asaph, the writer of Psalm 73, experienced exactly that. The destructiveness of envy is plainly set forth in Matthew 27:18; Acts 5:17; I John 3:12; I Samuel 18:7 ff.; Genesis 37:3, 4 ff.; in all of these passages envy leads to murder or attempted murder.

8. Self-pity is not always solitaire. Frequently gripe groups and pity parties develop. Temporarily, when expressing one's feelings, he feels relief, but ultimately he and his commiserators discover that griping feeds misery. Talking about others behind their backs in slanderous and malicious ways is one frequent consequence of self-pity and envy (cf. Psalm 37:8). One counselee said of his wife (who agreed), "She spends hours talking to anyone who would listen to her problems and complaints." Obviously, such persons do not focus on solutions. Sensitivity Groups and psychiatrists who stress "ventilation" tempt counselees to move in the all-too-familiar pattern of self-pity ⟶ anger ⟶ bitterness ⟶ depression. (Cf. Proverbs 25:23, NASB, margin.) Wise counselors look for the chain and break it at its earliest link.

justify their sin. The two must be distinguished. Counselors often can do so by asking such questions as: "What solutions came out of these thinking periods?" or "Do you find that these periods of thought make you a more radiant, capable, and better Christian?"

Self-pity is the stuff out of which depression, despair, murder, suicide, and other sins are made. The story of Elijah in I Kings 19 is illustrative of the destructiveness of self-pity. Elijah was bold as long as his mind was centered on God, but not when he began to focus his attention upon himself (cf. I Kings 19:4, 10, 14). Because he refused to turn from this self-orientation, his prophetic ministry was taken away and given to Elisha. Self-pity, envy, and brooding can lead to other serious results, as David warns (Psalm 37:8). The case of Amnon shows how through such brooding "he made himself ill" (II Samuel 13:2-4). This continual brooding led, at length, to disastrous consequences.

Brooding is thought without action. It is self-talk that does not focus upon God's solutions. It can have only bad effects.[9] When one broods over *past* problems, for instance, he allows that which is gone and has no existence (except in his mind) to make him miserable today. Past problems have no such power. *What* one does about them now determines his present state. When what he does is to brood in self-pity, he is *making himself miserable.*[10]

How to Change the Situation

What then can a counselor suggest to the brooding, self-pitying, fretting, envying counselee? In brief, help is to be offered in coordination with previous instructions about habit alteration and in the specific directions for alleviating the bad effects of the talk-minus-action patterns.

First, the counselor may give a general biblical overview of the problem using Psalms 73 and 37. Next, he may direct the counselee to break the *self-pity ⟶ anger ⟶ bitterness ⟶ depression* chain at the earliest link. Rather than allow brooding self-pity to begin, the counselee may be instructed to pray about the problem, putting the

---

9. Cf. II Samuel 13:2-4, 15. Amnon was a man motivated by feeling. His desire orientation was fostered and fed by brooding. First, he made himself ill through it, then this brooding led to further sin. Absalom also acted by feeling out of two years of bitter brooding (cf. vss. 22 ff., vs. 32).

10. For a facetious discussion of the problem that, nevertheless, clearly points out many sinful foibles, see Dan Greenburg, *How to Make Yourself Miserable* (New York: The New American Library, 1966).

matter into God's hands.[11] He also may pray for strength to break the destructive patterns of envy and self-pity.[12] Then, he should get up and (lastly) turn to present responsibilities that otherwise might have been neglected.

One youngster who had lost her father through a divorce found herself sitting for hours in self-pity and sadness. She was helped when the counselor designed the following procedure for her:

1. Whenever you begin to think about this sad occurrence, take two minutes (time yourself) to think about it. The fact is a sad one and the loss is real. But, since you cannot allow yourself to become bitter or immobilized,

2. conclude the two-minute period in prayer to God, leaving your cares in His hands, then

3. get up and turn to a present chore or responsibility and pour your energies productively into it.

Discovering the Presence of the Problem

Counselors may detect the presence of destructive self-pity, etc., in the counselee principally in these ways:

1. By asking him outright. Some counselors too frequently forget that the simple, direct approach is the most basic, and tend to rely too much upon secondary and devious methods.

2. By using a DPP form to help the counselee to discover how often he is spending periods of time sitting and thinking (such feeding factors must be removed and replaced by proper biblical activity).

3. By inquiring about *what* the counselee thinks about when he is depressed, blue, etc.

4. By noting language used in the counseling session. Look, for example, for the self-destructive language of defeat ("There's no hope; nothing can be done"); the language of the unique problem ("No one has ever had to face a problem like this; if you had to live with my husband. . . ."); the language of tragic exaggeration ("This is a calamity; how could this be worse?"—especially when minor setbacks are viewed as tragedies); the language of complaint ("Why did God let this happen to *me*; what did I do to deserve this?").

---

11. Such prayers ought to be crisp. Brooders can turn prayer itself into self-pity sessions.

12. Envy must be replaced by its reverse. Cf., for instance, Romans 12:15.

5. By noting an undue focus by the counselee upon *himself*. Self-pitying persons are absorbed in themselves, need to be shown that the world was not created for them personally, and that it is their pride and self-centeredness that lies at the root of their problems. His focus of concern must be turned from himself to God and to others. Apart from such a thorough repentance (change of mind) there is no solution to his problem.

Self-pity is destructive; self-destructive. If continued it will lead to depression, which in turn is often the most direct route to despair and the ultimate self-destruction: suicide. To the subject of depression, therefore, we now must turn our attention.

Chapter Thirty-three

HELPING DEPRESSED PERSONS

What Is Behind Depression?

Almost anything can be at the root of the counselee's depression: a recent illness in which he gets behind in his work, hormonal changes, a reversal of his fortunes, the consequences of simple negligence, guilt over a particular sin, self-pity arising from jealousy or a disadvantageous turn of events, bad feeling resulting from resentment, worry, etc. The important fact to remember is that a depression does not result *directly* from any one of these factors, but rather comes from a cyclical process in which the initial problem is mishandled in such a way that it is enlarged in downward helixical spirals that eventually plunge one into despair.[1]

The downward cycle of sin moves from a problem to a faulty, sinful response, thereby causing an additional complicating problem which is met by an additional sinful response, etc. That pattern needs to be reversed by beginning an upward cycle of righteousness resulting in further righteousness. Here the reverse pattern may be seen: a problem met by a biblical response leads to a solution which strengthens one's ability to solve new problems. The downward cycle enslaves one in hopelessness and guilt, thus bringing on a slowing down or cessation of activity, called depression.

Proverbs plainly warns against the slavery of sinful habits:

> For directly before the eyes of the Lord are man's ways, and all his paths are well considered. His own iniquities seize the wicked, and he is held fast by the ropes of his own sin (Proverbs 5:21, 22, Berkeley).

Sinful habits are hard to break, but if they are not broken, they will bind the client ever more tightly. He finds that as sin spirals in a down-

---

1. Cf. *Competent to Counsel*, pp. 116 ff.

DOWNWARD SPIRAL   UPWARD SPIRAL
[enlarges problems]   [reduces problems]

(side view)

Good Feeling

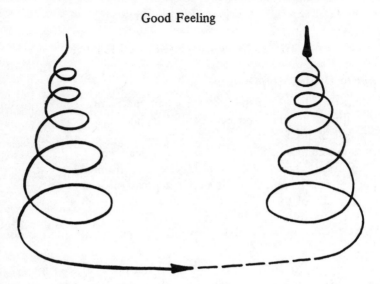

Bad Feeling

(top view)

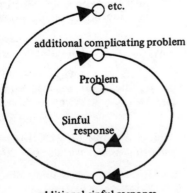

ward helix, pulling him along, he is captured and tied up by sin's ever-tightening cords. He is held fast by the ropes of his own sin.

The story of Cain illustrates the fearful dynamics of the downward cycle. The dimensions of the problem are plainly set forth in that passage by God Himself. Cain began badly by presenting a sinful offering before God. Abel gave God the best (the "firstlings" and the "fat"), whereas Cain merely brought an offering.[2] When God rejected his offering, Cain complicated the problem by responding wrongly to the rejection (he became angry and depressed: his face "fell"). The anger and depression were noted by God, who warned against the consequences of this wrong response. Instead, God graciously explained: "If you do right, you will feel right" (vss. 6, 7—your face will be "lifted up"[3]). He also warned Cain that failure to repent and offer the right kind of sacrifice would continue to complicate the problem and would cause him to fall into deeper sin (into the clutches of sin, which like a wild animal was crouching at the door anxiously waiting to devour him). God offered hope by saying that he could reverse the spiral and rule over sin by breaking out of the sinful pattern through repentance and a subsequent change of behavior.

Of course, the sequel to these words shows that Cain failed to heed Gods' warning and fell into deeper depths of sin just as God had said he would: the downward cycle led to the murder of Abel. Nursing his grudge, self-pity, and anger were all elements of the depressed look on Cain's face about which God strongly warned him.

Sin leads to guilt and depression, sinful handling of sin further complicates matters leading to greater guilt and deeper depression, *ad infinitum*. In the downward cycling the depression certainly contributes to further failures as it often becomes the excuse for a faulty handling of the sin itself. But, in contrast to those who would speak of changing the feelings in order to change the behavior, God reverses the order:

---

2. This is the only distinction implied by the text itself. To read back into the passage distinctions between a bloody and unbloody sacrifice may be reading too much into account. The reason for God's rejection of Cain's offering, however, is unimportant to the point of our discussion.

3. The King James rendering of verse 7, "If thou doest well, shalt thou not be accepted?" obscures the true intent of the passage, which literally reads: "If you do right, will there not be a lifting up [i.e., of Cain's face, which had 'fallen']?" The expression is universally true to life. One woman in counseling described her problem as "walking around with a long face on."

He declared, "do right" and "there will be a lifting up of your face."

Avoiding Depression

Such depressions never need result if the initial problem is met God's way. Depression is not inevitable, something that simply happens and cannot be avoided. Nor is it ever so far gone that the depression cannot be counteracted. The cycle can always be reversed at any point by biblical action in the power of the Holy Spirit. The hope for depressed persons, as elsewhere, lies in this: the depression is the result of the counselee's sin. If depression were some strange, unaccountable malady that has overcome him, for which he is not responsible and consequently about which he can do nothing, hope would evaporate. The fact is, however, though he may not be responsible for the initial problem (e.g., physical illness or a bad turn in his financial picture), he is responsible for *handling this initial problem God's way*. Because he hasn't, but instead has sinfully reacted to the problem (e.g., neglecting duties and chores; becoming resentful; complaining in self-pity), subsequently, *as a result of this reaction* he has become depressed. This depression is the result of the spiral of complicating factors;[4] it is not the direct result of the initial problem.[5] When the initial problem is mishandled, guilt and its miseries are added to the original problem. If, in turn, the counselee deals with these consequences sinfully, the spiral intensifies.

How the Counselor May Help

What does a counselor do to help depressed persons?

1. Counselors should check out complicating problems (letting down on chores: ironing, housekeeping, tasks at one's business, etc.) and set the counselee to work on dealing with these God's way. This should (at least) begin to lift the depression and reverse the spiral.

2. Next he should check out all factors (incidents, etc.) and/or life pattern(s) that may have led to the sinful reaction to the initial problem, urge and help the counselee to take biblical action in the power

---

4. Usually the failure to do what the counselee considers unpleasant tasks and chores: washing dishes, cooking meals, etc. "I just can't do it; I don't feel like it" is a typical response.

5. Of course, the initial problem often may be the result of the counselee's sin. When the initial problem is constituted by sinful activity, unless confession and forgiveness immediately result, the first sweep of a downward spiral has begun.

of the Spirit to replace these patterns (put off/put on) with biblical ones, and thus assure against future failure because of the same patterns.

3. The counselor must explain clearly the dynamics of depression to the counselee and set out for him (or her[6]) a plan to attack the sinful tendencies of the human heart that would surrender to feelings rather than follow the path of Christian responsibility. For example, in a case where ironing is always the first chore to slip, a counselor might advise: "The next time that you feel like not doing your ironing:

"1. Go ahead and do it anyway; NO MATTER HOW YOU FEEL.[7] Ask God to help you.

"2. Tell your husband that you are having initial problems so that he can encourage you and see to it that you do your ironing even though you do not want to.

"3. If you allow your ironing to get behind, cancel out all special events (TV, visits to neighbors, etc.) and allow yourself no other privileges until your ironing is done.

"4. Studiously avoid all daydreaming, TV watching, and self-pity sessions.[8] As soon as you find yourself drifting into these, set up the ironing board and get to work instead.

"5. At times like these, find a neighbor who will allow you to bring your ironing over to her house so that the two of you can iron together.

"6. Instead of feeling sorry for yourself or worrying about it, address yourself to the problem over which the initial feeling of concern arose. Write out these three questions and their answers:

a. What is my problem?

---

6. Women, ministers, and others whose week-day work must be self-structured more frequently become depressed than men whose tasks are spelled out for them on a 9:00-5:00 daily basis. This is because the cycle resulting from allowing chores and duties to slip more readily begins when there is no one else to insist that they be done. Feelings tend to take over.

7. Except for genuine sickness, of course. Illness and depression sometimes may be distinguished by noting the counselee's response to small bits of humor or to pleasantries (truly sick persons usually do not lose their sense of humor). A deeply depressed person typically will not respond.

8. I.e., be careful to discover and take steps to eliminate all *feeding factors.* Depression is fed by brooding, commiserating (mutual gripe sessions), failure to plan on eliminating onerous tasks from menstrual periods, getting behind, resentment, avoiding people, cutting corners, lying, excessive eating, refusal to eat, sleep loss, putting off decisions, and anything else that may lead to the unpleasant feelings of guilt that conscience triggers.

b. What does God want me to do about it? (The answer will be found in the Scriptures.[9])

c. When, where, and how shall I begin?

(1) Take the first step as soon as possible.

(2) Schedule the rest."

What About the So-Called "Manic-Depressive"?

It is probable that, as in the case of bizarre behavior of other sorts, persons exhibit what has been called manic-depressive (elated, then blue) reactions as the result of various underlying causes. There is at present no conclusive evidence that the etiology is ever organic. However, the possibility that the etiology of some such instances of behavior labeled "manic-depressive" is organic must be held open.

The counselor must think in terms of various possibilities when helping such persons. Among these, the following have been identified and successfully dealt with according to Christian principles:

1. *Camouflage.* All bizarre behavior can be simulated in order to throw others off one's track[10] See *Competent to Counsel*, pp. 29 ff., for further information concerning this phenomenon.

2. *Sinful solutions to depression.* Since the depression usually seems to occur first[11] and, even in the midst of elation, there often may be detected a fundamental tone of sadness, there is reason to believe that the so-called manic phase is basically a faulty, sinful attempt to overcome the depression that one feels, fears, and unsuccessfully seeks to alleviate. The problem may arise in several related but slightly distinct

---

9. It is not enough merely to *do something.* When Tennyson wrote, "I must lose myself in action lest I wither in despair," he was suggesting the non-Christian response to the problem. It is not merely *action—any* action—that will do. Although action temporarily may dispel despair, if it is not the proper biblical action the result will satisfy neither God, one's neighbor, nor oneself. Mere doing is inadequate also because there must often be an *undoing* (putting off) of what is wrong (unwinding the sin spiral), as well as a *redoing* (putting on) of that which God requires (rewinding a righteous one).

10. Cf. the case of Garrett B. Trapnell, the TWA hijacker who successfully feigned insanity again and again. The *New York Times,* Jan. 18, 1973, pp. 39, 49.

11. Cf. Robert M. Goldenson, ed., *The Encyclopedia of Human Behavior.* vol. II (Garden City: Doubleday and Co., Inc., 1970), p. 728. Masserman wrote: "In most instances, however, there is little true euphoria, and such reactions merely represent attempts to deny and overcompensate for the anxiety and depression." Jules H. Masserman, *A Psychiatric Odyssey* (New York: Science House, 1971), p. 333.

ways. Counselors, therefore, will want to investigate the following possibilities.

a. *Elation as overcorrection.* A driver whose wheels have run off the road into the ruts running along the side of it, in pulling the car back onto the road must guard against an overcorrection in which the car suddenly coming out of the rut may shoot across the medial line into the path of oncoming traffic. In attempting to pull oneself out of the rut of depression and despair, a counselee also may shoot across the road. Overcorrection in highly emotional states is neither unusual nor uncommon. Persons who tend to extremes anyway (and studies show some evidence that most "manic-depressives" [a bad label] are of this sort) react rather than act.

b. *Elation as solution.* Closely related to the foregoing is the erroneous idea that euphoria, whipped up and spread thickly, is the solution to depression. This concept parallels the whistle-in-the-dark view of life. It may be characterized as a laugh-when-you-are-down attitude. But guilt, failures to solve life's problems God's way, pressing decisions unmade, etc., cannot be laughed off. Hence, the cynical nature of what is known as the manic-depressive reaction.

c. *Elation as denial.* Paralleling the idea of elation-as-solution is the idea of elation-as-denial. "Look," the counselee tries to convince others and/or himself, "things are not so bad after all! I was wrong to be depressed; here is the real situation." But his attempt is too noticeable, he is trying too hard, and at length he too sees that a Christian Science approach to sin and its miseries always falls through. The more pressing the problem, the sooner the bottom drops out. Euphoria can be pumped up just so long.

d. *Elation as frantic straw-grasping.* A drowning man thrashes about in all directions seeking to lay hold on something to save himself. He may grasp at any straw. Frantic attempts to whip up euphoria often seem to be just that—attempts to keep from drowning in the sea of depression. Wild whooping it up, sexual advances, almost anything may be attempted . . . and will fail.

e. *Elation as one part of a way of life.* Some have never learned the middle way. All of their lives they have engaged in pendulum living. However, now the swing of the pendulum gradually has picked up momentum and the arc has grown wider. Or, perhaps, the pattern of swinging to extremes, heretofore reserved to minor problems, has at length become attached to a larger life issue. Perhaps this has happened suddenly. An emergency has arisen; the counselee did not know what to do. Without thinking, the basic sinful life pattern, lacking all scriptural balance, is brought into play. Frantically, he swings from one extreme to the other, seeking, but always missing the biblical middle.

Offering Help

What can a counselor do, once he has discovered the particular dynamic or combination of dynamics behind the ups and downs of the counselee? Obviously, the answer is similar to that which is involved in many other counseling situations. He must:

1. Bring the counselee to repentance by the effective use of the Word of God. It may be easier to achieve this when he is in the depressed (or more *realistic*) phase. It is possible that the excesses of the elation and the euphoria may have to be exposed for what they are—unscriptural behavior in the face of a serious dilemma. If the counselor takes seriously the fact that the elation is uncalled for and looks for and pulls hard on the basic thread of despair and depression that inevitably seems to protrude even in the most euphoric moments, he will soon unravel the problem. Since the elation is contrived, the counselor will need to eliminate it in order to help the counselee to handle the fundamental problem of depression in a biblical manner.

2. Reaching the counselee when he is in a state of despair, or having assisted him in putting off the erroneous or contrived elation, the counselor now can proceed to work with him as he would with any other depressed person.

3. One further factor is necessary to mention. In putting off the depression-elation-depression pattern, it is important to spell out clearly and help the counselee to learn how to meet problems with biblical soberness and reserve. The biblical center must be laid out plainly and, before dismissal from counseling, the counselee must demonstrate that he or she has learned by God's grace not only how to find it in solving the problems that led to the depression, but also that he knows how to apply it to new problems of life.

How Not to Handle Depressed Persons

In his monograph, "Treatment of Depression," Paul Huston has recommended two procedures in dealing with depressed persons that *must* be mentioned, since they are, perhaps, the most dangerous things that any counselor can do. He has suggested that (1) "The psychotherapy of the endogenous depressed patient is primarily supportive," and that (2) "If the patient has thoughts of hostility and guilt, the physician minimizes them."[12] *Support* and *minimizing*, for reasons discussed at length in other places in this book,[13] are likely to lead to suicide or despair. Use of support, as has been shown, says to the counselee: "There is no hope; God has no answers," or ideas akin to these. Minimizing tells him: "This counselor cannot help me; he does not understand the depth of my problem." Both of these faulty procedures fail to treat the counselee as responsible before God and thus take away his hope. Taking away any hope from a depressed person always is dangerous because it gives occasion for him to despair, even to the point of taking his life. If, instead, the magnitude of his problem is acknowledged (rather than minimized), but in spite of the greatness of the difficulty God is presented as able to handle even so difficult a problem as this, the counselee is more likely to believe that the counselor may be able to provide a reliable basis for hope. Despair may be dispelled, also, by assuring the counselee that despite the grave nature of the problem, God has an answer. By laying out a biblical plan and sketching the scriptural course that may be taken during the days ahead, the counselee can see that, rather than offer "support," there is in the gospel of Christ a way out of circumstances that before seemed to lead only to despair.

---

12. Paul Huston, "Treatment of Depression," *Handbook of Psychiatric Therapies, op. cit.*, pp. 230, 231. Huston also suggests lying to him by telling him that his problem is "a temporary malfunction of the nervous system," *ibid.* Not only is lying sin, but it is no basis for trust in the counseling relationship.
13. Chap. 16.

Chapter Thirty-four

HELPING THE "SCHIZOPHRENIC"

What Is "Schizophrenia"?

What about people, for instance, who suspect that others are after them? Can a Christian counselor help them? What if they freeze up in a catatonic state? Other persons also may talk about visions, claim to hear voices inaudible to others, etc. What can the Christian counselor do for them? To begin with, a good medical checkup is the place to start. Counselees with problems of this sort may have an organic problem; perhaps a tumor on the brain or, as may be more likely, a perceptual disorder resulting from chemical malfunction in the body.[2] Chemical malfunction also may be a result of the use or abuse of drugs. Again, perceptual problems may result from toxic chemical buildup in the body caused by acute sleep loss. Christian counselors who are aware of the effects of sleep loss (often as a result of sinful abuse of the body) have been able to get to the root of the problem when physcians could find no cause. At times some of these causes may be combined: the counselee could be taking drugs to keep him awake at night. He may have been on "up" pills (amphetimines) to keep himself awake (as do some students during exam periods; truck drivers, etc.). But if in doing so he misses two or three days of sleep, he may become very irritable, then suspicious, and then even begin to hallucinate. Significant sleep loss (loss of Rapid Eye Movement [R.E.M.] sleep) can cause every effect of LSD. There are, then, at least three known *organic* possibilities behind the bizarre behavior labeled "schizophrenia": bodily (glandular) malfunction, drug abuse, sleep loss.

All of these causes have been lumped under the unfortunate classi-

---

1. Cf. Appendix C for further discussion of organic/nonorganic problems and a discussion of cooperation with physicians.
2. The P.D.I. contains a series of sample questions designed to pick up such possibilities.

fication, schizophrenia.[3] When a counselee suffers from organic problems of a perceptual sort, it is important for both him and the counselor to recognize that nothing is wrong with his mind; he is *not* mentally ill. The problem is with the data that are fed to the mind by the senses. The brain operates properly but on the basis of incorrect data. In other words, if it looks (wrongly) to me like a chair has left the ground and is now moving rapidly through the air toward my head, my brain (*rightly, on the basis of these wrong data*) signals my body to jump aside. The data are false, so the movement seems bizarre. The behavior is *not* bizarre, however; it is perfectly intelligible on the basis that has just been explained. There is no *mental* illness involved. Understandably, others who are getting true data by their senses, begin to wonder about my sanity; before long I may wonder too.

Many people for various reasons get into situations where they have perceptual difficulties. If, for example, a counselee runs his hand over a table top that he knows (by looking) has a smooth surface, but it *feels* hairy, he may begin to wonder about his sanity. Yet there is nothing wrong with his *sanity*. The problem is that his sense of touch is providing inaccurate data as the result of a chemical disorder arising either from an original inside malfunction in his body chemistry, or as the result of chemical malfunction that has been caused by drugs, lack of sleep, etc. Perception may be affected at any or all points. Sight, when distorted, can cause one severe problems. If the faces of others (friends and strangers alike) seem to be scowling at him much of the time, he quickly may grow suspicious and at length become asocial. When depth perception fails to function properly, one bumps into tables, chairs, garbage cans, and people. It is not long before he not only may be

---

3. This is a poor word. The term is similar to the words "red nose." One may have the latter for any number of reasons: boozing, growing a pimple on it, being punched in it, or getting it sunburned. *Schizophrenia*, like the words *red nose*, is a non-specific term that says nothing of *causes* but speaks only of *effects* (bizarre or strongly unpleasant behavior). Its use, particularly as the designation for a so-called mental *illness*, ought to be discontinued. Hoffer and Osmond are unwise to continue this word to speak of a specific organic bodily malfunction. (Cf. the *Journal of Schizophrenia*; Abraham Hoffer and Humphrey Osmond, *How to Live with Schizophrenia* (New York: University Books, 1966); Carl C. Pfeiffer, ed., *The Schizophrenias, Yours and Mine* (New York: Pyramid Books, 1970). Karl Menninger recently quipped, "Schizophrenia to me is just a nice Greek word." "12 Admissions of Mental Error," *Medical World News*, February 9, 1973, p. 18.

forced to stop driving (because of frequent accidents), but he may also become reluctant to frequent places where even small crowds gather.[4] This withdrawal can complicate the original problem.

Mystics: Visionaries or Sinners?

If in the ascetic life early morning prayer was combined with late night vigils, there is little wonder that many early mystics saw what they thought were visions and heard what they supposed were revelations from God. Since they held a strong belief in present direct revelation and miracles, it is not surprising that the perceptual disturbances resulting from sleep loss that brought about hallucinations often took the form of (or were interpreted as) revelations.[5] A study of the practices of the ascetics forces one to conclude that it was probably sin against their bodies, rather than holiness derived from ascetic practices, that was at the bottom of the mysticism so often associated with hermits, monastics, and others. It seems, therefore, to be not merely a coincidence that mysticism grew tall in the soil of ascetic communities. The adaptation of sinful Greek thought that divided between the sacred and the secular and considered matter evil led to many practices that seriously harmed the body. In contrast, God declares that the body must be cared for as the "temple of the Holy Spirit."[6] They violated the commandment, "Thou shalt not murder," with the resultant perceptual problems that develop whenever the body is pushed beyond its limits.

Counselors should be aware of the existence of contemporary Protestant ascetics who attempt to become holy by similar unholy practices. It is not frequent that one meets pietistic Protestants who have sinned against God and their bodies in this manner; the greater number of genuine Christians sin by spending too little time in prayer. But occasionally—and they will tend to end up in the counseling room (so that there they will be met with greater frequency)—he will run across

---

4. Be sure to check reasons why people stop attending church services; it is not *always* because of poor sermons!

5. Cf., for example, the ascetic-prophetic-revelational movement called Montanism. See also Frederic W. Farrar, *Lives of the Fathers* (New York: Macmillan and Co., 1889), vol. II, pp. 159-172. Among other things, he wrote: "The weakened brains of the hermits were disturbed by visitations of hellish monsters and their sleepless nights affrighted by sights and sounds," p. 166. Even Augustine devoted half of the night to meditations, *ibid.*, pp. 337, 338.

6. Cf. I Corinthians 6:19; Exodus 20:13.

such persons. When one suspects that sleep loss may be at the bottom of the problem, he may need to ask questions about prayer and other devotional habits. Significant sleep loss is always one key area for investigation whenever one encounters counselees with heavy strains of mysticism or who purport to have direct revelations. Check out the hours of actual connected sleep attained each night. Note whether long periods of sleep loss preceded the "revelational" experience. Two or more days of sleep loss may lead to any or all of the effects of LSD.[7]

Sleep Loss

It is important to point out to such counselees that there is no evidence in the Scriptures that Jesus ever lost as much as two days' sleep. Although it is plain that He arose early in the morning for prayer,[8] two other facts are evident (1) He "arose," i.e., He had been asleep beforehand. It does not seem to have been His practice to spend whole nights in prayer. (2) There is no indication of the hour at which Jesus went to bed at night. He may have retired quite early.

Counselees often complain of tiredness that results from loss of sleep. Sleep problems should be traced to their source. Counselors should probe until the cause (or causes) are clear. Some of the most frequent causes of sleep loss are: (1) bad scheduling—irregularity can cause serious sleep difficulties; (2) concern over unsolved problems—the answer here is to solve each day's problems each day (cf. comments on worry elsewhere);[9] (3) bad habits, like watching the late TV show each night; (4) failure to complete chores at proper times: washing, ironing, homework, etc.; (5) late dating.

Sometimes counselees object, "But I *can't* get to sleep at night; my mind keeps on racing even after I go to bed." What can be done? Several things: (1) *prayer* for God's blessing upon sleep (cf. Proverbs 3:24; Psalm 4:8; 127:2) including confession of sin and committal of problems into God's care; (2) *exercise* to perspiration before retiring (especially if one has been worried or tense); the body is designed so that exercise and worry are normally exclusive of each other; (3) *relaxa-*

---

7. Cf. Gay G. Luce and Julius Segal, *Sleep* (New York: Lancer Books, 1967), pp. 81-100.
8. Cf. Mark 1:35.
9. Cf. *What to Do About Worry, op. cit.*

tion;[10] (4) the use of *night notes*; if a pad and pencil are placed within reach of the bed, one can jot down notes (not write essays) that will retain vital thoughts so that he will feel free to go to sleep. It is important not to get up and eat or read or watch TV, as this further stimulates the mind. Satisfy it rather than stimulate it.

Much more could be said about helping with counselees who have bizarre behavior problems, but it is perhaps sufficient to remark that these can be divided into two sorts: organic and non-organic (of course, the two also may interact). I have stressed thus far the importance of cooperation with a physician to make sure that the behavior does not stem from organic sources. When it has been ascertained by adequate tests that the *basis* for the difficuly is almost certainly non-organic, then it is the counselor's task to break through the camouflage or the sinful life pattern or attitude that has been developed. He must do this in order to help the counselee to solve his problems in a biblical manner.[11] He may then proceed as in any other case.

The diagram which follows (see next page) illustrates the "red nose" problem involved in the unhelpful designation *schizophrenia*.

The term schizophrenia, then, is inadequate in that it fails to distinguish widely differing causes of similar behavior. It does not indicate when body chemistry or the brain affects or is affected by attitudes. It ought, therefore, to be abandoned as confusing rather than helpful.

"Catatonic Schizophrenia"

When there is a diagnosis that the counselee has not suffered any physical paralysis or shock and that there is, presumably, no physiological cause behind the behavior that is commonly called a catatonic state,[12] the counselor must assume that the state is self-induced and may be broken by the proper procedures. Perhaps the best way to indicate what must be done is to describe a recent case. Barbara had received the unpleasant news that her son, George, had gotten his girlfriend pregnant. This came on the wake of other problems that had been piling up in the

---

10. Cf. David H. Fink, M.D., *Release From Nervous Tension* (New York: Simon and Schuster, 1943), p. 66. Note the chart for proper positioning of a pillow under the neck in order to relax it. Fink discovered that if the corners of the pillow were pulled up over the front of the shoulders, one's neck was best supported for sleep.

11. Cf. *Competent to Counsel*, pp. 29 ff.

12. A state in which one becomes rigid and immobile and may not speak or even attend to his bodily necessities.

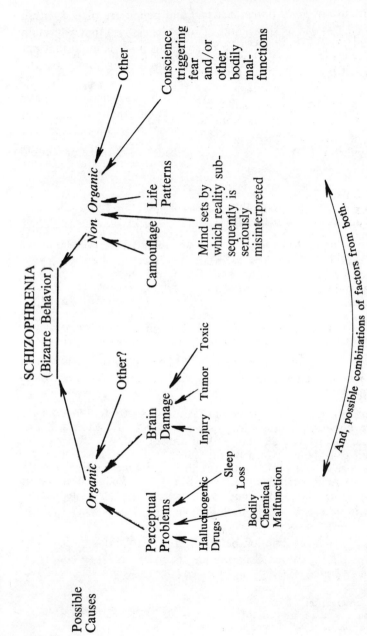

Figure 11

family. Jon, Barbara's husband, phoned the office of a nouthetic counselor and described the scene: Barbara had gone to their bedroom, sat down on the bed, and became frozen, stiff as stone. She had been in that position, staring ahead at the wall, totally uncommunicative, acting as if she were out of touch with reality, for seven hours. The counselor arrived and did three things:

1. From the account (much more fully given) surmised that there was no organic cause for this behavior.

2. Assumed that Barbara was *not* out of touch and, therefore, could hear all that he was about to say.

3. Spoke to her directly in a firm and yet loving manner:

> Barbara, I know that you can understand everything that I am saying, and I want you to listen carefully. First, you are running away from your problems this way. That is wrong; that is not God's way of handling life's difficulties. I recognize that your problems are serious, and I do not want to minimize them one bit. Yet, your Lord, Jesus Christ, is greater and if you will let me, I shall try to help you work out the answers to them from His Word. Part of your difficulty may be that you see them all at once, looming up before you like a dark forest through which you can see no daylight. We are going to chop down one or two trees at a time. Eventually— sooner than you think—we shall begin to see daylight.

Barbara stirred a bit, but did not respond. She continued to sit silently as before. The counselor went on to describe the consequences of failing to respond:

> If you do not meet your problems, you will force Jon to take the far more unpleasant alternative that lies ahead. First, he will find it necessary to let you sit here as you are for a day.[13] In that time if you fail to respond, you will find that lack of food and your regular toilet needs will make your situation quite uncomfortable. If, even under those circumstances, you still do not budge, Jon can do only one more thing—he must send you to a mental institution. Do you have any idea of what it is like in a mental institution? Let me describe. . . .

It was not far into the description before Barbara broke down. She wept in relief, then spilled out her disappointments and fears. The counselor, as a result, was able to help her meet these God's way.[14]

---

13. Under observation, of course.
14. Cf. also a similar case related in John Bettler, "The Pastor's Casebook," *Nouthetic Confrontation*, vol. I, no. 3, Winter, 1973, p. 3.

Chapter Thirty-five

RESOLVING SEXUAL DIFFICULTIES

In Marriage

Counselors should recognize that there are relatively few "mechanical" or organic problems with sex. In almost every case, if there is an organic problem, the physician already will have discovered it or may do so quickly. In almost every instance when the counselor sends counselees for physical checkups, the findings are negative. Yet many, many counselees speak of sexual difficulties as the presenting problem. In the vast majority of cases, there will be sexual difficulties, it is true, but these will be symptomatic of *other* difficulties from which they stem and of which they are one clear sign.[1]

Probing usually will promptly uncover the underlying relational difficulties. These usually will consist of any or all of the following: fear,[2] anger and resentment,[3] worry, guilt, jealousy and suspicion, and fatigue.[4] The emphasis in early questioning should be put upon anger and resentment, since this problem most frequently seems to underlie sexual difficulties. For help in resolving this problem, the counselor should consult the section on "How to Handle Anger."[5]

Whenever dealing with underlying relational difficulties, counselors also should take time to discuss the fundamental biblical principles of sexual relations. Basic to these is Paul's discussion of the subject in I Corinthians 7.

Biblical Principles of Sex

In that passage certain principles are clear. Among those are the following:

---

1. Counselors will find this to be true contrary to Freud's pan-sexualism theory.
2. Fear of pregnancy; fear that the other party may abuse a child (if born), as he (or she) has been maltreated.
3. Tension, abhorrence, or even revenge (getting even) may stem from this.
4. Fatigue often demands rescheduling of time; schedules also may represent attempts to stay apart.
5. Chap. 31.

1. Sexual relations within marriage are holy and good. God encourages relations and warns against their cessation.

2. Pleasure in sexual relations is not sinful but assumed (the bodies of both parties belong to each other). See also the Song of Solomon and Proverbs 5:18, 19.

3. Sexual pleasure is to be regulated by the principle that one's sexuality is not to be self-oriented but other-oriented ("rights" over one's body are given in marriage to the other party). All homosexuality and masturbation are out of accord with this fundamental principle. The idea here, as elsewhere, is that "it is more blessed to give than to receive."

4. Sexual relations are to be regular and continuous. No exact number of times per week is advised, but the principle is that both parties are to provide such adequate sexual satisfaction that both "burning" (sexual desire) and temptation to find satisfaction elsewhere are avoided.

5. The principle of satisfaction means that each party is to provide sexual enjoyment (which is "due" him or her in marriage) as frequently as the other party requires. But, of course, other biblical principles (moderation, seeking to please another rather than oneself, etc.) also come into play. Consideration for one's mate is to regulate one's requests for sexual relations. But this must not be used as an excuse for failing to meet genuine needs. On the other hand, requests for sexual satisfaction may not be governed by an idolatrous lust.

6. In accordance with the principle of "rights," there is to be no sexual bargaining between married persons ("I'll not have relations unless you. . . ."). Neither party has the right to make such bargains.

7. Sexual relationships are equal and reciprocal.[6] Paul does not give the man superior rights to the woman. It is clear, then, that mutual stimulation and mutual initiation of relations are legitimate. Indeed, the doctrine of mutual rights involves also the obligation of mutual responsibility. This means, among other things, mutual active participation in the act of intercourse.

In counseling, these principles may be used as benchmarks for dealing with the great variety of particulars that may be presented.

---

6. Women need not be timid about taking the initiative in requesting or suggesting sexual relations. Paul's words plainly indicate that there is a mutual need that *each* partner is required to satisfy. Nor should women hesitate to cooperate in or even to initiate foreplay in sexual relations.

General Counseling Procedures

In conjunction with the use of the biblical principles for sexual relations found in I Corinthians, a plan for handling the specific underlying difficulties must be followed. A general procedure such as the following is one possibility.

1. Discover the areas of conflict, difficulty, both foundational and ancillary, to the sexual problem. The counselor may begin with setting up a conference table, helping the counselees to make lists of conflicts and teaching them how to deal with problems daily in a biblical manner.[7] Early questioning and probing may be fairly extensive. When he has discovered the "hot spots" and has probed these intensively, he will work on each one of these areas in order to eliminate all of the underlying problems.

2. Meanwhile, problems with sexual relations usually will begin to disappear without much direct attention to this matter. The change will usually take place as the relationship between the husband and wife improves. This *may* occur very early in counseling, even before major changes in some of the problem areas have been effected. The reasons for this are clear. For one thing, both parties, at bottom, may earnestly desire to resume good sexual relations. When this is true (and it often is), it takes little encouragement to make the difference. In addition, when any amount of hope arises through a change in personal relationships and a change in the direction that the marriage is taking, this can make all of the difference in sexual relations.

Whenever this early change occurs, it is wise for the counselor to anticipate the possibility that the counselees will settle for too little too soon. He may point out that the problem of poor sexual relations has been solved so readily *only because* it was never the basic problem. Distinguishing between the *issue* (poor sexual relations) and the *relationship* (interpersonally poor), the counselor will point out that it is difficult to have good sexual relations in a bed that is loaded with baggage. Contrary to Ephesians 4:26, in which Paul wrote, ". . . do not let the sun go down on your anger," they had been dragging the day's baggage into the bed with them at night. When they began to deal with some of these problems, and when the channels of communication were cleared daily through practicing confession and forgiveness, and they

---

7. Cf. *Competent to Counsel*, pp. 231-236, 220 ff.

had begun to check the baggage before going to bed, there was room once again for normal sexual relations.

3. Having persuaded them that their entire relationship *is* their sexual relationship, the counselor will continue to establish the proper relationship on every front. Specifically relating to the sexual side of the relationship, he will instruct them about the principles found in I Corinthians 7 and any applications of these that may seem pertinent to their particular situation. Because of the sins of self-concern, pride, lust, etc., many poor habit patterns in sexual relations may have been established that may need separate handling. When the basic relationship between the husband and wife has been reestablished on biblical grounds, they are ready for direct help relating to sexual difficulties.

4. Finally, the counselor will endeavor to instruct them in what was wrong, what made the difference and what, therefore, they must do both to prevent and to recoup from future failure.

Specific sexual problems of many sorts will arise. They all cannot be anticipated here. The two that follow are offered as samples from which inferences regarding principles and procedures possibly may be gleaned.

Guilt Over Sins

Often, sexual relations deteriorate (or never develop) because of growing guilt over sexual promiscuity either prior to or during marriage. Confession, forgiveness, and reconciliation which includes the building of a new interpersonal relationship between husband and wife is God's answer. First the relationship to God, then to one's partner, must be reestablished. The following case, quoted in part from *Competent to Counsel*, is an example of what needs to be done.

Both Tom and Mary before and after marriage had engaged in extra-marital sexual affairs. When they married, neither was a Christian; until very recently they had known nothing of Christianity. But now in the eighteenth year of their marriage they became Christians. Tom, over the last year, had been seeing another woman. He didn't want to give her up. Mary found out about it and made Tom promise to break the relationship. He agreed; but he didn't do it. For nearly a year Tom's broken promise and double life had eaten away at him, and the more his Christian faith had become a pressing reality, the more guilt of his actions weighed upon him. What could he do? He came for counseling. He came under the guise of talking about his son, but in the first interview it was not long before the discussion turned to the real problem. "Tom," his counselor said, "you've got to repent of your sin and give her up. If you want to straighten out your marriage, you're going to have to tell your wife about it. You'll have to tell her that you've been lying; that you've really been seeing this woman. You'll have to ask her forgiveness, assure her that this time you mean business, and ask her to help you stick to your promise."

Tom said, "I can't do it."

"Tom, we can't help you if you don't."

After a discussion of God's commandments and His grace, Tom agreed: "All right, I'll do it." Tom asked God's forgiveness and help. The counselor prayed about the outcome. Tom scheduled another visit for that afternoon, and brought Mary along.

During this counseling session Tom told Mary the truth. He confessed that he had lied and that at this very moment he had the keys to the other woman's apartment in his pocket. Mary was shattered, but she was gratified that he had told her, and she took it well (she probably took it better because it happened in the presence of a counselor who was able to help them take the next step). She said, "What can we do?" Tom said, "I want you to forgive me and help me to become the kind of Christian husband I ought to be." Mary said, "Well, I will forgive you Tom, if you mean it, if you really want to save our marriage." Tom said, "I do" (it sounded almost as if he were taking his marriage vows again). So Mary forgave Tom. As a matter of fact, before the session had ended, Mary too had asked for forgiveness for some previous escapades of her own, and had received it. "What do we do next?" Tom asked. Everyone talked this over. It was decided that then and there Tom should phone the other woman and tell her he would not see her again.

The next week Tom and Mary came back for further counseling. During the week an issue had arisen between them about those keys to the other woman's apartment. Both agreed that he should dispose of them— but how? Should he take them back to the woman and give them to her? Should he throw them away? What should he do about them? Everyone felt that it was important to do something immediately. The matter disturbed Mary considerably. The counselor said, "Tom, hand over those keys right now." He did. Dramatically he placed them one after another on the table in a solemn commitment that helped Mary know that he meant business. She was a new woman after that. This very act, this burning of his bridges, meant a great deal to her. Those keys are in the counseling files to this day, as evidence that Tom meant business. Sometime in years to come, if it is ever necessary to do so, those keys could be shown to Tom or to his wife as a reminder of the commitment he made that day. It probably won't be necessary to do so. The keys remain as a landmark in their lives; they are like the pile of stones which the old patriarchs erected, noting a milestone along the road of sanctification.[8]

Often in response to this biblical solution the objection is raised, "Why do I have to tell? Won't that cause more problems? Why should I bring my wife (husband) into this? It is my guilt; let me bear it."[9] This objection may stem from fear of consequences or from genuine concern. In one sense, the motive is irrelevant; the objection cannot stand up. As the proverb says, "You will never succeed in life if you try to hide your sins. Confess them and repent; then God will show mercy to you" (Proverbs 28:13, T.E.V.). In the long run, trying to avoid these problems only allows them to continue to destroy relations between you and your spouse. The effects of guilt upon a relationship cannot be avoided. The fear of being found out, then the stresses and strains and their misunderstandings all mount up and at length lead to the breakdown of the guilty party, of communication, or of both. Counselors say to the counselee: "You cannot avoid the issue because you are no longer two but one. It is no longer your guilt alone; you are now 'one flesh.' You are too intimately related to one another to face *any* large problem separately, not to speak of this one. When two persons must be neighbors as close as a husband and wife, their relationship will suffer unless it is established upon the basis of truth (Ephesians 4:25). Guilt held in by one will be felt by both. Guilt will

---

8. Cf. God's use of "reminders" in Numbers 15:37-41. His people were to wear tassels on their garments as a reminder to obey His commandments. One client was helped by affixing a large "T" (constructed of masking tape) to his front door to remind him to take out the trash as he left. Masking tape for such purposes is a nearly universal aid in counseling!

9. Counselees must be told, "Of course 'the truth hurts,' but it *never* hurts like a lie. Sin always causes pain and misery. But repentance leads to peace. When you tell the truth, the hurt comes quickly, but healing soon follows. If you put off telling the truth, you will suffer longer and in the end suffer the pain of facing it after all. When one wrongly handles the truth, it *really* hurts!"

out.[10] Marriage removes privacy from this matter. It is a matter between the husband and wife. Indeed it has *come between* you and must be removed. You cannot handle the problem solely on your own." The counselor then can point out ways in which the problem already has come between them.

A man, when faced with his Christian obligation to deal with his adultery, protested,"No! No! A psychiatrist told me it is the worst thing I could do." Finally he agreed. Both he and his wife came later and he told her the truth. After the initial shock, the wife said, "My greatest hope for the future is that he *told* me; if I had found out first, I would have no reason to believe that he wanted to do anything about it."

The issue is not *whether* to tell the truth, but only *how* he will do so. Forgiveness and reconciliation must be sought. Forgiveness must be genuine; it must be viewed as a promise to remember the confessed wrong against another no more. It is only when the issue has been brought out into the light that the relationship can be restored. Moreover, apart from confession leading to reconciliation, any original difficulties in the marriage that might have become occasions for such sin could be resolved only when both parties were able to look at them candidly. Often it takes the hard reality of the effects of problems to get people to face them: "Sometimes it takes a painful experience to make us change our ways" (Proverbs 20:30, T.E.V.).

Sexual Ignorance

How much of the biology of sex is a Christian counselor obligated to discuss? The question is hard to answer. While it is not his prerogative to pull down anatomical charts and give illustrated lectures, and he will certainly not want to devote counseling time to such matters as an analysis of the various forms of exotic positions that it is possible to assume during sexual relations, there *may* be occasions on which he will find it necessary to discuss *something* of even anatomy and technique.

Bob and June, married only a few months, had overcome the interpersonal problems between them. When they first came for counseling they complained of extreme physical difficulty in relations, which left her very sore and sometimes bleeding. Yet the physician said that there

---

10. Cf. Proverbs 22:12 (T.E.V.). Truth will become known; God will disprove liars.

was no physical *cause*; the problem was extreme tension on her part. "It was," as the counselor put it, "as if Bob were trying to enter a door that June had shut and bolted and that he gained access only by forcibly entering." This condition had been caused by jealousy and suspicion. When *those* problems were solved, the tension ceased, June relaxed, and sexual relations without physical injury became possible for the first time. However, after the resolution of those two difficulties, it became apparent that there was a third. Because of the previous difficuties, both parties had developed a hasty approach to relations, which afterward continued. The pattern involved little or no lovemaking and foreplay and was distinctly unsatisfying to June. Along with that problem, June had developed a defensive posture rather than a participatory one, that persisted. This led the counselor to discuss the need for *mutual* stimulation and participation in sexual relations according to the principles in I Corinthians 7. As the counselor *applied* these to the particulars in the case, he found it necessary to counsel them about the importance of lovemaking prior to intercourse and the need for clitorial stimulation, since June had never reached a climax.[11] June had to be encouraged to participate actively in intercourse by making forward upward rhythmical bodily thrusts during clitorial stimulation.

Thus, without long, detailed instruction in biology and technique, the principles of sex as other-oriented, sexual relations as legitimate pleasure, and the doctrine of mutual rights and responsibilities led *in one specific case* to a minimal amount of such instruction.

All discussion of sexual relations in counseling, since it involves both parties intimately, should be in the presence of *both* the husband and the wife. Discussing such matters *privately* with a wife alone can lead to unnecessary temptations and/or accusations. If in very rare circumstances sexual matters must be discussed with the woman alone, it is always wise to do so in a team counseling situation.[12]

---

11. Often female counselees will say that they are not sure whether they have ever experienced an orgasm. When they say this, the counselor may be nearly sure that they have not. Orgasm is a pleasure experience, readily identifiable. When a woman properly *prepares* for sexual relations throughout the day, she is most likely to achieve satisfying results. If she *plans* how she will entice her husband, stimulates his desire, cooperates in foreplay, and thinks of *him* throughout—i.e., how she can be most pleasing to him—she is most likely to succeed. Nothing helps bring about an orgasm like knowing she is pleasing to her partner.

12. Cf. *Competent to Counsel*, pp. 203 ff. Elders, other ministers, and sometimes wives (rarely, but perhaps in an emergency) can serve as team counselors. The

Christian counselors need not be prudish about discussing sexual relations; the biblical writers certainly were not. Yet, in their frankness they never showed a spirit of undue curiosity, nor did they write about sex with a view to titillate the reader or themselves. Counselors, remembering Galatians 6:1b, likewise must refrain from such temptations.

Helping Young People to Handle Masturbation

Masturbation Is Sin

There does not seem to be any *direct* reference to masturbation (as such) in the Scriptures. There is, to be sure, one verse that some people (especially Roman Catholics) have taken to refer to masturbation, but it is certain that it does not.[13] So, if we do not have specific reference to the matter, we must turn to the broad biblical principles that apply to this subject. One very important principle is found in I Corinthians 6:12, where Paul says: "All things are lawful for me, but I will not be *mastered* by anything." This is an important principle. It means that even those things that are right must not be allowed to get such a hold over a Christian that they become his master and he becomes their servant.

Anyone who has had anything to do with counseling young people, particularly young boys, knows that many of them are *trapped* by this habit. Masturbation can get such a hold on a child that it can almost drive him out of his mind.[14] Today there are aspects of the problem that parents as young people did not have to face. Children are maturing sooner now than they used to mature in the past. This means that the sex drive arrives sooner. They are maturing some time around the ages of 11, 12, or 13. And on the other end of adolescence, their schooling has been lengthened. College education is now the equivalent of a high school education a generation ago. There was a time when a sixth grade education was all that was necessary to get by; then it was high school, and now, college. Fewer are getting married as early as before;

---

counselor himself must always remain in charge and must caution the team member not to break into what may be the steps of an argument.

13. Genesis 38:9. The sin referred to in the passage is not masturbation but Onan's failure to raise up children to his brother's wife according to the Levirate marriage law. Cf. Deuteronomy 25:5, 6.

14. Cf. John Schindler, *How to Live 365 Days a Year* (Greenwich: Fawcett Publications, 1954), pp. 135, 136, for other effects of masturbation.

and so the unmarried period during which this desire is strong (and for males possibly the strongest) has been lengthened, causing intensified difficulty. It was hard enough to endure that period in an abbreviated form, but now it is even more difficult to do so.

Paul says that a Christian must not let anything gain the mastery over him. But counselors regularly see young people (*Christian* youth) who are so tangled up in the masturbation problem that they hardly can think about anything else but sex all day long. And the more they engage in masturbation, the more they depend upon it, the more they want it, and the more they feed it. And the more they feed it, the more they are trapped by it. They are caught up in one big vicious circle. Masturbation can gain such a tenacious control over them that it saps their energies, takes their minds away from their studies, and sets them to thinking about sex everywhere they go and with every person they see. Masturbation is a serious problem, much more serious than many may think. Children, therefore, often need help in dealing with this problem.

Because of the meagre public and private discussion that is devoted to the subject of masturbation, it is easy for counselors to forget their own adolescent problem and for them to minimize its importance. But just because the problem of masturbation is not discussed often in society does not mean that it is not an explosive problem. As an additional complication, our society uses sex commercially on every billboard, in every magazine, and as a part of nearly every television program. Everywhere women dress provocatively because that is what the billboards, magazines, and TV dictate. Counselors must realize that young men have an exceedingly difficult time.

Now look at a second principle that is found in Matthew 5:27, 28. There Jesus said that it is not just the outward act of adultery that God is concerned about, but that God also considers the inward thought-and-consent of the heart to be adultery. A child who becomes tangled up in the masturbation spiral eventually cannot avoid becoming involved in this sin as well.[15] In a very young child masturbation may be only exploratory, but before long it gets plugged into fantasizing about sexual relations with imagined sexual partners. Jesus said that this is sin. Adultery of the heart, He said, is just like hatred, which is murder in

---

15. Idealists have contended that the two are separable; counselors know better. The sinful human heart may want to rationalize the matter.

the heart. To kill with a knife or a gun is not the only way to become guilty of murder before God. It is better for the other fellow, of course, if one murders him only in the imagination, but it is no better for the murderer in the sight of God. The same holds true for adultery.

The third factor that must be considered in any discussion of masturbation is that it is not presented (as Herbert J. Miles[16] wrongly supposes) as a biblical option. When Paul wrote: "If they do not have self control, let them marry; for it is better to marry than to burn" (I Corinthians 7:9), the alternatives are clear: self control or marriage. There is no third option. Paul does not say that masturbation is a proper relief for sexual desire (burning). He does not say, "It is better to masturbate than to burn." Quite to the contrary, he lists self-control as the only alternative to marriage. Paul knew, of course, that which everyone who practices masturbation discovers sooner or later: masturbation does not put out the fire but only adds fuel to it. It could never be set over against "burning" as an alternative.

Lastly, masturbation is clearly wrong since it constitutes a perversion of the sexual act. In I Corinthians 7:3-4 one thing is plain: one's sexual capacity does not exist for himself. God has provided one's sexuality for the benefit of his lawful partner. In sex, as elsewhere, it is always true that it is more blessed to give than to receive. Self-directed sex, therefore, constitutes an unlawful use of sexuality. The rights over one's body belong to another, not to himself. He must see, therefore, that sexual activity is (1) never to be conducted as a solitaire activity, and (2) properly may be used only in conjunction with one's lawfully married partner. These two fundamental factors clearly forbid masturbation as a biblically legitimate release of sexual tension.

Masturbation Can Be Overcome

But specifically, how can the counselor help? He must do at least two things: (1) Explain the biblical basis for sex to the child, including the sin of masturbation. He may also need to explain the function of the organs of the body that are involved and how God expects them to be used properly. That is the first thing that he may need to do. This explanation often may culminate in repentance. (2) The second thing

16. Herbert J. Miles, *Sexual Understanding Before Marriage* (Grand Rapids: Zondervan, 1971), pp. 137-162. Miles's advice is plainly out of accord with the Scriptures and must be rejected. With this exception, Miles's books have much to commend them.

that the counselor can do is to talk through the problem to a biblical solution. Notice, he must not just talk; he also must lend genuine help. He must recognize how hard it is to break a habit that may have been established long before. He should find out the facts about his problem (how severe, longstanding, etc.) and give him the precise help that he needs. What he is going to need is some sort of structure that meets his specific situation. And he will need the power of the Holy Spirit to operate within the structure. The Holy Spirit Himself sets forth the need for structure (in the Bible). He talks about "putting off" old patterns and "putting on" new ones. He insists on "discipline." He speaks of "training" (by practice) in godliness. He gives structural principles by which to guide our lives. And when the structure of these principles is translated into concrete action in the child's situation and his determination is to serve God in this matter, he will be on the right track toward breaking that habit and establishing instead the correct biblical pattern for his life.

One of the things the counselee needs is a very specific, concrete structure adapted to his particular situation. Counselees often come in agony begging for help to stop. They often feel so guilty that they plead, "*Do* something for me, *help* me some way." They do not want talk; they want action. Well, there are all kinds of things that can be done to help. For example, the counselor can find out when and where masturbation occurs most frequently. He may want to explain (as he asks) that he is not seeking such information out of curiosity, but in order to help construct a specific plan and program for meeting the problem. If he finds that masturbation regularly occurs after the counselee goes to bed before going to sleep, he may encourage him to engage in vigorous exercise after prayer and before retiring so that he falls into bed exhausted. If, instead, masturbation ordinarily occurs in the morning, he may suggest putting the repeating alarm clock across the room where he must get out of bed in order to turn it off. The next move is to make the bed right away.

The homework assignments should structure the counselee's desire to stop in ways appropriate to *his* situation. As in all cases, the counselor must learn to be creatively concrete in assigning homework.

In all cases, prayer must be coupled with structure. The standard for the latter is the Scriptures, and the result of the former is the power of the Holy Spirit.

How to Counsel Persons Involved in the Sin of Homosexuality

Treat It As Sin

Homosexuality is a growing problem for the Christian counselor. Recently a young man from another state wrote, saying that he has been a Christian for three years, and asking for help concerning the problem, which he says that he "can no longer find an excuse" to avoid. Increasingly the need for help intrudes itself. Nouthetic counselors rejoice in sharing God's adequate answer to this problem. Because they recognize homosexuality as a sin, they can offer hope.[17] God forgives this sin and cleanses men from it: "Such were some of you; but you were washed, but you were sanctified, but you were justified" (I Corinthians 6:11).

It is tragic, in contrast, to observe Wayne Oates's feeble efforts to circumvent clear scriptural data in dealing with the sin of homosexuality. I cite Oates because his is typical of the insipid response that ministers have been trained to make to the problem. He rejects the straightforward biblical condemnation of homosexuality for a moderating approach in which he tries to take the edge off the scriptural view that refers to the act as "an abomination" and declares the homosexual "worthy of death."[18] As a result, he fails to offer real help to the homosexual.

Rather than call homosexual activity sin as God does (there is hope in this, for Christ died for sins and helps us to overcome sinful practices), Oates instead speaks of persons with "homosexual needs."[19] If one has such inherent "needs," because of genetic factors or parental socialization over which he can have little or no control and for which he is not responsible, then there is little or no hope.[20] Indeed, Oates does not hold forth much hope. One can see why. He would rather blunt the Scriptures so that homosexuality no longer need be considered

---

17. Excellent success has been the result of the counseling of homosexuals at the Hatboro Counseling center.

18. Leviticus 18:22; Romans 1:32.

19. Wayne Oates, *The Bible and Pastoral Care* (Grand Rapids: Baker Book House, 1971), p. 46.

20. One seminary student wrote of his condition as that of an "irreversible homosexual" and went on to justify his sin: "homosexual love, when practiced according to the more central Christian principles, is a valid form of eroticism," in "The Misguided Conscience of a 'Christian Queer,'" *The Outlook*, August, 1972.

a "taboo."[21] He finds a farfetched reason for the so-called taboo in the threat to the "perpetuity of the race." That is why the Hebrews (not God) were so upset about homosexuality, Oates opines. Yet Paul in Romans does not mention any such reason. Rather, the entire emphasis there is upon the *perversion* of sexuality. Homosexuality is said to be "against nature" (which, incidentally, militates against any genetically determined view[22]). Oates clearly seems to be hedging, probably out of kindly motives and a well-meaning attempt to help the homosexual. But it is unwise to think that one may be more humane than God. Any attempt to do so actually makes one less humane in the long run. Indeed, inventing the fiction of "homosexual needs" gives the impression that the counselee is uncontrollably dominated by such drives and virtually dooms him to hopelessness and despair.[23]

---

21. *Ibid.*, p. 47. For further discussion of homosexuality, cf. *Competent to Counsel*, pp. 35-36, and *The Big Umbrella*, pp. 219-221. Homosexual practices may begin in many ways, but always constitute learned behavior (sin). In prison or on shipboard, where men are denied access to females for lengthy periods of time, homosexual sin is rife. Lesbianism often develops among women who fail to find husbands.

22. Oates is not specific about his view of the etiology of homosexuality, but his reference to "needs" and to "latent tendencies" (p. 48) seems to indicate that he adopts (perhaps with reservations) the genetic concept. This is a false, non-biblical understanding of homosexuality. God plainly speaks of the sin as an "error" (Romans 1:27), an "abomination" (Leviticus 18:22), etc. Although Narramore rejects the genetic view, he does not speak plainly about the *sin* of homosexuality in his book, *The Psychology of Counseling*, but rather softens the biblical position by suggesting that counselors must help the homosexual offender to see that "life experiences and other factors have caused him to turn to unnatural patterns." Clyde N. Narramore, *The Psychology of Counseling* (Grand Rapids: Zondervan Publishing House, 1960), p. 229. This view again tends to remove responsibility and reduce hope. G. C. Scorer's view is quite unbiblical in a peculiarly harmful way. He wrote: "A clear distinction needs to be made between homosexuality and homosexual acts. The former describes the constitution of a man or woman, for which he or she cannot be held responsible; that is the way they are made or the way they have developed." *The Bible and Sex Ethics Today* (London: Tyndale Press, 1966), p. 118.

23. Paul's words, "against nature" (Romans 1:26), plainly indicate that Oates is wrong in speaking about "homosexual needs." Homosexual drives are not the result of innate needs; they are secondary, learned drives associated with habitual perversion growing out of a sinful way of life. It is just as misleading to speak of "homosexual needs" as it is to speak of "adulterous needs" or "intoxicating needs." Vincent also errs when he writes: "We must realize that in denying the homosexual . . . his 'natural' sexual outlet we are asking a great deal of him." Merville Vincent, "A Christian View of Homosexuality," *Eternity*, August, 1972, p. 25. It is quite wrong to suggest that homosexuality is natural in any sense in

The newest escape among Christians that has come to attention is the propagation of the idea that Satan is in a special way directly responsible for homosexuality. While Satan surely rejoices in its prevalence and encourages its spread by holding the temptation before men, he cannot be blamed for homosexual sin in such a way as to remove the responsibility of the one who commits it. Homosexual behavior is sin, not the product of irresistible Satanic influence or demon possession or control. Such an idea involves an attempt to moderate the plain biblical position regarding homosexuality and, as a result, again removes hope from those who accept this faulty explanation. In no passage in which homosexuality is condemned is it ever especially linked to Satanic or demonic influence.

A further evasion of clear scriptural teaching about homosexuality is set forth in a recent publication, *The Returns of Love*.[24] In this illuminating series of letters between two men who have a homosexual attraction toward one another, the discussion of the problem issues in an uneasy consensus in which they settle for a physically unfulfilled relationship. They are able to do this by distinguishing between the homosexual act and homosexual desire and calling only the former sin.[25] This brings no answer to the problem, however, since they are willing to "burn" in a kind of sacrificial suffering. Nonsense! Indeed, sinful nonsense! The desire *as well as* the act is condemned as sin in the Scriptures, which fail to distinguish the one from the other as acceptable and unacceptable. Paul described the sin of homosexuality (as Christ described adultery and murder) as including *both* the desire ("lusting after," "desiring") and the act (Romans 1:27).

Although the letters purport to show progress in the handling of the sin of homosexuality, there is, in this reviewer's opinion, no real progress at all. Since the writer settles for "my homosexuality enduring for the rest of my life,"[26] there seems to be no real hope; merely a stoical

---

view of Romans 1. It is significant that Vincent's gloomy article fails to speak of hope or help beyond attitudes of "understanding."

24. Alex Davidson, *The Returns of Love* (London: The Inter Varsity Press, 1970). The title is particularly offensive. Homosexuality with its perverted egocentric emphasis upon sexual self-gratification is diametrically opposed to the biblical concept of love as *giving*. One wonders whether the author is not also continually using his reader to titillate his sexual lusts. For instance, was the choice of the pseudonym Peter altogether without significance? Many dodges appear in this booklet, such as calling homosexuality "mental illness," p. 5.

25. Pp. 6, 38, 39. It is his very distinction that takes away all grounds for hope.

26. Last letter, *ibid.*, p. 88.

grimness about it all that in no way approximates the Lord's "washing" from homosexuality (I Corinthians 6:11[27]).

One's heart must go out to these two anonymous young men whose understanding of their problem and of God's solution to it is so faulty. Let me use this page to address them directly. Men, there is a better answer; you do not have to continue in your homosexual habits. If you truly are serious about overcoming the problem, you *can* do so by God's grace. We have seen deliverance happen more than once in our counseling of those who have been caught up in the homosexual way of life. God has the answer. If we can help you at our counseling center, we should be happy to do so. Perhaps, God willing, the day will come when you can write a sequel to the former book from a truly biblical stance, beginning with I Corinthians 6:11.

What to Do to Help

The question increasingly arises, "How does a Christian counselor help the homosexual?" Challenges to the Christian norm abound everywhere; more and more Christian youth are being ensnared. There are several elements composing the answer to that question.

First, the Christian counselor gives hope by acknowledging homosexuality to be what it is—a sinful way of life—rather than a matter determined by genetic or social factors.[28] The Bible is explicit about

---

27. Paul uses the past tense: "such *were* some of you." The verse abounds in hope not only for those who have become ensnared in homosexual habits, but for all sorts of persons mentioned in the two preceding verses.

28. Cf. Romans 1:26-28, 32. In verse 26 Paul speaks of homosexuality as a "degrading passion," in verse 27 as an "indecent act" and "an error," in verse 28 the improper activity of a "depraved mind," and in verse 32 declares it is "worthy of death." One is not a homosexual constitutionally any more than one is an adulterer constitutionally. Homosexuality is not considered to be a condition, but an act. It is viewed as a sinful practice which can become a way of life. The homosexual act, like the act of adultery, is the reason for calling one a homosexual (of course, one may commit homosexual sins of the heart, just as one may commit adultery in his heart. He may lust after a man in his heart as another may lust after a woman). But precisely because homosexuality, like adultery, is learned behavior into which men with sinful natures are prone to wander, homosexuality can be forgiven in Christ, and the pattern can be abandoned and in its place proper patterns can be reestablished by the Holy Spirit. Some homosexuals have lost hope because of the reluctance of Christian counselors to represent homosexuality as sin. For an excellent recent discussion of homosexuality, see Hebden Taylor, *The New Legality* (Philadelphia: Presbyterian and Reformed Publishing Co., 1967), pp. 36-49.

this question. In many places God talks plainly about homosexuality. In Leviticus 18:22, He calls homosexuality an "abomination." In Leviticus 20:13, God says that two Israelites caught in this act were to be put to death. In the New Testament, Paul declares that because men gave up God, God gave up men! Those men who deserted God and His Standard were deserted by God and, as a consequence, wandered into shameful practices. And when he talks about these degrading passions and practices, he specifically talks about homosexuality. He says:

> For this reason God gave them over to degrading passions, for their women exchanged the natural function for that which is unnatural, and in the same way also the men abandoned the natural function of the woman and burned in their desire toward one another; men with men committing indecent acts and receiving in their own persons the due penalty of their error (Romans 1:26, 27).

He calls homosexual acts "things that are not proper" (vs. 28) and concludes that "Those that practice such things are worthy of death" (vs. 32). Homosexuality also is mentioned in I Corinthians 6:9, in Genesis 19, and in I Timothy 1:10. In each instance, it is always considered a sin, not a sickness. In every biblical reference, homosexuality is considered an irresponsible way of life, not an irresistible state that results from genetic factors or social conditioning. It is called an "error," a wrong way of life.

You may ask, "Why do effeminate-looking people so often get involved in homosexuality? Is it because of genetic factors?" Well, the effeminate aspects of the person may be genetic, but the fact that he got involved in homosexuality is not. It is the effeminate-looking person that the practiced homosexual is looking for.[29] He is the one that the latter will seek to seduce. The Bible is clear: homosexuality is a *sin;* it is not a sickness. And that is why there is hope. What hope is there of changing genes? But God is in the business of dealing with sin.[30]

---

29. Contrary to many explanations of homosexuality, the choice of a partner that approximates (as closely as possible) a member of the opposite sex shows that the problem does not exist in a lack of interest in heterosexual characteristics, but just the opposite. Other factors are basic to the perversion. But note, interest in an effeminate person by another male shows his basic need and even desire (though warped) for a female rather than male.

30. The genetic view is widespread among homosexuals themselves. One "Christian Queer," as he styles himself, describes himself as "an irreversible homosexual." *Stromata,* May, 1972, in *The Outlook,* August, 1972, p. 5. The concept

Secondly, counselors must show the homosexual offender that Christ holds the answer to the sin. It is He that "washes" and "sanctifies" one from its pollution and power (I Corinthians 6:11). Evangelism may figure into the picture here. But, assuming that the offender has become a Christian and, in true repentance, seeks to withdraw from all homosexual activities and wishes to pursue the normal course of finding a husband or wife, what may he do? He may complain about persons of the opposite sex holding no attraction for him. How, he may ask, can he overcome this problem?

To begin with, the counselor must assure the homosexual counselee that, like any other sinful way of life, homosexuality may be eliminated by putting off past sinful patterns and learning to live by God's patterns of life instead. This change involves several procedures. First, he must break all past associations, cutting off any associations or friendships that he has made with other homosexuals. The counselor may need to have him phone them from his office and break off the relationship then and there.[31] Nothing is more important than to make this break early and clean.

Secondly, he must so restructure the course of his life as to avoid places in which homosexual contacts frequently have been or may be made. Rescheduling daily activities as fully as possible also aids.

Next, he must recognize that homosexuality is a life-dominating sin which permeates every phase and activity of his life. One may begin with homosexuality as one aspect of his total life,[32] but before long a fixed pattern develops, and once having become a habit, homosexuality becomes a total way of life.

The habit may become so firmly established that homosexuality *appears* to be a genetic problem. Homosexual propaganda, coupled with

---

of irreversibility is hope-shattering. The anonymous writer acknowledges this when he speaks of his "resolve" to "accept the facts about himself and go from there to live in the way most pleasing to God of which he is capable." What God calls an "abomination" can never please Him, but the hope lies precisely in the fact that Christ changes abominable people.

31. Incidentally, during counseling sessions the telephone may be used whenever the counselor considers it helpful to make an immediate commitment, obtain information necessary to the *present* session, etc. Many counselors waste time by forgetting the phone on the desk.

32. In some instances, homosexual solutions to the problems occasioned by adolescent sexual drives may have been sought as "safe" solutions that alleviate the fears of pregnancy which accompany illicit heterosexual activity. Before long, the practice became a life in itself.

the acting and showmanship involved in many homosexual relationships, may tend to authenticate this false view. But there is no reason for viewing homosexuality as a genetic condition in the light of the Scriptures, which declare that the homosexual act is sin. Apart from the work of Christ in their lives, all sinful men will distort God's marvelous gift of sex in one way or another. The particular style of sin (whether homosexual or heterosexual in its orientation), however, is learned behavior. Homosexuality is the sinful way in which some counselees have attempted to solve the sexual difficulties of adolescence and later life.

Usually one who commits homosexual sin develops a grossly distorted view of sex and other interpersonal relations. He finds, for instance, that in order to get away with his sin he must lead a double life. So he carries a heavy load of fear and guilt. Part of the homosexual pattern is lying. Anyone leading a double life usually becomes an astute liar. It is very difficult to believe what he says, because he will make promises that he fails to keep. This is particularly frustrating to counselors. They will find it necessary to confront him about patterns of falsehood, which may have become so much a part of his way of life that his first response to stress may be to lie. The characteristics of homosexuals accord fully with what we know of other learned behavior and, therefore, must be handled accordingly. Yet, since homosexualism, like adultery, drunkenness, drug abuse, etc., soon becomes a life-dominating sin, it is necessary to focus not upon homosexuality alone, but upon every aspect of life. This, then leads to the next point.

Total Structuring

To counsel homosexuals, counselors must get a commitment for *total structuring*. It is not only those who have lived a life of general irresponsibility who need structuring. Whenever a counselee's problem turns out to be one large, glaring sin like homosexuality, he may believe, wrongly, that he has only one problem to solve. He may even be impatient with a counselor who attempts to look at other aspects of his life. "Why don't you get to *the* problem?" he may ask. But in such cases, *the* problem cannot help but affect every other aspect of his life. Its effects doubtless have bled over into social life, married life, work, physical and financial matters, etc. All of these areas must be investigated and restructured biblically. The following diagram may help to visualize the situation.

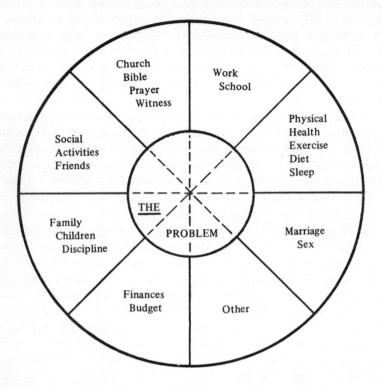

TOTAL STRUCTURING means looking at *the* problem in relationship to all areas of life. The problem affects all areas, and whenever all areas are in proper relationship to God, the dotted lines become solid lines and *the* problem dissolves. The above diagram is not intended to be comprehensive, but suggestive.

If the counseling focuses upon only the issue of homosexuality, usually it will fail. Poor health or lack of sleep (to consider only one area) can lead to a general inability to withstand temptation and a tendency to revert to old patterns, since they offer the course of least resistance and effort. Even rectal problems often associated with homosexual sin can become a trigger for failure. Medical attention may be required. Failure to perform properly at work, worries over financial incompetences, poor family or social relationships, and lack of prayer and Bible study all may lead to similar reversions. On the other hand, homosexual activities have so interpenetrated and affected each area of life that social and family failures, etc., inevitably result. Unless he shores up each of the areas of his life before God, they will constantly tend to drag him back toward homosexual sin in spite of good intentions. The counselee, therefore, must be shown the importance of total structuring and must be urged to work hard in each area of his life by the power of the Spirit.

First, the counselor must gather data on each area; then he must help the counselee to restructure that area God's way.[33] This probably will involve such assignments as straightening out relationships with parents, rescheduling his daily life patterns so as to get adequate sleep (homosexuals often do their prowling at night), etc.

Positively the pursuit of new patterns at length may lead to the only God-given solution to the problem of strong sexual desire: "It is better to marry than to burn" (I Corinthians 7:9). Marriage is God's answer to immorality: "Because of immoralities let each man have his own wife, and let each woman have her own husband." The old sinful pattern must be broken and replaced by the new godly one. Successful, happy marriages can be achieved by the earnest, sincere, and godly pursuit of the opposite sex.[34]

There is hope for the homosexual. That hope, then, lies in the following.

1. Christian conversion

---

33. Cf. suggestions about Data Gathering. Here an extensive approach to discover problem spots, followed by intensive consideration of each, is the usual order.

34. Before entering into marriage, the former homosexual should tell his intended wife of his past which has been cleansed by Christ, but which, if others raised the issue in the future, could cause untold pain and agony after marriage. Moreover, concern that may develop out of fear that one cannot consummate his marriage or satisfy his mate may need to be met. An understanding spouse who is willing to help her husband can be of great comfort and assistance in enabling him to make the transition. He also must learn a wholly new orientation toward sex in which self-gratification (evidenced by the astounding amount of self-pity among homosexuals) must be replaced by the gratification of his spouse. The new orientation will grow from the discussion of I Corinthians 7:3-5, in which one's sexuality is shown to exist *not for himself* (or herself), but *for his* (her) *spouse*. The life of desire must be put off for the life of love in sex. He must learn to seek to bring sexual satisfaction to his wife rather than to himself. If he endeavors earnestly to do so by the power of the Spirit, soon he will discover that it is true also that "it is more blessed to give than to receive."

2. An acknowledgment and confession of the sin of homosexuality leading to forgiveness
3. Fruits appropriate to repentance, such as
   a. Abandonment of homosexual practices and associates (I Corinthians 15:33)
   b. Rescheduling of activities, etc.
   c. Restructuring of the whole life according to biblical principles by the power of Christ's Spirit
   d. Less emphasis upon sexual experiences[35]
4. Unless God gives the gift of continence, seeking to learn and manifest a life of love by giving oneself to his spouse within the bounds of heterosexual marriage.

---

35. For many homosexuals, sex has become the idolatrous pursuit of life. Its life-dominating influence violates the Christian resolve: "I will not be mastered by anything" (I Corinthians 6:12). Therefore, behavior therapist Alan Goldstein of Temple University, who purports to transform homosexuals into heterosexuals by teaching them how to woo, win, and seduce a woman (not to mention the sin of fornication, which he encourages), has failed to deemphasize sex as the dominant factor. In fact, his "solution" to the problem only reemphasizes it (in a different direction). He has erected a new god for his counselee to worship. The lack of concern about value in his system is clear when he says: "We merely help our people go in the direction they want to go." This means that if a homosexual wants to continue in his homosexual sin, Goldstein will "help him to become a better homosexual," the Evening Bulletin, December 16, 1972. In effect, Goldstein says he will help one become a better sinner, regardless of how he prefers to sin.

Chapter Thirty-six

HELPING THOSE WHO FEAR

Love and Fear

Love looks for opportunities to give; it asks: "What can I do for another?" Fear keeps a wary eye on the possible consequences and asks: "What will he do to me?" Love "thinks no evil"; fear thinks of little else. Love labors doing today's tasks and is so busy that it has no time to worry about tomorrow. Because it focuses upon tomorrow, fear fails to undertake responsibilities today. Love leads to greater love—fulfilling one's obligations brings joy and peace and satisfaction and greater love and devotion to the work. Fear, in turn, occasions greater fear, since failure to assume responsibilities brings additional fear of the consequences of acting irresponsibly.

"What a strange way to begin a discussion of fear," you might think. "Why contrast *love* and fear as you have? Why not fear and peace, or fear and security, or fear and serenity?"[1] The answer to that question

---

1. Love and fear are multidimensional. The fuller and richer that a word is, the more *sides* it has. Love (or fear) are large parts of life. They, therefore, do not look like this:

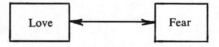

Rather, being many-sided, they bear more relationships than one, and might look more like this:

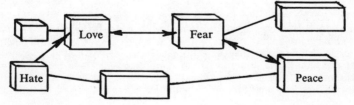

is found in I John 4:17, 18, where John himself sets fear and love over against each other as mutually exclusive. While John specifically is concerned about the fear of the judgment to come and shows how assured love from God and for God erases all such fear, his words also demand broader application. John seems to be applying a general principle ("perfect love casts out fear") to a specific case (the fear of judgment). This is apparent, since he analyzes the nature of fear and its effects *in general* "fear (not the fear of judgment in particular) involves punishment."

The wall plaque correctly reads, "The fear of God is the one fear that removes all others."[2] The enemy of fear is love; the way to put off fear, then, is to put on love. Counselors who recognize this basic fact are on their way toward reaching the biblical solution to many problems connected with fear, including what have been called the phobias.

In what ways are love and fear mutually opposed? Notice this:

Love is self-giving; fear is self-protecting.[3]

Love moves toward others; fear shrinks away from them. But the counselor must remember (and persuade the counselee that) love is the stronger since it is able to "cast out" fear. In dealing with fear, nothing else possesses the same expulsive power.

Although under other circumstances she might be frightened by a

---

2. The expression "the fear of God" originally had reference to an awesome respect growing out of the greatness and power of God; it meant being afraid of what He can do to you. In time it came to mean something like "the life of the faithful" or "the true faith" or "faith in the true God" (cf. Nehemiah 1:11, to "delight to fear"). Yet it seems never to have lost completely the notion of awe and respect for One who has power to judge and punish. According to Psalm 112:1, 7, 8, the man who fears the Lord (note: the parallel in the other half of the verse calls him a Bible believer: "who greatly delights in His commandments"), "will not fear evil tidings," his heart will be "steadfast" and will be "upheld" so that "he will not fear." In all three verses the same Hebrew word is used, (*yare*). Cf. also Isaiah 8:11-13 (in I Peter 3:14, the words "do not fear their fear," are interpreted to mean, do not fear their *intimidation*).

3. Fear began in the Garden (Genesis 3:10). It led to running and hiding from God (Genesis 3:8-10, this is the first occurrence of the word fear). Adam and Eve tried to cover up their sin. In brief, this is the paradigm of the fear that results from sin. It is not difficult to see how love brings about the opposite:

Fear ⟶ moving away from (problems, persons), hiding and covering up, self-protection

Love ⟶ moving toward (problems, persons), revelation and openness, vulnerability (cf. I Corinthians 13).

mouse, a mother is not immobilized by the fear of a wild animal attacking the child that she loves. Foolishly or otherwise, her love overcomes fear and casts it out as she throws herself into the fray. Love thus demonstrates itself as greater. A man with a phobia for crossing bridges, upon hearing of an automobile accident involving his children drove heedlessly over two bridges to reach them, experiencing no fear whatever in the process. A few days before he had refused to cross those very same bridges.

According to I John 5:19, that which enables Christians to love is God's prior love to them. Through loving fellowship with God, this responding love matures (is "perfected"). That one is fearful is indicative of the fact that his love is yet imperfect (vs. 18b). Growth in love produces a boldness (vs. 17—"confidence") in approaching the Father. Conversely, the more that one walks with Him, the less fear and the more confidence he has in coming before Him, both in the judgment to come and *now* (cf. I John 5:14).

Fear and love vary inversely. The more fear, the less love; the more love, the less fear. They tend to seesaw. But the encouraging fact for all counseling is that love is the heavier.

It is interesting to notice that in the Scriptures Jesus never is said to be afraid.[4] The obvious reason for this was that His love was perfect.

Fear and Punishment

John notes that fear "involves punishment." John's discussion of fear provides for the Christian counselor a certain answer to Skinner when he attempts to distinguish between punishment and aversive reinforcement. Skinner makes a euphemistic distinction without a difference. Skinner wishes to distinguish between punishment and aversive controls. But aversive control is what one fears. John says, "Fear *involves* punishment." Skinner is wrong.

Punishment in fear is seen perhaps most clearly in the fear of death.

---

4. Fear, per se, is not wrong. God implanted all emotions in man. Even that which lies behind the phrase "the fear of God" indicates how proper fear can be when rightly aroused and directed in the proper contexts. Fear of dangers (e.g., falling over the cliff) that leads one to take necessary precautions is right and holy so long as it rests upon and grows out of a faith and trust in the providence of God. In this sense Jesus undoubtedly entertained the sort of precautionary concern that is necessary for righteous living.

It is the "sting" in death (I Corinthians 15:55-57[5]). According to Hebrews 2:14-15, unsaved men are "held in bondage" (the element of punishment is plain) to such fear all their life long. Only Christ, by His love, can release His people from this bondage (cf. also Romans 8:15). In Him, love overcomes fear. Evangelism in counseling is the basic act of love necessary to overcome the greatest fear, the fear of death. Those who through His first love have come to love Him have no need to fear Him; they are able to "assure their hearts" before Him in confidence as they think of the Day of Judgment. Love removes the stinger from death. Matured love thus enables the Christian to look forward to death (or Christ's return) with joy and expectation (cf. Philippians 1:20; II Timothy 4:7, 8; II Thessalonians 1:10, 12; I Peter 4:13). The man who can do that is well on his way toward the elimination of other fears. Through such faith Christians have fearlessly faced lions, the stake, and every manner of hardship and deprivation (Hebrews 11).

The Christian has not received the "spirit of slavery leading to fear again" (Romans 8:15).[6] He no longer needs to be "terrified" over facing God (Hebrews 10:31). Therefore, three times Christ commands him "do not fear" (Matthew 10:26, 28, 31). Such fear is sin. This same emphasis appears frequently in the Scriptures. Hebrews 13:6, quoting Psalm 118:6, epitomizes all that is said elsewhere:

> . . . we confidently say, "The Lord is my Helper, I will not be afraid. What shall man do to me?"[7]

Eliminating Fear by Love

In the passages that have been quoted, fear seems to stem from fear of what either God or man may do. The summary of the law should be of great interest since, in contrast, it consists of *love* toward God and man. Love toward God means focusing upon how one may trust, worship, and serve Him; love toward one's neighbor likewise focuses upon a giving relationship to him.

In the light of the above, Christian counselors must determine the *source* of fear and meet it by a proper call to repentance and love. Is the fear basically a fear of God or of man? If the counselee fears God,

---

5. Cf. *The Big Umbrella*, pp. 63 ff., for a discussion of the passage.
6. Other significant passages relating to fear and the Spirit are Haggai 2:5 and II Timothy 1:7.
7. Cf. also Proverbs 29:25.

his relationship to God must be explored. The counselor should consider these questions: Does the counselee genuinely believe? Does he understand the biblical teaching about assurance and peace? Is there sin in his life disrupting his relationship to God and chilling his ardor for Him? (Cf. Deuteronomy 28:65-67 for a sober description of the dread and fear that God may send as the consequence of sin.) Repentance and renewed loving service for God is in order.

If the counselee's fear fundamentally is a fear of men, then the answer lies in encouraging him to engage in loving ministry, in which he may give of himself to others. Granted, more may be involved, but ultimately, fear will vanish only when he has learned to live the life of loving concern for his neighbor.

If, like Brad, a counselee expresses a fear of meeting people, the counselor may help him to discover and use his gift in ministering contexts. Brad overcame his problem by using his piano playing ability in youth meetings and in a coffee house. However, the counselor must guard against advising ministry *in order to rid one of fear*. With John, he must see fear as an index of a lack of love (in this case a loving exercise of one's gifts toward others. The piano had previously been used selfishly) and must call the counselee to repentance over this matter. He must be helped to see the need to minister to his neighbor; he must not minister merely in order to meet his own lack. As always in Christian service, he will *find* his life in *losing* it. His fears of men will diminish as his loving service to them increases. It is more blessed to give than to receive. Personal blessing comes not by seeking blessing, however, but by becoming a blessing to others.

Fear of Consequences

"The wicked flee when no man is pursuing" (Proverbs 28:1; cf. also Leviticus 26:36). This statement forms the basis for a great number of problems relating to fear. It shows clearly how a guilty conscience can cause great emotional distress, and even bizarre behavior. Some persons who have been tagged with that omnidirectional label, "schizophrenia," are afflicted with nothing more than a bad case of fear stemming from a guilty conscience. This fear over the consequences of guilt can so color one's way of thinking and living that (in time) he may even develop a fantasy world that in some ways is quite far removed from reality. If, like Rick, a counselee tells a far-fetched story of government narcotic agents following him day and night, of his phone tapped and his room bugged, the counselor need not merely write off the whole story as fantastic and label the counselee as a paranoid. Instead, by careful questioning, working on the assumption that some persons who have learned to walk through life looking over one shoulder do so because of a guilty past, the counselor might (as in Rick's case) discover that at one time he was involved in the sale and use of narcotics. The world of suspicion in which he lived and moved during those days, leading a double life, always fearing detection and its consequences, continued on even after he had abandoned the former practices. The wary life of fear had become a way of life for him. *Real* occasions for fear in the past leading to a way of living and interpreting reality, had so molded him that he interpreted his new situation in terms of old categories. Again, a new life, based upon forgiveness, leading to love and loving service in which he began to experience opposite responses from those around him, was the basic answer to Rick's need.

Fears should not quickly be labeled unrealistic. Janet complained that God was going to kill her. Her pastor treated her as if she had no basis for such a fear. However, when a nouthetic counselor dealt with her, he took her fears quite seriously ("You must have done some pretty serious things to think that!"). To such an approach she revealed that she had borne two illegitimate children and was framing a man with whom she was now having sinful relations into marrying her by saying (a lie) that the second child was his. Christian counselors know that a man who flees when no one pursues is "wicked."

Phobias

All of which leads to a discussion of the thorny problem of what have been called phobias (from the Greek word *phobos*, "fear"). The problem is thorny because, to the best of the writer's knowledge, the Bible never speaks of such occasions for fear as a separate category. The solution to the problem, therefore, seems to lie (as in the case of "schizophrenia") in considering phobias not as a distinct category, but merely as a catch-all term that describes a group of fears that can be traced to many cause-and-effect situations with quite distinct etiologies. Counseling experience seems to verify this hunch.

For instance, doubtless there are people who use fear manipulatively. They claim to be afraid of mice or cats or worms and put on quite a demonstration whenever confronted with such creatures. In some cases there may have been a rationale for the fear (e.g., a frightening experience in the past involving the specified animal). But in others, those who talk too much about the problem or who avoid going to certain places because of the presence of the offending creatures, by their words and actions demonstrate to a careful observer that the little mouse, cat, or worm has become a convenient foil against which they can gain attention and/or sympathy. They also may use such "fears" to punish others or to get their own ways. Such persons often have a repertoire of such foils (which can range from foods to certain situations or activities, etc.) that they may use as a backdrop against which they act out their little plays for various audiences. In time, like all good actors, they may learn to *feel* the part that they play and thus actually experience real fear of the object (rarely ever out of control for these persons).

Other phobias are occasioned by faulty associative links. Paul became fearful of crossing bridges as the result of a terrifying experience while crossing a bridge, that was caused by significant sleep loss. Loss of two or more days of R.E.M. (rapid eye movement) sleep can lead to any or every effect of L.S.D. by its effects upon bodily chemistry. While on a bridge, he took a "trip" occasioned by sleep loss. Knowing nothing of this bodily dynamic, he (wrongly) associated the frightening experience with the bridge that he happened to be crossing. On approaching bridges afterward, he became agitated and uncontrollably fearful. The latter problem was not the result of sleep loss, but rather stemmed from fear of the previous experience. He had associated the experience with bridges, and in his anxiety over whether it would occur again while crossing the bridge, he had emotionally spiraled himself into a panic. Thus, this derivative experience was added to the problem of bridge crossing, which he came to fear and all the more associate with bridge crossing, *ad infinitum*. Thereafter, even the thought of crossing a bridge brought on a sense of apprehension. This man eventually reached a point where fear arose by crossing his bridges before coming to them.

What did this counselee need to do? He needed to recognize certain facts and act in a Christian manner in accordance with them.

1. His fear was real.

2. His fear was wrong and sinful. This wrong way of handling life had caused undue self-preoccupation, had curtailed his mobility and

usefulness, and was in many other ways a hindrance to godly, responsible, Christian living. It had to go.

3. His fear was not a fear of bridges; it was a fear that *had become associated with bridges*. This distinction is vital, and coming to recognize it often helps the counselee to overcome many such fears.

4. What he fears is the *experiences* that he has had on bridges.

5. Bridges do not produce these experiences; *he himself* does. He *literally* has *had* them; he *produces* them. That means he can stop *having* them; he can stop *producing* them. There are no strange outside forces in control of him.

6. What he fears *now* is fear.

7. What he fears is normal physical anticipation feelings of crossing bridges (associated with past fear experiences). These are feared rather than understood and used for what they are—the power to prepare him for courageous action in the face of possible danger. Fear of these anticipation feelings triggers more fear, which in turn produces more physical feelings that (wrongly understood as "*it* comes over me"[8]) he fears and thus triggers more . . . and so on into a state of panic.

Consider the following comments on the similar well-known problem of stage fright.

Tension and Fear (Stage Fright)

Tension is often the key problem that a beginning speaker must overcome. Sometimes he speaks of butterflies in the stomach, stage fright, or clammy hands. But nervousness, as someone has said, is the penalty that we pay for being race horses rather than cows. Tension is a normal anticipation reaction before a long-awaited trip, a sports event, and a test. Some have called such excitement the original emotion.[9] Tension has been noted in a child as early as the second week. It would seem that it cannot be avoided. Four thousand combat airmen in World War II were quizzed about their feelings prior to a flight. The result of that study showed symptoms that are strikingly similar to those commonly reported during stage fright. In the order of their frequency, here are the top six: (1) a pounding heart; (2) muscular tension; (3) easily irritated, angry, or sore; (4) dryness of mouth; (5) perspiration; (6) butterflies in stomach.

What actually happens in stage fright? A normal bodily state of an-

8. Note the victim motif that must be shattered.
9. Floyd L. Ruch, *Psychology and Life* (Scott, Foresman and Co., 1948), p. 411.

ticipation or tension may be all that is necessary to start a vicious circle that will make one incapable of speaking well. The normal bodily state of anticipation arouses feelings in the body that may be misunderstood and thereby cause fear, which, in turn, causes the body to grow more tense, which creates more pronounced feelings, which again may be misinterpreted and bring about more fear, ad infinitum. In tension situations, the body, by psychological impetus, prepares itself for an emergency. Wise speakers know this and they know also that it is good and necessary for the body to be so prepared for speaking. They know that good speaking is dependent upon bodily alertness, so they harness the tension for service. Tension often helps ideas to jell during delivery. The best sermons are those in which the jelling factor is prominent. If they jell earlier in the study, they may lose some of the fire that they might otherwise have at the moment of delivery.

In an emotionally tense anticipation situation, the mind reflecting on the task ahead telegraphs the various parts of the body to prepare to the fullest, and the body mobilizes its resources. That is what the speaker needs: a body fully prepared. In relaxed situations the sympathetic system operates. Its function is to build up and conserve bodily supplies. But, when the parasympathetic system is called into service, the breathing rate, the heartbeat, circulation, and other physiological functions respond appropriately. The adrenal glands (adrenal means on top of the kidneys) secrete adrenalin hormone into the blood. This hormone circulates throughout the body and affects many organs. People in stress have found themselves capable of performing tasks that they are unable to do normally. Adrenalin is a kind of a supercharger that soups up the body for action. For example, a man carried a safe across the room and threw it out of the window during a fire. After the fire was over, he was asked how he did this and attempted a repeat performance. He found that in a normal state of tension he could hardly budge the safe.[10] When adrenalin reaches the liver, it helps release sugar into the blood to make more energy available for the brain and the muscles. It also speeds the heartbeat so that the blood can carry on its functions more rapidly. It converts sugar resources into sugar to be utilized more rapidly by the skeletal muscles. As the body diverts blood from the digestive system to exterior muscles, the peristaltic movements of the stomach and intestines (those warm, comfortable ripples that move our food along during the more relaxed state of the body) stop and thereby cause the butterfly feeling. The mouth may dry up, the hair may stand on end, and the hands may feel clammy.

---

10. Ruch, *op. cit.*, p. 166.

Tension cannot be avoided, need not be feared, but must be understood. Tension is bodily preparation, the way God has made us to enable us to meet emergencies and difficult situations. Tension makes us alert. Speakers should not seek the reduction of tension, but only of the kind of excessive tension that spirals out of control because of fear. Fear can usually be avoided by understanding the beneficial function of tension and thus brought under control of content. This means that tension, to be used properly by a speaker, must be controlled so that it varies with the variety of subject matter. Content controls the amount of tension and makes it appropriate to itself at each point. Tension problems, then, are fundamentally a matter of degree.

Tension: A Matter of Degree

So long as tension is the speaker's servant, tension is good. In order to preach well or speak well in any circumstance one must be alert, not overly relaxed, not overly tense. A certain amount of normal tension is necessary for this alertness. Normal keying up is good because it helps, but whatever hinders is abnormal and must be dealt with. Understanding is the first of several factors that may be brought into play. The first step in learning to use tension as a servant is coming to understand its purpose and its function. That's why we have been taking the time to explain the psychosomatic effects of anticipation. When lack of understanding is the source of the problem, the fear of the unknown and the resulting undisciplined tension will disappear. When a speaker feels the butterflies in his stomach, feels his muscles tense, and has a feeling of apprehension, and understands why, he will not fear these normal feelings and thus escalate tension to an abnormal level.

But after a speaker acquires a thorough understanding of the normal bodily sensations, if stage fright persists, there may be another problem. His difficulty may stem from pride or possibly from cowardice and guilt. Possibly he is afraid of the audience's response. Fear of this sort boils down ultimately to undue personal self-concern. Assuming that his preparation is adequate, that he has spoken frequently enough to become acquainted with the speaking situation, and that he understands the dynamics of normal keying up or tension, if stage fright still persists, the speaker must plainly ask himself: "Am I afraid of my audience?" He may be concerned about his appearance. A speaker's appearance becomes an object of scrutiny, and perhaps he is concerned about audience response to it. Or, more likely, he may be concerned about audience response to his performance. Or, he may be concerned about audience response to his ideas, particularly about the response of those who disagree with him. He may fear the subsequent consequences of what he has to say. Or he may feel guilty for having failed to say what he knows God wants him to say. In that case, his anticipation is about committing the sin of cowardice. Each of these possibilities notes that a shift has occurred in the speaker's thinking. Instead of thinking of the welfare of the audience, rather than thinking about being faithful to God, he has started to think about himself. The subject matter that he wishes his audience to believe has become secondary to self concern. When a speaker begins to think, "How do I look? How am I speaking? How am I going across?" he has opened the door to the possibility of a bad case of stage fright. There is only one cure for this malady—straightening out these matters with God before preaching. The speaking situation must be put into the hands of God so that when actually preaching the speaker is lost in his subject and his concern for the audience. If one is rightly concentrating on the subject matter, he has no time to think about himself. Such thought is diversionary, it hinders concentration on the subject matter and it, therefore, hurts good speaking.[11]

8. Nothing mysterious has been happening; nothing out of God's control; nothing that by His grace cannot be overcome fully.

9. Normal anxiety is good and needs to be understood and used rather than feared or removed. This God has provided to enable men to live responsibly. It is only *the fear spiral*—and at its end the debilitating panic—that is wrong and must be overcome. Indeed, it is through this normal anxiety preparation that God will give courage to face and conquer the problem.

10. Courage growing out of faith (trust) in God will be required. Christians have faced lions. He can face the fear experience.

11. In Paul's case, the facts about his sleep loss and its effects were uncovered and explained. He came to see how this was falsely associated with crossing bridges.[12] Armed with these facts, in faith he prayerfully crossed a bridge. He was anxious but did not panic. This initial experience helped him. He recrossed it with even better results. Then, again and again and again he went over the bridge until the problem was solved.

Such fears often begin at times when one is in poor physical condition. In times of sickness, grief, depression, sleep loss, etc., such

---

11. *Pulpit Speech*, pp. 154-157.
12. It is not necessary or possible always to discover the original cause. Simply separating the fear of the *experience* from the fear of the *object* is sufficient.

patterns may tend to develop. A fearful experience ensues. The mind fixes on something (or someone nearby) and associates the two. On the next similar occasion, fear of a repetition of the fearful experience triggers it. Thus, the fear becomes a self-fulfilling prophecy. The pattern has begun.

Christians, out of love for God and in trusting obedience to His Word[13] can overcome these problems by

1. prayer and repentance;
2. separating the fear experience from the fear object;
3. understanding the spiral;
4. Christian courage in grappling with the problem.

Point four perhaps needs some further comment. If Paul had not *actually crossed* the bridge (grappled with his problem) he would not have overcome it. The faith and knowledge must lead to action. The formula, then, for dealing with this type of phobia is quite simple. It boils down simply to this: *trust and obey*. Love for God in faith answers "yes" to the Scriptures that say, "If you love me, keep my commandments."

Distinguishing Objects of Fear

Another way for counselors to look at fear is to distinguish whether its object is proper or improper. Does the fear stem from a truly fearful object that it is biblically legitimate to fear (e.g., a tiger), or was it generated from within in the presence of an object that it is not biblically legitimate to fear (e.g., a congregation feared by a preacher *because he is not adequately prepared to preach*. Take another similar example: Sally fears Martha. Why? Because of guilt. She does not wish to see her, talk to her, or be in her presence because she has wronged her. It may be legitimate to fear a tiger and hide and run under the proper circumstances. There is good reason to fear Martha, but neither running nor hiding from her is Christian. The proper action in this instance is the confession of sin and reconciliation. Avoidance only multiplies and enlarges the sin)?

Sleep loss may stem from fear (cf. Psalm 3:5-6) or, as we have seen,

---

13. Cf. such wonderful verses as Psalm 34:4 (Berkeley): "The Lord . . . freed me from all my fears."

fear may stem from sleep loss. As in other habits, once the pattern has been learned, fear no longer is triggered consciously. It just *comes*. Therefore, some fears may seem strange, unfounded, or generalized. This is because the associative bond has become obscure.

To *break* the pattern, it is helpful to distinguish and discover *what* one is afraid of. Is the fear occasioned by (1) an object legitimately fearful; (2) the experience of fear erroneously associated with what should be a non-fearful object; (3) the presence of certain persons, places, or things that remind the counselee of possible fearful consequences of his sin; (4) a way of life developed under truly fearful conditions that has persisted although these conditions no longer do; or (5) a way of responding originally as a manipulative act that, now, has become a reality?

Whatever the cause, the Christian counselor, armed with the Word of God from which he can present the love of God in Christ, has the ultimate answer to fear both in this life and in the life to come.

Chapter Thirty-seven

COUNSELING THOSE WHO FEAR THAT THEY HAVE COMMITTED THE UNPARDONABLE SIN

From time to time Christian counselors are called upon to help persons who are deeply distressed because they think that they have (or may have) committed the unpardonable sin. How does the counselor deal with such persons?

What Is This Sin?

First, the counselor must know specifically *what* the unpardonable sin is. The passages referring to this sin occur in Mark 3:29, 30 and Matthew 12:31, 32, where it is described as attributing the work of the Holy Spirit to the devil. It is clearly identified in the context by the following facts: (1) the unpardonable sin is a sin against the Holy Spirit; (2) it is blasphemy against the Spirit; and, most specifically, (3) it consists of calling the *Holy* Spirit an "*unclean* spirit" by (4) attributing His work to Beelzebub.

What Can Be Done?

Armed with this understanding of the passage, the counselor may begin by asking the counselee to describe the sin that he has committed. When he does so (or as he is helped to do so by careful questioning), the counselor will be able to ascertain precisely what the counselee's (faulty[1]) understanding of this sin may be. Having come to an understanding of the sin that *has* been committed (adultery, homosexuality, incest, etc., frequently are considered by some persons to be unpardonable; others who fear this fate may do so because of obsessive thinking[2]), the counselor now is in a position to do two things. Both are vital.

---

1. Clearly so; persons who commit the unpardonable sin, like the Pharisees, are hardened against God so that neither are they concerned about having committed the sin, nor do they seek out counselors for help about the matter.

2. Cf. A. Alexander, *Thoughts on Religious Experience* (London: Banner of Truth, 1971), pp. 150 ff.

First, he can explain the true nature of the unpardonable sin as it is set forth in its context: hardened religious leaders declared that Jesus performed His miraculous works not by the power of the *Holy* Spirit, but rather by the power of Beelzebub, an *unclean* spirit, thus attributing the work of the Spirit of *holiness* to the devil. This biblical picture may be compared and contrasted to the sin of the concerned (not hardened) counselee.

However, *it is altogether essential* that *at the same time* the counselor in no way minimize the guilt and the heinous character of the sin that was committed by the counselee. He may even want to say to him: "I can understand how you came to believe that you had committed the sin against the Holy Spirit, since what you have done is very serious." In distinguishing between the unpardonable sin and other sins, there is hope; in minimizing the guilt there is no hope. The failure to do the latter while emphasizing the former accounts for much of the failure in handling such persons. The counselor should switch quickly to the sin (or sins) actually committed, note their tragic effects upon all parties involved, and call the counselee to repentance, faith, and the need to put on a new manner of life. Rather than focus upon the unpardonable sin, the counselor should turn to the pardonable ones!

Reassurance is not the answer at this point. The counselor may go even further. In addition to what was suggested above, he may press the point: "I can recognize how you might well think that you had committed the sin against the Holy Spirit after hearing of what you have done, and I certainly cannot offer any comfort or peace to you until you have confessed, repented, and done all that you can to rectify the wrongs that you have done. A person with your guilt may have little reason to believe that he is saved until he has dealt with his sin. Your hope lies in the goodness of God, who has caused you to become concerned over your sin. Conviction of sin, you may be thankful to learn, is the work of God the Spirit (John 16:8), who is at work in your life since he has convicted you of sinning. He has not left you. That same God graciously said (when commenting about the blasphemy against the Holy Spirit): '*Every kind of sin* and blasphemy shall be forgiven to men, except the blasphemy against the Holy Spirit.' That promise includes the heinous sin that you have committed. Our Savior is great enough to forgive even *that*."

As in the case of other problems, like the loss of assurance, one must focus upon the sins that he has committed, rather than upon the lack of assurance or the fear that he has sinned unpardonably. Otherwise the devil may cleverly occupy the counselee's mind with the theological problem, while his sins remain unconfessed. Repentance and its fruits, rather than theological argumentation, is the path down which the counselor must lead the counselee. He may need to say words to this effect: "I know you do not interpret the passage as I do, but let us assume for awhile that I am correct and that you are wrong. On my interpretation, the solution to your problem lies in cleaning up your life before God and others. Let's work on that and then see if the problem of your lack of assurance persists."[3]

More could be said, but fundamentally the method for handling the problem of fear of having committed the unpardonable sin is easily explained. The persistence with which one may stubbornly refuse to hear cogent exegesis and sober theological argumentation is not easily handled. Prayerful counter persistence on the part of the counselor is required. He must insist strongly upon understanding fully what the sins of the counselee are and then upon forgiveness and taking biblical courses of action in conjunction with each.

Confidence in his own exegetical stance on the part of the counselor often constitutes the most potent factor of all. By this he often raises the minimal amount of hope that can become the hole in the dike.

Finally, it is important to note that sometimes counselees pretend to be concerned about this matter when it is the furthest fear from their minds. The supposed fear can mask other problems and be used to erect strong walls between the counselee's real problem and the counselor. By not allowing himself to be diverted into long theological or exegetical discussions (after having stated his biblical position clearly and firmly), the counselor who moves on to the actual sin in the counselee's life will find himself on the right track. The counselee, realizing that his diversionary strategy has failed, may then (and only then) be willing to come to terms with the real problems in his life.

---

3. Assurance of salvation is a crucial factor in productive Christian living. It is the rule, not the exception. It is essential to the discovery, development, and fruitful use of one's gifts. It is basic to the development of proper habit patterns. Apart from assurance, destructive, introspective patterns may develop. These patterns may inhibit ministry and evangelism by idolatrously fixating one's concerns upon himself.

Chapter Thirty-eight

CONCLUSION

No one could recognize more fully than this writer how incomplete and inadequate this book is. Nevertheless, it is a beginning. It is my hope, however, that in subsequent volumes and revisions of this work the pastor and other Christian counselors will find help of a sort that up until now has been virtually unavailable.

I also recognize that no one can become an adequate counselor by reading books. But books, aimed at practicality in Christian counseling, are an advance over merely theoretical discussions. At the Christian Counseling Center in Hatboro, Pennsylvania, and through Westminster Theological Seminary in Philadelphia, additional training in actual counseling sessions is available.

May the gracious God whom we serve so use this book that many counselors, encouraged to try, will become a blessing to the wounded, bleeding Church of Jesus Christ.

APPENDICES

Appendix A

PERSONAL DATA INVENTORY

IDENTIFICATION DATA:

Name .... Phone ....

Address ....

Occupation ....

Business Phone ....

Sex .... Birth Date .... Age .... Height ....

Marital Status: Single .... Going Steady .... Married .... Separated........

Divorced .... Widowed ....

Education (last year completed): .... (grade) Other training (list type and

years ....

Referred here by .... Address ....

HEALTH INFORMATION:

Rate your health (check): Very Good.... Good.... Average.... Declining.... Other....

Your approximate weight .... lbs. Weight changes recently:

    Lost .... Gained ....

List all important present or past illnesses or injuries or handicaps:

....

Date of last medical examination .... Report: ....

....

Your physician .... Address ....

Are you presently taking medication? Yes.... No.... What ....

Have you used drugs for other than medical purposes? Yes.... No....

What? ....

Have you ever had a severe emotional upset? Yes No.... Explain ....

....

Have you ever been arrested? Yes .... No ....

Are you willing to sign a release of information form so that your counselor may

write for social, psychiatric, or medical reports? Yes.... No....

Have you recently suffered the loss of someone who was close to you? Yes.... No....

Explain: ....

Have you recently suffered loss from serious social, business, or other reversals?
Yes.... No.... Explain: ....
....

RELIGIOUS BACKGROUND:

Denominational preference: .... Member ....
Church Attendance per month (circle): O 1 2 3 4 5 6 7 8 9 10+
Church attended in childhood .... Baptized? Yes.... No....
Religious background of spouse (if married) ....
Do you consider yourself a religious person? Yes.... No.... Uncertain....
Do you believe in God? Yes.... No.... Uncertain....
Do you pray to God? Never.... Occasionally.... Often....
Are you saved? Yes.... No.... Not sure what you mean....
How much do you read the Bible? Never.... Occasionally.... Often....
Do you have regular family devotions? Yes.... No....
Explain recent changes in your religious life, if any ....
....

PERSONALITY INFORMATION:

Have you ever had any psychotherapy or counseling before? Yes.... No....
If yes, list counselor or therapist and dates: ....
....
....
What was the outcome? ....
Circle any of the following words which best describe you now: active   ambitious
self-confident   persistent   nervous   hardworking   impatient   impulsive   moody
often-blue   excitable   imaginative   calm   serious   easy-going   shy   good-natured
introvert   extrovert   likeable   leader   quiet   hard-boiled   submissive   lonely
self-conscious   sensitive   other ....
Have you ever felt people were watching you? Yes.... No....
Do people's faces ever seem distorted? Yes.... No....
Do you ever have difficulty distinguishing faces? Yes.... No....
Do colors ever seem too bright? .... To dull? ....
Are you sometimes unable to judge distance? Yes.... No....
Have you ever had hallucinations? Yes.... No....
Are you afraid of being in a car? Yes.... No....
Is your hearing exceptionally good? Yes.... No....
Do you have problems sleeping? Yes.... No....

MARRIAGE AND FAMILY INFORMATION:

Name of spouse .... Address ....

Phone .... Occupation .... Business phone ....

Your spouse's age .... Education (in years) .... Religion ....

Is spouse willing to come for counseling? Yes.... No.... Uncertain....

Have you ever been separated? Yes.... No.... When? from .... to ....

Has either of you ever filed for divorce? Yes.... No.... When? ....

Date of Marriage .... Your ages when married: Husband .... Wife........

How long did you know your spouse before marriage? ....

Length of steady dating with spouse .... Length of Engagement ....

Give brief information about any previous marriages: ....

....

Information about children:

PM*	Name	Age	Sex	Living Yes No	Education in years	Marital status

*Check this column if child is by previous marriage

If you were reared by anyone other than your own parents, briefly explain:

....

How many older brothers .... sisters .... do you have?

How many younger brothers .... sisters .... do you have?

BRIEFLY ANSWER THE FOLLOWING QUESTIONS:

1. What is your problem?
2. What have you done about it?
3. What can we do? (What are your expectations in coming here?)
4. As you see yourself, what kind of person are you? Describe yourself.
5. What, if anything, do you fear?
6. Is there any other information we should know?

Appendix B

COUNSELOR'S CHECK LIST

1. Determine whether evangelism is indicated.
2. Sort out responsibilities.
3. Gather concrete data.
4. Stress *what* rather than *why* for data.
5. Distinguish presentation, performance, and preconditioning problems.
6. Talk not only about problems; talk also about God's solutions.
7. Check motivation (ultimately it must be *loving obedience*: because God says so).
8. Insist on obedience to God regardless of how one *feels*.
9. Check out Agendas.
10. Give concrete homework at every session. (Explain "how to"; begin with single-stranded problems.)
11. Check on homework.
12. Would a medical checkup be advisable?

(Cut out or Xerox and post in counseling room,
or slip under glass on desk)

Appendix C

THE ORGANIC/NONORGANIC PROBLEM
AND COOPERATION WITH PHYSICIANS

Man is a complex whole. He cannot (in this life) be separated into his parts, except for purposes of analysis. All attempts, therefore, to divide man as body, soul, and spirit in order to allocate these several parts to the physician, to the psychologist, and to the preacher, respectively, must fail. They fail because the concept of a tripartite nature of man is not biblical (despite a superficial reading of I Thessalonians 5:23 and Hebrews 4:12). The obvious point that is made by the writer of Hebrews, for instance, is that only the Word of God is sharp enough to make the subtle distinction (not separation) between soul and spirit.[1] Yet those who facilely divide between these believe that the division is obvious and should be apparent to all. Careful exegetes understand the Bible to speak of man dichotomistically, not trichotomistically.[2]

Yet, even the twofold division of man that becomes clear in biblical comments pertaining to life in the intermediate state is not, in this life, easy to distinguish. While alive and in the body (which is man's proper state; apart from his body he is "unclothed" [II Corinthians 5:4]), he is a psychosomatic whole. Throughout the Scriptures he is treated as such.

---

1. The writer of Hebrews is stating that it is difficult to make this fine distinction. His whole argument hangs upon the extreme subtlety of the distinction. Presumably, trichotomists find the task easier, and by the way that some write, one would think that they scarcely need help from the Word of God to accomplish it. It would seem that the non-material element is called "soul" in the Scriptures when viewed *in relationship to* the body; it is called "spirit" when viewed as separated from the body.

2. Cf. Leon Morris, *I Thessalonians, The New International Commentary on the New Testament* (Grand Rapids: Wm. Eerdmans, 1959), p. 181; William Hendrickson, *I Thessalonians, New Testament Commentary* (Grand Rapids: Baker Book House, 1955), pp. 141-150. In such passages as Romans 8:10; I Corinthians 5:5; II Corinthians 7:1, and Colossians 2:5, Paul's basic dichotomistic view of man emerges.

It is no surprise, therefore, to discover that when one attempts to deal with man in ways that demand some distinction between the organic and the nonorganic, he runs into problems. These problems cannot be solved either by Skinnerian reductionism: man is only an animal (all is organic), or on the other hand by simplistic categorizattion: the nonorganic is the province of the pastor; the organic is the province of the physician.

While the latter solution is preferable to the former, and in a limited and carefully guarded fashion must become the working model for biblical counselors, they can never shirk their responsibility for dealing with ethical matters of bodily use and abuse, nor can they allow physicians unhampered freedom to advise Christians in ways that tend to ignore or exclude this dimension. James 5:14-16, for instance, puts the organized church squarely in the business of dealing with organic illness.[3]

That the body affects the soul and the soul the body in so many obvious, as well as subtle, ways is a fact that the Christian counselor must always remember. His work, therefore, constantly involves the organic

---

3. If, as James avers, sin can be a cause of bodily sickness, and confession and prayer its cure, the Christian counselor must recognize the psychosomatic dimensions of the work that he is called to perform. For further discussion of James 5:14-16, cf. *Competent to Counsel*, pp. 105-110. Under whose care is the counselee? Fundamentally, the counselee is under the overall care of the pastor and the elders of his church. This is a care that must be exercised prior to, *during*, and after the care of the attending physician. Pastoral care is *ongoing* and *total*. It is to be seen as extending over the body, not only with reference to psychosomatic illnesses, in which ulcers are caused by worry, colitis by resentment, and heart attacks by anger, but also to the general care and welfare of the body. Pastors, for instance, should (*à la* James 5:14 and I Timothy 5:23) urge medical treatment upon members as a biblical principle, condemn abuses to the body ("You shall not murder"), and work with the physician as an aid to total pastoral care. Whenever biblical pastoral care conflicts with medical practices, the pastor must urge the counselee to acknowledge the former over the latter. Pastors must not prescribe medical treatments or meddle in matters about which they know little or nothing, but they must always consider the biblical implications of medical treatment. Other examples of bodily matters that must be handled directly by Christian counselors are: direct harm or injury to the body (suicide, etc.), significant sleep loss, diet problems, cancer producing activities, drug abuse, failure to see a physician when necessary. One way of viewing the matter (although somewhat simplistic) is to say that the counselor is concerned about *what the counselee does to the body* and that the doctor is concerned about the breakdown of the body and *what the body does to itself*. (Of course, *both* are concerned about both sides of the organic problem in differing ways. At times, e.g., the physician treats the injured liver of the drunkard, while the counselor deals with the drunkenness behind the bodily injury.)

dimension. He will strive always to work from this biblical presupposition in ways that are consistent with it.[4] He should take the time and trouble, therefore, to study the fundamental functions of the human body.

Because the problem of the dividing line between problems caused by organic factors and nonorganic factors is often fuzzy, the best solution to this problem (to date) seems to be for the counselor to cultivate a close alliance with a Christian physician with whom he can work closely. Such teamwork recognizes and gives expression to man's fundamental psychosomatic unity. The following article, which appeared in the *Christian Medical Society Journal*, Fall, 1971, sets forth in outline some guides to such cooperation:

"The Christian Physician and Counseling

"Many of your patients suffer from more than medical problems, as you well know. Even if you tried to forget or ignore the fact, that guilty depressed woman or that resentful colitis patient who will appear in your office tomorrow will raise the matter afresh.[5] You *cannot* avoid the issue. The problem, of course, involves the further question: 'Should I take the time to counsel, should I refer the patient, or should I by-pass the issue of counseling by treating symptoms alone?'

"Suppose you opt for counseling; by assuming the role of a counselor immediately you will stir up several additional problems. For instance,

---

4. John was the brunt of an office prank that clearly exhibits the strong effects of thought upon body. Knowing that he always checked the thermometer, a fellow employee held a match under the thermometer immediately before John's daily routine check. Upon reading the temperature, John broke out in perspiration. Fink cites the case of psychosomatic asthmatic attacks occasioned by roses. The counselee insisted that roses organically affected him. An attack was induced by the counselor through the use of artificial roses, thought by the counselee to be real, thus demonstrating the psychosomatic nature of the ailment. David Fink, *Release From Nervous Tension* (New York: Simon and Schuster, 1943), p. 2. An interesting book dealing with psychosomatics is John Schindler, *How to Live 365 Days a Year, op. cit.* Chapter 4 is of particular interest. Because Schindler does not write from a Christian perspective, much that he writes must be rejected (e.g., weakening *sin* to *immaturity*; seeing *education and training* as the answer rather than *salvation*). Yet his comments on the relationship of emotion to body are useful.

5. "Cf. William DeLay, 'Survey Tells What Mrs. America Wants to Know,' *American Family Physician*, August, 1971, vol. 4, no. 2, p. 113: 'The type of problem most often seen among young women (20-39 years) was "emotional problems." '

you must face the issue of *time*: where, in your busy schedule, can you find the time to devote to counseling? An average routine office visit may take no longer than ten minutes, while a complete physical might take no more than forty minutes to an hour. Most effective counseling sessions take from forty to fifty minutes.

"One way to get the time is to limit the number of patients you see. But this suggestion will hardly be found acceptable because of the obvious financial difficulties that this may cause for either the physician or for his patients. Such a radical decision in favor of counseling may also curtail his principal activity as a physician in a day when such activities are needed so desperately.

"More likely, as a devoted Christian physician you may determine to find time for counseling by attempting to stretch your already overly expanded schedule. But this solution may cut short your social life, reduce your activities in the local church, and most of all inevitably lop off another chunk from the all too little amount of time that you have allotted to your family.

"Possibly if you already have opted to do counseling, you are dissatisfied with these solutions and find yourself vacillating between both of them. Chances are that you also have chopped counseling sessions down to what has become a frustratingly inadequate length of time. While such solutions may dissolve some problems, they tend rather to give rise to new and more serious ones. Then, too, you need to determine what sort of counseling you are going to do. Some non-Christian forms of counseling (e.g., psychoanalytic or reflective counseling) take enormous amounts of time with highly questionable results.

"Instead of undertaking counseling yourself, you largely may have opted for referral. This, of course, is the easiest solution. And yet so frequently it is no solution at all (as you know only too well). So often patients either find little or no help at all or return in worse condition. Referral raises the crucial question: *to whom?* Shall the patient be referred to a psychiatrist? So few are Christians (and of these still fewer have based their practice upon Christian presuppositions and principles). Can you, in good conscience, refer a patient to such a psychiatrist when it is his task to attempt to change behavior and attitudes through value change? If his values are not Christian or if he divorces his personal faith from the Rogerian, Skinnerian, or Freudian presuppositions and methods by which he practices psychiatry, how can you justify referral?[6]

"Of course, you might refer your patient to a Christian minister. Perhaps this is what you would prefer to do, but you dare not; you are afraid of his incompetence. Possibly if you did he might refuse to accept the referral! There are so many incompetent ministers and, in particular, ministers who are incompetent counselors. One of the reasons for this is because of their inadequate and faulty training based upon the erroneous belief that they must refer people with personal problems more serious than a psychic scratch to psychiatrists. And, the pastoral counseling most widely taught has been of an unbiblical and almost totally ineffective non-directive sort. No wonder Christian physicians hesitate to refer their patients to ministers.

"But that is a tragedy! It is time for ministers to confess and to apologize for their sin against God and their Christian brethren in the medical profession. By their incompetence, conservative clergymen (with notable exceptions) have forced physicians into the present dilemma that I have just described. Christian physician, let me say it again: the counseling dilemma is not of your own making. The Christian physician (with confidence) *ought* to be able to refer cases that demand extensive counseling to Christian ministers. But sadly, this has not been possible in our society recently. On behalf of myself and many of my brethren, let me apologize.

"However welcome a belated ministerial apology may seem, confession and forgiveness are not a solution to the problem. Happily, I can go further. Indeed the situation is changing rapidly. Over the last five years a new awareness of the minister's proper biblical role as a counselor has been developing among conservative (and in particular among reformed) ministers. Evidence of this may be seen in the response of ministers who have been trained in courses at Westminster Theological Seminary and at the Christian Counseling and Educational Foundation to the biblical approach to counseling that is sometimes called *nouthetic*

---

6. "I have discussed in detail the problems of non-Christian presuppositions in my books *Competent to Counsel*, Presbyterian and Reformed Publishing Company: Nutley, N. J., 1971 and *The Big Umbrella*, Presbyterian and Reformed Publishing Company: Nutley, N. J., 1971. All that I have said in this brief article presupposes what I have said there.

confrontation.[7] There has been wide favorable response to this approach by others.[8]

"Let me partially describe this new pastoral counselor. First and foremost he will have an unshakeable confidence in the power of the Spirit working through His Word to solve the nonorganic problems of living caused by the eventual failure of sinful living patterns into which men drift. Secondly, he will use the Scriptures in counseling in a practical fashion that at the same time exalts Christ and meets human needs. He will not give out passages like prescriptions or dispense platitudes like pills. Rather, he will use (and teach his counselees to use) the Bible in a plain and practical manner that enables them to see *how* God has provided solutions to their problems. Thirdly, he will have a humble confidence, acknowledging that any benefit accruing from his counseling is ultimately attributable to the work of God and not to himself. Yet, at the same time he will strive continually to improve his knowledge and technique, recognizing that God ordinarily works through human agency. When he does not understand a problem, he will honestly admit it, but he also will search the Scriptures to discover the answers that previously eluded him. He will tackle nearly any problem that previously might have been referred to a psychiatrist, probably with a significantly higher rate of success and certainly in much shorter periods of time. He will work enthusiastically with Christian physicians and will frequently send counselees for medical checkups.

"Brethren, something has been happening, and you should be aware of the fact since you may be able to enlarge the effectiveness of your own ministry as a physician by achieving a significant alliance with a minister (or ministers) to whom you confidently can refer patients for counseling.[9]

---

7. "The names and addresses of the increasing number of ministers who have received such training are available upon request. Please write to Christian Counseling and Educational Foundation, 151 West County Line Road, Hatboro, Pennsylvania, 19040. For a physician's viewpoint on nouthetic confrontation, contact William O'Rourke, M.D., 150 West Main Street, Westminster, Maryland. Dr. O'Rourke is a member of the board of C.C.E.F., as well as a member of C.M.S.

8. "Cf. reviews of *Competent to Counsel* in *The Presbyterian Journal*, November 4, 1970, p. 19; *Christianity Today*, November 6, 1970, p. 23 and June 4, 1971, pp. 16, 17; *The Alliance Witness*, March 17, 1971, p. 14; *The Christian Reformed Outlook*, July 1971, pp. 17-19. At the time of writing this article the book is in its third edition. The book was adopted as a text in several colleges and seminaries.

9. "If your own pastor is unaware of this movement, it might be of importance

"Do not expect this new pastoral counselor to have all of the answers, anymore than you would claim answers to every organic problem, but look for a man who can do far more to help complement you in your medical ministry than many pastors whom you previously have known.[10] I encourage you to explore this possibility to the full."

---

to both of you to discuss this matter with him. For further help he may write to C.C.E.F. I have not had the time to investigate the legal ramifications of such referrals. It is possible that genuine courage may be called for in this regard.

10. Biblical aids to counseling of which you should have become aware are now available. At present three inexpensive pamphlets called *Christ and Your Problems, What to Do About Worry*, and *Godliness Through Discipline* (Presbyterian and Reformed Publishing Company) that may be used as handouts to patients are available.

Appendix D
(Sample)

WEEKLY COUNSELING RECORD

Counselor's initials

Name .... Date ....

Session No. ....   AGENDA

Evaluation of Last Week's Homework

Drift of the Session

Appendix E

FINANCIAL PROFILE

Salary (take home pay) per month ....

Additional Income per month ....

TOTAL ....

Outstanding debts (list all debts and total)

TOTAL ....

Regular Monthly Obligations (convert all other quarterly or yearly payments to monthly figures)

Church ....

Insurance ....

Savings and Investments ....

Gas, electricity, heat ....

Telephone ....

Food and household items ....

Family recreation ....

Doctor, dentist, medicine ....

Clothing ....

Auto payments and maintenance ....

House payments (or rent) ....

Incidentals ....

Other ....

TOTAL ....

Questions to ask when preparing a Budget

Can I get along without it? (steaks, cigarettes); Do I need to use as much? (toothpaste, detergent); Can I substitute a cheaper item when quality is not essential? (waxed paper for baggies); Is there another way to do it? (sew rather than buy dresses); Can I suspend the practice for a time? (amusements, newspaper).

(On sheet provided, draw up a proposed monthly budget.)

PROPOSED BUDGET

Appendix F

On pages 16 and 17 are ten statements, some of which a Christian counselor could make; others he ought not to make. Let us look at the thinking behind the decisions concerning each.

Statement number 1: "Confess this sin to God and forsake it." If the practice (e.g., adultery, lying) is a transgression of a plain commandment of God, the counselor not only *may*, but *must*, speak with this sort of finality. There can be no suggestion of situation ethics. Statements 6 (concerning homosexuality) and 8 (concerning worry) are of the same order. Statement 10 corresponds to Luke 17:3-10 and may be made just as baldly. Biblical injunctions like 3 (regular Scripture study and prayer) must be stressed with equal firmness.

The other six statements are of a different sort. Statement number 2, "Sell your car and pay off the loan," may be offered as a piece of wise advice under certain circumstances, but must be given along with room for other possible solutions. The biblical principle to "owe no man anything" must be fulfilled, however it may be accomplished. If selling one of two cars is the *only* way to obey, then that must be done. However, there may be another way.

Statement 4 again might be offered as a good suggestion. Much may be said for morning Bible study and prayer of the length indicated. But since the Scriptures do not so clearly define the time for such activities, the statement *as it stands* should not be made. The "must" of statement 3 is biblically legitimate; the "must" of statement 4 is not.

Statement 5 is a good one. It recognizes that there may be more than one way to implement God's commandments (the words "one way . . ." substituted for "must" in statement 4 would make it acceptable) and offers a concrete suggestion for a minimal beginning.

Statement 7 may be beyond the counselor's competence to make. Although he may be of this opinion (rightly) he would do well to phrase the matter differently: "While I cannot prescribe medically, I can see no good in depending upon tranquillizers. In our counseling we will be concerned about getting you off of them." Or, perhaps, in some cases:

"I find that I am talking to a pill more than to a real person. Until you decide to get off of those tranquillizers, I am afraid that we can go no further in counseling." Or, "Shall I call your physician and tell him that we agree that you should be taken off of tranquillizers while coming for counseling?"

Statement 9 may be made as a typical homework assignment and urged upon the counselee as one plain application of the commandment to do *all* one's work in six days. Yet, if there are *other* more pressing matters to catch up on, it is possible that debate about the assignment might lead to a decision to "catch up on" those first.

**REFERENCE
SECTION**

Reference 1

Typical Counselee Remarks	*Typical Counselor Responses That May Be Used*
1. "I can't!"	1. "Do you mean can't or won't?" or, "*God* says that you *can*."
2. "I have done everything that I could."	2. "Everything? What about. . . ."
3. I've tried that but it didn't work."	3. "Did you *really* try? How many times? For how long? In what way? How consistently?" (Get the details: "precisely, what *did* you do?")
4. "I did my best."	4. "Are you sure? Tell me precisely *what* you did." or, "Remember, the *best* is what God says to do. Did you . . . ?"
5. *No one* believes me, etc."	5. "Can't you think of *one* person who does? How about some more?" or, "I believe you. . . ."
6. "I could *never* do *that*."	6. "Never is a long time. Really, how long do you suppose it might take to learn? By the way, if you think hard enough you will discover that you have learned to do a number of things that are just as hard (or harder). Take for instance. . . ."
7. "If I had the time, I'd do it."	7. "You do. We all have 24 hours each day; it all depends on how you slice the pie. Now let's work on drawing up a schedule that honors God."
8. "Don't blame me. . . ."	8. "Are you saying that you are not responsible? God says. . . ."
9. "Don't ask me. . . ."	9. "But I am asking you. Who else would know? I am sure that you know the answer. Think hard; I'll help you by asking some other related questions, and perhaps we can come up with it."
10. "I guess so."	10. "Are you really guessing or is that what you believe (think)?"
11. "You know how it is. . . ."	11. "No, I don't know; can you explain it more fully?"

Typical Counselee Remarks	*Typical Counselor Responses That May Be Used*
12. "But I've *prayed* about it."	12. "Fine! Then what did you *do?*" or, "Have you prayed for help to discover what God's Word says to *do* about the problem?" or, "What, exactly, did you pray?"
13. "I'm at the end of my rope."	13. Which end? Perhaps you are beginning to uncoil your problem for the first time."
14. "I have a need to. . . ."	14. "Is it a need or only a desire? (or, habit)."
15. "I'm just one of those people who has to. . . ."	15. "Yes, I'm sure you are; but Christ wants you to become a different sort of person."
16. "That's just the way I am."	16. "Doubtless, but God says that you can be different."
17. "That is impossible."	17. "What you mean, of course, is that it is very difficult."
18. "There are all sorts of [too many] objections to doing that."	18. "Would you mind naming six or seven so that I can see what sort of things you have in mind and determine what it will take to answer them?"
19. "You can't teach an old dog new tricks."	19. "Perhaps that is true—but you are not a dog. You were created in the image and likeness of the living God! He knows you and commands you to change."
20. "It'll never work."	20. "It is God's way and it *always* works when people abandon that attitude."
21. "I'll never forgive him!"	21. "If you are a child of God, as you claim, you will. You are going to live with him for eternity; why don't you forgive him and begin to get used to it now?"
22. "I don't do anything half way, so. . . ."	22. "Are you sure? Can't you think of some things that you do? For instance, what about . . .?"
23. "Everything [one] is against me. . . ."	23. "No, you are wrong. If you are a Christian the Bible says the opposite: 'If God be for us, who can be against us?' (Romans 8:31)"
24. "How do you feel about . . .?"	24. "May I tell you what I think, or may I only discuss my emotions?"

Reference 2

THE COUNSELOR'S LIST OF PATTERNS
AND THEMES OF SIN

Sinful Patterns and Themes	Corresponding Bible Passages	Corresponding Counseling Cases (use code names and give thumbnail sketch)

(over)

Reference 2 (continued)

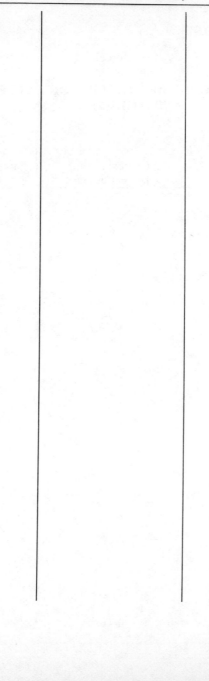

Reference 2 (continued)

(over)

Reference 2 (continued)

Reference 3

THE COUNSELOR'S PERSONAL LIST
OF PUT-OFF's AND PUT-ON's

Dehabituate (Put Off)	Rehabituate (Put On)	Scriptural References

(over)

Reference 3 (continued)

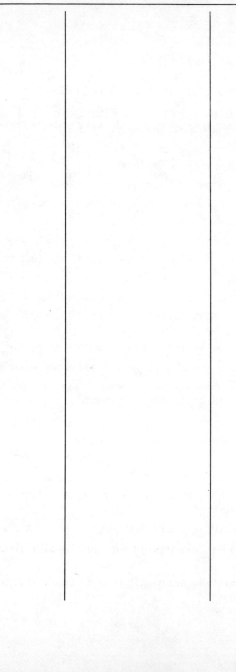

Reference 4

FIFTY FAILURE FACTORS

For a quick check on what *may* be behind counseling failure, consider the following factors:

1. Is the counselee truly a Christian?
2. Has there been genuine repentance?
3. Is there a vital commitment to the biblical change?
4. Are your agendas in harmony?
5. Do you have *all* of the necessary data?
6. Are you trying to achieve change in the abstract or concretely?
7. Have you been intellectualizing?
8. Would a medical examination be in order?
9. Are you sure that you know the problem(s)? Is more data gathering necessary?
10. Are there other problems that must be settled first?
11. Have you been trying to deal with the *issue* while ignoring the *relationship*?
12. Did you give adequate scriptural hope?
13. Did you minimize?
14. Have you accepted speculative data as true?
15. Are you regularly assigning concrete homework?
16. Would using a D.P.P. form help?
17. If this is a life-dominating problem, are you counseling for total restructuring?
18. Are you empathizing with self-pity?
19. Are you talking about problems only or also about God's solutions?
20. Have you carefully analyzed the counselee's attitudes expressed in his language?

21. Have you allowed the counselees to talk about others behind their backs?

22. Has a new problem entered the picture, or has the situation changed since the counseling sessions began?

23. Have you been focusing on the wrong problem?

24. Is the problem not so complex after all, but simply a case of open rebellion?

25. Have you failed to move forward rapidly enough in the giving of homework assignments?

26. Have you as a counselor fallen into some of the same problems as the counselee?

27. Does doctrinal error lie at the base of the problem?

28. Do drugs (tranquilizers, etc.) present a complicating problem?

29. Have you stressed the put-off to the exclusion of the put-on?

30. Have you prayed about the problem?

31. Have you personally turned off the counselee in some way?

32. Is he willing to settle for something less than the scriptural solution?

33. Have you been less aggressive and demanding than the Scriptures?

34. Have you failed to give hope by calling sin *sin?*

35. Is the counselee convinced that personality change is impossible?

36. Has your counseling been feeling-oriented rather than command-ment-oriented?

37. Have you failed to use the full resources of Christ? (e.g., the help of the Christian community).

38. Is church discipline in order?

39. Have you set poor patterns in previous sessions? (e.g., accepting partially fulfilled homework assignments).

40. Do you really know the biblical solution(s) to his problem? (Can you write it out in thematic form?)

41. Do you really believe there is hope?

42. Has the counselee been praying, reading the Scriptures, fellow-shipping with God's people, and witnessing regularly?

43. Could you call in another Christian counselor for help? (with the counselee's knowledge, of course).

44. Would a full rereading of your Weekly Counseling Records disclose any patterns? Trends? Unexplored areas?

45. Have you questioned only intensively? Extensively?

46. Have you been assuming (wrongly) that this case is similar to a previous case?

47. Has the counselee been concealing or twisting data?

48. Would someone else involved in the problem (husband, wife, parent, child) be able to supply needed data?

49. Are you simply incompetent to handle this sort of problem?

50. Are you reasonably sure that there is no organic base to the problem?

SOME DON'TS IN COUNSELING
(Sometimes useful to reread before each period of counseling)

DON'T ALLOW COUNSELEES TO:

1. Act on feeling
2. Avoid problems
3. Blame others
4. Lose hope
5. Remain undisciplined and disorganized
6. Harbor grudges
7. Simply talk about problems
8. Stop with forgiveness
9. Talk about another behind his back
10. Shut off communication
11. Give up when they fail
12. Goof off on homework
13. Settle for solutions to immediate problems when wrong underlying patterns remain
14. Neglect regular prayer, Bible study, and church attendance
15. Leave without hearing the gospel
16. Generalize rather than specify
17. Use any other basis than the Bible for belief or action
18. Make major decisions when depressed or greatly pressured
19. Use inaccurate language to describe their problems
20. Call sin sickness
21. Hurt others in solving their own problems
22. Wallow in self-pity, envy, or resentment
23. Become dependent upon the counseling session
24. Set unbiblical agendas for counseling
25. Continue counseling in an uncommitted manner

Reference 6

SIGNS OF TEN COMMON PROBLEMS

PROBLEMS

SIGNS	1 Anger	2 Blame Shifting	3 Depression	4 Envy, Jealousy	5 Fear	6 Guilt	7 Rebellion	8 Self Pity	9 Sexual Deviation	10 Organic Problem
CROSS REFERENCES	(2),(4),(5),(6),7,(8)	1,(4),5,6,(8)	2,(4),6,8	1,(3),(5),8	(1),2,(4),6,(8)	(1),2,(3),5,(8)	1,2,6,8	1,(2),3,4,5,6,(7)	(2),(3),5,6,8	(3),(1)
Failure to do daily chores			•					(•)		•
Slackening of interests			•				•		•	•
Withdrawal, avoidance	•		•		•	•		(•)	(•)	•
Frequently asks why? Dwells on past			•	(•)		(•)		•		
Loneliness			•	(•)	(•)	(•)	(•)	•		
Disorder of person, in home, on job			•	(•)	•	•		•		•
Muscular tension	•	•			•	•	•	(•)	•	•
Dry mouth, clammy hands, heart palpitation					•	•				•
Tiredness	(•)	(•)	•	(•)	(•)	•	(•)	•	(•)	•
Shyness		(•)			•	•			(•)	
Blue, sad, tears	(•)		•	•	•			•		•
Sensitive, touchy, irritable	•	•	•	•	•	•	•	•	•	•
Bitterness	•	•	(•)	(•)		•	(•)	•		
Suicidal tendencies	•		•	•	•	•	(•)	•	(•)	?
Violence (verbal or physical)	•	(•)		(•)	•	•	•	(•)		•
Communication breakdown	•	•	•	•	•	•	•	•	•	•
Immobility	(•)	(•)	•		•	•	•	•		•
Sleeplessness	•	•	•		•	•	•	•		•
Loss of appetite (weight loss)	•	•	•	•	•	•	•	•		•
Excessive eating (weight gain)			•	•	•	•	•	•		•
Headaches	•	•		•	•	•	•	•		•
Sexual impotency	•	(•)	•		•	•			•	(•)
Hallucinations										•
Anxiety	•	•	•	•	•	•	•	•	•	•
Bizarre behavior	(•)			(•)	•	•		•	•	•
Excuses, lies		•	•		•	•		•		•
Trouble with people	•	•		•	•	•	•	•	•	•
Suspicion				•	•	•		•	•	•
Ulcer	(•)	•			•	•		o	(•)	•
Colitis	•	(•)	(•)	•	•		•	•		•

Key:
Numbers = cross references to items listed across top of table (e.g., 1 = anger).
• = probable presence of sign.
( ) = possible presence of sign.

463

INDEXES

INDEX OF SCRIPTURES

INDEX OF PERSONS

LIST OF DIAGRAMS & FORMS

INDEX OF SUBJECTS

To help you become "competent to counsel"

THE CHRISTIAN COUNSELOR'S STARTER PACKET

The items in this packet have been selected for the purpose of helping Christian counselors structure their counseling more effectively along biblical lines. The packet includes a supply of sixteen different forms, plastic folders, and appointment pads, and has been designed to provide professionally effective aids for carrying on Christian counseling.

These materials have been tested by, and are in actual use at, the Christian Counseling and Educational center, 151 County Line Road, Hatboro, Pa. 19040. They are referred to frequently throughout this book.

The Starter Packet provides materials for at least ten extended cases. Additional supplies in desired quantities may be obtained as needed from the publisher. It lists for $10.00